D1456637

# FROM SATELLITE TO SINGLE MARKET

In 1982 satellite broadcasters delivered the first pan-European television services to European viewers. European unionists saw in this new communication technology a means of eroding national differences and uniting a fragmented continent, while others saw satellite television as a malign force which threatened to destroy European public service broadcasting.

Satellite television also introduced competition and commercial services to television markets previously controlled by monopoly public service broadcasters. With the assistance of the European Broadcasting Union, public broadcasters launched their own public service channels – Eurikon, Europa, Eurosport and Euronews – as alternatives to commercial satellite television.

Richard Collins explores television's role in fostering European cultural identity and the extent to which European public service broadcasters were able to meet the challenges posed by the introduction of new communication technologies. *From Satellite to Single Market* is based on extensive primary research, interviews with participants, and analysis of key European programmes. It documents the lessons learned by public broadcasters, their alliance with Rupert Murdoch's commercial Sky network and the strictly limited extent to which television could serve the integrationist project of the European Union.

**Richard Collins** is Head of Education at the British Film Institute. From 1993 to 1997 he was Research Director of the Media and Communication programme at the Institute for Public Policy Research (IPPR). He has taught media and communications at universities in the UK and overseas since the early seventies and latterly at the London School of Economics and Political Science.

ROUTLEDGE RESEARCH IN CULTURAL
AND MEDIA STUDIES
Series advisers: David Morley and James Curran

# FROM SATELLITE TO SINGLE MARKET

New communication technology and
European public service television

*Richard Collins*

London and New York

First published 1998
by Routledge
11 New Fetter Lane, London EC4P 4EE

Simultaneously published in the USA and Canada
by Routledge
29 West 35th Street, New York, NY 10001

Typeset in Galliard by Routledge
Printed and bound in Great Britain by Biddles Ltd., Guildford and King's Lynn

*British Library Cataloguing in Publication Data*
A catalogue record for this book is available from the British Library

*Library of Congress Cataloging in Publication Data*
Collins, Richard
From satellite to single market : new communication technology and European Public
Service television / Richard Collins.
p. cm.–(Routledge research in cultural and media studies)
Includes bibliographical references and index.
1. Public television–European Union countries–History.
2. Direct broadcast satellite television–European Union countries–
History. I. Title. II. Series.
HE8700.79.E85C65  1998
384.55` 094–dc21    98–6977

ISBN 0–415–17970–X

TO CHRISTINE, FOR WHAT WAS AND
WHAT WASN'T

# CONTENTS

# CONTENTS

# TABLES

# PREFACE

This is a study of the development and demise of European public service broadcasters' ventures in pan-European satellite television in the decade from 1982, when the first satellite television services began (and key European institutions – the Council of Europe and the European Community – first began to develop broadcasting policies), and 1992, when the European Single Market was completed. A research grant (R 00023 2159) from the Economic and Social Research Council (ESRC) enabled me to undertake this study and bring it to completion. Not only do I feel keenly the pleasure customarily experienced by recipients of the Council's bounty who, like me, take pleasure in the conventional acknowledgement of their indebtedness, but I also remember vividly the constructive and sympathetic action (taken when I most needed it) by ESRC officials, notably Catherine Roberts and Stephen Schwenk, which made possible my return to the UK and thus this study. Indebted though I am to the ESRC and its officers I could not have written this study without the generous hospitality of two academic homes: the Department of Media and Communications at Goldsmiths' College, University of London and the Department of Film Studies at Queen's University, Kingston, Ontario. I am particularly indebted to Ivor Gaber and James Curran (and other Goldsmiths' colleagues) who took me in when I needed a home. I retain very fond memories (gilded little, I am convinced, by the passing of time) of the long hours at Goldsmiths' spent scuffling through endless European Community papers and at the wordprocessor. I also owe much to Queen's, where I held the Canadian Commonwealth Fellowship in 1996, and which provided the perfect balance of seclusion and stimulation which enabled me to ruthlessly blue pencil all the detail I still loved but which had to go. The Research Fund of the London School of Economics and Political Science enabled me to secure Dave Steinberg's bibliographical assistance. I am pleased to acknowledge my gratitude to it and him.

Bill Melody, though geographically distant, had an important influence on this work. One measure of his influence is that the whole of this book could be conceived as a reply to a question of his; a question which now introduces this study. But Bill's influence has been deeper and wider than that. Without his invention of the ESRC's PICT programme I should never have been able to develop my interests in new communication technologies and their impact. And without Bill's professional and personal support I should never have had the circumstances and opportunity to conduct this study. Nor could I have done so without Neville Clarke's help. Neville led the Eurikon Operations Group and it was a chance conversation with him in the late 1980s that led to the genesis of this work. He kindly ensured both that his Eurikon and Europa files reached me, rather than the recycling bin, when he left the IBA and that I had access to the Eurikon programme tapes deposited at the National Film Archive. Without Neville there would have been neither Eurikon nor this book. I am also grateful to Stelios Papathanassopoulos who permitted me to read his MA dissertation on the EBU's first satellite television initiatives. His published work (Papathanassopoulos 1990, Negrine and Papathanassopoulos 1990), and Wright's (1983), Stoop's (1986 and 1986a) and Wendelbo's conference paper (Wendelbo 1986) all assisted me.

Of course I could not have written this without the help and support of other friends and colleagues. The most important of these were my sons, Matthew and Luke, who saw me through some turbulent and troubled times. But I take great pleasure in thanking all (not least Routledge's anonymous academic referee, whose comments were unfailingly helpful) from Eagle Cottage to New Fetter Lane, from Grand Sacconex to Montreal Street, without whose help this book would never have seen the light of day. All named above and below have a share in the credit but of course all the blame is mine!

Blaine Allen, Colin Aggett, Jane Arms, Monique Auban, David Barlow, Peter Baxter, Murielle Belliveau, Ulf Bruhann, Janey Buchan, Joan Burch, Jean Cerentola, Chris Cudmore, Harry Dennis, Jane Dinsdale, Susan Elkington, Michael Elliott, Susan Emanuel, Patrick Fallon, Gerry Fitzmaurice, Beverley Friedgood, Margot Frohlinger, Avis Furness, Alf Game, Saturnin Munos-Gomez, Alison Griffiths, Louis Heinsmann, Pierre Hivernat, Stig Hjarvard, Linda Hunt, Anne Jäckel, Elizabeth Jacka, Ian Jarvie, Michael Johnson, Jean-Pierre Julien, Laurie Keating, Pam Logan, Mariano Maggiore, Matteo Maggiore, Les Massey, Peter Meneer, Jackie Morris, Bertrand Mouiller, Jean-Bernard Münch, Frank Naef, Jerry Palmer, Stelios Papathanassopoulos, Richard Paterson, Caroline Pauwels, Jean-Paul Pelieu, Christian Pinaud, Anthony Pragnell, Stacey Prickett, Patricia Rawlings, Rachel Reynolds, Ryclef Rienstra, Elisabeth Röhmer, Kevin Saldanah, Philip Schlesinger, Dietrich Schwarzkopf, Sheila Sheehan, Roger Silverstone, the late Joanna Spicer, Wolfgang Stindel, Jack Stuart-Clark, Jeremy Taylor, Jeremy Tunstall, Michael Type, Roy Vickery, Keith Waghorn, George Waters, Harald Wendelbo, Karen Williams, Mallory Wober, John Woodward.

This study draws on my previously published studies of Eurikon and Europa in *Screen*, Vol. 34, No. 2:162–75 and on Eurosport in *Media Culture and Society*, Vol. 20, No. 4: 653–63.

# ACRONYMS

| | |
|---|---|
| ABC | American Broadcasting Corporation |
| ACT | Association of Commercial Television in Europe |
| ARD | Arbeitsgemeinschaft der öffentlich-rechtlichen Rundfunk-anstalten der Bundesrepublik Deutschland. Germany |
| ARTE | A Franco-German cultural television channel based in Strasbourg |
| ASBU | Arab States Broadcasting Union |
| AVRO | Algemene Omroepvereninging. Netherlands |
| BBC | British Broadcasting Corporation |
| BR | Bayerischer Rundfunk. Germany |
| BRT | De Nederlandse Radio-en Televisie-uitzendingen in Belgie. Belgium |
| BRU | Broadcasting Research Unit |
| CBS | Columbia Broadcasting System. USA |
| CDMM | Comité directeur des moyens de communication de masse |
| CET | Central European Time |
| CLT-RTL | Compagnie Luxembourgoise de Télédiffusion-Radio-Télé Luxembourg |
| CNN | Cable News Network |
| CYBC | Cyprus Broadcasting Corporation |
| DBS | Direct Broadcast Satellite |
| DG | Directorate General |
| DR | Danmarks Radio. Denmark |
| EBU | European Broadcasting Union |
| EEA | European Economic Area |
| EEC | European Economic Community |
| ERT | Elleniki Radiophonia-Tileorassi SA. Greece |
| ERTU | Egyptian Radio and Television Union |
| ESA | European Space Agency |
| ETN | European Television Networks |
| EVN | Eurovision News |
| FR3 | France 3 |

| | |
|---|---|
| GRF | Groupement des Radiodiffuseurs Françaises. |
| HDTV | High-Definition Television |
| HTV | Harlech Television. UK |
| IBA | Independent Broadcasting Authority. UK |
| IBA | Israel Broadcasting Authority |
| IBU | International Broadcasting Union |
| IOC | International Olympic Committee |
| IRIB | Islamic Republic of Iran Broadcasting |
| ITCA | Independent Television Contractors Association. UK |
| ITN | Independent Television News |
| ITU | International Telecommunications Union |
| ITV | Independent Television. UK |
| JRT | Jugoslovenska Radiotelevizjia. Yugoslavia |
| KRO | Katholieke Radio Omroep. Netherlands |
| L-Sat | Large Satellite |
| LWT | London Weekend Television. UK |
| MAC | Multiplexed Analogue Component |
| MBA | Malta Broadcasting Authority |
| MEDIA | Measures to Encourage the Development of the Industry of Audiovisual Production |
| NOS | Nederlandse Omroepprogramma Stichting. Netherlands |
| NRK | Norsk rikskringkasting. Norway |
| OIRT | Organisation Internationale de Radio et Télévision |
| ORF | Österreichisher Rundfunk. Austria |
| ORTF | Office de Radiodiffusion-Télévision Française |
| OTS | Orbital Test Satellite |
| PAL | Phase Alternation Line |
| PETAR | Pan-European Television Audience Research |
| PSB | Public Service Broadcasting |
| PTT | Post Télécommunications, Télégraphs |
| RAI | Radiotelevisione Italiana. Italy |
| RTA | Radio-Télévision Algerien. Algeria |
| RTBF | Radio-Télévision Belge de la Communauté Française. Belgium |
| RTE | Radio Telefis Eireann. Ireland |
| RTL | Radio-Télé Luxembourg |
| RTL+ | Radio-Télé Luxembourg Plus |
| RTL4 | Radio-Télé Luxembourg 4 |
| RTP | Radiotelevisao Portuguesa. Portugal |
| RTT | Radiodiffusion-Télévision Tunisienne. Tunisia |
| RTVE | Radiotelevisión Española |
| RUV | Rikisutvarpid-Sjonvarp. Iceland |
| S4C | Sianel Pedwar Cymru. Wales |
| SES | Société Européenne des Satellites |

| | |
|---|---|
| SR | Sveriges Radio. Sweden |
| SRG | Schweizerische Radio – und Fernsehgesellschaft. Switzerland |
| SSR | Société Suisse de Radiodiffusion et télévision. Switzerland |
| STL | Satellite Television Limited |
| SVT | Sveriges Television Ab. Sweden |
| SWF | Sud West Funk. Germany |
| TDF | TéléDiffusion de France |
| TF1 | Télévision Française 1. France |
| TMC | Télé Monte-Carlo |
| TROS | Televisie Radio Omroep Stichting. Netherlands |
| TRT | Turkiye Radyo-Televizyon Kurumu. Turkey |
| TSS | Televidenie Sovietskovo Soiuza. USSR |
| TVE | Televisión Española. Spain |
| TVS | Television South. UK |
| UKIB | United Kingdom Independent Broadcasting |
| UPITN | United Press Independent Television News |
| VARA | Omroepvereniging Vara. Netherlands |
| YLE | Oy Yleisradio Ab. Finland |
| ZDF | Zweites Deutsches Fernsehen. Germany |

# INTRODUCTION

With the introduction of pan-European commercial TV by satellite, why
have the dominant national public service broadcast institutions in
Europe not responded with an aggressively supported European public
service alternative? Is this not where one would look for the potential
positive cultivation of the desired common European cultural values that
are now so often discussed as abstract theoretical notions?

(Melody 1988: 271)

Europe will not make any headway in building its unity without the
backing of television, today's prime vehicle of culture.

(Chenevière 1990: 17)

In this book I explore two principal themes: television's role in fostering
European cultural identity (and promoting European union) and the extent to
which European public service broadcasters were able to meet the challenges
posed by the introduction of a new communication technology – satellite television.[1] I do so through an analysis of the pan-European satellite television
channels sponsored by the European Broadcasting Union (EBU) in European
satellite television's first decade and of the first two channels, Eurikon and
Europa, in particular. Satellite television loosed a succession of profound
changes in European broadcasting. It unleashed commercial broadcasting,
destroyed public service broadcasters' long-standing monopolies and permanently changed the nature of European broadcasting. It aroused intense hopes
in European unionists, who saw in the new technology a medium to unite a
fragmented Europe, and equally intense fears in others, who saw in satellite television a malign force which threatened to destroy European public service
broadcasting.

In this study I answer Melody's question: 'Why have the dominant national
public service broadcast institutions in Europe not responded with an aggressively supported European public service alternative?' I show that European
public service broadcasters *did* launch the public service alternatives to commer-

cial satellite services which Melody enjoined, but that these services were poorly adapted to the challenges to which they constituted a response and bore out Melody's speculation that 'existing public service institutions are having difficulty adapting effectively and defining a clear role for public service television in the new institutional environment'.

Through the historical case study of Eurikon and Europa I explore several distinct but related themes: the impact of new communication technologies on broadcasting; the reciprocal shaping of broadcasting and cultural identity; the role and status of public service broadcasters; and the theoretical rationale for public service broadcasting. Eurikon and Europa failed, but their failure is instructive. These channels constituted a kind of laboratory in which to test the possibilities, first, of transcending national broadcasting in Europe by transnational, pan-European broadcasting, and, second, of public service broadcasting both meeting, and defeating, commercial broadcasting on new ground. As it turned out they were tested to destruction.

European audio-visual policy between 1982 and 1992 was haunted by a stubborn ghost: the growing penetration of European markets by American films and television programmes.[2] This ghost continues unexorcised and is perceived to threaten both the economic base of Europe's film and television programme production industries (industries which are seen as more and more important if Europe is to become an 'information society'), and the development of the pan-European consciousness and culture on which the development of a European political community is deemed to rest.

The recent publications of European Union (EU) testify to these concerns. The European Commission's white paper on *Growth, Competitiveness and Employment* (Commission of the European Communities 1993b) identifies the audio-visual as one of three European sectors which have the potential for growth in jobs and wealth creation in the twenty-first century; and the Bangemann report, properly titled *Europe and the Global Information Society. Recommendations to the European Council* (Bangemann *et al.* 1994); and the Audiovisual Green Paper properly titled *Strategy Options to Strengthen the European Programme Industry in the Context of the Audiovisual Policy of the European Union*[3] (European Commission 1994) echo it. In its first paragraph the Bangemann report unequivocally urged that 'the European Union . . . put its faith in market mechanisms' and explicitly rejected the use of 'public money, financial assistance, subsidies, dirigisme, or protectionism' as policy instruments (Bangemann *et al.* 1994: 3). In contrast, the authors of the Green Paper emphasise the comprehensive failure of audio-visual markets and advocate intervention to secure policy goals. They define the central policy problem as: 'How can the European Union contribute to the development of a strong, forward-looking programme industry (both for the cinema and for television) that can compete on world markets and help European culture to flourish and create jobs in Europe?' (European Commission 1994: 53).

The Green Paper's authors refer to film and television's impact on 'national

2

and regional cultures' (1994: 4); to the importance of 'cultural and linguistic diversity' (1994: 5); to the deficiencies of the European audio-visual sector and to the threat posed by imports from the USA (1994: 6). The Green Paper particularly emphasises the problems posed by 'television production [which] has focused on satisfying national audiences with very little by way of programme circulation within the Community' (1994: 7).

The introduction of satellite television in Western Europe in 1982 unleashed a vicious conflict between the institutional and ideological champions of market forces and intervention in which the role of television in shaping European identity and as an economic force was bitterly contested. Analysis of the response of European public service broadcaster to the challenge of satellite television provides an illuminating case study in which concepts which have been the subject of much theoretical consideration – concepts of public service and the market and European identity (see, *inter alia*, Garnham, 1984, 1986, 1990; Keane 1991; Schlesinger 1991; Smith 1991) – informed a concrete institutional history which, in turn, illuminated the character and relative power of rival institutional/conceptual formations. In the pan-European satellite television initiatives of public service broadcasters between 1982 and 1992, analyses which continue to dominate the European broadcasting policy discourse were translated into action.

This study is thus an attempt to identify the lessons, if lessons there be, from a recent moment in European broadcasting history when the limits of the possible were tested experimentally. My object of study, the pan-European satellite television channels Eurikon and Europa, and their successors Eurosport and Euronews, represented the flagships of the European audio-visual sector's response to what the European Union's Audio-visual Think Tank identified as a qualitative change in the European broadcasting and audio-visual domain. This change, which followed from the 'deregulation of the hertzian waves which brought in its wake a whole multitude of private stations, also before the proliferation of satellite and cable' (Vasconcelos 1994: 7), continues to underpin the structure of the contemporary European broadcasting and audio-visual sector.

Between 1982 and 1992, the temporal limits of this study, European broadcasting changed dramatically. In 1982 the first satellite television broadcasts began, the first directly elected European Parliament resolved to enlist television to foster European union and the Council of Europe established a permanent committee on mass media issues as part of the Council's Directorate of Human Rights. Ten years on, 1992 was the target date for completion of the European Single Market and the year in which the Treaty on European Union (the Maastricht Treaty), was signed by the European Community's Member States. Between these dates, European public service broadcasters had to respond to what the Secretary General of the EBU, Jean-Bernard Münch, described as the 'four contemporary phenomena that concern all EBU members without exception: increasing competition, calling the public service into question, financial crisis, the new technological revolution' (*Espace* No. 21 November [1993]: 1).

The satellite channels Eurikon and Europa (followed by two further EBU satellite channels Eurosport and Euronews) constituted public service broadcasters' most important collective response to these challenges. These channels bore the hopes of both public service broadcasters and European unionists for successful renewal of public service broadcasting's historical vocation and for the Europeanisation of television, and television viewers, in a new technological era.

## Technological change

Testimony to the dramatic character of the changes brought about by new technologies came from the Study Group on the Future of Public Service Broadcasting established by the EBU in 1982. This group (named the Wangermée Group after its chair the Belgian broadcaster Robert Wangermée) stated: 'We are witnessing a true *technological explosion* whose effects are already being felt, particularly in television but also in radio. We are moving from a situation of scarcity to one of abundance where the traditional broadcasters are no longer, and will in the future no longer be, the only ones to have available the technological facilities for distribution and broadcasting of programmes' (APG 551 SPG 2642 June 1984: 2). Although spectrum scarcity was never the only ground for public provision and regulation of broadcasting,[4] the diminishing importance of spectrum regulation, a consequence of technological change, threw into question the legitimacy and necessity of broadcasting regulation and thus of the time-honoured European public service broadcasting monopolies.

The technological explosion to which the Wangermée Group referred was anticipated by Arthur C. Clarke in his visionary article 'Extra-Terrestrial Relays', published in October 1945 by *Wireless World*.[5] Clarke argued that a space station (what we would now call a communication satellite) lodged in a geostationary orbit above the earth could 'act as a repeater to relay transmissions between any two points on the hemisphere beneath, using any frequency which will penetrate the ionosphere ... moreover, a transmission received from any point on the hemisphere could be broadcast to the whole of the visible face of the globe' (Clarke, A. 1992: 274). A satellite's position relative to the earth is determined by the height, velocity and location of its orbit. Clarke reasoned that a satellite 'parked' 42,000 kilometres above the Equator would orbit the earth so that its position relative to the earth's surface would remain constant: 'unlike all other heavenly bodies [it] would neither rise nor set' (Clarke, A. 1992: 273).

In the 1960s and 1970s satellites began to be used for the distribution of television signals. But because these satellites were small and relatively weak in power, the earth stations required to transmit and receive signals were large and costly. They were used only by wealthy broadcasters and telecommunications enterprises. However, by the early 1980s the costs of satellite television had fallen and new services were launched by entrepreneurs – often encouraged by satellite operators embarrassed by a surplus of transmission capacity. Brian Haynes, formerly an executive of Thames Television, was the first in Europe to launch such a service. In April 1982 Haynes' Sky Channel began transmissions using the European Space Agency's Orbital Test Satellite 2 (OTS2). Public service and commercial broadcasters rapidly established other services. By the end of the decade there were more than forty satellite television services. Consequently, European public service broadcasters lost their national monopolies and had to devise responses to a radically new broadcasting environment. One such response was made by several European public service broadcasters who collaborated, at different times and in different combinations, to establish pan-European satellite services.

Satellite television decoupled the relationship between cost and distance, thus enabling service providers to deliver point to multi-point broadcast services as cheaply to a viewer far from the point of origination of the signal as to one next to the point of origination. It has also mitigated the scarcity of radio frequencies which previously limited the number of television services in particular European television markets. Moreover, satellite television abolished the 'communication sovereignty' of European states and destroyed European public service broadcasters' monopolies. Between 1982 and 1992 public service broadcasting in Europe had lost its dominance and public service broadcasters became embattled and, for the most part, marginal forces. Patricia Hodgson, Director of Policy and Planning at the BBC, testified to the measure, and pace, of these changes: 'Ten years ago, there were only four commercial television services in the whole of Europe; now there are 58' (Hodgson 1992: vii).

### Technological change, threat and opportunity for public service broadcasters

The primary changes – expansion of distribution capacity and decoupling of cost and distance of transmission – provoked second order changes. The 'abolition' of spectrum scarcity, consequent on the expansion of distribution capacity delivered by the new satellite technology, delegitimised political intervention in broadcasting markets. Arguments for the organisation of broadcasting using market principles grew in force and were strengthened by the perceived failure of public service broadcasting, which was trenchantly criticised for its waste of resources, poor matching of programme supply to audience demand, and capture by political and cultural elites (see, *inter alia*, Keane 1991: 54–7; Kimmel 1982; Kumar 1986). Not only did public service broadcasters lose their monopolies but the philosophical foundations of public service broadcasting were increasingly strongly challenged, with the intellectual high ground formerly held by collectivist doctrines of 'positive liberty' – or 'freedom to' – captured by individualist doctrines of 'negative liberty' – or 'freedom from' (Berlin 1969).[6]

Melody (1988: 271) implied that European public service broadcasters were masters of their own fates in the mid-1980s. However, whilst they may have appeared to be so at the beginning of the decade, they were not at its end. Technological change had made possible the practical realisation of what Clarke envisaged only as a theoretical possibility. His prediction that such a 'broadcast service, giving constant field strength at all times over the whole globe would be invaluable, not to say indispensable, in a world society' (Clarke, A. 1992: 272) remains unfulfilled. Clarke envisaged a world society realised through satellite broadcasting. Instead, European unionists saw satellite television as a means to achieve a seemingly more modest, but in the event equally unrealised, end: a common European culture and collective identity.

Satellite television appealed to those who either (and there were few who favoured both possible consequences) wished to introduce more competition into national broadcasting markets or wished to use satellite television to create genuinely transnational, European, publics bound into a European collective identity through their consumption of common European programming. Thus public service broadcasters from countries which feared the introduction of competition into their broadcasting markets had strong interests in establishing defensive, or pre-emptive, public satellite television services, a trend based on a 'if you can't beat them join them' basis. Those who wished to create new communities of television viewers, and to bind those viewers into a new European collective identity through European programming showing European political institutions and events, European culture and European sports, saw in satellite television the opportunity to do so.

Different consortia of European public service broadcasters under the auspices of the EBU launched a succession of pan-European services – Eurikon, Europa, Eurosport and Euronews – between 1982 and 1992. These channels embodied European public service broadcasters' chief response to the changed circumstances which confronted them. The history of these channels, the principal focus of this study, illustrates the extent to which European unionists' hopes of using television to build a collective European culture and identity could be realised and the adequacy of public service broadcasters' response to the collapse of their monopolies.

Technological and regulatory change has opened broadcasting markets to new entrants and provoked an enormous increase in the number of programme hours broadcast. Not only has the number of channels transmitted increased, but so too has the number of hours broadcast. To take a representative example: in the early 1970s television programmes were transmitted in the Netherlands for an average of eleven hours daily. But by the mid-1980s transmission time had risen to an average of fifteen hours daily (Bekkers 1987: 32). The volume of television available to Dutch viewers has increased substantially.[7] But the increase in broadcasting hours, driven by this dual dynamic, has not been matched by a commensurate increase in funding for broadcasting.

Dibie (1993: 10) estimates that between 1986 and 1990 broadcasting time more than doubled, increasing by 104 per cent, whereas television broadcasters' revenues increased by only 28 per cent. Necessarily, funding per hour of broadcasting fell and broadcasters perforce adopted various measures to reduce the cost of an average programme hour: more repeated programmes, more imported and co-produced programmes and new production and commissioning methods to secure programmes more cheaply. But, overwhelmingly, the funding gap was bridged by importing more programmes from producers outside Europe – notably from the USA. Paradoxically, the advent of a broadcasting technology which promised to carry television services to viewers across Europe and thus, potentially at least, to integrate Europe, delivered more and more non-European programming to European viewers.

European politicians sought to harness satellite television's potential to foster the 'ever closer union' prescribed in the Treaty of Rome and to inhibit the Americanisation of programming on European screens. Paralleling the development of European political institutions, political demands for a Europeanisation of television grew between 1982 and 1992. The European Community both 'widened' as new members joined (Greece had joined in 1981 and Portugal and Spain in 1986), and 'deepened' as the 'Single Market by 1992' programme was spurred on with the appointment of Jacques Delors as President of the Commission of the European Communities in 1985. The first European Parliament elected by Community citizens had taken office in 1979 and pressed for progress towards fuller European integration. European unionists hoped to further their cause by accelerating the Europeanisation of television as technological obstacles to pan-European television disappeared.

## Cultural screens

Many of the hopes of European public service broadcasters and proponents of European union rested on the pioneering pan-European satellite television initiatives of the EBU in the 1980s. But, in spite of the technological potential to establish satellite television, and the creation of a European Community regulatory order conducive to transnational satellite television few of the threats (or promises) of internationalisation of television via satellite came to fruition. However, it was barriers of language and culture, rather than those of technology and regulation, which proved decisive. As Henri Perez (formerly of the French broadcaster Antenne 2 and latterly Head of the EBU Television Programme Department), stated:

> Despite all the talk of the single market, viewers still prefer the domestic product . . . deep rooted cultural phenomena must be taken into account . . . and they change very slowly.
> 
> (Perez interviewed in *Espace* No. 12 [1992]: 4)

Moreover Perez emphasised that, even in polyglot European countries, little foreign language television is watched, and thus there are only poor prospects for transnational services.

> In Switzerland, for example, where French, German and Italian are spoken and taught, the French-language channels represent 82% of the audience in French-speaking Switzerland as compared to 6 per cent of that audience for the German – and Italian – language channels. The situation is the same in German-speaking Switzerland.
>
> (Perez interviewed in *Espace* No. 12 [1992]: 4)

The critical importance of language and culture as 'cultural screens' inhibiting the flow of television programmes and services across national boundaries was not well understood in the early 1980s. It was widely assumed that the new communication technology of satellite television would fundamentally transnationalise European broadcasting. The EBU's Secretariat identified the challenge posed by satellite television to established public service broadcasters.

> The challenge confronting the public service broadcaster today, and which he will have to counter with increasing acumen in the future, is twofold – though its two principal constituents are interrelated. On the one hand, the invasion of the TV programme market by commercially orientated competitors is tending to deprive the traditional broadcaster of his position of monopoly or virtual monopoly. On the other hand, the evolution in distribution methods – satellites, cable systems, videograms – while encouraging the emergence of such competitors is also opening up new possibilities for the traditional broadcaster, which will not only enable him to diversify his activities and hence resist his competitors more effectively, but will also provide him, if he is willing to use them, with the fresh sources of income he so urgently needs. . . . There would appear to be two possible spheres of action; on the one hand the development of closer and more pertinent cooperation in programme production and exchanges, and on the other hand the initiation of new programming ventures, particularly at European level.
>
> (SPG 2130 9.12.82: 1)

Entrepreneurs, both public and private, launched new services. In response to the threats posed by commercial services and the opportunities for public service broadcasting, European public service broadcasters and European political institutions fostered new programme production and exchange ventures. The EBU further developed its established Eurovision system and launched four new pan-European satellite television services (Eurikon, Europa, Eurosport and Euronews) and new joint ventures, such as the European Coproduction Association, Eurimages and the MEDIA Programme were also established.

8

## Culture

Culture was a major consideration in the Europeanisation of television. European unionists sought to use pan-European television to create a pan-European 'nation state'. They sought a political-cultural order in which political institutions and identities would mirror cultural communities and identities. But, whereas most accounts of the development of the classic nationalist congruence between polity and culture emphasise the historical primacy of the cultural community which seeks self-realisation and self-rule by establishing its own state, European political institutions sought to create a European cultural community in its own image. Rather than the nation creating its own state, the European 'state' sought, through television, to create a 'nation' in its own image.

Satellite television in Europe was perceived to threaten public service broadcasting monopolies and the dominance of endogenous programming on European screens. It was seen to promise a pan-European culture and identity shared by citizens of the widening and deepening European Community. It promised to accelerate development of the 'ever closer union' specified in the Treaty of Rome. Thus, it was not surprising that embattled public service broadcasters and enthusiastic European unionists joined forces and attempted to establish pan-European public service satellite television channels.

If, as Smith (1991: 14) has argued, a common mass public culture and common myths are required for a collective national identity, then the discovery (or creation) and dissemination of a common European public culture and mythology was required if a collective European identity was to be realised. The failure of pan-European public service television mattered most to those who were most committed to European union. These European maximalists, seeking European political and cultural integration to complement, consolidate and surpass the economic integration advocated by minimalists (who sought to limit European integration to the minimum necessary to realise mutual economic interests), believed that the classically nationalist isomorphism between polity and culture was necessary, not only for European union but also to sustain the precarious economic common market. They were alarmed by European citizens' weak identification with European political institutions and believed that a strong sense of collective European identity was necessary if Europe was to build a stable and legitimate political order.

European unionists sought a pan-European culture and a pan-European public sphere.[8] They saw in pan-European television a marvellous instrument for the realisation of their goals. As the EBU contended: 'Broadcasting in the widest sense (radio or television) also, and primarily, forms part of the cultural life of a country, and is sometimes the most effective and universally accepted means of upholding and developing the national culture, that is the identity and ultimately the very existence of the country concerned. As such it is a far cry from the concept of a 'service' akin to some kind of merchandise' (Great Britain. Parliament. House of Lords. 1985: 38).

## Public service broadcasters and their audiences

Hervé Bourges, during his time as Chairman of France Television,[9] recently contended that 'Just as the film industry does not work for empty cinemas, public service television, with two-thirds of its funding obtained from licence fees paid by the viewers, must not offer programmes inconsistent with the expectations of those who do, in fact, watch. This is a service concept, valid in all areas involving the community, such as public transport, telecommunications, or public health' (Bourges 1993: 5).

Many European public service broadcasters resisted change. Bourges' emphasis on viewer entitlements was uncharacteristic of European public service broadcasters in the 1980s. Broadcasters' characteristic outlook, moulded through decades of monopoly, had led them to pay insufficient attention to what Tracey (1992) has called 'the public as audience'. Instead of their *actual* audiences European public service broadcasters too often served a reified ideal public which existed only in their imagination and not in the living rooms, kitchens, bedrooms and cafes of Europe's television viewers.[10] Public service broadcasters' share of the audience declined in *national*, single country, markets as well as transnationally, in pan-European markets.

Not surprisingly the EBU's pan-European television services were informed by the same programming philosophies and attitudes to audiences as those which were leading to public service broadcasters' loss of audiences in national European markets. The pan-European satellite television channels, which public service broadcasters launched to occupy the broadcasting high ground before it was colonised by their commercial rivals, were therefore ill-suited to the competitive circumstances into which they were propelled. Throughout the 1980s, European public service broadcasters (their ventures into satellite television notwithstanding) generally followed a conservative course in their programming and their institutional arrangements. In 1990 they drew their wagons into a laager at the EBU Marino conference and voted to exclude commercial broadcasters from EBU membership. Pan-European public service television channels, albeit strikingly innovative in other respects, have followed the 'top-down' agendas of political and cultural elites rather than the 'bottom up' demands of viewers and listeners which commercial broadcasters addressed. Viewers' tastes fitted neither the presumptions European public service broadcasters had inherited from their halcyon days of monopoly nor the expectations of European unionists.

European public service broadcasters disdain (in varying degrees) the cultural tastes of the European masses. Their programming policies were classically devised to, at best, assist viewers and listeners in their ascent of what a Director General of the BBC memorably described as 'the cultural pyramid' (Haley 1948). Cultural mountaineering is by no means a quaint period phenomenon. Indeed, the proposals to move the BBC 'upmarket' canvassed by its new Director General, John Birt, after he took up office in 1993 were irreverently but appositely known in the BBC as the 'Himalayan option'.[11] Under the conditions of national broadcasting monopolies which long prevailed throughout Europe, viewers and listeners had no alternative (short of ceasing to watch television and to listen to radio) to involuntary cultural mountaineering. Public service broadcasting seemed to work well enough in such circumstances. But once audiences had an alternative – the consumption of public service broadcasting fell away dramatically. Maintenance of the historical-cultural mission of public service broadcasting seemed to be incompatible with the ending of monopoly.

This study of European public service broadcasters' responses to the challenges of competition and Europeanisation brought by satellite television and the European Single Market illuminates how far public service broadcasters were able to meet these challenges, and the extent to which their time-honoured assumptions and ideological inheritance fitted them for changed circumstances. It also casts light on the extent to which television can provide an effective instrument for European unionists who use the modern mass media to advance a collective European identity. Implementation of pan-European services demonstrated that there were formidable difficulties in the path of a fully Europeanised television. Initiative after initiative foundered on European viewers' obdurate insistence on watching, first, entertaining television, second, national television and last, if at all, European television. The EBU's pan-European satellite television services provide graphic examples of the limitations arising from the unresolved contradictions between a television market which is formally integrated but which in fact is profoundly divided by the linguistic and cultural differences of its television viewers.

The Eurikon and Europa satellite television channels, established by separate consortia of EBU members in the early and mid-1980s, were high points in the history of cooperation between European public service broadcasters and in attempts to use television as an instrument of European integration. They were developed at a time uniquely favourable to such initiatives. Satellite television technologies had matured sufficiently to realise the potential for pan-European television which had been apparent since Arthur C. Clarke's demonstration of the theoretical possibility of establishing transnational communication services in 1945. Moreover pan-European political institutions had also been developing rapidly. Satellite television seemed to offer the possibility of effectively propagating a European culture which was presumed to be required if robust European political institutions and identities were to strike root.

Pan-European television proved in practice to be less successful in fostering and expressing a collective European identity and culture than European unionists had wished. European viewers' responses to the pan-European channels that were launched in the early 1980s suggested that the tastes and interests – the cultures – of European television viewers were so dissimilar as to make the term 'European culture' a misnomer. Neither public service channels such as Eurikon

11

and Europa, nor contemporary commercial satellite television channels such as Sky Channel and Super Channel, commanded sufficient audience approval for commercial viability but the reception accorded the public service channels suggested that the programming offered by public service broadcasters was particularly ill suited to the attraction and retention of viewers. As audience research showed the programme offer of public service satellite channels ill matched viewer's desires. Eurikon, the first of the EBU sponsored channels, was perceived as:

> An international, non-violent, serious and humourless channel . . . British test persons considered Eurikon most different from their national television; Dutch and Italian test persons least. In all three countries, however, was Eurikon's test profile unfavourable with regard to audience attractiveness. The Irish test persons showed a somewhat more favourable profile. Thus Eurikon had the image of a predominantly serious, information channel and its characteristics [*sic*] profile indicated only a modest audience attractiveness compared with national television stations.
>
> (EBU/OTS Operations Group 1983: 26–7)

Once it was recognised that the putatively European sentiments of television viewers across Europe were not easily to be focused and liberated by the pan-European services (which new communication technologies had made possible), a theoretical possibility remained that pan-European satellite television services might offer viewers a minoritarian alternative to national services. But even this hope, that television might capture and realise the latent European, rather than national, sentiments of Europe's television viewers, was frustrated. There was little evidence that viewers wanted a European alternative to national television or that, if an alternative to national public service television was wanted (in 1982 most European viewers' television diet was dominated by national public service channels) that the desired alternative was a pan-European public service channel. The alternatives to national public service television which actually proved attractive to viewers were national commercial entertainment television.

My emphasis on the reception context in accounting for the failure of pan-European television is not universally shared. Shaughnessy and Fuente Cobo (1990) have argued that the failure of pan-European television should rather be attributed to regulatory deficiencies. They contend that, were a more congenial regulatory framework to be established, pan-European television would thrive. I disagree, and believe that the shared European culture necessary to pan-European television (which Shaughnessy and Fuente Cobo (1990: 146) believed they saw in the 'growing awareness among manufacturers of a "consumer convergence" in habits and culture') is much less evident than Shaughnessy and Fuente Cobo have supposed. My analysis then, places a greater emphasis on reception (demand-side) factors than have Shaughnessy and Fuente Cobo. But, like them, I recognise that supply-side factors have been very important. Not only the factor of regulation (to which they rightly drew attention), but also the embedded 'culture' and ensemble of assumptions of European public service broadcasters, their 'habitus', which left the public service broadcasters uniquely well equipped, but fatally ill prepared, to deal with an explosion of competition from commercial broadcasters.

When writing history it is easy to forget that what, with hindsight, seems obvious was seldom obvious at the time a decision was made. Robert Frost's poem, *The Road Not Taken*, evokes both the indeterminacy of the present – where future options are open – and its character of being determined by its own past. 'Two roads diverged in a yellow wood. . . . And both that morning equally lay . . . .' (Frost 1946: 117). Seeing the past with hindsight may give the false impression that the costs and benefits of a range of historical options, and the number and extent of the options themselves, were clear. And historical re-constructions like this one may imply that the paths leading to success and failure were clearly marked. But this is seldom the case. That the reasons for European public service broadcasters' failure to successfully establish pan-European satellite television services now seem obvious may suggest that failure could, and should, have been foreseen. Certainly there was more than a dash of self-deception by the proponents in this story. It is *now* clear that the changes described here are paradigmatic of the major historical shift in the relative importance of European commercial and public service broadcasting which took place in the 1980s. But fifteen years ago few would have predicted the outcomes that now seem to have been almost inevitable.

# 1

# EUROPEAN CULTURE AND IDENTITY

La télévision restera toujours le lieu d'affrontement de deux logiques, celle de la culture et celle de l'entreprise qu'il faut bien arbitrer sauf à s'en remettre totalement aux lois du marché. [Television will always be the site for the confrontation of two opposed logics, that of culture and that of business between which we have to navigate or abandon ourselves wholly to the laws of the market.]

(Jacques Boutet in *Le Monde* 10.1.92: 15)[1]

It is now universally accepted that the development of audio-visual creativity in Europe, in both the cinema and television, requires the strengthening of co-operation between the professionals in the various European countries. Such a requirement, which is necessary to meet the challenges raised by the world-wide expansion of communication, also offers a chance for Europe. Co-productions, co-financing, exchanges and other forms of co-operation provide many different opportunities for conceiving and producing works which contribute to creating a greater awareness of both the cultural specificities of each European country and the common heritage of our continent.

(Catherine Lalumière [Secretary General of the Council of Europe] in Dibie 1993: 1)

## Television, government and culture

In the decade between 1982, when satellite television services began in Europe, and 1991, when the Maastricht Treaty on European Union was signed, the relationship between television and political institutions in Europe changed dramatically. The customary correspondence between national governments and national broadcasting systems, which had prevailed since the beginning of European public broadcasting services in the 1920s, was doubly disrupted. Increasingly, European states shared sovereignty as their participation in the European Union and Council of Europe broadened and deepened and European broadcasting became pluralised and internationalised as new commer-

14

cial satellite television services challenged terrestrial services which had long been insulated from competition.

Simultaneous progress towards ever closer European union and ever more intense competition in, and internationalisation of, television disrupted the complementarity between national cultures disseminated and fostered by national television systems and national political institutions. A process seen as deeply threatening by adherents of what Underhill (1966: xvi) called the 'dominant twentieth century religion' – nationalism. Nationalists believe that (to use Gellner's [1983: 43] terms) if the congruence between polity and culture is disrupted then political institutions lose strength and legitimacy. Hence, the alarm occasioned by the growth of US films and television programmes on European screens.

However, what most saw as a threat, others saw as an opportunity. European unionists saw in satellite television the means to return polity and culture to a new congruence. If, as Smith proposes, 'Nations must have a measure of common culture and a civic ideology, a set of common understandings and aspirations, sentiments and ideas, that bind the population together in their homeland', and, as he further contends, 'The task of ensuring a common public, mass culture has been handed over to the agencies of popular socialization, notably the public system of education and the mass media', then the creation of Europe, whether a community of communities or a culturally and politically integrated super-nation, depends on television, the most important of the contemporary mass media (Smith 1991: 11).

Satellite television promised to establish a pan-European mass medium which would cement citizens of the European Community together. The shared European culture delivered by satellite television would sustain Europe's nascent political institutions. Yet, whilst the problem nationalists saw in a mismatch between polity and culture could be defined easily, finding a practical solution proved elusive. Simone Veil's lament, that 'a hundred million Europeans could unerringly identify Monument Valley but would have trouble in recognizing Mont Blanc' (Veil 1988: 9), seemed to point to a straightforward solution – more programmes showing Mont Blanc and fewer showing Monument Valley. But, as Maidment[2] and others stated, solving supply-side problems did little to address demand-side issues. European viewers too seldom chose to watch European films and television programmes – even when given the opportunity to do so – except those made in their own language and representing their own culture (see also Porter 1985):

> it is a fact of life that cinema audiences have rarely taken to films made by other European producers because they have not been able to relate to the subject matter, style and comprehension. This comment applies particularly to non-documentary works. The television broadcasters however have frequently shown foreign language films albeit usually to minority or very selective audiences. It must also be borne in mind that

television broadcasters frequently make what they call co-production arrangements with other broadcasters but in fact they are more in the nature of financial participations and not genuine co-productions.

(Maidment 1985: 1)

Moreover, solving supply-side problems, delivering more images of Mont Blanc or, less flippantly, more representations of European experience and perspectives, proved less than straightforward. In television news, to take a different case to that of fiction which Maidment considered, existing European news-gathering infrastructures were found to be ill suited to the needs of pan-European television services. Reuters' wire service proved to be the 'backbone of the scripting operation' (Barrand 1982: 3) during the Eurikon experiment. But, as Charles Barrand (the British editor who became head of news for the EBU-sponsored operational satellite service Europa) stated: the Reuters service 'reflects only the top European news stories . . . it is designed with newspaper deadlines as priority' (1982: 3). Many stories which would be of interest to European *viewers* were not covered by Reuters. The EBU's Eurovision television news exchanges 'proved an inadequate source of European material' (1983a: 5).

Many initiatives aimed at increasing the presence of European programming were specifically national. Indeed, the strongest pressure to 'Europeanise' European screens has come from France which, until the late 1980s, prioritised its own national services, and those undertaken with fellow members of La francophonie, rather than the ambitious multilingual pan-European satellite television services sponsored by the EBU. But national particularities (not, of course, confined to France) and the difficulties of European collaboration familiar to Maidment and other European film and television professionals notwithstanding the increasingly important political imperative of 'Europeanisation' (see, *inter alia*, European Parliament 1985b) stimulated a variety of pan-European ventures.

Melich identified four European responses to 'la faiblesse des télévisions nationales à faire front seules à l' offensive des produits médiatiques extra-européens' [the vulnerability of national television before the assault of media products from outside Europe] (Melich 1990: 124–5): the Europa pan-European satellite television channel; the MEDIA programme of the Commission of the European Communities; the BABEL re-languaging programme of the EBU and MEDIA; and co-production of pan-European television programmes which was promoted through the European Co-production Association (see Chenevière 1992, Ungureit 1988: 20) and the Eurimages co-production fund (established under the auspices of the Council of Europe).

The satellite television ventures of European public service broadcasters in the 1980s were the most important of these initiatives. For the new technology of satellite television seemed to offer a solution to the long-established problem of national particularism, and the EBU, with its long established and highly successful record of pan-European collaboration, seemed the perfect instrument to ensure that European viewers' familiarity with the topography of Mont Blanc would surpass their awareness of Monument Valley. As Lorenzo Natali, the senior of Italy's two Commissioners of the European Community in 1982, stated:[3]

> Without fear of exaggerating we can say that the achievement of a European programme channel – of various pictures and languages which can be understood by the population of the Community – represents a cultural revolution and may give rise to the birth of the new European man.

## The new European man

For pan-European satellite television to succeed in making a 'new European man', two conditions must be satisfied. Both rest on contested premises. First, the culture in question, European culture, must be shared by Europeans, and television must have the formidable powers which many believed it to possess. It is not my purpose here to consider the vexed question of the effects of television; suffice it to say that the dominant – but not the only – theme in contemporary media effects scholarship has been to emphasise the active role of viewers, and thus to minimise the imputed effects of television (see, *inter alia*, Ang 1996; Becker 1995; Becker and Kosicki 1995; Fiske 1987; Hall *et al.* 1980; Katz and Liebes 1985; Morley 1980, 1992; McQuail 1994). And to note that, as Becker states, 'elites – and individuals generally – often overestimate the effects of the media on people other than themselves' (1995: 4). My discussion of audience responses to pan-European satellite television below lends support to the active audience/weak effect thesis.

Second, that there is, actually or potentially, a common European culture. Either a common European culture already exists or one has to be created. In either case there are difficult problems to be negotiated. Notably, the differences in history, language and cultural tastes of different European groups. Seen thus, European culture exists only at a very general level. Anthony Smith has referred to European culture as 'the heritage of Roman law, Judeo-Christian ethics, Renaissance humanism and individualism, Enlightenment rationalism and science, artistic classicism and romanticism and above all traditions of civil rights and democracy . . . have created a common European cultural heritage' (Smith 1991: 174). Shirley Williams (a former UK Labour Cabinet Minister), in a popular daily newspaper, similarly referred to 'a commitment to democratic institutions; a belief in individual freedom, racial and religious tolerance and a market-based economy; and a civil society in which the rights of each individual are respected and the obligations of each individual are discharged' (*Evening Standard* 14.12.92: 9).

Thus defined, European culture is unlikely to be powerful enough to act as a real pole of attraction rivalling the specificities of Europe's national cultures.

Indeed, as much as uniting Europeans their shared heritage separates them through confessional, linguistic, culinary, historical and like differences. For example, major European groups are excluded by these definitions: European Muslims by Smith's definition and communists, and perhaps socialists, by Williams'. Anthony Burgess, a British novelist who spent his last years resident in France went even further than Smith and Williams in denying the existence of a European culture of the 'vécu' and the power of culture to bind together political communities. He stated:

> I've despaired of finding a culture – other than that of Barbara Cartland, Batman, Indiana Jones and the Coca-Cola can – which should bring Europe and Asia closer together, so I accept, with no sense of despair at all, a Europe united only in its substructure. . . . If we wish to speak of a single European culture, we shall find it only in a tolerant liberalism which accepts those impulses which seem to be disruptive. National culture has nothing to do with political nationalism. . . . We are making an error of logic if we think that political and economic unity automatically signifies cultural unity. Culture is somewhere else.
>
> (Burgess 1990: 21)

It may reasonably be objected that citing British commentators proves little. But pan-European sources are able to put little more flesh on the bones of the concept than have the two British commentators cited above. When the EBU's Television Programme Committee met to consider the future of Eurovision in the early 1980s (and considered, *inter alia*, establishing a pan-European television channel) it stressed the differences between audiences in different member countries and thus the difficulties of constructing a programme schedule which would be attractive to a pan-European audience made up of distinct audience components and only nominally pan-European:

> Such a project [a pan-European programme] would, if it came to fruition, mean mounting a complete public service television operation, with a balanced programming policy structured along the lines of a national public service channel, but with a European outlook. This ambitious venture would certainly present the audience with a new viewing option not available elsewhere. But how are individual viewers going to react, each in his/her own country with his/her particular mentality?
>
> At the present time, however attractive the prospect of a 'European' programme may look, such a programme is sure to come up against the social, economic and political conditions in the various countries concerned and have to vie with consumer habits, for each national audience is used to a certain kind of television product. This applies

particularly for news . . . any future moves towards joint programming would at this stage appear more easily geared to linguistic or regional groupings than to a pan-European audience.

(EBU 1982: 9)

The EBU's scepticism drew on deep roots. In the late 1940s, when the European Movement sought to distinguish a European identity, only very general definitions were offered. The European Movement defined a common morality (derived from Christianity); a political tradition of the rule of law and self-government; and a common, if ill defined, symbolic and intellectual culture (notably the invention of science by 'the western nations' – European Movement n.d.: 133) as the distinguishing characteristics of European culture. Latterly, the European Community has experienced the same difficulty. In seeking to define European identity it has contrived only a bland formulation which is insufficient to differentiate Europe from other liberal democracies: 'the rejection of war, the fight against poverty and unemployment, protection of the environment; Human Rights, freedom and democracy; the wealth and diversity of European culture' as the values which 'could form the basis of a European identity' (Commission of the European Communities 1993: 2).

The definitions of European culture cited above are not specific enough to differentiate Europeans from citizens of the 'fragments of Europe' (Hartz 1964) from which the 'new societies' of North and South America, South Africa and Australasia grew – it is no coincidence that Europe's audio-visual imports overwhelmingly originate from these societies. Jack Lang (formerly Minister of Culture and Communication of France) recognised that the membranes separating the different European linguistic and cultural groups were universally permeable only to works originating in the most powerful of 'Les Enfants de l'Europe' (as the French translation of Hartz's book is titled) – the USA:

> The countries of Europe, encumbered as they are with all sorts of historic, linguistic and sociological barriers, were more or less impervious to each other, while the European market – unified – existed only for the Americans.

(Lang 1988: 18)

Of course, Lang's article in the semi-official European Community publication *European Affairs* (from which this citation comes), argues for strong European measures to resist US penetration of European audio-visual markets. He argued that:

> At a time when Europe, the cradle of Western civilization, loses control over one of the main areas in which contemporary culture is being

made, the audiovisual, one can no longer react aesthetically to such liberal or ultra liberal ideologies. Reality demands that concrete steps be taken.

(Lang 1988: 20)

Whereas contemporary commentators, and Lang and Weil are unrepresentative only in the vigour of their prose, deplore the consequences of the shared patrimony enjoyed by Europe and its children and argue for a European cultural identity which unites Europe and differentiates it from the USA, former theorists of European identity openly acknowledged that the European patrimony was not Europe's alone. In 1948 the European Movement (as the International Committee of the Movement for European Unity came to be called) held a Congress in The Hague. The Political Report and Political Resolution which issued from the Congress advocated a European union (to include Germany, Turkey and Eastern Europe) and stated:

> The Nations of Europe must create an economic and political union in order to assure security, economic independence and social progress; and for this purpose they must agree to merge certain of their sovereign rights.
>
> (European Movement n.d.: 47)

From the Hague Congress Resolution, and the Declaration of Political Principles of European Union determined at the Brussels meeting sponsored by the European Movement the following year, the Statute of the Council of Europe was promulgated, and in 1949 the Council of Europe was born. It was followed by the first of the European Communities, the European Coal and Steel Community, in 1951.[4] Delegates to the Hague Congress stressed the open and non-exclusive character of Europe. For example, the French Delegate to the Cultural Committee, Professor Étienne Gilson (a member of the Académie Française and the Sénat), described the distinctiveness of European culture as 'its being receptive to outside influences and ready to give freely in return' (European Movement 1948: 86). The Congress defined European identity as the 'heritage of Christian and other spiritual values and our common loyalty to the fundamental rights of man, especially freedom of thought and expression' (1948: 88).

Thus, in contrast to contemporary emphases in the European Union on European cultural particularism, the post-war European Movement defined European culture as pluralistic, based on democratic traditions and shared with communities *outside*, as well as inside, the geographical boundaries of Europe. The Brussels Declaration of Political Principles of European Union stated that 'European culture is expressed through that tradition of democracy which is shared by all our nations'; the European Movement stated that 'the richness of European culture depends on its diversity' (European Movement n.d.: 136) and

20

(referring to the major political project of the Movement during the period of its inception) that 'It is very much to be hoped that the fall of Hitler will make possible an ideological reuniting of Germany with the culture of France and England and the United States' (n.d.: 131).[5]

That the European Movement included the USA within the domain of European culture clearly differentiated its conception of Europe, and of European culture, from that which later developed in the European Communities. Many post-war pan-European initiatives emphasised the shared, Enlightenment, values of Europe and the USA. For example, the European Convention on Human Rights includes a European equivalent to the First Amendment to the Constitution of the United States. The Convention was signed on 4 November 1950 and came into force on 3 September 1953. Article 10 provides, *inter alia*, that:

> Everyone has the right to freedom of expression. This right shall include freedom to hold opinions and to receive and impart information and ideas without interference by public authority and regardless of frontiers.

In spite of the European Convention on Human Rights' emphasis on freedom of expression, the Council of Europe did not first formally recognise the importance of the mass media until the mid-1970s and only in 1981 charged its Directorate of Human Rights with formal responsibility for the mass media. The Directorate of Human Rights, through its Steering Committee on the Mass Media (CDMM[6]), was made responsible for media matters because of 'the close tie between the mass media and the defence of democracy and human rights' (Council of Europe 1982: 6). Nonetheless, although the Council's formal acknowledgement of the mass media's importance was belated, its influence on European television regulation cannot be doubted.

The Council of Europe's broadcasting regime is grounded in the libertarian principles enshrined in the Convention on Human Rights. Thus it has been friendly to free flows of information across national frontiers and to the rights of access of European listeners and viewers to new, monopoly busting, broadcasting services. Indeed the Council's *European Convention on Transfrontier Television* explicitly defines its purpose as 'to facilitate . . . the transfrontier transmission and retransmission of television programme services' (Council of Europe 1990: 60) on the basis of the 'principles of the free flow of information and ideas' (1990: 59). The competition provisions of the Treaty of Rome, in which are rooted several European Community regulatory decisions friendly to commercial satellite television services and thus to delivery of channels dominated by American programmes, can also be seen as based in a similar libertarian enlightenment intellectual nexus and in US precedents.

## The 1980s: a time of change in European television

A Council official (interviewed 18.12.91) characterised the 1980s (when the Council formally took up media issues) as a time of 'tremendous technical change', a time when members of the Council had become alarmed by doctrines which they thought threatening to freedom of expression and communication. Publication of the UNESCO-sponsored MacBride report *Many Voices One World* in 1980 focused these concerns. In contrast to the MacBride doctrine of 'prior consent', the Parliamentary Assembly of the Council of Europe adopted a recommendation (n 926) in 1981 which welcomed satellite television and affirmed that the development of policy for these new media must be based on 'freedom of the press and television, as a fundamental component of freedom of expression' (Council of Europe 1991: 34).

In 1982, the Committee of Ministers of the Council of Europe adopted a *Declaration on the Freedom of Expression and Information* (Council of Europe 1991a: 63) grounded in Article 19 of the Universal Declaration of Human Rights and Article 10 of the European Convention on Human Rights. The CDMM was established within the Council's Directorate of Human Rights the same year. The 1982 Declaration (sometimes known as the European Media Charter) was notable for its commitment to the free flows of information across borders and to the 'protection of the right of everyone, regardless of frontiers, to express himself, to seek and receive information and ideas, whatever their source'. The Declaration specifically rejected 'arbitrary controls or constraints on participants in the information process'. The twenty one (as the membership of the Council then was) members of the Council of Europe thus explicitly and unequivocally rejected the doctrine of 'prior consent' advanced in the contemporary UNESCO MacBride Report.

The effect, therefore, of the Council's intervention was to reinforce the erosion of national regulatory authority in broadcasting and to support the growth in transnational satellite television services. National regulation, which had kept television a monopoly of the national public service broadcaster in most European countries, could no longer do so if it was not to offend against the European Convention on Human Rights and the European Media Charter. The Council's support for 'negative freedom' in broadcasting was decisively affirmed in the Convention on Transfrontier Television (which came into force on 1.5.93) the preamble of which enshrines 'freedom of expression and information, as embodied in Article 10 of the Convention for the Protection of Human Rights and Fundamental Freedoms' as the basis of the Council's broadcasting regime and specifically provides for 'freedom of expression and information . . . freedom of reception and . . . retransmission . . . of programme services' (Council of Europe 1989).

## 'Freedom to' and 'freedom from'

The concepts of positive freedom and negative freedom come from Isiah Berlin's essay 'Two concepts of liberty' (Berlin 1969). Berlin defines negative freedom (or liberty) as 'The area within which the subject . . . is left to do or be what he [*sic*] is able to do or be, without interference by other persons', whereas positive freedom (or liberty) is 'the source of control or interference that can determine someone to do, or be, this rather than that' (1969: 121–2). The extent of negative freedom depends, Berlin argues, on 'how many choices are open to me (though the method of counting these can never be more than impressionistic)' (1969: 130).[7]

The extent to which positive freedom, 'the wish on the part of the individual to be his own master' (Berlin 1969: 131), can be realised is a matter of an individual's (or group's) social power to achieve goals. In principle, positive freedom is not limited by others, though the extent to which a particular individual can be his or her own master is dependent on the extent to which the realisation of her or his positive freedom conflicts with the attempts of others to realise theirs.

However, although Berlin shows how the well intentioned exercise of positive freedom by a group on behalf of its members (the coercion of 'men in the name of some goal (let us say, justice or public health) which they would, if they were more enlightened, themselves pursue' (Berlin 1969: 132–3) may become despotic, ('sovereignty of the people could easily destroy that of individuals' [1969: 163]), he also shows that freedom is a matter of self-realisation – freedom to – rather than simple absence of restraint – freedom from. Moreover, the realisation of both positive and negative liberty (or freedom) is a social matter. Because humans are interdependent, 'freedom for the pike is death for the minnows' (1969: 124). The freedom of one (or some) may be diminished, or extended, in consequence of the actions of others.

Berlin's distinction between positive and negative liberty is helpful in that it highlights the one-sidedness of the conceptions of liberty which inform European political institutions. In both the European Community[8] and the Council of Europe, doctrines of negative freedom predominate, and are at best neutral, at worst hostile, to the positive freedom which informs the institutions and practices of European public service broadcasting, and to the development and self-realisation of viewers and listeners

## Technological and cultural determinism

Two related presumptions were put forward consistently in discussions of broadcasting and audio-visual policy during the early 1980s. First, new communication technologies would profoundly affect market structures and the social and cultural relationships which derived from them. Second, the changed cultural relationships and identities, which were presumed necessarily to follow changes in audio-visual and broadcasting markets, would have adverse political and social consequences. These presumptions can be characterised as technological and cultural determinism and can be exemplified in Community documents of the 1980s and 1990s. In 1986 the Commission described the audio-visual policy field thus:

> At the end of 1986 the whole European television scene will be transformed by the appearance of Europe's first direct television satellites. . . . The choice is clear: Either a strengthening of exchanges within Europe and a deepening of Community cooperation to promote the identity of our continent in all its diversity; or a surrender to powerful competitors and their cultural models, be it the Americans today, or the Japanese tomorrow.
>
> (Commission of the European Communities 1986: 3)

This formula implied a stronger, more interventionist, Commission policy than that in the *Television without Frontiers* Green Paper which stated that 'Cross-frontier radio and television broadcasting would make a significant contribution to European integration' (1984a: 28) implying that market forces in broadcasting would be sufficient to cement European union.

For some the ideological reunification of Europe and the USA, anticipated by the European Movement in the late 1940s, was a dream; for others it was a nightmare. The European Parliament took the lead in fostering European television services to counter growing US influence, to foster a shared European culture and to promote the congruence between polity and culture deemed to be necessary for the survival and legitimacy of European political institutions and to strengthen European public service broadcasters – many of whom faced competition for the first time thanks to satellite television. The European Parliament, which took office in 1979, was the first to have been directly elected by citizens of the Community. It was led by the veteran Italian European unionist Altiero Spinelli (whose draft treaty on European Union the Parliament approved).

Spinelli (who had been a Commissioner of the European Communities from 1972 to 1976) and other Parliamentarians believed that European union could only develop and thrive if European Community citizens shared a sentiment of collective identity. They looked to television to foster sentiments of European union because television was presumed to be a powerful social glue. By bringing information about the political institutions and practices of the Community to Community citizens, television could foster their support for the Community and the goal of 'ever closer union' defined in the Treaty of Rome. And by circulating representations of the culture and civilisation of Europe to Community citizens, television would engender a truly European consciousness and a collective European identity transcending the established limited, national, identities of Community citizens.

24

## The Hahn Report and Resolution

In September 1980 the Parliament referred to its Committee on Youth, Culture, Education, Information and Sport a resolution tabled by Wilhelm Hahn[9] and others on 'radio and television broadcasting in the European Community'.[10] The Committee appointed Hahn as *rapporteur* and received his *Report on Radio and Television Broadcasting in the European Community* (European Parliament 1982) which was subsequently submitted to the Parliament on February 23rd 1982.

Hahn identified the mass media, and television in particular, as instruments through which the Community could become a genuine 'political community'. The Hahn Report stated 'Information is a decisive, perhaps the most decisive factor in European integration' and argued that '[t]he instruments which serve to shape public opinion today are the media. Of these, television, as an audio-visual means of communication is the most important'. It judged that the political integration it desired was unlikely to be achieved whilst 'the mass media is controlled at national level' (1982: 8). Accordingly the Parliament and the Commission enthusiastically supported transnational European audio-visual initiatives such as the EBU's satellite television services Eurikon and Europa (established 1982 and 1985, respectively).[11]

The Hahn Report offers striking evidence of commitment to political unification, of belief in the role of culture in fostering union and in television as a powerful instrument through which unification could be advanced. It gave particular attention to the new technology of satellite television. As well as *threatening* a broadcasting war in which European culture would be annihilated, satellite television also *promised* – if suitably guided – hope to European integrationists. The Hahn Report proposed 'television satellites will lead to a reorganization of the media in Europe; the new technical facilities will break down the boundaries of the national television networks and enforce the creation of wide-ranging transmission areas' (European Parliament 1982: 8). Common to both the pessimistic vision and the hopes expressed in the final Hahn Report was a profound belief in the power of a new communication technology – satellite television – to foster European cultural and political union.

The Report was followed by the Arfé Resolution of 1984 where a comprehensive programme for the Europeanisation of television was proposed which endorsed both the Hahn Resolution's support for the European television channel (and Hahn's subsequent proposal for a European fund for television programmes [EP Doc 1–1219/83]) and the EBU's contemporaneous plans for the establishment of a successor to Eurikon – the Europa channel. Arfé recommended that a unified television transmission system be established as 'an essential prerequisite for the production of multilingual European programmes', that the Community assist the EBU in establishing its satellite television channel (i.e. the proposed successor to Eurikon named first Olympus and subsequently Europa). Concurrently Alastair Hutton, a UK MEP, tabled a Resolution on the

Threat to Diversity of Opinion posed by Commercialisation of the Media (European Parliament 1984a). Hutton's Resolution testified to the Parliament's belief that new broadcasting technology would help in increasing mutual European understanding, and both his and Arfé's Resolutions advocated establishment of a European television news service – an initiative which was ultimately realised in the EBU's Euronews channel in 1993 (European Parliament 1984b: 8).

The EBU commented that Arfé's report included 'bold ideas [which], although they may seem theoretical, are significant of current thinking in European quarters. As such they raise an all-important question of policy for the EBU and its Members'. However the EBU also noted that 'financing of these schemes is never mentioned' (CA 1719 SPG 2787 22.11.84: 6). Not only were the policies advocated in the Arfé Resolution lacking (as the EBU recognised) in financial support, but they were also lacking in effective political support. A year later, the Parliament's proposal for a fund for European television co-productions was blocked and was only resurrected by France by using 'European variable geometry' to establish the Eurimages fund under the aegis of the Council of Europe rather than the European Community.

The manifest commitment of both the Council of Europe, the European Parliament and the Commission of the European Communities to fostering closer European integration, combined with a pervasive acceptance of the double determinism attributed to television, explains the material assistance given to Eurikon by the television service of the Council of Europe and the testimony of support from the European Parliamentary Assembly.[12] Eurikon's perceived success laid the ground for the European Community's subsequent support for Europa: as Franz Froschmaier, then Director General of Information of the Commission of the European Communities, wrote to Neville Clarke:

> your project, as well as its predecessor Eurikon in 1982, has since its inception been closely followed by the Commission as one of the most promising and worthwhile efforts to promote a truly European television service. The Commission's views in this field were expressed in our interim report to the European Parliament, along with a general indication of our willingness to support a joint international organisation of broadcasters.
>
> (Froschmaier to Clarke 22.12.83)

Support for the establishment of pan-European television services continued even after the demise of Europa a year after its launch in 1985. In 1990 the European Community's Economic and Social Committee proposed that 'appropriate technical measures should be introduced to ensure that radio and television programmes could be distributed throughout the Community countries to reach all Europeans' (Bull EC 9–1990: 53–4).

## The economics of Europeanisation

If there were clear political imperatives for the development of European co-operation in television, so too were there powerful economic reasons to do so. One important reason for the persistence of European broadcasting monopolies was the diminishing affordability of high quality European programmes in markets where several broadcasters competed for revenues. As more services are brought to the market, any disparity between programme production costs and revenue tends to grow. As less and less money is available per hour of program-ming the incentive to import programmes grows. European public service broadcasting monopolies recognised the benefits of pooling programme resources, exchanging programmes and combining to acquire rights as a monopsony. The EBU effectively did all these things and European public service broadcasters benefited accordingly. However, commercial broadcasters were excluded from enjoying these benefits and their programming needs, particularly when starting a new service, led to dramatic increases in Europe's acquisition of programmes from the USA and other extra-European sources to fill new programme streams.

The entry of new enterprises into established broadcasting markets and a consequential fragmentation of the audience between channels led to increased imports and, as they viewed increasing numbers of high-cost productions, European audiences' expectations of television rose. Broadcasters were caught in an inescapable inflationary spiral as programme costs rose both absolutely (as audiences demanded more and more costly programmes) and relative to revenues (as the growth in the total volume of programmes shown outpaced the growth in revenues). To amortise programme costs in circumstances where revenues remain, at best, constant or (as more competitors enter particular broadcasting markets) often decline, broadcasters increasingly had recourse to a variety of international cost sharing initiatives: [13] to programme sales, to co-productions and all manner of inventive twinning, presale and co-venture agreements. These permitted broadcasters, in theory if not always in practice, to spread the costs of programmes over larger and larger markets which, of course, increasingly crossed national boundaries. Both programme co-productions and joint ventures between European broadcasters to establish new channels were instances of this general strategy of spreading costs and risks by extending markets. However such cost sharing initiatives were, and are, neither costless, necessarily successful nor invariably European.[14]

Realisation of the theoretical economic (and political) benefits conferred by European television co-ventures, whether through collaboration on individual programmes or on entire television channels, is conditional on successful solu-tion of the problems posed by the cultural (and linguistic) differences which distinguish distinct European television audiences. The hazards posed by co-produced programmes using a kind of televisual Esperanto, comprehensible to many but engaging to few, have proven hard to overcome. If, as Wolton stated 'there is no communication without identification' (1992: 155), then successful identification by European television audiences with programmes and services emanating from outside their national linguistic and cultural community is likely to be more difficult to achieve than economic rationalists and European unionists have wished.

An Anglo-French co-production, even if made in English and French, is likely to be less attractive to distinct French and British audiences than a domestic production. Such works may seem to result in televisual 'Esperanto' and, to use the customary contemporary European metaphor, produce an unappetising 'Europudding'. Guillaume Chenevière humorously testified to the difficulties of bringing joint ventures to a successful conclusion; stating that 'we Swiss have 700 years of harmonious coexistence among diverse cultures. How many television programmes have we co-produced between the three linguistic regions of the country during all these years? Not a single successful one' (1990: 17). The EBU's pan-European satellite television channels provided further empirical support for Chenevière's contention – few viewers chose to watch them in preference to national alternatives. As the EBU's Television Programme Committee itself recognised, there were scant opportunities to build pan-European television:

> What is meant by the term 'European programme'? Is a mixture of a Spanish bullfight, a German opera and a cricket match enough to make a programme European, as broadcasters tried to demonstrate during the 1982 experiments with the OTS satellite?
>
> (EBU 1982: 9)

However, although it's clear that European television viewers do generally prefer domestic television productions there is, as is well known, a marked presence of US television programmes and films on European screens. A pan-European research team, assembled by the Italian Council for the Social Sciences and led by Alessandro Silj, analysed 'the contents and narrative structures of television fiction in European countries' (Silj 1988: 1). They found that 'national programmes occupy the top positions in the audience ratings, [but] the public's second choice *never* [original emphasis] falls on programmes produced by other European countries. American is the lingua franca of the European market of television fiction' but that '*reality was much more diversified than we had expected*' [original emphasis] (Silj 1988: 199).

Moreover, European television viewers tend neither to watch the same television programmes, nor to value similarly those programmes to which they share access (see, *inter alia*, Collins 1990b: 72–5). That is, even though American may be the lingua franca of European television viewers, it is not necessarily the same US programmes that different European television viewers have as their second choices after their national first preferences. Silj and his colleagues found that there were particularly striking differences between the television fiction diet of Europe's anglophone states and the other European states (notably France and Italy): 'the non-homogeneity of the sample stems mainly from the presence of British (but also Irish) serial fiction, which presents very different characteristics from the fiction of other countries. . . . These differences are anything but accidental. They reflect the tastes and culture of the various countries and the characteristics of their programming schedules . . . to offer another example, while many films will be found at the top of the audience ratings in France and Italy, they hardly appear at all in the English ones' (Silj 1988: 199–200).

Guillaume Chenevière[15] referred to his experience as a television scheduler in Switzerland and recognition that European viewers do not necessarily find European programming attractive:

> I had the idea of running a schedule à la carte where viewers would be able to choose a series each week from among a selection of some 50 repeats of French, British and US productions. Not only were the US series the triumphant winners chosen by viewers, but they had considerably higher viewer ratings during the summer than those we had obtained with similar productions over the rest of the year. I was forced to recognize the fact that US productions were preferred by our viewers, and that the problem was not one of imposing the European product but of making it competitive.
>
> (Chenevière 1990: 18)

Ryclef Rienstra meanwhile, when Executive Secretary of Eurimages, stated that comparable problems existed in film: the biggest problem of the European film industry, he stated, was European cinemagoers' disinclination to watch European films (interview 17.12.91).

There is considerable debate about the reasons for the striking success of US programmes on European screens. Guback (1969) has emphasised the USA's first mover advantages, Schiller (1969 and 1992), the power of US government to secure advantages for its audio-visual sector, Hoskins and Mirus (1988), the economic advantages conferred by the size of the US domestic market and Chenevière (1990), the attractiveness of US programmes. Whatever the reason, or combination of reasons – for the explanations cited above are non-exclusive – for their success, the presence of US programmes on European screens has occasioned a pervasive alarm among European cultural and political elites. Growth in this alarm accelerated in intensity in the early 1980s among European political circles and European public service broadcasters predisposing them to support initiatives promising to strengthen the position of European, and particularly pan-European, services.

For example, the EBU's Study Group on the Future of Public Service Broadcasting (established in 1982 and chaired by Robert Wangermée [RTBF]) had explicitly recommended development of European joint ventures under the

EBU umbrella. However, Wangermée's proposals were not implemented in spite of the support of Jean Autin (a former President of the EBU) at the EBU's Administrative Council meeting in May 1984 (CA 1704 SPG 2653 May 1984: 34–5). At the same meeting of the Administrative Council Eric Jurgens, the chief executive of NOS, proposed that the EBU increase its participation in co-ventures and programme exchanges in order to strengthen the competitive response of public broadcasters (especially the smallest and most vulnerable) to commercial broadcasting and to the perceived erosion of European identities by exogenous programming. He told the Council that:

> programmes cost the small and medium organisations more than they did the large organisations, so that the former produced little and purchased a great deal. He wished that the small and medium organi-sations could have more possibilities of working and producing together within the Union. A flexible structure ought to be envisaged permitting a more convergent action of broadcasting organisations of the smaller European countries, taking as an example the initiative of the organisations of the Netherlands, Austria, Belgium, Ireland, Switzerland, Scandinavia (key word NOBIS). They could thus better maintain their cultural identity and better face the competition of enterprises with essentially commercial aims.
>
> (CA 1704 SPG 2653 May 1984: 34)[16]

Jurgens', Wangermée's and others' injunctions came at a time when the EBU, and Jurgens' own organisation the NOS itself, had made strong commit-ments to developing pan-European satellite channels. It had done so with the support of the European Community which, in the 1980s, saw the EBU as the obvious agency through which its desire to promote European cultural exchange and European unification might be promoted. In 1983 the Commission's Report *Realities and Tendencies in European Television* (Commission of the European Communities 1983) had referred to the EBU as the instrument through which the Community's initiatives should develop: 'If European television by satellite is to be set up, the Community's cooperation with European television organisations working together on it within the EBU framework should . . . ' (Commission of the European Communities 1983: 28).

## Cultural differences

Fostering a common European culture was a major imperative for European policy makers in the 1980s. But broadcasters were often less sanguine than politicians. When the EBU's Television Programme Committee met to consider the future of Eurovision in the early 1980s, and the extension of Eurovision via a pan-European television channel, it stressed what divided the audiences in different countries and the difficulties of constructing a programme schedule attractive to a pan-European audience.

> Such a project [a pan-European programme] would, if it came to fruition, mean mounting a complete public service television operation, with a balanced programming policy structured along the lines of a national public service channel, but with a European outlook. This ambitious venture would certainly present the audience with a new viewing option not available elsewhere. But how are individual viewers going to react, each in his/her own country with his/her particular mentality?
>
> At the present time, however attractive the prospect of a 'European' programme may look, such a programme is sure to come up against the social, economic and political conditions in the various countries concerned and have to vie with consumer habits, for each national audience is used to a certain kind of television product. This applies particularly for news . . . any future moves towards joint programming would at this stage appear more easily geared to linguistic or regional groupings than to a pan-European audience.
>
> (EBU 1982: 9)

The Television Programme Committee doubted whether EBU members were sufficiently committed to a pan-European programme for it to be successful.

> What value does a 'cooperative' system grouping public service broadcasters anxious to provide pan-European television really have when one recalls that such cooperation has been the EBU's hallmark for years now and one looks at what has happened to 'solidarity' among EBU members? If, in the event, the above misgivings proved unfounded and the European programme were a success, would there not still be a risk of organisations selfishly defending their right to contribute an allotted percentage of material to the pan-European programme service, which would end up as a laborious search for proportional balance among 'Competing' broadcasters during which sight is lost of the original pan-European programming concept?
>
> (EBU 1982: 9)

Régis de Kalbermatten, when Secretary General of the EBU, referred to such differences in 1983 when, seeking support for the EBU's pan-European service Europa, he acknowledged that some EBU members prioritised services for their co-linguists rather than the EBU's more ambitious pan-European venture. Some, he wrote, 'are preparing pan-European programme projects on this satellite, others believe more in a multiplication of experiments within homogeneous cultural groups (French language experiments for example)' (EBU 1983: 4).

In spite of members of the EBU's Television Programme Committee's

31

doubts, doubts which subsequent events demonstrated to be well founded, a succession of EBU sponsored pan-European services were launched. The most important of these services, the Eurikon and Europa satellite television channels, established by separate consortia of EBU members in the early and mid-1980s, were high points in European public service broadcasters co-operation and in the use of television for European integration. Yet pan-European television proved to be less successful in fostering and expressing a collective European identity and culture than European unionists wished.

European viewers' responses to the pan-European public service channels of the early 1980s suggests that European television viewers' tastes and interests (their cultures) were so dissimilar as to make the term 'European culture' nonsensical. Neither public service channels such as Eurikon and Europa, nor contemporary commercial satellite television channels such as Sky Channel and Super Channel, had sufficient viewers to be commercially viable. Not only did viewers generally prefer the services which were available in their own languages and which were tailored to their tastes and interests but the reception they gave the public service pan-European channels was a particularly frosty one. Viewers' responses suggested that these channels were ill suited to attracting and retaining viewers. Yet the logic of establishing such channels seemed obvious, both to the pan-European political institutions of the European Community and to the pan-European association of public service broadcasters – the EBU.

# 2

# THE EUROPEAN
# BROADCASTING UNION

> If there is one danger greater than any other in middle-age, it is the
> danger of being satisfied. Lately I have begun to feel, at certain sessions
> of the Television Programme Committee, that the attendance was
> coming to resemble a shareholders' meeting, gathered together simply
> to go through the annual rituals.
>
> (White 1980: 59)

White's judgement on the EBU, in an article provocatively titled, 'At 30 the
EBU needs Creative Fire' (written when the author was Director of Broadcasting
Resources at RTE), was both validated and falsified by the events of the
following decade. Between 1980 and 1990 the EBU redefined its own role, and
the role of public service broadcasting in Europe, but it did so under conditions
that were not of its own choosing. The stable ecology of European broadcasting
in which the EBU had been formed, where public service broadcasting systems
enjoyed monopolies within national territories, was doubly disrupted. European
broadcasting was both commercialised and transnationalised through the introduction of a new communication technology – satellite television.

## The role and origins of the EBU

The EBU,[1] was established in 1950. It and its Cold War twin, the OIRT, were
born out of the IBU, established in 1925.[2] The OIRT and EBU, created sepa-
rately as a consequence of Cold War political rivalries, reunited on 1 January
1993 when the OIRT submerged its identity in the EBU.[3] The EBU makes no
programmes, nor does it direct production networking or other kinds of collaboration between members. It exists to facilitate its members' activities on a
voluntary basis. And, as Jean d'Arcy stated, it does so by substituting 'co-ordination for direction, leaving each [member] the complete freedom to offer,
accept, or refuse a program' (Eugster 1983: 102).

The EBU has two kinds of members: active members from what the ITU
defines as the 'European Broadcasting Area' (the 41st parallel divides the

European and Asian broadcasting areas) and associate members from the rest of the world (Type[4] 1990). In 1950 the EBU had twenty-three members, drawn from Europe and the Mediterranean, by 1990 it had grown to ninety-three members in sixty-four countries stretching from Australia to Canada. Broadcasting organisations are eligible for EBU membership if they are based in a country which is an ITU member, are authorised to operate a broadcasting service in their home country, and provide a service of national character and importance (Eugster 1983: 59).

The Union's Secretariat (the Permanent Services) is directed by the Secretary General – a Swiss national, Jean-Bernard Münch – who is responsible to the Administrative Council which is in turn responsible to the General Assembly. The Secretary General supervises five directorates (technical, legal, radio programmes, television programmes and general affairs) the first four of which are linked to committees (technical, legal, radio programmes and television programmes) of the Administrative Council. The General Assembly meets annually and elects the Administrative Council which comprises fifteen representatives of the Active Members, a President and two Vice Presidents.[5] Members of the Administrative Council are elected for a four-year term and may be re-elected (Eugster 1983; Type 1990). The Administrative Council appoints an Executive Group to provide against the 'need to take decisions quickly' (interview EBU official 24.2.92). Each country represented on the Administrative Council has an Administrator and an Alternate member. Thus, when both ITV/IBA and the BBC were members at times the UK was represented by the BBC as Administrator and the IBA as Alternate and vice versa.[6]

The General Assembly and the Administrative Council make decisions on the basis of proposals from Committees and Study Groups which are, in turn, supported by the Union's Permanent Services. Votes are allocated to countries (rather than to broadcasters) and each member country has twenty-four votes (thus Monaco and Germany have equal voting power in the Union's business). A country's votes are divided between its member broadcasters (thus, for example, the ZDF and ARD share Germany's votes). Both active and associate members may participate at meetings of the General Assembly but only active members may vote. However, except for the elections of members of the Administrative Council (and the President and Vice Presidents), matters are seldom put to the vote.

The EBU performs a wide range of tasks on behalf of its members, ranging from a quasi-diplomatic lobbying function to acquisition of programme rights. Whilst the EBU is not a broadcaster it is more than a trade association of European public service broadcasters. Its operations – and especially the sharing of programmes and news through Eurovision and acquisition of programme, especially sports, rights – have become indispensable parts of European public service broadcasting. By fostering the development of a succession of pan-

European satellite television channels in the 1980s the EBU notably extended its traditional role and remit.

To a considerable extent, it is due to the EBU that European public service broadcasting, as Nicholas Garnham claimed, has been able to make 'available a far wider range of cultural experience to a far wider range of people than the cinema or the popular press' (Garnham 1990: 126). The EBU provided an organisational umbrella enabling European public service broadcasters to pool and exchange programmes and to acquire programme rights at a lower price than members would otherwise have been able to secure had they acted as independent agents. In consequence, European viewers and listeners have enjoyed access, free at the point of use, to a wealth of programming which would otherwise have been denied them or would only have been available at a higher price.

Garnham further stated that 'European public service broadcasting has represented a real step forward in the attempt to create a common culture' (1990: 126). Here the achievement of European public service broadcasting can, perhaps, be doubted. Certainly, one of the most salient reasons for the lack of success of both the public service and commercial pan-European satellite television channels were the different tastes, languages and habits – cultures in short – of European television viewers. But there can be no doubt that many of the public service broadcasters, and the EBU's, initiatives were directed towards the creation and dissemination of a common European culture. And European unionists saw in the EBU the perfect instrument for fostering the shared European collective cultural identity they thought necessary for the consolidation and deepening of European union. In Eurovision the EBU had already established a pan-European system of television programme exchanges and satellite distribution of television signals directly to European viewers promised to amplify the power of the EBU's and its members' established initiatives.

Klaas-Jan Hindriks, a Dutch broadcaster who took a central part in the satellite television ventures sponsored by the EBU, argued that 'Our only chances of survival and of being recognised as European lie in bringing together European television programmes adapted to the many different languages' (Hindriks n.d.: 3). He expressed his hope that Eurikon and its successor Europa would enable public service broadcasters to escape what he described as a 'deadlock which must be broken if the public broadcaster isn't to sign its own death-warrant' (Hindriks n.d.: 3).

Hindriks testified to the intimate connection between the EBU's transnational satellite television enterprises and the contemporary search for both a stronger European cultural identity and for a new role and relevance for public service broadcasters. Such statements echoed widely through the publications and the public statements of the EBU and its members throughout the decade between the inception of European satellite television and the signing of the Maastricht Treaty on European union.

## Programme exchanges and rights

### *Eurovision*

European public service broadcasters' programme sharing through the EBU was foreshadowed in the co-operative arrangements they devised in the inter-war period under the IBU's mantle. Eugster states 'The IBU's creation was also an expression of founding members' desire to organize program exchanges. As Captain Peter Eckersley, (one of the founders of the IBU and a prominent figure in the early BBC until his dismissal by Reith after disclosures about his private life), told the delegates at the 1925 London Conference, "to make broadcasting more interesting, the exchange of programs is going to be an important thing"' (Eugster 1983: 36).

The 'important thing' to which Eckersley referred came to fruition in 1954 with Eurovision. Eurovision began when eight EBU members shared, via a complicated terrestrial network created for the occasion, coverage of the Fêtes des Narcisses from Montreux (see Wilson 1994). SSR's coverage of the Fête des Narcisses was followed by contributions from each of the seven other participating broadcasters and culminated in coverage of the soccer World Cup final.[7]

Eurovision is, as Eugster puts it: 'not an institution, but an arrangement that has been internalized into much of the EBU's work' (1983: 102). Its importance may be estimated from the resources devoted to it. Albert Scharf, the EBU President, described Eurovision as 'one of the EBU's most important activities, with a special consolidated budget in 1984 nearly eight times as high as the EBU's ordinary budget' (Great Britain. Parliament. House of Lords. Evidence. 1985: 38).

If the EBU is 'a co-operative to help small organisations' (interview with EBU official 24.2.92) then it is Eurovision that is the principal means for it to do so. Through its programme exchanges the EBU has enabled co-operating broadcasters to more fully realise the value embedded in television and radio programmes and to share that value with other broadcasters and their viewers and listeners. Because information goods such as radio and television programmes are not exhausted in consumption, they are available for consumption in locations other than those where they are first transmitted. Thus a broadcast originated (and funded) in the UK is available for relay and/or recording and retransmission in Denmark without depriving UK viewers and listeners. Moreover the EBU's systems for more fully realising the value of broadcasts have effectively transferred value from large broadcasters (but without thereby depriving these broadcasters or their viewers and listeners) to small broadcasters. The utility of these arrangements from which all members benefit, but from which small EBU members benefit more than proportionally, is evident from the flows of programmes and news items exchanged through Eurovision.[8]

In 1989 10,141 Eurovision programmes (excluding news) were relayed to members, of which 87.4 per cent were sports programmes (EBU 1990: 23).[9] But impressive though the EBU's commitment to sport has been, its news exchanges were the biggest single element in the EBU's television programme exchanges.[10] Moreover, the cooperative character of EBU activity is most clearly seen in the Eurovision news exchanges. A rapidly growing number of news items are exchanged between EBU members via the Eurovision news exchanges[11] – in 1988 10,573, in 1989 14,399 and in 1990 16,509. The Eurovision system of daily news exchanges has been copied by Sky News and CNN, the commercial news services challenging EBU members' television news services.[12]

News items are offered to the exchanges by participating EBU members, by the EBU office in New York, by international television news agencies (such as Visnews) and by other broadcasting organisations such as Asiavision. The Eurovision news co-ordinator in Geneva selects items for the exchanges, usually about ten stories of not more than five minutes in length which have only natural sound (i.e. no commentaries) on the sound tracks. A news item is included in the exchange if at least three members express interest in it. All participants in the news exchanges pay a share of the costs of the exchange (see Eugster 1983: 110–11; Denys 1991).

Following trials beginning in 1958, the first regular daily Eurovision news exchange began in the early 1960s (Type states that the news exchange began in 1961, Eugster gives 1962 as the starting date). The second (EVN-2) and third exchanges (EVN-0) began in 1968 and 1974, respectively. A fourth exchange, for breakfast television (EVN-M) began in 1989 and a fifth, IVN (or EVN-W), in 1991. In September 1993 the EBU began an experimental satellite-linked permanent news network. All full EBU members receive more programming from the Eurovision news pool than they contribute to it but small members receive proportionally much more. Eurovision also provides members with further 'invisible' economies. For example, knowing that Eurovision news exchanges will cover major news stories means that EBU member broadcasters can provide adequate and comprehensive European news services with fewer crews maintained in foreign locations or transported to the scene of news stories than would otherwise be the case. The willingness of commercial broadcasters to purchase access to the Eurovision system testifies to the benefits conferred by the news exchanges.[13]

The costs of Eurovision are divided according to a complicated formula using 'basic units' and 'vision units' for the calculations. Members are liable to pay basic units (or strictly 'rectified basic units') in proportion to the size of their television viewing population (and therefore, notionally, their ability to pay). Small poor members thus pay less than do large wealthy members.[14] Vision units are based on the costs of circuits. Members far from the network centre will be liable to pay more in vision units than will members close to it.[15] The cost of EBU services is therefore not usage sensitive. And, as the Eurovision system is used more and more, so the average price of programmes available through Eurovision has fallen. So too have the costs of providing Eurovision circuits as satellite links replace terrestrial circuits.[16]

The EBU has an unusual structure, albeit one which it shares with other organisations such as Intelsat[17] and (until its recent reorganisation) the UK's ITN. It is owned by its users and supplies services to those who own and control it. However such organisations sometimes have an anti-competitive character. The users/controllers may either (or both) exclude outside users from access to the co-operative's services or charge higher rates to outsiders than are charged to insiders. Even when prices are constant outsiders are likely to be disadvantaged, for any surplus accruing from pricing above cost accrues to insiders and not to all users. However, whilst arguably discriminating against outsiders in favour of insiders, the EBU has benefited small insider broadcasters more than big broadcasters.

Whilst, from the point of view of competition regulation and theory, the EBU's administrative and institutional arrangements may seem anti-competitive and an abuse of the EBU's dominant position, from another point of view they may be seen to promote competition and the interests of viewers and listeners (the consumers whose interest is ultimately the foundational value competition is supposed to serve). They did so by enabling small broadcasters to enter and/or remain in markets from which they would otherwise be excluded. Nonetheless, the structure of Eurovision and the preferential access to Eurovision (and programme rights) granted to EBU members provoked a series of disputes between the Commission of the European Communities' Competition Directorate and the EBU. The Secretary General of the EBU, Jean-Bernard Münch, described these conflicts as 'potentially fatal' to the EBU (interview 27.2.92).

## Rights

Perhaps the most important of the services that the EBU discharges on behalf of its members is that rooted most deeply in its past – namely, collective acquisition of programme rights. The EBU's origins lie in European public service broadcasters' recognition of their mutual interest in collaborating to acquire programme rights (notably for sport) rather than buying rights as individual agents (and sometimes competing against each other to do so). As Eugster states: 'At Torquay [where the EBU held its founding conference in 1950] in 1950, West European broadcasters were worried that they would have to pay higher royalties to directors, artists, authors and musicians. . . . The seriousness of the matter made necessary a formal examination of ways by which broadcasters can protect themselves from higher program rights costs' (Eugster 1983: 71).

The conflict of interests between broadcasters and rights holders had therefore been recognised by the EBU and its members from the beginning of the EBU's existence. Certainly, competition for rights (following the de-monopolisation of European broadcasting) meant that the prices broadcasters paid escalated rapidly. In 1960 the EBU paid $380,000 for European rights to the Rome Olympics. By 1980 the price for European rights to the Moscow Olympic Games had risen to $5.95 million (much less than the $85 million paid for American rights). The EBU paid $28 million for the rights to the 1988 Olympics in Seoul whereas NBC paid $300 million. In 1992 the price the EBU paid for European television rights to the Barcelona Olympics rose to $75 million (American rights cost $401 million) and to $240 million for the 1996 Atlanta Olympics (Barnett 1990: 131; Clarke and Riddell 1992: 203; Wilson 1994: 22).

The change in the price of rights is a measure of the change in the European broadcasting environment which took place as public service broadcasters lost their monopolies. Not only did this change, or cluster of related changes, threaten European public service broadcasting and its collective expression the EBU, but the EBU's responses to the changed circumstances intensified the difficulties heralded by the advent of competition. If creation of a rights monopsony accounted for the birth of the EBU then, for much of the 1980s, it appeared as if the EBU's death might arise from the same cause. European public service broadcasters' long-standing success in countering the power of rights holders by establishing the EBU as a monopsony to acquire rights led to a succession of difficult conflicts with the Competition Directorate of the Commission of the European Communities.

Given the EBU's record as a monopsonist (see Eugster 1983: 71)[18], it can easily be understood why collecting agencies and talent unions were cautious in their enthusiasm for EBU's satellite television initiatives of the 1980s. However in the 1980s the chief locus of conflict over rights shifted from conflict between broadcasters and rights holders to conflict between two classes of broadcasters: those who enjoyed membership of the EBU and those who were excluded from membership. The pressures unleashed by satellite television and the consequential explosive growth of competition in European broadcasting provoked intense self-examination within the EBU, formulation of a variety of rival possible responses to the dramatically changed circumstances in which public service broadcasters found themselves, and a series of conflicts between the 'modernisers' and 'traditionalists' for the soul of the EBU.

Should the EBU adapt to changed circumstances by admitting commercial broadcasters to membership, not least because doing so would soften the hostile impact of the Commission of the European Communities' Competition Directorate's adjudications on the EBU's working arrangements? Or should the line be held against the forces of commercial broadcasting? The issue was less straightforward than it seemed because, for historical reasons, the EBU numbered several nakedly commercial broadcasters among its membership and admitted others. Why should RTL (Luxembourg) be an EBU member and Sky Channel not? Why should Canal Plus be admitted to EBU membership and CNN be refused?

## Reassessment of the role of public service broadcasting

In 1978 the EBU established a study group to consider and advise on the its future. The study group, the Statutes Revision Group, presented its report in mid-1981 (EBU 1982a). The Statutes Revision Group was established to consider how far the EBU's established structures, goals and administrative arrangements were compatible with 'the predictable development of new technologies and their consequences for broadcasting organizations' (EBU 1982a: 2). However, no changes were made to the EBU's Statutes, and thus to the official aims of the Union, until 1992.[19]

The Statutes Revision Group recommended changes to EBU Statutes in the light of recent changes to European broadcasting. It identified three factors which demanded particular attention. They were:

- national direct broadcast satellites in western Europe and their effects on the activities of the EBU and its members;
- the use of the ECS satellite and its effects on the activities of the EBU and its members;
- schemes for European programme channels or European broadcasting organizations tabled in the Council of Europe and the European Communities Parliament, and their effects on the EBU.

(EBU 1982a: 15)

The Statutes Revisions Group counselled the EBU to adapt to change. 'Of course', it stated, 'the Union could take an attitude of ostracism towards these new services and ignore them. But it was thought preferable to see under what conditions it could integrate them' (EBU 1982a: 4). Nonetheless, the Statutes Revisions Group's proposals were rather modest. On the crucial issue of opening membership of the EBU more widely it recommended softening of the, formerly rigorously prescriptive, membership criterion of 'providing a service of national importance and national character' which, it proposed, should be applied in future 'with discernment' (EBU 1982a: 19). But it asserted that only a broadcaster that produced 'a significant part of its programmes' should be eligible for membership. 'Organizations which are merely distributors' would be ineligible as would be 'purely technical broadcasting entities' (EBU 1982a: 20).

There were minor changes to the EBU's Statutes during the 1980s but fundamental changes did not take place until 1992. The revised statutes (EBU 1992) opened the door to commercial broadcasters. Whereas the 1982 Statutes had stated: '[t]he EBU has no commercial aim', the 1992 version stated that '[t]he association has no commercial aim'. The new Statutes also explicitly affirmed the 'diplomatic' role of the Union as an 'interlocutor' of European institutions by including a new aim:

to act as professional interlocutor of European institutions and international organizations and, where appropriate, to contribute to the drafting of legal instruments and the establishment of standards and norms relating to broadcasting, in the overall interest of the development of broadcasting.

(EBU 1992: 2)

However, other changes to the Statutes, notably to the criteria defining eligibility for membership, underlined how *little* the EBU had changed. Although the door had been opened to commercial broadcasters these changes were more to rationalise existing anomalies in the EBU's membership rather than to admit the new commercial services to which many EBU members had lost a substantial part of their audiences. Only broadcasters which satisfied the following criteria were permitted to be active EBU members:

- under an obligation to cover the entire national population and in fact already cover at least a substantial part thereof, while using their best endeavour to achieve full coverage in due course
- they are under an obligation to, and actually do, provide varied and balanced programming for all sections of the population, including a fair share of programmes catering for special/minority interests of various sections of the public, irrespective of the ratio of programme cost to audience
- they actually produce and/or commission under their own editorial control a substantial proportion of the programmes broadcast.

Moreover, active members were obliged to 'contribute actively to radio and television programme exchanges and other EBU activities' (EBU 1992: 3). The redefinition of the goals and eligibility for membership of the EBU in the 1992 Statutes reflected extensive, and highly controversial, discussions within the EBU between the establishment of the Statutes Revision Group in 1978 and the promulgation of the new statutes in 1992.

## Modernisation or more of the same?

The most intense phase of internal discussions about the future role and conduct of the EBU began in May 1982 – the same month that European satellite television began. That month, at its 68th meeting the EBU's Administrative Council formally requested its permanent committees to consider the 'future of public service broadcasting in the light of technological developments in Europe' (CA 1638 SPG 2107 December 1982: 55). In fact this request was a formal ratification of initiatives which had already been put in train. The previous month, in April 1982, the Television Programme Committee had recommended that a 'Group of Experts' be appointed to organise a conference on the future of public service broadcasting,[20] and at its 69th meeting (in Tunis in December 1982) the Administrative Council recommended that a multidisciplinary group be established 'to draw up the principles of a Union policy with regard to the future of public service broadcasting in view of the new technological developments (in particular satellites, cable, videograms, teletexts . . . )' (CA 1638 SPG 2107 December 1982: 55).

This group, the Study Group on the Future of Public Service Broadcasting, was chaired by Robert Wangermée (RTBF) and included the chairmen of the Union's four committees (Vittorio Boni of RAI was chairman of the most important of the committees, the Television Programme Committee[21]), the Secretary General and the four most senior members of the EBU Permanent Services (the Directors of the four departments which served the Union's four main committees) and a small Group of Experts (including Holde Lhoest, then of RTBF and later head of the Commission of the European Communities' MEDIA programme). It consulted 'active member organisations'[22] and tabled its initial report to the Administrative Council in May 1983, an interim report in November 1983 and a final report to the Administrative Council in May 1984.

However, the Television Programme Committee, an EBU 'ginger group', established its own working group to address the question of the EBU's future. This group, known as the Perez Group, included several radical voices. The core of the Perez Group was Henri Perez himself (then a senior official at Antenne 2 and latterly Head of the Television Programmes Department of the EBU's Permanent Services), Carel Enkelaar of NOS, Michael Johnson of the BBC, Hans Kimmel of ZDF, and Muiris MacConghail of RTE.[23] The 'modernisers' in the Perez Group developed a powerful analysis which differed in many respects from that of the 'traditionalists' in the official Wangermée Group to whom they formally reported.

The Perez Group subjected the monopolies enjoyed by most European public service broadcasters and their funding from state sources, which they identified as the chief characteristics underpinning European public service broadcasting, to a trenchant and iconoclastic critique. Perez acknowledged that these factors had permitted 'a balanced programme diet of largely original output which has been geared to a variety of audience categories' but hinted at their evaluation of the results by admitting only that 'certain standards of excellence' had been satisfied (Perez 1983: 2). It is striking how firmly committed to radical change the members of the Perez Group were – a commitment which is more nakedly evident in the group's internal documents than in their public report. Muiris MacConghail (RTE), asked: 'What precisely is it we are to defend? It cannot be the status quo. It must not be the EBU in its present form or membership. If the viewers with whom the real choice is going to lie detect a protectionist philosophy on our part then they will reject us. We must bring a real sense of value for money. We must not oversell the "high culture" aspect' (MacConghail telex to Vilcek 23.9.82).

Another member of the Perez Group, Hans Kimmel (ZDF), was no less heretical. He asserted that:

> The EBU has been a successful and exclusive club of monopolist (or almost monopolist) PSB. It has reflected PSB standards back into national constellations and acted as a conservative agent, maintaining PSB philosophy and standards and being used, in rational issues, as an argument against any departure from PSB patterns. Wherever commercial television came up in Europe mainly in smaller and smallest countries it had to accept the overwhelming PSB behaviour sanctified by the EBU club. . . . As a club of monopoly TV producers and distributors it has successfully organised itself for a non-market place constellation, its parliamentary[24] way of functioning being based on the general assumption of a state of peace in the world of broadcasting. A question of whether EBU should or should not take a position in defending the survival of PSB and its standards in a period of revolution is therefore a tautology. EBU in its present shape is a perfect projection of classical PSB metaphysics. It therefore cannot but coincide with PSB and is therefore unfit to serve as a survival kit for PSB in any immanent crisis of PSB itself.
>
> [note added] (Kimmel 1982: 7)

Although its public utterances were never as iconoclastic as its internal musings the Perez Group's recommendations were considerably more radical than were those of the Wangermée Group. It signalled that the EBU should review its membership policy: 'it was felt that any new approach on the part of the EBU ought to prompt it to review the question of its membership. Should the Union in fact revise its Statutes so that the new "entrepreneurs" can join – and be subjected to its influence with, hopefully, beneficial results?' (Perez 1983: 7). In contrast, the Wangermée Group unequivocally excluded commercial broadcasters from the EBU. Moreover, the Perez Group affirmed both the importance of impartiality in news services and the economic and technological importance of broadcasting – matters on which the Wangermée Group was silent. Wangermée envisioned the maintenance of public service broadcasting on traditional lines, with state and broadcaster closely connected and the market anathematised. The Perez Group envisioned a pluralistic, market-oriented system with much weaker links between public service broadcasters and political authorities.

Striking differences between the two groups were also evident in other respects. The Wangermée group advocated support for a variety of pan-European initiatives,[25] including an EBU co-production policy (one of the favourites of European unionists in the European Community). The Perez Group was more cautious about both the EBU and public service broadcasters taking their agendas from political circles and about whether the pan-European ventures advocated by the unionists could be successfully implemented. The Perez Group judged that 'except in very rare cases, it is difficult to mount large-scale multilateral co-productions produced and directed by teams of professionals from several countries, particularly where fiction programmes are concerned' (SPG 2409 9.11.83: 4). Here, the Perez Group drew on the lessons learned from the EBU's experiment in pan-European television. One of its members, Carel Enkelaar, had played a key role in Eurikon, and the Perez Group specifically referred to the need to find 'ways of surmounting the language obstacle less burdensome than the simultaneous interpretation employed during the 1982 OTS European programme experiments' (SPG 2409 9.11.83: 6) if the EBU was to foster European services and programme exchanges.

The subsequent cooperation between the EBU and the Commission of the European Communities in BABEL (the re-languaging initiative of the European Union's MEDIA programme long chaired by Michael Johnson another member of the Perez Group[26]) was foreshadowed by the Perez Group's identification of the community of interest between the EBU and '[t]he European institutions . . . interested in a solution to the language problem and . . . prepared to make funds available for research' (SPG 2409 9.11.83: 6).

The Perez Group criticised the Wangermée Group's interim report (tabled in November 1983) which, it believed, had baulked the central question facing the EBU – how should the EBU respond to competition? – by considering this issue as one among many issues rather than, as the Perez Group believed, prioritising it. The Perez Group stated that the Wangermée Group's report 'leaves the impression – unintentionally – that these problems are nearly of equal importance, and perhaps does not sufficiently show the broad strategic choices confronting the EBU' (Perez 1983a: 1), and that '[t]his need for a choice of policy to be formulated does not seem to have been raised with sufficient clarity by the Wangermée Group' (1983a: 2).

Rather than sidelining the issue of competition the Perez Group stated clearly that the EBU should seek to 'achieve a situation of semi-controlled competition' (Perez 1983a: 2). However it was the Wangermée Group, rather than the subordinate Perez Group, which reported to the Administrative Council. It was not the Perez Group's firm advocacy of the admission of commercial competitors to EBU membership and that of innovation by public service broadcasters to facilitate competition that was presented to the Administrative Council but the Wangermée Group's final report. Wangermée recommended only that the EBU undertake a:

- recasting of the administrative, technical, financial and legal basis of Eurovision.

And, without firm recommendations, suggested only that the EBU should consider:

- the problems surrounding the acquisition of rights with a view to establishing rules of cooperation;
- the advantages and disadvantages of opening up the Union;
- the terms of a possible revision of the Statutes and internal rules of discipline.

(CA 1704 SPG 2653 18.10.84: 33)

## Commercial competitors: in or out?

The centrality of the membership issue, and thus of the future identity of the EBU, was further watered down in the Administrative Council's discussions. However, discussion of admission of commercial competitors to the EBU gave rise to a 'lively discussion' (the minutes of the Administrative Council record [CA 1704 SPG 2653 May 1984: 35]). Jean-Bernard Münch (then of SSR and later the Secretary General of the EBU) argued that commercial broadcasters be excluded: 'It was . . . important . . . to organise the opening of the Union on very severe terms'. Albeit Münch qualified his statement by insisting that 'new enterprises should not be left to organise outside the Union and against it' (CA 1704 SPG 2653 May 1984: 37).

The policy of exclusion was advocated, *inter alia*, by the IBA whose Director General, John Whitney, had written to de Kalbermatten on 3.4.84 stating: 'We do not favour broadening the membership of the EBU to include organisations which are not public service broadcasters but whose main aim is through the provision of programme services, possibly of a specialist nature, to maximise profits'. Another response, from Eric Jurgens the Voorzitter (Director General) of NOS, observed that 'the name of the Interim Report "the future of Public Service Broadcasting" should have "the future of EBU" as a permanent subtitle' (letter to de Kalbermatten 3.4.84: 1). Jurgens echoed the IBA's emphasis and observed that 'it is wiser, when reflecting on possible changes, to take notice of the maxims of BBC's founding father Reith than of the press bulletins of Mr Rupert Murdoch' (letter to de Kalbermatten 3.4.84: 4).

Alasdair Milne, Director General of the BBC, emphasised however that 'competition from newcomers need not be feared unduly. It could have stimulating effects: had not the RAI for example when threatened some years ago been stimulated by the competition and had it not been able to meet it in a remarkable way?' (CA 1704 SPG 2653 May 1984: 37). Eric Jurgens was less sanguine and publicly echoed the line he had put in his letter to de Kalbermatten stating: 'The problem . . . was indeed that of transnational enterprises of the Sky Channel type and it must therefore be asked first of all whether these were public service organizations: in his view only the latter were eligible for entry into the Union. The NOS . . . had accepted the internal competition coming from colleagues such as the BBC or French Television . . . but it did not favour external competition from organisations whose objectives were not to serve the public but only to make profits' (CA 1704 SPG 2653 May 84: 36).

The Administrative Council's discussion further diluted the issue by concentrating on Wangermée's recommendations for co-ventures in television programming. These were advocated by Eric Jurgens of the NOS and Vittorio Boni of RAI (CA 1704 SPG 2653 May 1984: 34). Boni and Jurgens argued for the extension of the EBU's established co-operation in news and sport into areas such as relations with the film industry. Jurgens stated that 'National solutions were necessary but a solution at Union level now seemed indispensable since the EBU had a role to play in creation and coproduction in a European context' (May 1984: 34). But the specific proposal, that an EBU cultural investment fund be established, (on which realisation of the co-production policy depended), was opposed by two of the most influential members of the Administrative Council: Alasdair Milne (Director General BBC) and Jean Autin (President of the EBU from 1979–83 and head of the French ORTF [later GRF] delegation to the EBU).

The debate about the role of public service broadcasters and the strategy of the EBU, which the Wangermée Group's report provoked, culminated in the Administrative Council's formal adoption of the Wangermée report. It concluded that the Union needed new membership rules and that members should develop new types of collaboration in programming, though the Administrative Council specifically rejected an EBU cultural investment fund. Adoption of the Wangermée report neither put an end to dissent about the role of public broadcasters in the EBU nor did it enable the EBU to control its own destiny throughout the 1980s.

Increasingly the EBU had to respond to agendas set by others in circumstances which became less and less favourable to maintenance of the principles embodied in the Wangermée report. A former EBU official (interviewed 17.9.91) described the Union's difficulties as stemming from two areas of neglect: (1) the Commission of the European Communities and; (2) commercial broadcasting. The EBU had, the former official stated, 'a cavalier attitude to the Commission' and senior EBU officials had long regarded the European Community as representative only of twelve European states and therefore as less representatively European than the EBU itself. This hubris proved as damaging to the EBU as was its continued exclusion of new commercial broadcasters from membership.

## The Marino Charter

In 1990, a decade after White's jab at the EBU's complacency was published, the EBU concluded the review and reassessment which had began in the early 1980s. At its conference at Marino the EBU adopted a new Charter, which embodied 'remarkably convergent opinions', for European public service broadcasting: the so called Marino Charter[27] (CA 2064 SPG 4971 9.5.90: 1). The Marino conference, a meeting of Directors General, was itself an innovation arising from Eric Jurgens' proposal that a meeting of Directors General be established as 'a consultative body for questions of general policy' (CA 1704 SPG 2653 May 1984: 38).

The EBU's Marino Conference followed the founding (on 12 July 1989) of the Association of Commercial Television (ACT), formed by five European commercial broadcasters, CLT-RTL, Fininvest, ITV, Sat-1 and TF1, three of which (CLT-RTL, ITV and TF1) were also EBU members![28] At Marino the EBU resolved the conflict between modernisers and traditionalists which had raged within the organisation since European public service broadcasters' television monopolies had first been challenged by the new technology of satellite television. At last it took a position on the issues which it had devolved to the Study Group on the Future of Public Service Broadcasting (the Wangermée Group) eight years before. In the Marino Charter the EBU firmly excluded commercial broadcasters from EBU membership – unless they were already inside.

The distinctions which enabled the EBU to discriminate between the public service broadcasters and the commercial broadcasters were by no means obvious. Not only did the Charter of the ACT define commercial broadcasting in terms rather similar to public service broadcasting,[29] but the criterion which an EBU official stated to be the definitive measure of eligibility for EBU membership – namely, whether a broadcaster 'was providing programmes to all sections of the community irrespective of the cost of production and number of viewers watching, the real crunch is whether programmes for minorities are provided' (interview 24.2.92) – was satisfied more in the breach than the observance by some EBU members.

However, the decisions taken at Marino echoed long established EBU values. The EBU had affirmed, at its Brussels Symposium (part of the European Cinema and Television Year) in 1989, the year preceding the Marino Conference, that 'public service organisations have no intention of abandoning broadcasting to the laws of the marketplace. They remain aware of the cultural mission devolving on them. Competition has ultimately been beneficial in that the public service channels are now firmly convinced that they must remain strong to assume all their roles: political, educational, informative entertaining. The EBU sets out to be the spokesman for this mission' (EBU 1989a: 10). And, earlier in the 1980s, the EBU had resolved that its 'careful and very well supervised opening' to new members should be confined to new members which produced significant numbers of programmes, 'simple distributors of programmes could not be admitted, the creative element remaining one of the basic criteria for membership' (AG 551 SPG 2593 June 1984: 3). Thus the EBU maintained a definition of public service broadcasting designed to exclude from membership a particular class of broadcasters, that of the new European commercial broadcasters. It did so even though commercial broadcasters were

EBU members and with a definition of eligibility for membership which, if rigorously applied, would have excluded the UK public service broadcaster Channel 4.[30]

More important, the Marino decision is not easily reconciled with the long-established presence of Radio Monte Carlo, TF1 and CLT-RTL as active members of the EBU.[31] CLT-RTL's membership of the EBU was described (by a former EBU official interviewed on 17.9.91) as 'hideous, it breaks every rule in the book'. The same source argued that the EBU decision was in essence a decision against the admission of Silvio Berlusconi's broadcasting enterprises to membership and was motivated by domestic rivalry with Berlusconi's television channels. He described the EBU as 'being manipulated by RAI to fight its battles with Berlusconi'. This persuasive analysis suggests that the Marino decision is better understood as a ploy in a struggle between established public service broadcasters and emergent commercial competitors rather than a rigorous defence of the principles of public service broadcasting and rejection of commercial broadcasting.

The strength of RAI's influence within the EBU derived from its long and diligent membership of the EBU; as the former EBU official (interviewed 17.9.91) stated: 'RAI is particularly good and active within the Union whereas the BBC and ITV have behaved with slight arrogance over a long time'. A (non Italian) EBU official (interviewed 24.2.92) made a similar point and testified to RAI's long standing commitment to the collective development of public broadcasting in Europe, instancing the establishment of the Prix Italia as evidence of the strength and longevity of RAI's commitment. Formally however the EBU's decision to exclude new broadcasters, such as Sky Channel, can be explained in terms of the EBU's statutes which prescribed that member broadcasters must have a 'national character and national importance' (Article 3 Paragraph 1).

The EBU's exclusion of new commercial broadcasters from membership is made more absurd, and seemingly more arbitrary, by the 'back door' route to membership later taken by the French Pay TV service Canal Plus. France established a 'Groupement des Radiodiffusers Françaises', the GRF, as a vehicle to enable French broadcasters, whether commercial or public service, to achieve admission to membership of the EBU. The GRF embraces TF1, Canal Plus, France 2 and France 3.[32]

One EBU official (interviewed 26.2.92) characterised the Marino decision as a choice to exclude commercial broadcasters and accept problems coming from outside the Union – notably from the Competition Directorate of the Commission of the European Communities – rather than to admit commercial broadcasters and have fights inside the EBU. The modernisers sought an active EBU response to changed circumstances while the traditionalists advocated firm adherence to public service broadcasting's established competencies and practices.

Development of public service satellite television in Europe can be seen as an index of the modernisers' strength. The dogged resistance to admitting commercial broadcasters to EBU membership is an index of the traditionalists' power. Responsibility for the failure of the EBU's first satellite television channels must be attributed to both factions. To the modernisers for their excessive optimism about the potentiality of a new technology and to the traditionalists for the persistence of views of programming and of the relationship between broadcasters and audiences which were inappropriate to the new circumstances.

## The EBU and the European Community

The EBU's relations with the Commission of the European Communities dramatically deteriorated in the decade between 1982 and 1992 – between the first pan-European television services and the establishment of the European Single Market. In 1982 the European Community and the EBU were closely allied; by 1992 the EBU perceived itself to be lethally threatened by the Community's competition policies. In 1982 the European Parliament proposed that the EBU operate the 'joint European channel' (European Parliament 1982: 11) which Hahn believed to be the key to the integration of Europe. In 1992 a senior EBU official (interviewed 24.2.92) stated that the stance of the Competition Directorate of the Commission of the European Communities 'could lead to a catastrophic collapse of Eurovision'.

Relations between the European Community and the EBU cooled considerably after the high point reached in 1982 when the European Parliament passed the Hahn Resolution. The EBU had rejected the cornerstone of the Community's television policy – the *Television without Frontiers* Green Paper and Directive (Commission of the European Communities 1984a; Council of the European Communities 1989) which the Secretary General of the EBU described as a 'interference by the European Commission in an area outside its jurisdiction' (*Espace* No. 14 September [1992]: 1). And, although *Television without Frontiers* and its 'ultra liberal' emphasis on the economic integration of the European broadcasting market had powerful *dirigiste* opponents within the Community,[33] divisions within the EBU's membership meant that the EBU was unable to deliver any of the *dirigistes'* favourites (for example, a European co-production fund, collaboration between film and television producers and, of course, a pan-European satellite television channel.

After promulgation of the *Television without Frontiers* Directive (Council of the European Communities 1989), which decisively destroyed the legitimacy of any regulatory measures to protect public service broadcasters' monopolies, and in the face of an increasingly adversarial relationship between the EBU and the Commission's Competition Directorate the EBU sought to mend its fences with the European Community. It began an attempt to be recognised by the Commission as a 'privileged partner for the European Commission in the audio-visual sphere' (*Espace* No. 14 September [1992]: 1). As the Secretary General, Jean-Bernard Münch, had stated to the Administrative Council

It is difficult to conclude since nothing stands still, everything changes rapidly and all questions become more complex. But we hold excellent cards in our hands. We must try to play them in a spirit of cooperation and solidarity which has always been ours, with an acute sense of the realities of the world today, with an open mind and with determination, ready to take all necessary measures to meet the challenges of the hour.

(Secretary General of the EBU to the Administrative Council 1986. CA 1852 SPG 3612 13.5.87: 6)

The fate of pan-European television hung on several distinct factors: the regulatory environment being shaped by the European Community, the varying priorities and commitments of EBU Members, the strength of competition from emerging commercial services, the balance of power within the EBU (and the pan-European channels) between traditionalists and modernisers and, above all, by the extent to which European television viewers were endowed with a common culture sufficient to make a common European television service possible. The relative strength of these factors became apparent in the history of the successive satellite channels sponsored by the EBU: Eurikon, Europa, Eurosport and Euronews. As did the strength of the largely unquestioned assumptions about their role (and thus about the nature of public service broadcasting) which European public service broadcasters had inherited from their long heyday of unchallenged monopoly. Assumptions which were to come under great pressure as the European broadcasting environment changed rapidly and comprehensively.

# 3

# PUBLIC SERVICE
# BROADCASTING

Does public service broadcasting cut such a poor figure? The end of its
monopoly and the advent of television from space, enabling satellites to
relay a vast quantity of programmes from elsewhere, in multilingual
versions, on channels that digital compression has made less scarce – do,
in fact suggest that the vocation of national stations must evolve in both
public and private sectors.

(Bourges 1993: 2)

Between 1982 and 1992, European public service broadcasting experienced an
unprecedented comprehensive and intense two-fold regime of change: technological change, in the form of communication satellites, and regulatory change,
in the form of the integration of the European Community's (later European
Union) television market under the jurisdiction of the European Commission's
Competition Directorate). These interdependent forces shifted the European
broadcasting paradigm and transformed a long-established European regime,
based on national broadcasting markets which were dominated, if not monopo-
lised, by a single national public service broadcaster, into a new, pluralised (and
in some areas genuinely competitive) transnational system.

Satellites made it possible for new services to be established and for new
services to cross national frontiers. The creation of a single European market in
television among the Member States of the European Community meant that
television, hitherto regulated under national (and largely non-commercial)
regimes, was henceforth conceived as a service traded within and between
European Community Member States and subject to European Community
competition regulation. These changes revealed fissures in, and between, the
institutional and ideological definitions of European public service broadcasting
and showed that European public service broadcasters did not always agree on
what public service broadcasting was.

Satellite (and cable) television made possible an increase in competition
within established national markets in two ways: by increasing supply of a
resource – the radio frequency spectrum – that was believed (on grounds of

uncertain validity) to be scarce; and by supplying signals from outside national markets (thanks to satellite footprints crossing national frontiers and enabling viewers to receive signals which, unlike those relayed by cable networks, were not readily controlled by national regulatory authorities).

The perceived scarcity of the basic resource used for broadcasting (the radio frequency spectrum) meant that free entry (a necessary condition of a well-functioning market) to the broadcasting market could not take place; the broadcasting market was thus thought to be a clear, and classic, instance of market failure. Accordingly, government intervention in European broadcasting markets was general and uncontroversial. To ration the scarce spectrum resource[1] and prevent spectrum pollution a limited number of authorised users – generally a national public service monopoly – were given access to the spectrum. However market failure is not necessarily permanent. Technological change can turn a hitherto failed market into a well-functioning market, and thus compromise the legitimacy (at least for those who see markets as appropriate mechanisms for the allocation of resources) of political intervention in the relevant market. Broadcasting is a prime case in point.[2]

The introduction of a new ICT (information and communication technology) satellite television, in Europe in the early 1980s transformed the conditions under which television broadcasting had hitherto been arranged. It provoked widespread debate about the ends and means of broadcasting policy and a recognition that broadcasting policy could no longer be made on the old, largely national, terms. Abolition of spectrum scarcity seemed to delegitimise political intervention in broadcasting markets; no matter that there were, and are, other grounds for intervention in broadcasting markets.[3] New services were slowly established which eroded the privileged positions enjoyed by national public service broadcasters. Accordingly, the case for the organisation of broadcasting on market lines grew in force and salience – not least because the formidable *Television without Frontiers* Green Paper (Commission of the European Communities 1984a) provided solid arguments for considering television a traded service.

Such arguments were strengthened by the perceived failure of public service broadcasting. New services and new possibilities focused attention on public service broadcasters' performance, which was trenchantly criticised for wasteful use of resources, poor matching of programme supply to audience demand and susceptibility to capture by political and cultural elites, (see, *inter alia*, Peacock 1986; Keane 1991: 54–7; Kimmel 1982 *passim*; Kumar 1986). Indeed, the BBC itself has acknowledged the force of such criticisms stating: 'For much of its history, the BBC has been part of a high cost industry. ITV and ILR as well as the BBC were characterised by entrenched working practices, cumbersome organisation structures, over-staffing and poor industrial relations' (BBC 1992: 52).

In contrast, advocates of market principles of organisation claimed that provision of broadcasting services via markets (even if imperfect markets[4]), better matches offer to demand (thanks to a signalling system via price which registers consumers' preferences and the intensity of their preferences), uses resources more efficiently and is less subject to capture by cultural and political elites than is, and was, public service broadcasting (see, *inter alia*, Peacock 1986). Their theoretical case seemed to be vindicated empirically by a substantial shift in viewing in favour of the new commercial services. The combination of technological and regulatory change thus altered the landscape of European broadcasting both empirically, through the establishment of new services, and theoretically, by posing a powerful intellectual and ideological challenge to established public service rationales.

These challenges led to re-examination of the project and performance of public service broadcasting, both by the broadcasters themselves and by academic commentators, and to a variety of attempts, enjoying varying degrees of success, to re-invent public service broadcasting. The satellite television services of the 1980s, sponsored by the EBU, were prime cases in point which provided empirical tests of the contemporary viability of the sanctified principles of European public service broadcasting and of the flexibility and resilience of its institutions and traditions. The acid test was, of course, the ability of public service broadcasters to attract and retain audiences.

The 'ratings' test was important for several reasons. First, if public service broadcasting provided what economists call 'merit goods' – that is goods that are good for people, which have intrinsically meritorious qualities – then it was in the public interest for these merit goods to be pervasively consumed. What benefit could there be for society if the meritorious public broadcasting services were not consumed? Second, the legitimacy of public service broadcasters' claims on resources – whether allocations from state budgets (via licence fees or direct subventions) or advertising revenues won in direct competition with commercial services – depended on the extent to which their services were consumed. Third, if public service broadcasting were to be an instrument for the creation of a new European consciousness and culture, its effectiveness was likely to be directly proportional to its consumption.

## Definitions of public service broadcasting

What then is the 'public service broadcasting' that was threatened? Perhaps we all know what we mean by the term. But what is customarily taken for granted customarily proves troublesome. What one believes a term to mean may not correspond to what others understand by it. Induction and deduction offer possible routes to a definition of public service broadcasting: induction via codification of what public service broadcasting 'is'; deduction via theoretical systematisation of what public service broadcasting 'ought' to be. Characteristically, inductivists have been concerned with the actual historical practice of public service broadcasters, whereas deductivists have focused on a theoretical ideal of public service broadcasting. Blumler (1992) provides an inductive, empirical, approach to the question, as do the Broadcasting Research

Unit (BRU n.d.) and some of the cogitations of public service broadcasters themselves (see, for example, Perez Group 1983 and 1983a). Garnham (1990 and 1992), Keane (1991) and other neo-Habermasians offer a deductive, theoretical, approach.

These approaches can be characterised respectively as studies, and defences, of public service broadcasters and of public service broadcasting. The first type of approach has an admirable concreteness but, for good or ill, weds its exponents indissolubly to the practice of actual and existing public service broadcasters. The second, for good or ill, emancipates its exponents from the challenging task of defending the historical practice of public service broadcasters but risks the idealist invocation of 'oughts' with only a tenuous connection to real historical 'ises'. Of course, distinguishing between those concerned with public service broadcast*ers* and those concerned with public service broadcast*ing* is to make an analytical distinction. Few are exclusively concerned with either theory or practice just as few are exclusively within either a deductivist or inductivist camp.

## The 'ises' of public service broadcasting

The modern era has seen the emergence of three distinct forms of state. Monolithic, often absolutist, states (such as the former Soviet Union or the People's Republic of China), in which the boundaries between a centralised state apparatus, a political party and control of economic activity are absent or indistinct. States where government and its apparatus perform a 'nightwatchman' function in respect of the economy and in which political parties and the apparatus of the state (often a plural apparatus) are clearly differentiated, where economic activity takes place within a framework of law established and guaranteed by political authority, but where political authority (in theory at least) has no direct part in economic activity (such as the US). And a third, intermediate, form of state, (such as the states of Western Europe), where economic activity is characteristically but not exclusively conducted by the private sector, where political authorities intervene more actively in the economy than is characteristic in the second kind of state but less comprehensively than is characteristic of the first, and where the state apparatus is customarily distinct from political parties. This third, intermediate, type of state customarily has a pluralistic and decentred structure and often has a rich, and sometimes confusing, plurality of state and para-statal structures.

These three types of state have distinctive and characteristic forms of broadcasting organisation. In the first, broadcasting is customarily organised as an arm of government, in the second it is customarily located in the private sector (and is therefore absent from government and any state sector), and in the third it is part of the state, but part of a decentred and pluralistic structure of political power and authority. European public service broadcasting organisations have been the locus of state institutional power in broadcasting and are characteristically separate from government but part of a loose and pluralistic state structure.

European states characteristically established their broadcasting services as national public sector monopolies. Although broadcasting in several European countries (including the UK) was begun by commercial interests (seeking to create a market for radio receivers), for the most part private interests soon lost their hold on broadcasting. True, in some countries such as Germany (where the Reichs Rundfunk Gesellschaft had significant participation from the private sector) and France (which had a number of commercial stations in the interwar years, including some for foreign listeners transmitted in languages other than French) the private sector retained a presence. But after the Second World War, French broadcasting came to be dominated by a public sector national broadcaster, the ORTF, while German broadcasting was reconstructed by the Allied Control Commissions on exclusively public service lines. However, exceptionally, Luxembourg, perennially the black sheep of European broadcasting, maintained a profit-making public company delivering advertising-financed services (services which, moreover, were directed to listeners outside Luxembourg). It was subsequently joined by other European states, first the UK and Finland in the 1950s, in permitting commercial services. In spite of these exceptions, however, European television was dominated by national public service monopolies until the 1980s.

The European experience contrasted with that of other developed countries. In the US broadcasting was commercial. In Australia and Canada and South Africa, public service broadcasting was belatedly established to complement and compete with established commercial services. Europe was thus the heartland of what came to be known as 'public service broadcasting', a distinctive institutional form which characteristically combined three elements: publicly owned not-for-profit organisation, a monopoly of service provision and a strongly normative programming policy emphasising national and high cultural themes. It is perhaps only from a contemporary perspective – which has a strong anti-statist flavour (it is not only east of the Elbe that the doctrine of '*Perestroika*' has come to dominate) – that the organisational form which so many states chose for broadcasting requires to be explained and justified.

Yet justification is required in the context of a dominant official European Community ethos hostile to public enterprise. This hostility derives from the mismatch between a fundamental assumption of Community policy – that competitive markets are normal and normative – and the legacy of long-established institutions, including public service broadcasters, which simply do not fit that paradigm. For example, the Commission of the European Communities has identified public libraries as a problematic exception to a normative commercial mode of service provision. In its proposal for a Council Directive on rental right, lending right and certain rights related to copyright the Commission stated:

With respect to competition, rental and lending are economically connected: nowadays, commercial rental shops and public libraries compete with each other and this competition will certainly grow in the future. The establishment of non-commercial public lending libraries at the beginning of this century resulted in the field of books in the virtual disappearance of the then prospering commercial rental libraries. A similar development in relation to the new media, which are to an increasing extent lent out in public libraries, cannot be excluded.

(Commission of the European Communities 1991f: 5)

The implication is clear enough. Public sector enterprise is a problem because its methods and institutions do not conform to the norms of competitive markets. Not only do public sector enterprises represent unfair competition, they threaten the normative status of competitive markets and the institutions specific to them. Indeed, a European public service broadcaster, RTP in Portugal, stood accused, under the provisions of the European Treaty, of improper receipt of state aid in the form of public finance for broadcasting. True, RTP was exonerated, but the judgement defined the legitimate boundaries of public finance for broadcasting very narrowly – essentially as permitting only activities that a profit-seeking firm would not undertake.[5] The consequences of this mismatch between the values enshrined in Community law and the values institutionalised in European public service broadcasters will be explored below. I refer to it now to signal that not all the changes to European broadcasting that have taken place during the decade 1982 to 1992 can be laid at the door of technological change.

In Europe, as elsewhere, understandings of the term public service broadcasting have been shaped by the memory and past experience of the services that have gone under that name. In Western Europe quite different institutional forms are all known as public service broadcasting; from institutions where broadcasting is closely associated with the state (and used as an instrument of central state power) to highly regionalised and pluralistic systems. Even in the UK, where, thanks to the international prestige and longevity of the BBC, what comes closest to an internationally accepted normative institutional definition of public service broadcasting is to be found, there is scant consensus on the meaning of 'public service broadcasting'. The most recent official enquiry into broadcasting in the UK, the Committee on Financing the BBC (the Peacock Committee[6]), stated that there is no 'simple dictionary definition' of public service broadcasting (Peacock 1986: 6). Indeed, all established terrestrial television channels in the UK – the advertising-free BBC, the for-profit advertising-financed Channel 3 (ITV) and Channel 5, and the not-for-profit advertising-financed Channel 4/S4C – have claimed the status of public service broadcaster.

The Peacock Committee (Peacock 1986: 7) cited eight characteristics of public service broadcasting borrowed from a BRU study (n.d.; see also Keane 1991: 117). The BRU had identified these characteristics in a classically inductive fashion by polling established British broadcasters and commentators. The eight characteristics are as follows:

- geographic universality – everyone should have access to the same services;
- catering for all interests and tastes;
- catering for minorities;
- catering for national identity and community;
- detachment from vested interests and government;
- one broadcasting system to be funded directly from the corpus of users;
- competition in good programming rather than for numbers;
- guidelines to liberate programme makers and not to restrict them.

Other contemporary European notions of public service broadcasting are broadly similar. Two sources (one academic, one professional) provide convenient compendia of European views: Jay Blumler's *Television and the Public Interest. Vulnerable Values in West European Broadcasting* (1992) and the report of the EBU's Perez Group (Perez 1983) on the nature and role of public service broadcasting.[7]

Blumler (1992: 7–14) defined the most salient characteristics of public service broadcasting as: comprehensive remit; generalized mandates; diversity, pluralism and range; cultural roles; place in politics; and non-commercialism. His formulations are particularly noteworthy for they derive from discussions at a pan-European conference (of a predominantly academic character) held in Liège in 1990 where the problems of, and policies for, public service broadcasting in eleven European states[8] were discussed. The aim of the conference, titled 'Vulnerable Values in Multichannel Television Systems: What European Policy Makers seek to Protect', was 'to identify the principal values and related programming forms that European policy makers are striving to protect from marketplace pressures' (Blumler 1992: 4). As the conference title suggests, public service broadcasting (and the values it embodied) were perceived to be threatened by recent changes to European broadcasting.

Because of their provenance, Blumler's findings have a general European representativeness and correspond closely to the BRU's definitions of public service broadcasting. For example, the 'comprehensive remit' (which Blumler cited as a defining characteristic of public service broadcasting), refers chiefly to range in programming, rather than to the geographical universality of service to which the BRU drew attention. Yet, overall, Blumler's formulation is compatible with the principle of universal service as defined by the BRU.[9]

Blumler's term, 'generalised mandate', refers to the characteristic delegation of authority to public service broadcasters by political authorities, and corresponds to what the BRU defined as 'detachment from vested interests and government' which, Blumler argues, has given rise to a distinctive high minded professional broadcasting culture. Blumler's terms 'diversity, pluralism and range' closely correspond to the BRU's 'catering for all interests and tastes' and to the BRU's 'catering for minorities'. All of these prescriptions are based on a notion of broadcasting as an emancipator of its audience through the provision of diversity, and thus of choice. Blumler contrasted the minoritarian, choice-enhancing, ethos of public service broadcasting with what he identified as a majoritarian, choice-restricting, ethos of commercial television.[10]

The other characteristics of public service broadcasting which Blumler identified are less certain vehicles for the emancipation of the audience. His fourth category, 'cultural roles', charges broadcasting with responsibility for providing a national cultural cement by disseminating culturally valuable programming. By discharging its cultural role public service broadcasting will, Blumler argues, act as a 'centripetal, societally integrative force' (1992: 11). Blumler explicitly couples this characteristic of public service broadcasting with the related characteristic of providing programme quality (captured in the BRU's list of characteristics as 'good programming'), and thereby transposes views Arnold advanced in the latter half of the nineteenth century to a contemporary context. Arnold saw dissemination of the 'best that had been thought and said' (1963: 6) as a social glue for 'culture is the most resolute enemy of anarchy because of the great hopes and designs for the State which culture teaches us to nourish' (1963: 204).

Blumler is not, of course, so explicitly authoritarian as Arnold. But, unlike Arnold, he did not recognise the significance of cultural stratification (notably on class and ethnic lines) and that, consequently, there may be scant social consensus on questions of cultural quality. Arnold explicitly proposed a resolution of the problem of cultural stratification through cultural homogenisation from above ('sweetness and light' was recommended as a prophylactic against the anarchy Arnold feared, although in default of effective cultural prophylaxis he recommended 'the old Roman way . . . flog the rank and file and fling the ring-leaders from the Tarpeian Rock' [Arnold 1963: 203]). Blumler does not recognise the problem for public service broadcasting posed by cultural difference. For public service broadcasting's cultural mission may divide, rather than integrate, the target community to which its programmes are transmitted.[11]

## Public service broadcasting and the cultural mandate

Public broadcasters had, and have, an intractable problem in that their mandates provide that they should lead, rather than follow, public and popular taste, and yet their social productivity (and institutional legitimacy) depending on the degree to which their programmes and services are used and valued by viewers and listeners. In conditions of monopoly this contradiction did not prove troublesome – audiences took what they were given and, in the absence of alternatives, for the most part liked what they got. Once alternatives were available, however, the contradiction at the heart of European public service broadcasting became palpably evident as viewers (and listeners) migrated to new commercial alternatives and public broadcasters found themselves skewered on the contradiction of satisfying what Tracey has called the 'public as audience' (1992: 21) and fulfilling their public and, broadly defined, educational mandate.

The constitutions of many European public service broadcasters explicitly charged broadcasters with a cultural mission, while those public service broadcasters not explicitly so charged customarily have long traditions of discharging high cultural responsibilities. The importance of tradition, rather than law, in determining broadcasters' cultural conduct is probably best exemplified by the case of the BBC, but the BBC is far from the only case. In theory, as Shaughnessy and Fuente Cobo (1990: 88) state, the BBC enjoys 'complete freedom' in programming and neither the BBC nor ITV and Channel 4 were specifically charged with cultural responsibilities. Yet, the BBC and Channel 4 (and, to a somewhat lesser extent, ITV) have vigorously maintained an extensive commitment to programmes about culture and to programmes of high cultural quality. Nonetheless, the relatively high proportion of entertainment programmes screened by the UKIBA participant in the EBU Eurikon experiment (and the UK broadcasters' decision not to participate in Europa) suggests that public service broadcasting's cultural mandate was less important to public service broadcasters in the UK than it was to the other participants in the EBU's European satellite television services, all of whom were mandated, to greater or lesser degrees, to discharge cultural responsibilities.

In Germany, too, the cultural responsibilities with which public broadcasters, that is ZDF and members of the ARD network, have been formally charged are not onerous. For example, Bayerischer Rundfunk, the second largest member of the ARD, is enjoined to exercise 'a sense of cultural responsibility' and West Deutscher Rundfunk, the largest member of the ARD, to take into account 'artistic factors' in the discharge of its responsibilities (Shaughnessy and Fuente Cobo 1990: 44). Nonetheless, German public service broadcasters have characteristically given cultural programmes important places in their television schedules and cultural programmes departments have enjoyed prestige and high levels of resources. More importantly, the production and construction of entertainment dramas (such as feature films, single and series dramas) have been strongly marked by 'high cultural' values – notably by a pre-eminence of the authorial voice. Certainly, there are counter-indications; of which *Schwarzwaldklinik* is only the best known.[12] Nor are 'high culture' values and popularity necessarily antipathetic; witness Edgar Reitz's *Heimat* (1980–4). But despite counter-indications like *Schwarzwaldklinik*, primetime German drama on German television has been decisively shaped by the doctrine of the *Autor*: the notion that 'the film maker should have autonomy in giving shape to his film idea without having to take legal or serious financial risks. He [*sic*] was to retain control over the direction and the entire production process' (Hermann Gerber, cited in Johnston 1979: 68).[13] Elsaesser named German television's Heads of Drama as 'godfathers of the New German Cinema' (1989: 109). Other European public service broadcasters have even more exacting and explicit cultural remits.

The Austrian public service broadcaster, ORF, is charged with the promotion of arts and sciences, to offer a service of high quality and to provide comprehensive information about culture (Shaughnessy and Fuente Cobo 1990: 32). The RAI, in Italy, is specifically charged with fostering cultural pluralism and regional and national culture. Moreover the RAI has a general obligation to promote the diffusion of the Italian language and culture abroad (Shaughnessy and Fuente Cobo 1990: 102–3).

Ireland's RTE is charged with promoting Irish culture (to 'ensure that programmes reflect the varied elements which make up the culture of the people of the whole island of Ireland, and have special regard for the elements which distinguish that culture') *and* with 'developing public awareness of the values of other countries, especially those which are members of the European Economic Community' (Shaughnessy and Fuente Cobo 1990: 107).

Dutch public broadcasters are subject to extensive cultural mandates (including an obligation to allocate 20 per cent of broadcasting time to cultural items [See discussion in NOS 1990: 4–5 and NOS 1991: 4–5]). But the requirements[14] to which broadcasters became subject following promulgation of the 1987 Media Act did not apply before 1987: prior to that date broadcasters were responsible to the Minister of Culture and, moreover, Shaughnessy and Fuente Cobo state that the 1987 Media Law was promulgated to 'reflect the importance the Government attaches to the cultural obligations of public broadcasters' (1990: 123). Like their colleagues elsewhere in Europe, Dutch public service broadcasters have interpreted their formal and informal mandates as both requiring and permitting their discharge of extensive cultural responsibilities.

The Portuguese Broadcasting Act of 1979 mandates RTP to promote and defend the national culture and language, to promote Portuguese culture internationally and to strengthen relations with other nations. Moreover RTP is obliged to 'reflect in its programme schedule the diversity and pluralism of classical works, modern cultural and artistic expression' and to 'offer events and programmes of high quality and diverse content' (Shaughnessy and Fuente Cobo 1990: 130).

The broadcasters (the ARD, IBA, NOS, ORF, RAI, RTE, RTP), participating in the EBU's first satellite television initiatives (Eurikon and Europa) were thus all mandated, either by tradition or by law or both, to discharge a cultural role. Three were also explicitly charged with promoting their respective national cultures. These considerations, whether manifested in explicit constitutional imperatives or in the habits accumulated in decades of public service broadcasting, markedly influenced the character of the programming of the EBU's Eurikon and Europa satellite television channels – the examples on which this study focuses.

However, it is important to recognise that components of public service broadcasting's mandate may sometimes be contradictory. Implementation of any particular broadcasting policy may therefore involve choices about the relative priorities to be attached to any individual goal. For example, catering for minorities may be at the expense of catering for national identity and community; efficient use of resources may be hostile to provision of an extensive range of services under diverse ownership and control. Competition provoked reflection, within and outside the ranks of public service broadcasters, on these contradictions and how they should be managed.

## The Wangermée and Perez Groups

The Wangermée and Perez Groups, established within the EBU in the early 1980s, to consider the nature and future of European public service broadcasting, produced definitions which parallelled those of Blumler and the BRU. The Perez Group[15] characterised public service broadcasting as the:

- provision, at a moderate cost, of a service accessible to all;
- varied and balanced programming designed to meet the needs of all sections of the public and all age groups;
- impartiality in the presentation of news;
- good balance between informative and artistic programmes;
- predominance of original productions;
- the entrepreneurial character of public service organisations – employing highly qualified technical staff, more often than not also training them, frequently constituting the country's major employer of performers, and collaborating with national electronic industries in research and development.

(Perez 1983: 4)

Perez identified universality and diversity, impartiality and (smacking rather of special pleading) the role of public service broadcasting as a patron and author of original productions and a trainer and educator of professional broadcasters as the defining characteristics of public service broadcasting.

The Wangermée Group (the parent EBU committee to which the Perez Group reported)[16] also defined public service broadcasting and stated that public service broadcasting should:

- provide in a national community for the intention [sic] of the general public, diversified and balanced programming for all categories of the population, including minorities;
- ensure in particular that the various currents of opinion and thought are present in their programmes;

- ensure an important part of the original production which they broadcast, and in any case be fully in control of it;
- serve the public by the most appropriate technical means;
- to reinvest the main part of the results of their operations in the development of broadcasting.

(AG 551 SPG 2642 June 1984: 6)

The two EBU groups emphasised rather different elements in the portfolio of public service broadcasting's attributes. Wangermée's list lacks Perez's insistence on impartiality (and therefore on broadcasters' independence from government). However Wangermée, like Perez, strongly emphasised universality and diversity. Moreover, the Perez Group believed that public service broadcasting could only realise these goals if there was 'a sound financial basis for public service organisations' which was conditional on public service broadcasters moving 'into new sectors of activity, pay TV, videograms etc' (Perez 1983: 5). Clearly the two groups' visions had much in common, but the Perez Group advocated innovation and a re-orientation of public service broadcasting to new circumstances whereas the Wangermée Group counselled continued adherence to the time-honoured practices of European public service broadcasting.

There is then, if not complete consensus, a high degree of communality in the content of the lists of attributes of public service broadcasting generated inductively by academics and broadcasters. The core attributes of public service broadcasting identified by the BRU, Blumler, Wangermée and Perez were diversity, universality and impartiality.

## Diversity

Diversity has increasingly been constituted as the key value in the name of which public service broadcasting is defended. The primacy ceded to diversity (above other potential values such as universality and impartiality) reflects an apprehension that this is the value most vulnerable to recent changes in European broadcasting. Public provision of broadcasting and information services is defended on the grounds that market mechanisms may lead to concentration of ownership and thus a diminished diversity in programming.[17]

Measures to ensure diversity are characteristically enshrined in the constitution and organisational structure of European public service broadcasting. The Italian public service broadcaster RAI is required to reserve at least 5 per cent of television and 3 per cent of radio broadcasting time for 'important political, social, cultural, religious and ethnic groups' (Commission of the European Communities 1984a: 66). German broadcasters are charged (by the judgement of the Federal Constitutional Court of 28.2.61 on television) with ensuring that broadcasters 'organize their programmes in such a way that all organisations representing the community will be able to influence and express their views in them, and which lay down general principles with regard to the content of the overall programme to ensure a minimum of balance, objectivity and mutual respect' (Internationes 1989: 20). Moreover, the constitutions under which Länder public service broadcasters, (which make up the first German television network, the ARD) are established characteristically require that programming, as well as governing bodies, reflect the plurality of elements in German society. Dutch public radio and television was built around a plurality of organisations: broadcasting organisations (i.e. membership associations), candidate organisations and political parties (having at least one representative in Parliament), church, cultural, regional and ideologically based associations all of which have access to broadcasting time, budgets and resources (Commission of the European Communities 1984a: 69).

The organisation of public service broadcasting in the UK is less clearly pluralistic than in Germany and the Netherlands. But, like Italy, the UK has enshrined a measure of pluralism in its broadcasting system. Not only are radio and television services provided by organisations independent of each other, (albeit with a preponderant BBC), but each broadcaster is charged with delivering a diversity of programmes. Channel 4 is most clearly bound by this mandate for diversity. It was charged (in the 1980 Broadcasting Act) with 'encouraging innovation and experiment in the form and content of programmes'. Moreover emphatic measures have been taken in the last decade to support indigenous minority languages in Britain through the establishment of a Welsh language television service, S4C, and a Gaelic broadcasting fund.

However, we should note that commitments to diversity are not the exclusive prerogative of public service broadcasters. The Charter of the ACT[18] states that:

> Private television participates in European social and cultural changes. It not only reflects existing diversity but gives it an impetus by expressing the constantly evolving aspirations and expectations of the people. . . . Being obliged to respond to viewers' wishes, private television is both an expression of popular sovereignty and a guarantee of pluralism.
>
> (Maggiore 1990: 202)

Elsewhere the ACT claims commercial television develops 'the European identity and cultural heritage' and provides programmes which are 'varied and up to the quality expected by the public' (Maggiore 1990: 201). Commercial broadcasting, no less than public service broadcasting, has claimed to provide services which are diverse, of high quality, and which foster a collective European identity. Indeed, although the responsibilities with which commercial broadcasting in Europe is charged are generally less prescriptive than those which apply to public broadcasters, private broadcasters are seldom free of statutory responsibilities.

The UK Broadcasting Act of 1990, for example, provides that commercial licensees are to provide 'services which (taken as a whole) are of high quality and offer a wide range of programmes calculated to appeal to a variety of tastes and interests' (Broadcasting Act 1990: 2). And German private broadcasters too are required to ensure that 'all shades of opinion, including the opinions of minorities, should be able to find expression in private broadcasting' (Internationes 1989: 21).[19]

## Universality

In spite of its formal commitment to diversity public service broadcasting embodies markedly normative values. How could it not if universality is part of its mandate? Often the contradiction between diversity and universality has been fudged by identifying the universalistic vocation of public service broadcasting as provision of a signal universally available to viewers and listeners. With terrestrial broadcasting, universal service would not have been supplied by profit-maximising commercial broadcasting, financial returns accrued from an extension of service to remote and thinly populated areas being exceeded by the cost of providing services. However direct-to-home satellite broadcasting has made universal service both attainable and financially desirable for profit-maximising broadcasters. Latterly, however, the role of universality in programming and broadcasting services has become a prominent focus of theoretical discussion (Garnham 1992) and public policy concerns.[20]

Although nominally a medium of information, enlightenment (education) and entertainment (and thus of diverse programming), the historical practice of public service broadcasters (and the advocacy of its adherents) has often had a highly normative character. See, for example, Stephen Hearst's[21] opposition to the diversification of UK radio on the grounds that national unity and social solidarity would be impaired (Hearst 1988). Moreover when, with admirable honesty, Blumler (and his collaborator, Hoffman-Riem[22]) specified what they meant by quality programmes they produced an aesthetic recipe book of alarming prescriptiveness and conservatism. Their proposals for television entertainment conjure up an uninviting earnest future of well-made plays. 'Characters', Blumler and Hoffman-Riem prescribe, 'even when standing for something emblematic, should have those less resolved qualities of complexity, potential and uncertainty that stamp real life individuals. Its conflicts should invite reflection on interests, temperaments, taboos and preferences that originate in the real world and pose dilemmas that viewers can absorb as belonging to life as they know it or could imagine it' (Blumler 1992: 210). It would be too cruel to mine the sanctified texts of European culture to find the host of works that would be unscreenable on a public service television channel programmed under Blumler and Hoffman-Riem's injunctions.

In his contribution to Blumler and Hoffman-Riem's collection of essays, Stephen Hearst innocently gave the game away by admitting the social exclusiveness on which public service broadcasting in Britain was historically based. He observed that post-war British broadcasting recruited 'hundreds of university graduates, who in an earlier age would have joined the Foreign or Colonial services' (Blumler 1992: 66). So much for diversity in recruitment and outlook! Just as Hearst envisioned a conservative and socially exclusive composition for public service broadcasters, so do Blumler and Hoffman-Riem innocently enjoin a conservative and exclusive aesthetic for public service broadcasting. If one is of a conservative and exclusive turn of mind their aesthetic and social prescriptions might be thought desirable and perhaps even diverse. Coward one week, Wilder the next, Eton in one office, Winchester in the next? But those who neither enjoy an improving diet of well-made plays nor are graduates of the formation envisioned by Hearst are unlikely to find diversity in either the social composition of public service broadcasters or in the programming advocated by Blumler and Hoffman-Riem.

Here again we find proponents of public service broadcasting advancing a very Arnoldian vision. This patrician perspective has proven the Achilles heel of public service broadcasting, contributing to its loss of audiences to commercial broadcasters, and of the arguments made by proponents of public service broadcasting whose prescriptive cultural vision is inconsistent with their advocacy of political pluralism and broadcasting's role as a disinterested forum for political debate and intellectual and cultural exchange.

## Impartiality

The penultimate characteristic of public service broadcasting listed by Blumler – place in politics – partly corresponds to the BRU's 'detachment from vested interests' (and, in other respects, to the BRU's notion of 'good programming'). But here Blumler's emphasis is different to the BRU's (from whose list of attributes he otherwise has drawn so much). Blumler contends that public service broadcasters are 'creatures ultimately of the state' (Blumler 1992: 12) whereas the BRU emphasised public service broadcasting's 'detachment' from state power. The EBU's Perez Group was closer to the BRU than to Blumler in its vigorous assertion of public service broadcasting's impartial news coverage. Finally, Blumler asserts the non-commercial and programme-driven character of public service broadcasting (which he contrasts to commercial broadcasting's advertising-driven character). In Blumler's scheme, public service broadcasting's independence of, and therefore lack of partisanship for, commercial interests, corresponds to the BRU's notion of 'competition in good programming rather than for numbers'.

But, although there is a considerable degree of convergence in the definitions of public service broadcasting considered above, there are also striking differences of emphasis. Public service broadcasters themselves have sometimes seemed less conservative, and more ready to welcome change, than have broadcasting scholars. The conservative notions expressed by the, largely academic, contributors to the 'Vulnerable Values' conference were not shared by the modernising members of the EBU's Perez Group as the iconoclastic views of Muiris MacConghail and Hans Kimmel, cited earlier, testify.[23]

Moreover, although there are important similarities in these definitions of public service broadcasting, albeit mitigated by differences in substance and in emphasis, it is, as Negrine has observed, too seldom apparent whether the prescriptions of proponents of public service broadcasting refer to 'ises' or 'oughts' (1989: 106). Do they derive from an inductive analysis (in which case they must correspond to either, or both, the actual historical practice or to the present reality of public service broadcasting)? Or do they articulate an 'ideal type' defined deductively: a future ideal to the realisation of which policy should be directed? Are the criteria employed descriptive or evaluative, normative or aspirational? Here the 'ises' of public service broadcasting on which Blumler, the BRU and the Perez and Wangermée Groups concentrated have become 'oughts'.

## The 'oughts' of public service broadcasting

A second, deductive, approach to defining public service broadcasting has foregrounded not the historical practices of public service broadcasting (the *post hoc* 'ises'), but the role which broadcasting should perform – the 'oughts' of public service broadcasting. From the definition of broadcasting's role comes a specification which will, *propter hoc*, tell us how broadcasting 'ought' to be. There are clear merits to such an approach which is more open to innovation and reassessment of the structure and practices of public service broadcasting than an inductive approach. Moreover a deductive approach does not so readily fetishise the historical practice of particular institutions. A deductive approach has the signal merit of forcing into explicit definition the underlying social visions implicit in different models of how non-market public service broadcasting ought to be. There are at least two such visions, each of which has been ably put forward in the UK. The first, authoritarian, vision may be found in the Pilkington Committee's report of 1962 (Pilkington 1962); the second, libertarian, vision in the writings of British neo-Habermasians such as Garnham (1990 and 1992), Keane (1991) and Murdock (1990).

The Pilkington Committee put forward a clear vision of public service broadcasting representative both of the established ethos of British public service broadcasting (rooted in Reith's BBC) and of the broadcasting order which prevailed from its publication in 1962 to 1986 and the next major landmark in British official thinking about broadcasting policy: the *Report of the Committee on Financing the BBC* (otherwise known as the Peacock Report ). Pilkington believed that the audience for broadcasting was vulnerable and should be protected. Radio and, in particular, television, (which the Committee judged to be 'the main factor in influencing the values and moral standards of our society' [para 42]), had to be organised so that viewers (and listeners) were protected, not only from the baleful influence of a powerful medium, but also from themselves and their own tastes and desires. 'To give the public what it wants', Pilkington stated, 'seems at first sight unexceptionable' (1962 para 44). But in reality it is 'patronising and arrogant' (para 48) for giving the audience what it wants is justifiable only if it is assumed that viewers and listeners not only know what they want but also what is good for them. Such a view, Pilkington argued, mistakes 'what the public wants . . . for the public interest' (para 408).[24] It is hard to resist the view that Pilkington's notion of public service was one of Platonic guardianship. Servants of the public broadcasters (and regulators) they may have been, but they were servants who were certainly not expected to take directions from those whom they were appointed to serve: the masters were considered less competent to govern than were their servants.

## The Neo-Habermasian defence of public service broadcasting

Neo-Habermasian proponents of public service broadcasting adopt an approach different to Blumler's.[25] They provide not an apologia for the past achievements and established institutions of European public service broadcasting, ('ises'), but a priori arguments ('oughts') for public service broadcasting as its chief institutional guarantor and bearer of a modern public sphere. Their arguments offer potential for institutional innovation, because grounded in 'oughts', and recognise that authoritarian rationales for public service broadcasting, like Pilkington's, are insufficient to stand against the resurgent libertarianism of free market doctrines (see, *inter alia*, Brittan 1987).

Habermas' ideas were introduced to the English language debate on broadcasting by Nicholas Garnham in 1986 (Garnham 1986, reprinted in Garnham 1990: 104–14) and were developed by him and others (see, *inter alia*, Garnham 1990, 1992; Keane 1991). Although Garnham's 'The media and the public sphere'[26] first appeared in 1986 the term 'public sphere' (the core Habermasian concept borrowed by British neo-Habermasians) was first used by him in an earlier, very influential, article published in 1983 (Garnham 1983, reprinted in Garnham 1990: 115–35), titled 'Public service versus the market'.[27]

In 'Public service versus the market', Garnham argued against market, rather than public service, mechanisms as inimical to the public interest. For, he claimed, public service principles of organisation are superior 'to the market as a means of providing all citizens, whatever their wealth or geographical location, equal access to a wide range of high-quality entertainment, information and education, and as a means of ensuring that the aim of the programme producer is the satisfaction of a range of audience tastes rather than only those tastes that show the largest profit' (Garnham 1990: 120).

The market has, Garnham argues, led to diminished diversity in a reduction in the number of enterprises which control (or at least very strongly influence) the production and circulation of information and culture, and to inequitable relationships between dominant, and metropolitan, enterprises at the expense of subordinate, and peripheral, entities. These market-driven inequities and inequalities in turn have sustained pervasive and deep-rooted social inequality and inequity. Moreover, technological change promises, contrary to the libertarian rhetoric of its advocates, to accelerate these processes of actual and relative deprivation.

Whilst challenging the claims made for the market, Garnham argued that discussion of broadcasting policy has been stultified by a pervasive dualism which opposed the concepts of state and market (1990: 106, 1984: 6). He argued for a third term, the Habermasian notion of a 'public sphere', which offered an escape from dualism and a 'space for a rational and universalistic politics distinct from both the economy and the State' (1990: 107). Garnham's argument, however, was not simply for an abstract third category, distinct from the terms 'state' and 'market', but in favour of what he, and others (see, *inter alia*, Keane 1991), designated the institutional embodiment and guarantor of the modern public sphere – public service broadcasting.

Whilst Garnham's triad escapes from dualism it is not problem free. For, although a third term conceptually mediating between state and market may be intellectually productive and signify a distinctive ethos in (at least some) broadcasting institutions at (some) moments in history, the notion of the public sphere helps only to a limited extent when concrete questions of broadcasting policy and organisation arise. For how is broadcasting to be funded if not by either the state[28] or the market? Moreover, others have shown that public service broadcasters' actual practice is far from that which would characterise a well functioning public sphere (see, *inter alia*, Docker 1991; GUMG 1976; Hjarvard 1991). Indeed, the discontinuity between Habermas' own arguments about broadcasting and the concrete broadcasting context in which he wrote makes the appropriation of Habermas' term 'public sphere' for defence of public service broadcasting rather curious.

Habermas' *Strukturwandel der Öffentlichkeit* (*The Structural Transformation of the Public Sphere*) (1989 [1962]) was written in a society where broadcasting services were provided by perhaps the most perfect form of public service broadcasting yet institutionalised (see, *inter alia*, Collins and Porter 1981; Falkenberg 1983). Yet, Habermas asserts quite unequivocally the *necessary* inferiority of audio-visual media to print media for rational understanding and democratic exchange.[29] He stated, (with characteristic opacity):

Radio, film and television by degrees reduce to a minimum the distance that a reader is forced to maintain toward the printed letter – a distance that required the privacy of the appropriation as much as it made possible the publicity of a rational-critical exchange about what had been read. With the arrival of the new media the form of communication as such has changed; they have had an impact, therefore, more penetrating (in the strict sense of the word) than was ever possible for the press. Under the pressure of the 'Don't talk back!' the conduct of the public assumes a different form. In comparison with printed communications the programs sent by the new media curtail the reactions of their recipients in a peculiar way. They draw the eyes and ears of the public under their spell but at the same time, by taking away its distance, place it under 'tutelage', which is to say they deprive it of the opportunity to say something and to disagree.

(Habermas 1989: 170–1)

Habermas developed his notion of the public sphere in the course of a general critique of contemporary mass society and mass communications and not to defend public service broadcasting (to which he gave scant attention). Like most members of the Frankfurt School[30] Habermas disdains demotic culture and the mass media's reduction of human experience to, what Marcuse trenchantly described as, 'one dimensionality' and its reification of culture as a commodity (see, *inter alia*, Marcuse 1972: 24). Thus, appropriation of the term 'public sphere' for a defence of public service broadcasting may appear to have been rather arbitrarily chosen.[31] Not least because, as several commentators have observed, Habermas' category – the public sphere – is open to objection and qualification.

Keane (1991: 35–6), for example, has argued that Habermas sentimentalised the heroic bourgeois era,[32] an argument which Schudson (1992) has explored in an excellent concrete historical analysis. And Bauman has cruelly compared Habermas' conception of the public sphere to 'society shaped after the pattern of a sociology seminar, that is, that there are only participants and the one thing that matters is the power of argument' (1992: 217). Perhaps Nancy Fraser's definition of the category 'public sphere' as a 'conceptual resource' (1992: 110) rather than a term signifying a strong identity between Habermas' own intellectual system and that of the user best captures the nature of the debt to Habermas of neo-Habermasian proponents of public service broadcasting.

So too is the reality of European public service broadcasters' commitment to a public sphere somewhat equivocal. Broadcasters' commitment to informing and educating their public too often led them to serve an audience of their imagination rather than the real audience. Rather than a democratic public sphere, in which the actual experience and interest of a real empirical public was represented, monopolistic European public service broadcasters too often addressed the public experience and interests, the public sphere, of elites. 'Bottom up' public services, which gave voice to a real public (or, to use Reith's term, publics) and represented a demotic and genuinely democratic public sphere, were conspicuous by their absence until competition with commercial services compelled public broadcasters to address the real public rather than that of their imagination. Claims for public service broadcasting's success in satisfying audiences' tastes can be reconciled only with difficulty with the dramatic loss of audience share experienced by European public service broadcasters when their monopolies were first challenged by commercial competitors. Recognition of 'the public as audience' (Tracey 1992: 21) did not come about spontaneously but as a consequence of competition with commercial broadcasting: that is, through public service broadcasters' presence *in* the market.

## Culture and the public sphere

Habermas' etymological discussions in the *Strukturwandel* provide some useful clues as to the Arnoldian character of his conception of culture and to the consequences of advocacy of public service broadcasting based on Habermasian foundations. His conception of culture is unfortunately reminiscent of the outlook which identified 'culture [as] the product of the old leisured classes who seek to defend it against new and destructive forces' (Williams 1963: 306). He points out that just as 'public' and 'lordly' (the public sphere and the state) were irrevocably intertwined, so too were the roots of the cultural elements of a public sphere, a growing 'representative publicness', to be found in the culture of both the nobility and the bourgeoisie (Habermas 1989: 9). The culture of Habermas' emergent public sphere was an elite culture (albeit rooted in the tastes and experience of the new, as well as the old, upper classes): if the 'humanistically cultivated courtier replaced the Christian knight' (1989: 9), little change is likely to have been apparent to those enjoying membership of neither courtly nor merchant classes. The common man was not the same as the educated man and the culture of the 'public' was not that of the 'mass', and the only way of making it so was (as Matthew Arnold enjoined) by educating common men and women. Habermas follows Kant in proposing that humans are limited by their own incapacities (from which they could be emancipated by others) as well as by duress imposed by others.

However, as Kant stated, in a section of his essay 'What is Enlightenment?' (1959), tellingly cited by Habermas (1989: 104): 'Enlightenment is man's release from his self-incurred tutelage. Tutelage is man's inability to make use of his understanding without direction from another. Self-incurred is this tutelage when its cause lies not in lack of reason but in lack of resolution and courage to use it without direction from another. Sapere aude! "Have courage to use your own reason!" – that is the motto of enlightenment' (1959: 85). Emancipation from 'tutelage' is both a social activity in which individuals may learn from others, and thus be freed by them, and also an individual activity in which the individual must release her- or himself from a tutelage imposed by others.

Habermas recognised the necessity of a social and collaborative dimension to emancipation and enlightenment. 'Liberation from self-incurred tutelage meant enlightenment. With regard to the individual, this denoted a subjective maxim, namely; to think for oneself . . . enlightenment had to be mediated by the public sphere' (Habermas 1989: 104). Here he clearly offers a foothold for proponents of public service broadcasting – a foothold initially provided by Kant. Citing further from 'What is Enlightenment?' he (and Kant) states 'For any single individual to work himself out of the life under tutelage which has become almost his nature is very difficult' (Habermas 1989: 104; Kant 1959: 86). Clearly proponents of public service broadcasting (from Reith, through Pilkington to the neo-Habermasians) have seen public service broadcasting as a mediating institution in the public sphere for exactly this aim.

A statement by Reith captures this Janus-faced inheritance very well and aptly characterises the potential of public service broadcasting to be both an instrument of tutelage and a means of emancipation from it. Reith testified to the democratic effect of broadcasting, but defined this democratic effect in terms of an improvement in information flow from above to below. Reith wrote (in a statement where he explicitly compared broadcasting to the Athenian agora) that broadcasting brought 'the personalities of the leading figures to the fireside' (Reith 1949: 135) of (those whom elsewhere he called ordinary people) 'mini-men' whom he regretted 'have all got votes' (cited in Boyle 1972: 18).[33]

However, in his discussion of tutelage, Habermas did not cite other sections of 'What is Enlightenment?' which are relevant to a consideration of the role and purpose of public service broadcasting. Kant also stated, that:

> Laziness and cowardice are the reasons why so great a portion of mankind, after nature has long since discharged them from external direction (*naturaliter maiorennes*), nevertheless remains under lifelong tutelage, and why it is so easy for others to set themselves up as their guardians. It is so easy not to be of age. If I have a book which understands for me, a pastor who has a conscience for me, a physician who decides my diet, and so forth, I need not trouble myself. I need not think, if I can only pay – others will readily undertake the irksome work for me.
>
> (Kant 1959: 85)

This passage has the authentic, noble, smack of Kant's earnest Prussian pietism about it. It affords little space for fun, diversion or the seductions of being not of age. However it stands as a powerful rationale for benevolent social action to emancipate man from tutelage (to use Kant's category), a rationale chosen by European public service broadcasting which, when free of competition, opted to prioritise information and education over entertainment.

The intellectual matrices in which different European public service broadcasting systems were formed have their own national specificities, and the influence of their Kantian inheritance is more directly apparent in some than in others. One looks, for example, in vain for a mention of Kant in Reith's writings. Yet in his and his successors' definitions of public service broadcasting there is, surely, an unmistakably Kantian strain. Reith wrote thus of the BBC:

> The BBC had founded a tradition of public service and of devotion to the highest interest of community and nation. There was to hand a mighty instrument to instruct and fashion public opinion; to banish ignorance and misery; to contribute richly and in many ways to the sum total of human wellbeing.
>
> (Reith 1949: 103)[34]

The statements of Reith's successors (as Directors General of the BBC) resonated with similarly Kantian strains (see Charles Curran 1971, cited in Smith 1974: 190–1; Alasdair Milne, cited in Peacock 1986: 130; William Haley 1948, cited in Smith 1974: 83). Like Reith's simultaneous endorsement and negation of Kant's emancipatory vision, they testify to the contradiction at the centre of public service broadcasting's project: emancipation on the terms set by the broadcasting elites who, like Habermas, have seen popular taste as a problem to be rectified rather than a centre of value. Habermas stated:

> mass culture has earned its rather dubious name precisely by achieving increased sales by adopting to the need for relaxation and entertainment on the part of consumer strata with relatively little education, rather than through the guidance of an enlarged public toward the appreciation of a culture undamaged in its substance.
>
> (Habermas 1989: 165)

It is easy to see popular taste, and the commercial broadcasting which has served it, as embodying Kant's vision of being not of age, of immersion in a 'book which understands for me' and Habermas' attribution of a 'dubious name' to mass culture clearly refers directly to contemporary, for-profit, mass media. But we may also see public service broadcasting as embodying Kant's vision of an agency of tutelage. What more clearly exemplifies Kant's notion of 'a pastor who has a conscience for me, a physician who decides my diet' than Pilkington's definition of the role of the governors of broadcasting. See Pilkington (e.g. 1962 para 408, cited above) for eloquent testimony to this effect.

Habermas' locution, 'through the guidance of an enlarged public toward the appreciation of a culture undamaged in its substance', clearly does not refer to a relationship of equals but to a Pilkingtonian guidance of consumers by guardians away from what he calls 'consumption ready' cultural goods to 'serious involvement with culture' (Habermas 1989: 166). As Peacock (1986), Kimmel (1982), Bourges (1993) and others have recognised, public service broadcasting has paid too little regard to the needs and desires of those whom it has undertaken to enlighten.

Not only were public service broadcasters too little prepared to recognise the importance of demotic entertainment in their programme schedules (and paid a high price in loss of audience share and legitimacy when confronted with commercial competition, which supplied viewers' and listeners' taste for cakes and ale), but so too are proponents of public service broadcasting characteristically slow to recognise that broadcasting is more than a political medium – it is an aesthetic medium too. As Kant stated 'If we attend to the course of conversation in mixed companies consisting not merely of scholars and subtle reasoners but also of business people and women, we notice that besides storytelling and jesting they have another entertainment, namely, arguing' (Kant 1949: 250–1, cited in Habermas 1989: 106). Curiously, Habermas cites Kant's recognition that human conversation and social experience is animated by storytelling and jesting as well as by argument to appropriate Kant's invocation of argument, whilst neglecting Kant's acknowledgement of storytelling and jesting. European public service broadcasting has similarly given greater salience to argument than to jesting,

Common to the inductivist and deductivist proponents of public service broadcasting is a categorical opposition between public service broadcasting and the market. This opposition is clearly signalled in the title of Garnham's seminal article 'Public service versus the market' (1983), but Blumler is scarcely less explicit. He proposed a categorical difference between market and public service broadcasting systems. One, he contends, is rooted in a 'standpoint of social ethics' and the other animated solely by the 'capture of audience as market as the prime, normative and pragmatic goal of the broadcasting business' (Blumler 1992: 2). It is undoubtedly true that the formula 'capture of audience as market as the prime, normative and pragmatic goal of the broadcasting business' (1992: 2) justly characterises some contemporary European broadcasters. But it does not accurately represent the outlook of all theorists of (or apologists for) the adoption of market principles as a basis for the organisation of broadcasting. Indeed, part of the power of market ideas has been the ethical component which they contain (see, *inter alia*, Friedman and Friedman 1981). And it is difficult to reconcile many public service broadcasters' intransigent defence of their historical monopolies, their subordination to party political agendas or their own commercial practices with a 'standpoint of ethics': as 'modernising' public service broadcasters have recognised.

Indeed, Massimo Fichera[35] of RAI described the changes to RAI following the introduction of competition in Italy as leading to a 'fruitful balance between market forces and public service requirements' (Fichera 1989: 23).[36]

It is clear that public service broadcasters *did* respond to pan-European commercial television by satellite with the European public service alternative which Melody enjoined (Melody 1988: 271) – first with the experimental Eurikon service and later with Europa, a fully fledged operational successor to Eurikon. The question is how far was public service broadcasters' challenge appropriate to the reception context, (the preferences and behaviour of

European viewers), and to the institutional and political context (created by the re-regulation of European broadcasting by pan-European political institutions; notably the European Community and the Council of Europe), into which it was launched? Negrine and Papathanassopoulos judged that Europa's lack of success stemmed from a regulatory climate hostile to public service broadcasting:

> the demise of Europa Television reflected the problems of public service broadcasters in an internationally commercial environment and in the age of liberalisation and privatisation.
> (Negrine and Papathanassopoulos 1990: 177)

There is much in the institutional and political context in which Europa was launched which lends support to their judgement. But neglect of the public as audience, for some public service broadcasters a habit rooted in a long and comfortable experience of monopoly and for all an endemic risk arising from their role as agencies of tutelage, was also a key factor, as examination of the history of pan-European public service satellite television (and its reception context in particular) shows.

# 4

# EURIKON: THE DEVELOPMENT
# OF PAN-EUROPEAN TELEVISION

[An] increasing need for European programmes exists. For European
politics it is of enormous importance to be represented by journalists on
[the] European level and also to be able to present oneself direct to
national audiences. But there are so many more interests – social and
cultural – that are from a European standpoint crying out for more
intensive and extensive communication.

(Dankert in AVRO 1982: 4).

Pieter Dankert's statement,[1] made when he was President of the European
Parliament, goes far to explain European politicians' and European broadcasters' enthusiastic embrace of the new communication technology of satellite
television. Satellite television seemed to offer the means to cement the nascent
European Community by fostering a European consciousness among Europe's
television viewers.

Europe's first operational satellite television channels began in 1982 using
the European Space Agency's (ESA) Orbital Test Satellite (OTS).[2] In April the
commercial Sky Television started up and in May a consortium of European
broadcasters under the umbrella of the EBU responded with their Eurikon
experimental service. Following the Eurikon experiment, European public
service broadcasters launched a full operational service, Europa. Europa was
based at NOS in the Netherlands from 1985 to 1986 and was a full operational
service (in contrast to Eurikon, which was an experimental service seen only by
broadcasters). Europa, like Eurikon, was strongly supported by the EBU
(although neither were 'official' EBU ventures) and following Europa's demise,
two further EBU-sponsored channels were launched: Eurosport (beginning in
1989) and Euronews (beginning on New Year's Day 1993). The origins of all
major European public service satellite channels, including ARTE, the Franco-
German culture channel (several key members of which were actively involved
in the EBU-sponsored channels) can thus be traced to Eurikon.

## The origins of Eurikon

In 1980 the ESA offered the EBU (for at least three years), the second of two direct broadcast satellite (DBS) television channels (the first was allocated to Italy), to be established on what was first known as 'L-Sat' and was subsequently named 'Olympus'. L-Sat was described as 'a heavy platform that would carry in particular a 12Ghz broadcasting pay-load' (letter from E. Quistgaard, Director General ESA, to Jean Autin, President of the EBU, dated January 1981). Two-thirds of the cost of L-Sat were shared equally by Italy and the UK and the remaining one-third was shared between Austria, Belgium, Denmark, the Netherlands, Spain, Switzerland and Canada. The EBU accepted the ESA's invitation but made it clear that it would not contribute to the development costs of the L-Sat (Autin to Quistgaard 6.1.81). However, the EBU remained cautious. Two years later Autin stated (to the EBU's Administrative Council) that 'he was not convinced of L-Sat's utility. From fragmentary studies he had carried out himself, an operation of this nature would be ruinous from the point of view of the cost/operation ratio' (CA 1638 SPG 2107 10.2.83: 85).[3] Autin's scepticism endured and the following year he told the General Assembly that 'there should be a clear distinction between the European programme which he agreed with, and the vehicle that would be used in – this case [sic] L-Sat/Olympus – which he did not favour' (EBU 1984a: 68).

At first the EBU envisaged a three-stage development of an EBU satellite television channel. First, an 'experimental stage using OTS', a 'pre operational stage using L-Sat' and, from 1990, 'an operational stage using the national direct broadcast satellites' (report to the 32nd Ordinary Session of the General Assembly, 26–9 June 1981. AG 512. SPB 191). Eurikon was the 'experimental stage' of the initiative. It was planned and run by a small group of energetic and innovative broadcasters – the Group of Experts – working through the EBU's New Developments Group (itself a sub group of the EBU Television Programme Committee). Europa became the operational stage. But the EBU neither used the L-Sat nor a national DBS as had been envisaged originally. By 1984 (when Autin urged caution on the General Assembly) the EBU had benefited from the experience conferred by Eurikon, and saw the difficulties the ESA was experiencing with L-Sat. These were sufficient to persuade the EBU to use satellites operated by Eutelsat and Luxembourg's Société Européenne des Satellites (SES) for its subsequent services.

## The Group of Experts

The Group of Experts (formally known as 'The Group To Consider European Direct Broadcast Satellite Programme Experiments') overcame formidable organisational, technical and institutional difficulties to bring Eurikon to the screens of participating EBU broadcasters. The Group was established in November 1980 at a meeting in Venice, instigated by RAI, and which included the key figures in the development of public service satellite television over the next decade. Notably, Jean-Pierre Julien (Senior Assistant at the EBU and later the EBU co-ordinator for Eurikon), Adolf Aigner of ORF and Richard Dill of ARD (who subsequently led the Austrian and German contributions to Eurikon), Carel Enkelaar of the NOS and Neville Clarke of the IBA (who became the lynch pin of Eurikon and was appointed *rapporteur* to the group). The Group's chair, Edouard Haas, had played a notable role in establishing Eurovision and Clarke had played a similar part in respect of the EBU's Eurovision news exchanges. Clarke's exceptional contribution to Eurikon was recognised in April 1983 when he received the *Grand Prix de la recherche* at MIP-TV (the principal European annual television trade fair held at Cannes).

The time seemed ripe for pan-European television in the early 1980s. Technological change had made satellite television possible and European institutions sought a medium to communicate with European viewers and voters. The first directly elected European Parliament had taken office in June 1979 and its five-year term expired in 1984. MEPs wished to bring their own activities to voters' attention and the existence and work of the Parliament itself into greater public prominence. Pieter Dankert's statement, cited at the beginning of this chapter, is a case in point. Dankert, and here he was representative of the European Parliament for which he spoke, emphatically advocated 'a European standpoint' because 'Europe does not yet exist in the different national consciousness' (Dankert in AVRO 1982: 4).

Other European agencies had similar goals and were receptive to the EBU's proposals to establish a television service which would raise their visibility and promote 'Europe'. For example, in 1975 the Parliamentary Assembly of the Council of Europe (in Recommendation 749) had asserted that 'broadcasting can constitute an important means of furthering European unity' and recommended that 'a more active policy of programme exchanges between European states, where possible using subtitling rather than dubbing' be adopted. Further, that national broadcasters should promote 'regular and serious (rather than sensational) coverage of the current activities of the major European organisations' (Council of Europe 1991: 23). The Parliamentary Assembly's recommendation was but one of a growing number of Council of Europe initiatives (of which the most important was establishment of the CDMM – the Steering Committee on the Mass Media – in 1982) which signalled the increased importance which the Council attached to media issues.

But, important though the political imperatives were, the most important factor was the EBU's concern about the development of commercial satellite television. It is easy to forget that in 1982 commercial television hardly existed in Europe. European states' control of the radio frequency spectrum had, Finland, the UK and Italy excepted, kept public service broadcasters' monopolies intact. Satellite television, boosted by the European Communities' proposals for free circulation of television signals among Member States of the European Communities in the *Television without Frontiers* Green Paper (Commission of the European Communities 1984a) broke the monopolies. The minutes of the meeting of the Executive Group of the EBU Television Programme Committee (held in Geneva on 29 and 30 October 1981) testify to public service broadcasters' concern. The Television Programme Committee expressed 'disquiet at the activities of the British commercial company Satellite TV Ltd'. The EBU's anxiety about Brian Haynes' company continued. When Satellite Television Ltd was discussed in the Administrative Council, Robert Wangermée (RTBF) stated that he 'felt the EBU should take the initiatives of Satellite Television Ltd very seriously since they could lead to a destructuralisation [sic] of the Union' (CA 1588 SPG 1773 December 1981: 70).

Accordingly, proponents of satellite television urged the EBU to develop a satellite service (using the ESA's DBS L-Sat) to pre-empt competitive commercial services.[4] In January 1982, just a few months before Sky Television began its service, the Administrative Council of the EBU recommended that 'members . . . take the utmost caution if they are contacted by any enterprise such as Satellite Television Ltd and asks them to adopt the attitude suggested by the Secretary General in his telex of 7 May' (Decisions of the Administrative Council dated 18.1.82 SPG 1801 inf).[5] Satellite Television Ltd (STL) had applied for membership of the EBU on 18.12.81 and had been refused on the grounds that:

> Satellite Television Ltd is not a broadcasting organisation but an enterprise for the supply of audiovisual programmes of all kinds in the same way as major cinema film production firms may not produce not only cinema films but all kinds of audiovisual material such as telefilms, videograms etc. Hence STL does not meet the Statutes requirements for EBU membership.
>
> (GE Statuts SPG 1925 12.5.82: 2)

Moreover, STL's supply of programmes to cable networks was seen by the EBU as a threat to the interests of EBU members and to represent a trend which 'can only aggravate the competitive situation in which EBU members are increasingly engaged' (GE Statuts SPG 1925 12.5.82: 2). In this early skirmish between the emergent commercial satellite television services and European public service broadcasters, embodied in the EBU, two themes surfaced which were later to assume great importance.

First, the EBU refused membership to a new entrant to the broadcasting market. The Union's consistent refusal to admit new commercial members made it vulnerable to sanctions by the European Community's Competition Directorate, DG IV, on the grounds that its working practices were unfair and anti-competitive. Indeed, Sky Television, the successor to Satellite Television Limited, complained to the Competition Directorate in 1986 about the EBU's acquisition of sports rights and consequential foreclosure of access by non-EBU members to rights, (a complaint which was subsequently dropped when the EBU and Sky Channel, erstwhile adversaries, became partners in Eurosport).[6]

Second, the EBU used the same technical definition of a television satellite as that used by the European Community in its Directive on satellite television transmission standards (Council of the European Communities 1986). Thus, the OTS was regarded as a telecommunications and not a television satellite. Formally, the satellites used by almost all commercial television broadcasters from the inception of European satellite television in 1982 to the mid-1990s were telecommunications satellites. This meant that neither the EBU nor the European Community was able to resist or regulate commercial satellite television during the 1980s. The EBU's reasoning that, because STL used a satellite officially designated as a telecommunications satellite rather than a broadcasting satellite, STL could not be recognised as a broadcaster (even though the EBU used the same satellite for its Eurikon transmissions), rebounded on it.

However, although there can be no doubt that the EBU sought to deny STL access to EBU services (and thus was vulnerable to charges that it abused a dominant market position), the EBU's determination to launch a public service satellite television channel was not anti-competitive. Whilst Eurikon and Europa grew out of EBU members' defensive concern to pre-empt competition, in practice the establishment of the EBU's services extended viewer choice and intensified competition. But, in these early decisions the EBU adopted a strategy which ultimately served it ill. Not only did it take a path that led to a succession of damaging conflicts with the Competition Directorate of the Commission of the European Communities but the satellite services it fostered cost its participating members very dearly. And, in the most piquant of ironies, the EBU's subsequent satellite television partnership with News International in Eurosport strengthened News International's own commercial satellite services at a critical juncture and laid the foundation for the spectacular success of the BSkyB service dominated by News International.

## Programme planning for the OTS

Clarke and his colleagues in the Group of Experts were given a remit 'to design and present several tentative European TV programme schedules, allowing for all possible options and implications: operational, legal, technical and financial' (Clarke 1981: 2). If they decided that a service should be established they were to 'draw up a progressive plan covering a sufficiently long period to ensure that, by the time the experiments are over, the programmes really are being received by an audience. This means (a) that the programme proposed by the group will need to provide the variety European viewers are accustomed to and (b) that the group will need to take into account the results of the latest European audience surveys' (Unpublished RAI report of the Venice meeting, 'European TV Programme Experiments using Direct Broadcast Satellites – L-Sat in Particular' dated December 1980).

The Group of Experts identified three potential sources of programmes for an EBU satellite television service which would offer 'a balanced schedule of the best European television' (Clarke 1982: 42–4). These were Eurovision programmes which were not screened because of insufficient channel capacity (the group discovered that 700 programme hours of Eurovision programming per year were not used); programmes which were unsuited to Eurovision but were well fitted to a satellite channel; and co-productions and other new programmes made especially for a new channel.

The Group of Experts met again in London on April 10th 1981[7] and agreed on common principles for the 'European TV Programme Experiment'. These were:

- The service should disseminate informational, educational and entertainment programmes of high quality which are of interest and relevance to the widest possible European audience.
- There should be a suitable balance between different types of programme matter and between the geographical and linguistic origin of the programmes transmitted.
- A substantial proportion of the programmes should be produced or co-produced by the participating broadcasting organisations.
- As far as possible, the service should be complementary to, rather than competitive with, the existing national services of participating organisations.
- The service should take into account the totality of other national and international services available to the various national audiences.
- The service should aim to reflect the characters and cultures of the individual participating countries to a wider audience.
- The service should aim to establish a distinctive flavour and character of its own, the schedule should be flexible enough to include extended coverage of major events, encouragement should be given to repeats for a wider audience of programmes of merit and a suitable proportion of the programmes should be innovative and experimental in form and character.
- As far as possible, arrangements should be made so that all programmes included in the service are understandable to the entire audience that is covered by the transmissions.
- As far as possible, the content of the programmes transmitted should be compatible with generally accepted standards of impartiality and good taste in the participating countries.

Two aspects of these principles are particularly important. First, they clearly embody the core, historically defined, values of public service broadcasting – universality, range and diversity of services, high mindedness, innovation and responsibility in content. Whilst it was eminently understandable that public service broadcasters should seek to use a new medium to bring a familiar diet of programmes to viewers, their adoption of a conservative programming strategy when new commercial services were bringing European viewers new mixes of programming (and were arousing considerable alarm among established public service broadcasters for doing so) proved highly damaging. Second, whilst it was again eminently understandable that the new satellite service was charged to *supplement* rather than *supplant* established national public broadcasting services, subordination of the new service to established terrestrial services fatally hampered the EBU's new pan-European channels.

The Group of Experts identified three possible channel formats for Eurikon which embodied in different ways the public service principles they had specified. The Group of Experts considered a thematic sports channel (proposed by Jean-Pierre Julien of the EBU and later adopted by the EBU for the Eurosport channel); a 'vertically' streamed schedule, whereby each day was given a particular character (proposed by the ARD's Richard Dill and later used in the RAI week of Eurikon and for the Franco-German ARTE channel); and a mixed programme schedule (proposed by Neville Clarke and used subsequently on Eurikon and Europa).

Not only did the different channel formats indicate the different priorities of the different European public service broadcasters, but planning the new channel also revealed different conceptions of the appropriate relationship between the new service and its audiences. Dill proposed a target audience share of 5 per cent whereas Clarke argued that the service should not be conceived as 'a ghetto or over elitist' channel. In the event Eurikon's scheduling and programming combined the influences of both Clarke and Dill's conceptions. Its news programming and mixed scheduling echoed Clarke, and its complementary scheduling (arts and drama at the weekend, sport mid-week) and themed days followed Dill's notions.

## Overcoming the opposition inside

The Group of Experts concluded their discussions at their third meeting at St-Germain (in June 1981). Clarke drafted their report (submitted to the EBU's New Developments Group in September 1981) which recommended that a service using the ESA's OTS should be established. Clarke's report stressed the need for urgency because of the activities of 'the British commercial consortium Satellite Television Ltd', a ploy which doubtless contributed to the successful consolidation of support for the proposed channel. The Group of Experts' 'parent committee', the New Developments Group, supported Clarke's proposal at its Cannes meeting in October 1981. In turn, the New Developments Group's response, endorsing the Group of Experts' proposal, was considered by the Executive Group of the Television Programme Committee meeting in Geneva later the same month. Clarke presented the Group of Experts' findings and Enkelaar the views of the New Developments Group.

The Group of Experts' report and proposals came under attack in both the

Television Programmes Committee and the New Developments Group. Notably by Noble Wilson, the BBC's Controller of International Relations and representative on the Executive Group of the EBU's Television Programme Committee, who 'voiced serious doubts about the value of a European programme project in view of both the costs and the practical difficulties of organising the operation' (SPG 1653 October 1981: 3).

Wilson's comments had been foreshadowed in a letter to Clarke by Michael Johnson (then Chief Assistant to the Deputy Managing Director BBC Television and later Head of International Television Liaison at the BBC). Johnson stated: 'I share the idealism that you and other members of the Group have over this issue but I think it is important for the New Developments Group that reports which have its endorsement should be severely practical and relate to the real world of television finance'. Johnson attached a copy of the paper he had written to brief Wilson (and which resumed the arguments Johnson had made at the New Developments Group meeting in Cannes). Johnson compared Eurikon to 'test driving a Rolls Royce which is easily and cheaply arranged but which may not be a sensible operation if you cannot in fact afford the motor car in the end' (Johnson, letter to Clarke, copied to members of the New Developments Group, 20 October 1981).

Although there can be no doubt that events vindicated Johnson's judgement, the BBC's opposition to the EBU OTS initiative was strongly influenced by its own corporate interests. The BBC was about to be given the sole broadcasting responsibility for the planned UK DBS television service, following publication of the UK Home Office's (then the department of state responsible for broadcasting) report on satellite broadcasting (Home Office 1981). Early the following year the Home Secretary announced the BBC's role in developing the, ultimately abortive, Unisat project. Earlier (that is, before its role in UK satellite television was envisaged), the BBC had advocated use of an ESA satellite for EBU programme exchanges (displacing the EBU permanent terrestrial circuits) and proposed a feasibility study of an EBU pan-European satellite television service:

La BBC estime néanmoins que les programmes d'expériences de l'UER devraient insister davantage sur les aspects favorables du débordement de H-SAT qui, en dépit des obstacles juridiques et politiques, pourrait être mis à profit pour étudier l'échange bilatéral de programmes. On pourrait aussi examiner les possibilités de réalisation d'un programme européen supranational s'adressant à de vastes groupes de pays. [The BBC believes that the EBU's experimental programmes must above all recognise the positive aspects of the development of the H-Sat which, in spite of legal and political obstacles, could with advantage be used to investigate bilateral programme exchanges. It would also be possible to study the feasibility of a

supranational European programme transmitted to a large number of
countries.]

(EBU memo *Expériences de Programme Européen avec OTS*. SG
UER/ESA/RAI 12 Avril 1982)

Indeed the EBU traced the genesis of the OTS experiment (and thus the
Eurikon and Europa ventures opposed by the BBC) from the BBC's proposal!
Moreover, after the failure of Eurikon and Europa and its own successful with-
drawal from the abortive UK DBS initiative, the BBC took a leading part in
establishing the EBU's next pan-European satellite television service,
Eurosport.

However, the Group of Experts' recommendations to establish a satellite
television service survived the BBC's opposition and were endorsed by the
highest bodies of the EBU. The Administrative Council endorsed the Television
Programmes Committee's invitation to EBU members to express their 'intention to transmit programmes using L-Sat' as a first stage towards realising the
'possibility of a European TV programme for the general public transmitted via
direct broadcast satellite'. The Television Programmes Committee stressed that
its recommendations were influenced by 'disquiet at the activities of the British
commercial company Satellite TV Ltd' (source SPG 1653 October 1981). In
late 1981 the Administrative Council urged a 'speed up' of work on satellite
policy. It noted the challenges posed by commercial satellite initiatives and
stated that 'It will also be necessary to overcome the obstacle of RTL's[8] opposition to the use of channel 20 by this satellite'. Further, it warned members 'to
take the utmost caution if they are contacted by any enterprise such as Satellite
Television Ltd' (SPG 1801 18.1.82: 15). Thus, late in 1981 the battle lines
between the European public broadcasters embodied in the EBU and the
nascent commercial satellite industry were drawn – albeit there were divisions
within the EBU camp. From then on matters moved rapidly.

## The development of Eurikon

In early 1982 the Group of Experts was renamed the Group of Programme
Experts and later redesignated the EBU/OTS Operations Group. Clarke
continued to head the group and Eurikon was accorded the status of a 'full
EBU operation' (G.Ex/Perm.Sub-G.News (r) SPG 1797/ March 1982: 26).
The renamed group first met at EBU headquarters in Geneva on January 20–1
1982[9] and agreed to commission research; on viewer behaviour in a multi
channel situation; on programme schedules; on the legal and technical questions associated with a pan-European satellite service; on news and on different
methods of re-languaging programmes including teletext.

At its Geneva meeting the group recommended five weeks of experimental
transmissions with each of the 'active' members (of what later became known as
the Eurikon consortium) taking responsibility for one week of transmissions.

The active members were the IBA from the UK (UKIB), RAI from Italy, ORF from Austria, NOS from the Netherlands and the ARD from Germany. The Eurikon 'experiment' was to pilot the proposed L-Sat service: 'the proposed use for the L-Sat experiments could be extrapolated from the experiments planned for OTS this year' by:

- demonstrating and testing five different possible schedule patterns for a European television Service;
- carrying out research designed to assess possible audience reaction to such a service and its impact on existing national services;
- experimenting with and assessing the costs and effectiveness of multi-channel audio and teletext subtitling in different languages;
- seeking new ways of making programmes understandable of [sic] a multilingual audience;
- assessing the nature and cost of the central services including news and information services and other infrastructure that would be required for an operational European service;
- identifying and as far as possible resolving the technical, legal and financial problems that an operational service would present;
- drawing attention to the interest of European Public Service Broadcasters in cooperation in the field of Direct Broadcast Satellites.

(Minutes of Meeting of Programme Experts Geneva 21.1.82 SPG 1806)

The Operations Group realised that their initiative could thrive only if it appeared not to threaten EBU member broadcasters' services. Clarke emphasised that 'any news service included should neither compete nor conflict with national news services' and that the experiment was simply to identify 'the problems that would be involved in an operational European direct broadcast service' in which 'news and information about Europe in various styles and formats should be included' (G.Ex/Perm.Sub-G.News (r) SPG 1797/March 1982: 24). These emollient assurances testified to EBU member broadcasters' sensitivity about competition to their terrestrial services – even when this competition came from among their own members.

## The Operations Group

The Operations Group which turned Eurikon from fantasy into fact comprised Neville Clarke (Head), Adolf Aigner (ORF), Klaas-Jan Hindriks (NOS), Richard Dill (ARD), Vittorio Boni (RAI[10]), Jean-Pierre Julien, Werner Rumphorst, Louis Cheveau and Freddy van der Kerkhove (all from the EBU Permanent Services staff), assisted by advisers on research (de Bock of NOS), engineering (Waddington of the IBA) and multi-audio (d'Amato of RAI).[11]

At the first meeting of the Operations Group in London on 15 February 1982 Clarke laid out the basis on which Eurikon was to operate. He proposed that Eurikon programming should place in the foreground pan-European themes. Clarke instanced the 'links between cultural and linguistic groupings: for example the Celtic connections between Catalonia and Atlantic seaboard communities from Spain to Scotland, the connections between "new immigrant communities", and "New World" links such as Portugal/Brazil, Spain/Mexico, France and the UK/Canada'[12] (although the Irish and British connections to the USA were not mentioned!). Clarke also proposed links to Eastern Europe and 'pan-national' themes, such as anniversaries, (such as the centenary of James Joyce's birth and the 25th anniversary of the Treaty of Rome), as programming opportunities (Clarke memo 8.2.82).

On March 1st 1982 Clarke telexed Jean-Pierre Julien at the EBU in Geneva (for circulation to programme contacts of active participants in Eurikon) asking for programmes for the new service. The themes Clarke defined illustrate the mixed public service, somewhat highbrow, programming philosophy of the Operations Group. Clarke specified:

- documentaries, exhibitions, concerts, etc. associated with major anniversaries of European significance (e.g. Copernicus, James Joyce, Garibaldi etc.);
- national and 'fringe' theatre, opera and ballet;
- magazine items on little known aspects of your country – particularly regional aspects;
- rock and popular music festivals;
- programmes designed for immigrant and guest worker communities (Asian, Turkish, etc);
- farming magazine items;
- national or regional sporting events little known outside your own country (pelote, hurling etc.);
- new and 'museum' films;
- links between the old and 'new' worlds and between cultural and linguistic groups in other countries.

The Operations Group's programming proposals and the programmes actually screened on Eurikon experiment exemplify the top-down, supply driven, doctrines of European public service broadcasters in the early 1980s. Viewers' responses to the Eurikon programme offer (see Chapter 10) foreshadowed viewers' response to pan-European public service channels which were built on its foundations. Unfortunately, supporters of pan-European public service broadcasting did not act on the lessons so eloquently taught by the Eurikon experiment which their members undertook. Although remarkably intimidating difficulties were successfully surmounted by the proponents of the EBU-sponsored satellite television channels the scale of the difficulties, combined with the sometimes unhelpful values and assumptions inherited as part of the historical baggage carried by European public service broadcasting, meant that the

Eurikon experiment and its successors enjoyed, at best, a very qualified success. As Dankert, at least, had recognised

> getting this organized is extremely complicated, because Europe has very complicated problems. All sorts of legal problems have to be considered if one seriously looks at the question of the kind of context or structure that would be needed for such a European programme to be able to be implemented, or what kind of framework you would need.
>
> (Dankert in AVRO 1982: 4)

Dankert specifically identified legal problems as the most significant obstacle to the successful establishment of 'a European programme': that is, a pan-European satellite television service. The European Community addressed these legal problems – albeit not always to the satisfaction of the MEPs who most strongly advocated pan-European television – (through its *Television without Frontiers* Green Paper and Directive [Commission of the European Communities 1984a; Council of the European Communities 1989]). However, the successive pan-European satellite television initiatives of European public service broadcasters showed that there were far more intractable problems than the legal matters Dankert identified. Many of these problems became apparent as the first satellite television channel, Eurikon, launched by a consortium of European public service broadcasters, came on stream.

Eurikon was transmitted scrambled for five weeks between May and November 1982 with its five participating EBU members taking responsibility for a week in turn. The UKIBA was responsible for the first week, Italy's RAI[13] for the second, the Austrian ORF for the third, the Dutch NOS for the fourth and the German (ARD) for the fifth and final week.

## The Rome meeting of the Operations Group

The Operations Group met in Rome on 26th July 1982 after transmission of the IBA (24th to 30th May) and RAI (19th to 25th July) programme weeks. In spite of having received enthusiastic support from major European institutions[14] the professional broadcasters who made up the Operations Group were concerned about the viability of the service. Already the problems of re-languaging programmes for a multi-lingual audience had assumed intimidating proportions. The Operations Group judged that simultaneous interpretation and multiple sound tracks used for both the IBA and RAI transmissions were unsatisfactory. The ORF representative insisted that the service needed 'a new way' (Notes to minutes of Rome meeting 26.7.82: 1) and Richard Dill of the ARD saw translation as the key to the acceptability of the service. Looking ahead to 1986 (i.e. to the target launch date for the EBU's projected L-Sat, DBS, service), the Operations Group judged that a central translation unit would be needed and that interpreters would have to be specially trained in television programme interpretation (Minutes of EBU/OTS Operations Group Meeting, Rome 26.7.82: 4).

Moreover, ORF observed that the first two weeks of Eurikon had been 'aimed at a fairly high intellectual and social level' (Minutes of the EBU/OTS Operations Group Meeting, Rome 26.7.82.: 7). ORF's judgement may seem remarkable, given that the IBA's week (the first week) included quotas of drama and light entertainment far above the average transmitted throughout the Eurikon experiment and that RAI's included whole evenings devoted to film, light entertainment and drama. However, viewing of the programmes transmitted bears out the ORF judgement.

The Operations Group met again in Vienna on 24 August 1982 (before the ORF week of 27 September–3 October). It reviewed the financial and technical aspects of Eurikon. The technical and engineering review was positive: some problems were evident but nothing compromised continuation of the Eurikon experiments or threatened future services. The technological potentiality for successful satellite television services undoubtedly existed. The financial review was more troubling however: 'the experiments were proving very expensive'. But although the cost of an experimental service was high, this cost was considerably lower than the cost of an operational service: Eurikon neither contributed to the costs of the EBU centres in Brussels and Geneva on which it depended nor did it pay for its programmes (Minutes of Vienna meeting of the Operations Group 24.8.82: 3–4).

## The Strasbourg meeting of the Operations Group

At its penultimate meeting in Strasbourg on 14 October 1982 (after the ORF week and before the NOS week, 25–31 October and the final ARD week of 22–8 November), the Operations Group recommended continuing development of an operational satellite service but recognised that the cost of the experiments was troubling. Frank Tappolet (the Television Programme Coordinator of SRG and SRG/SSR's representative on the Operations Group) pressed for information on 'the hidden costs borne by the co-ordinating organisations' (Minutes of Strasbourg meeting 14.10.82: 2). The pertinence of his question was underscored by Dill's remark that 'the co-ordinating organisations were having to meet enormous indirect costs' (Minutes of Strasbourg meeting 14.10.82: 6).[15] However the five participating broadcasters, joined by SSR, agreed to go ahead with further initiatives once the Eurikon experiment had run its course.

Clarke identified news and information services as the 'most politically sensitive part of the programme experiments' (Minutes of Strasbourg meeting 14.10.82: 2). 'After three weeks' experiments', the Operations Group concluded, 'there is a growing awareness among the participants for the need to find a new transnational criterion for assessing news values. In both organising the coverage and putting the day's events into perspective, the broadcasters have found it necessary to depart radically from the particular attitudes which they are normally called upon to adopt by their national employers' (Minutes of Strasbourg meeting 14.10.82: 2/3). This delicate formulation signified the objective difficulties of finding news relevant to potential viewers in an area bounded by the Arctic, the Mediterranean, the Baltic and the Atlantic. Also, the difficulty journalists experienced in maintaining their traditional separation from government when the future of the service was so dependent on the financial support and goodwill of Brussels and Strasbourg.

Charles Barrand, a journalist and editor for UPITN who led the UK Eurikon News team and who subsequently became Head of News and Current Affairs for Europa, wrote an official report (Barrand 1982) on his experiences in Eurikon news and a franker and more revealing private letter to Clarke (Barrand 1983a). In his letter to Clarke (Barrand 1983a: 5) Barrand contended that Eurikon had been excessively dependent on the major European political institutions and that the independence of its news services had been compromised. He stated: 'I winced when ORF without one vestige of a news peg, ran a handout film on Strasbourg and when ARD led its first bulletin on a deadly dull story from Brussels. It may please political masters, but it would do nothing for the ratings'. Barrand's concerns echoed those of members of the EBU's Television News Working Party who were jealously concerned with the preservation of the independence of European public service broadcasters' independence from government, whether national or transnational.

Clarke (at least in public) did not share Barrand's judgement. In his report to the EBU Television News Working Party in February 1983 explicitly argued that Eurikon's 'Editorial independence was maintained' and that 'Although the European Institutions gave both moral and financial support, only 0.4 per cent of news items concerned the Council of Europe and 0.5 per cent the European Parliament' (Clarke, manuscript draft report: 3). The minutes of the EBU News Working Party meeting reflected Clarke's emphasis and noted that 'Mr Clarke reassured the Working Party that both the European Parliament and the Council of Europe had left the EBU complete freedom to use, edit or transmit the material provided by them and that this attitude would not change in the future, even if funds should be allocated to the EBU by these organisations' (Com.TV/GT TV News (r) SPG 2136/February 1983: 20).

Clarke's confidence in the impartiality and independence of Eurikon news was not shared by all and Barrand was not the only journalist who believed that the need to secure support for Eurikon from European funding agencies had affected the channel's news selection and news values. A memo (dated 13.12.82) from Hugh Whitcomb (Editor ITN) to Bill Hodgson, General Manager of ITN, on *Status of the OTS project* stated: 'One Chief Editor involved in the tests told me he was shocked to find Neville leaning on the editorial staff to ensure the inclusion of stories favourable to the European politicians' (see also Hjarvard 1991).

Barrand also tellingly identified the problems of actually constructing a news programme likely to be of interest to a target audience so widely defined as to include the whole of Western Europe. Eurikon news was, he stated, 'of a very general nature'. He exemplified his charge by citing a Eurikon weather report which commented 'Holland, Belgium, Luxembourg, Germany and Switzerland will be warm and sunny both today and tomorrow, but in Austria there will be some rain today'. He asked: 'just what information the viewer would extract from this information. Is so general a forecast credible when weather can be so local? Can the viewer in Munich confidently leave his umbrella at home, whereas the Salzburg viewer must wear his raincoat outdoors?' (Barrand 1982: 14).

Similar problems arose in respect of the road reports transmitted by Eurikon (none were received from the AA which was unable to work out criteria for selection) and changes in the exchange rates of European currencies – the figures were 'lifeless, uncommunicating and uncommunicable' (Barrand 1982: 14). Eurikon news was thus seen to be vitiated both by the difficulties of representing a pan-European experience so it would be relevant to Europeans and by an excessive influence exerted by pan-European political institutions on the news.

## Eurikon presents itself

On October 13th 1982, before its own meeting took place, the Operations Group presented Eurikon to members of the European Parliament in the Palais de l'Europe. Pieter Dankert (President of the European Parliament) Lorenzo Natali (a Vice President of the Commission of the European Communities) and about 100 MEPs attended (as did representatives of the Council of Europe and the press). The centrepiece of the presentation was a screening of 'Connexions'; a video designed to give a taste of Eurikon programming. 'Connexions' described audience responses to Eurikon and looked forward to the development of a future pan-European television service. It was shown in English and French and each screening was followed by a discussion led by Wilhelm Hahn MEP, Neville Clarke (Eurikon) and Andreas Caruso (Secretary General of Eutelsat).

'Connexions' began with the choral movement of Beethoven's Ninth Symphony, the European anthem, and showed the launch of the OTS by the ESA launcher, Ariane. The commentary stated:

> Europe is a continent – fragmented by language, by culture, by geography. A mixture of people sharing the same hopes, needs, and emotions, yet isolated by the mechanics of language and radio waves which will only travel in a straight line. We can talk to space – but not to our neighbours. Until now.

It continued with a history of Eurikon stressing its European character and the great potential of new communication technologies. Eurikon programmes thought to be particularly well suited to fostering European union were strongly emphasised. RAI's single theme evenings, drawing on programmes from different European sources, were described as creating 'the necessary bridge across the chasm of national prejudice. National identity fades away as common bonds are struck irrespective of frontiers'. The ORF week was given a high technology gloss and ORF's use of teletext foregrounded. New communication technology both humanised and Europeanised television. As the script stated: 'As well as putting a human face on this form of bilingual translation ORF invested much time and effort into the use of teletext subtitling. Similarly European information is instantly made available through the teletext pages. Weather, exchange rates, the latest news headlines were available in two languages throughout the week'. However the claims made for teletext paled beside those made for satellite television itself: 'Tomorrow's future is already being determined by today's technological decisions. . . . The permutations offered by the new technology are virtually boundless. . . . What is made possible by the connexions of technology only means anything when the connexions become human connexions'.

'Connexions' cited fulsome testimony to Eurikon's importance from leading European political figures. Pieter Dankert, the President of the European Parliament, stated:

> There is enormous importance for European politics to be represented at the European level and I would say that also as far as communication journalism is concerned there is a need for increased European programmes.

Jose Maria de Areilza, President of the Parliamentary Assembly of the Council of Europe, said:

> I believe this venture is extraordinarily important because it represents a major step forward in building Europe. On the occasion of this experiment starting today, Europe acquires a new dimension.

The Strasbourg lobby preceded the EBU Television Programme Committee's meeting which took place a week later. At this meeting, they endorsed the Eurikon experiments which were judged to have been 'extremely positive' (SPG 2081 n.d.: 1). Accordingly, the Television Programme Committee recommended that further initiatives should continue. Thus, by the middle of the experiment the Eurikon Operations Group had won significant public relations victories. The final weeks of the experiment saw further innovation in linguistic re-presentation (notably, the NOS week) and (in the ARD week) a second public relations spectacular, to follow the success of 'Connexions'.

# 5

# EURIKON PROGRAMMING

The only thing that really matters in broadcasting is programme content; all the rest is housekeeping

(Fowler 1965: 3)

Programmes are the test of the authorities' success

(Pilkington 1962: 13)

## Pan-European television programming

Too often television is discussed as a thing rather than as a complex system of symbols through which viewers and producers interact. Viewed from the top-down or the outside-in, from the broadcasting headquarters to the home, the decade 1982–92 was a decade of Europeanisation. Yet viewed from the inside-out or from the bottom-up, from the home to the broadcaster, that decade was scarcely more European than any other. At the level of the programme or the broadcasting schedule, Europeanisation had yet to take place.

How did the Eurikon Operations Group tackle the unprecedented problem of programming for a pan-European audience? As might have been expected, by and large, they devised pan-European versions of the programming they, and their colleagues, had been accustomed to screening on their parent terrestrial services. These programming services, with the partial exceptions of Italy and the UK, were still unchallenged by commercial competitors. This was an unfortunate choice, which ran contrary to the shift towards demotic and entertainment programming which characterised European television viewing behaviour during the decade in which commercial alternatives became available to most European television viewers.

## Eurikon programming

Unfortunately, however important programmes are in making or breaking broadcasting services, it is not easy to give a satisfactory account of them.

91

Analysis of even so small a sample of television as the programmes transmitted during the Eurikon experiment (five weeks of television) is time intensive and fraught with difficulties. In spite of cheap recording technologies, television remains an extraordinarily ephemeral art and I have only secured access to tapes of the programmes transmitted on Eurikon for this study. The discussion of Europa programming is based on analysis of the written record of the programme schedules.[1]

I classified Eurikon programming into eleven categories: news, documentary, drama, arts, sports, light entertainment, children's, adult education, feature films, religion and continuity. Analysis shows that Eurikon programming emphasised news, which accounted for 26 per cent of its programming. Documentary represented a further 18 per cent of programming, (informational programming, news and documentary, together accounted for 44 per cent of all programming on the channel). Light entertainment accounted for 14 per cent, drama 9 per cent and feature films 7 per cent of programming. Entertainment (broadly defined) therefore accounted for 30 per cent of the Eurikon schedule and arts a further 10 per cent, children's programming 7 per cent, sport 6 per cent, continuity 3 per cent and religion 1 per cent, adult education featured only in the IBA and ARD schedules and overall accounted for less than 1 per cent of programming (figures are rounded and do not sum to 100).

However, within the overall envelope of the Eurikon schedule, programming priorities of each of the five participating broadcasters were very different (see Table 5.1). The NOS screened more documentary programming than its partners (38 per cent more than the average). ORF accounted for an overwhelming preponderance of time committed to continuity programming (410 per cent more than the average) and an above average (52 per cent more than average) proportion of Eurikon arts programmes. RAI screened relatively less documentary (66 per cent of the average) and feature films (87 per cent of the average) than other Eurikon broadcasters but otherwise (religious and continuity programmes excepted) showed more than average amounts of programming in other categories (not surprisingly as RAI took more airtime than any of its partners). The ARD screened strikingly more news programmes (44 per cent more than average) and much less drama (about 12 per cent of the average) than other broadcasters. While the IBA screened more than average amounts of drama (71 per cent more) and light entertainment (61 per cent more than average), it also screened a very high proportion (400 per cent more than average) of the (modest) quantity of religious programmes screened on Eurikon, but only 61 per cent of the average proportion of children's programming.

Even though the programme mix transmitted by each of the five broadcasters participating in Eurikon was not perfectly comparable – RAI transmitted for longer, ORF 'over-represented' continuity programming because of its novel approach to linguistic re-presentation, it is clear that the European public service broadcasters who collaborated on Eurikon had different views of the appropriate programme mix for pan-European television.

*Table 5.1*  Minutes of programming screened during the Eurikon experiment by programme type and broadcaster

| Programme types[2] | Scheduling broadcaster (not necessarily the producer of the programme) | | | | | |
|---|---|---|---|---|---|---|
| | NOS | ORF | RAI | ARD | IBA | Total |
| News | 397 | 376 | 556 | 698 | 395 | 2,422 |
| Documentary | 455 | 244 | 216 | 360 | 372 | 1,647 |
| Drama | 86 | 188 | 260 | 20 | 287 | 841 |
| Arts | 77 | 292 | 270 | 147 | 172 | 958 |
| Sport | 82 | 58 | 150 | 147 | 105 | 542 |
| Light entertainment | 194 | 192 | 320 | 154 | 407 | 1,267 |
| Childrens programming | 138 | 185 | 176 | 90 | 82 | 671 |
| Feature films | 90 | 221 | 110 | 97 | 112 | 630 |
| Religious programming | | | | 15 | 60 | 75 |
| Continuity | | 221 | 2 | 20 | 24 | 267 |
| Total | 1,519 | 1,977 | 2,060 | 1,748 | 2,016 | 9,320 |

Quantitative comparison of programme types is illuminating, but does not capture the flavour of the distinctive programme mixes and presentational styles used by each of the Eurikon broadcasters. For example, the time devoted to feature films in the schedules of the IBA and RAI suggests that these broadcasters placed a roughly equal emphasis on cinema presentations. But RAI devoted a whole evening to the cinema and thus its movie programming had a very different flavour to that of the IBA. Accordingly I have supplemented Table 5.1 with further tables and extempore accounts of the first day of Eurikon programming transmitted by each of the participating broadcasters.

### The IBA week. 24–30 May 1982

The first programme screened by the IBA (and therefore the first to be screened by a pan-European public service satellite television service) was 'European Overture' (beginning 17:00, ending 17:24). European and broadcasting dignitaries welcomed viewers to the service and introduced performances by the winners of the principal pan-European talent contests: the International Young Musician of the Year competition and the Eurovision Song Contest. The speeches of welcome by Lord Thomson (the Chairperson of IBA), Pieter Dankert (the Chairperson of the European Parliament), Franz Karasek (the Secretary General of the Council of Europe) and Jose Maria de Areilza (President of the Parliamentary Assembly of the Council of Europe) stressed the Europeans' common heritage. Karasek emphasised European adherence to democratic values and de Areilza spoke of television's role in unifying Europe.

He referred to Eurikon as 'A major step in building a unified Europe. Only by using the full potential of European television can we build a culturally unified Europe'.

'European Overture' exemplified many of the characteristic themes of Eurikon and not a few of its problems. Five languages were used in the programme (Dutch, English, German, French and Spanish) and an English language simultaneous studio interpretation was overlaid on the original sound. Some speakers were not identified and the commentary on the International Young Musician of the Year neither explained nor introduced the event shown: an earnest, high cultural, tenor suffused the programme. After twenty-four minutes of speeches by male European dignitaries and high- and mid-European musical culture, the first evening of Europe's first transnational public service television continued with a documentary (in German) on Haydn, an interview (in French) with the Romanian director of the Wiener Fest Wochen bicentennial performance of the Staats Oper production of Haydn's *Orlando Paladino* followed by the first act of the opera. The eighty-seven minutes, or thereabouts, of *Orlando Paladino* were followed by an episode (twenty-four minutes long) of the UK soap opera *Coronation Street* (in English) preceded by a four-minute documentary item which showed Queen Elizabeth II's visit to the set of *Coronation Street*.

Following *Coronation Street* (the episode showed the fictional celebration of the 'actual' jubilee of Queen Elizabeth II) and its inventive but perhaps confusing intertextuality, the IBA showed a thirty-seven minute discussion (in French with English subtitles) between a Dutch feminist (and a princess of the Dutch royal house), Irene van Lippe and the French political philosopher Roger Garaudy. The programme (made by the Dutch broadcaster Katholieke Radio Omroep (KRO)) was titled 'On the Lack of Appreciation for the Feminine'. The IBA's own report on the first week of Eurikon noted that the Garaudy–von Lippe double act 'sent the press to the bar in droves on the night. Its atrocious title gave Sue Summers of the London newspaper, the *Evening Standard*, ammunition for a jolly piece titled "pass the drinks – this is Euro TV" '.[3]

'Lack of Appreciation for the Feminine' was followed by fifty minutes of pop music: 'Pop around Europe' compiled from popular music programmes made by EBU member broadcasters. It began with an item by Rod Stewart and continued through twenty items (almost all of which were sung in English) and closed with the song 'Little Bit of Peace' (sung in Dutch, English and German) which had won the most recent Eurovision song contest. A screening of the Granada Television *World in Action* current affairs documentary (which had been screened on UK television the same evening – 24 May 1982) and a transvestite cabaret, 'Mary und Gordy' (contributed by the ARD) were the last two programmes of the first day of Eurikon.

The *World in Action* (twenty-seven minutes) screened was about the responses of families of British servicemen (then on active service in the South Atlantic) to the Falklands campaign. It was strikingly dependent on natural language. Many statements were made via a voice-over soundtrack and (in 'World in Action's' characteristic style) there was often no motivated relationship between images and sounds. To many non-English native speakers the programme is likely to have been incomprehensible. 'Mary und Gordy' (fifty-five minutes) was similarly language dependent. Many humorous (and provocative) connotations of the programme were lost in translation. The first evening of Eurikon programming closed eight minutes late; its final image was a Eurikon caption shown reversed.

The first night of pan-European public service satellite television included programmes from four of the five members of the Eurikon consortium but technical problems precluded inclusion of news in the first evening's schedule. The absence of RAI programmes in the first evening's schedule was redressed the following evening when two RAI programmes were screened. One, the fifty-seven minute 'Historia senza parole', successfully dramatised an erotic modern melodrama without use of speech. It was thus intelligible to all viewers with the cultural competence to decode a well-made drama in a thriller–romance format about the contemporary European bourgeoisie. Unfortunately similarly positive claims could not be made for the hour-long RAI monochrome documentary which followed 'Historia senza parole'. This showed the Congo River through the eyes of the Italian novelist Alberto Moravia. 'Alberto Moravia in Africa' testified both to the European longing to exoticise the African other, and to the unsuitability of a programme which juxtaposed images and unmotivated (or tenuously motivated) commentary for an audience made up of different language communities. Like the IBA's *World in Action*, decoupling sound and image made 'Alberto Moravia in Africa' very difficult for non-Italian speakers to understand. The difficulties it presented the simultaneous interpreters who re-presented the programme were clearly serious. The IBA record notes that 'RAI apologised the next day . . . for its dullness!'. Clarke later noted that the RAI of this period was 'rigidly controlled and culturally elitist' (Clarke and Riddell 1992: 63).

The first Eurikon news programme was transmitted on Tuesday 25 May.[4] Stories from the Vatican, the South Atlantic, Argentina, the United Nations, from France and the Lebanon were covered. During the first week of Eurikon the IBA record showed ninety-seven items[5] as having been screened (in six separate fifty-minute news programmes, the number of items screened per programme ranged from thirteen to twenty-three items). Of these ninety-seven items, a majority (fifty-five) emanated from UK sources,[6] although by no means all of the material of UK origin showed events in the UK.[7] The larger European countries (Germany, France and Italy) were the next most important source of IBA news followed by the USA, Austria, Ireland, Iran and the Soviet Union. Portugal, Belgium, Finland, Yugoslavia, the Netherlands, Spain, Switzerland, Denmark and Cuba were each the source of one news item shown in the course of the IBA week.[8]

Overall about 73 per cent of programmes screened during the IBA week

*Table 5.2*     Programmes by country of origin. IBA week 24–30 May 1982

| | UK | France | West Germany | Italy | Austria | Nether-lands | Spain | Ireland | Switzer-land | Belgium | Other | Total |
|---|---|---|---|---|---|---|---|---|---|---|---|---|
| News | 364 | | | | | | 31 | | | | | 395 |
| Documentary | 110 | 73 | | 76 | | 37 | | 60 | | | 16 | 372 |
| Drama | 28 | | 86 | 117 | 56 | | | | | | | 287 |
| Arts | 31 | | | | 81 | 60 | | | | | | 172 |
| Sports | 105 | | | | | | | | | | | 105 |
| Light entertainment | 101 | | 115 | 56 | | 13 | 83 | 13 | 26 | | | 407 |
| Children | | | 20 | 10 | | 10 | 32 | | | | 10 | 82 |
| Adult education | | | 28 | 21 | | | | | | | | 49 |
| Feature films | | | | | 112 | | | | | | | 112 |
| Religion | | | | | | | | | | 60 | | 60 |
| Continuity | 24 | | | | | | | | | | | 24 |
| Total | 763 | 73 | 249 | 280 | 249 | 120 | 146 | 73 | 26 | 60 | 26 | 2,065 |

*Notes:* Programme times in minutes. Weather reports were coded as 'continuity' since they emanated from the host station. Attributions, for genre and country of origin, follow those in the IBA programme and schedule notes even when viewing suggests other attribution should be made. For example, 'Unterwegs im Europa' ('On the Road in Europe', shown in the NOS week, though attributed by the IBA to the ARD (and thus meriting a 'German' classification) was assembled with footage from Germany, Austria and the Netherlands. This method of attribution, though in some ways misleading, follows the method used by the UK regulator, the IBA (now ITC) which attributes the nationality of a television programme to its location of final assembly (thus a cartoon programme which packages Hollywood animated films within a presentation made and introduced by UK workers is deemed a UK programme). This system of classification meant that RAI's programme on Hungarian cinema (which included extensive extracts from Hungarian films) was deemed to be Italian. Programmes designated as compilations (e.g. Eurocompilation; sport) and attributed to more than one producer were credited equally to the contributing countries (e.g. the seventy-minute Eurosport compilation screened during the NOS week was attributed in equal proportions of twenty-three minutes to the Netherlands, UK and Italy).

Programming on Eurikon which originated from one of the participating countries did not necessarily originate from broadcasters which directly participated in the experiment. For example, the BBC contributed children's programming to the Eurikon schedule although the BBC did not directly participate in the experiment.

Tables are based on a single entry for each programme. Thus the children's news programme screened by NOS (18:20–18:26 25.10.82) scored once – as a children's programme. Similarly 'The Stolen Scarf', a children's drama (18:28–18:43 25.10.82) scored as a children's programme. News and drama were categories used only for programmes directed to adult viewers. The classification system used underestimates the diversity of origins of Eurikon programming in that it categorises news programming as emanating from a single national source and also records co-produced programmes, e.g. feature films, as the product of a single country.

originated from the member-countries of the Eurikon consortium: 13.3 per cent came from the UK, 11.9 per cent from Germany, 11.9 per cent from Austria, 11.5 per cent from Italy and 6.1 per cent from the Netherlands. Of the remainder, 11.7 per cent of programmes were 'Eurocompilations' and 18.7 per cent were UK programmes made especially for Eurikon by the news team which the IBA established at Visnews (EBU/OTS Operations Group 1983: 3 and 9).[9]

## The RAI week. 19–25 July 1982

RAI scheduled its programmes differently to the IBA. It dedicated each day of its week to a different theme. The first day centred on cinema, the second on current affairs, the third on serious music, the fourth on comedy, the fifth on drama, the sixth on sport and the seventh day on light entertainment. In keeping with the experimental mission of Eurikon, RAI 'used the Eurovision Conference and Vision networks to a greater extent than in the UKIBA week . . . this was an effective if at times hair raising method' (EBU/OTS Operations Group 1983: 3).

RAI introduced its Eurikon week (rather as had the IBA) with a package of honorific statements from celebrities; a seven-minute package of interviews with Sergio Zaroli (then President of RAI) and Lorenzo Natali (a Vice President of the Commission of the European Communities). Natali testified to the 'significant contribution to the construction of European unity' made by Eurikon but Zaroli posed the fundamental question on which the future of pan-European television depended: 'Is there a European television audience?'. Zaroli asserted that a European audience existed for 'great works' but that there was little in the day to day lives and customary television viewing of Europeans to interest a pan-European audience. Characteristically the broadcaster identified the practical problems which stood in the way of the political imperatives fluently advanced by the politician. Yet Zaroli's answer to the question he rightly posed reflected the high culturalism which, Clarke argued, suffused the RAI of the early 1980s before it was changed through competition from the channels established by Fininvest. Zaroli and Natali were followed by a short, seven item, news summary.[10]

The cinematic theme of the first day of the RAI week began with a British compilation programme (made by Granada 1982, twenty-three minutes) of recoloured Warner animations. The cartoons were linked by Derek Griffiths who played the parts of different members of the staff of a traditional cinema (the commissionaire, the manager, etc.). RAI continued with 'Buona Sera', a thirty-minute chat show on the theme of cinema (spoken in Italian with English voice-over interpretation) which discussed 'O Megalexandros' (Theo Angelopoulos) and 'Les uns et les autres' (directed by Claude Lelouch 1981).[11] The male presenter of 'Buona Sera' drew humorous distinctions between American and European cinema (Hollywood producers smoke big cigars and are interested in money, Italians smoke slim cigarettes and are interested in art) and was listened to by a mute blonde female. The (unpublished) IBA record commented:

> the theme of the first evening was cinema – that one overpowering addiction that pervades RAI and Italian television. Using their co-production muscle they looked at clips from several films which they had had a hand in . . . the extracts were lengthy and the discussions were quite erudite despite the gaudy staginess of the bright orange set. RAI has a very strong hand in this area of 'art' movies and this kind of programming would appeal strongly to the growing number of TV movie buffs currently tuning into BBC2 and Channel 4. Nevertheless, some problems became evident which should be noted for the future. The Italian presentation was very studio bound, ponderous and lengthy. Placido's speeches [the male Italian cinema chat show host], while very amusing in Italian suffered terribly in translation as all his ironic phrases came out in the interpretation as the opposite of what he meant.

'Buona Sera' was broken by a thirty-minute news and features programme after which it continued for a further fifteen minutes. The features programme (fifteen minutes) comprised a weather report, a slide show (with voice-over commentary) on Caravaggio (the anniversary of whose death fell on the day of transmission), a sexist cookery programme showing biscuit making (a woman did the work and a man commented and explained)[12] and a truncated item on human physiognomy.[13] The news (using the same studio set as 'Bueno Sera') also lasted for fifteen minutes. It covered the Iran–Iraq and Israel–Palestine conflicts, the meeting between the Pope and the Polish Foreign Minister Edward Gierek, the end of a UK train strike and the beginning of a UK health dispute, the decline in the international parity of the US dollar, conflicts between leisure and fishing uses of the Volendam (Netherlands), the Italian Red Brigade trial, a competition injury to a Soviet fencer and a British motorcyclist's successful jump over a record number of buses.

The main news on the first day of the RAI week began with an item showing Enrico Colombo and Helmut Schmidt (the heads of government of Italy and West Germany) in Brussels prior to a meeting with George Schultz (the US Secretary of State). The voice-over commentary enjoined 'Europeans need to be on the same wavelength'. The first day of RAI news exemplified what was to be a developing theme in Eurikon; programming showing pan-European, rather than national, matters became more and more evident. In RAI's week this European dimension was most clearly manifest in the commentary framing and interpreting news and some other programmes.

'Buona Sera' continued with an expert discussion of contemporary cinema (the presenter cited Ernst Bloch's *Das Prinzip Hoffnung* at one point) and an extract from the film *Padre Padrone*. Unfortunately viewers who were neither male (all RAI's discussants were male) nor expert cine-intellectuals were provided with few points for imaginative entry. The learned discussion was followed by a screening (one hundred and ten minutes) of the Taviani brothers' film *La notte di San Lorenzo* which was screened with its original soundtrack. However, the film was also transmitted with English subtitles and with an English language simultaneous interpretation. The simultaneous interpretation was redundant (because of the subtitling) and interfered with the original soundtrack. These absurdities graphically exemplified the intractable problems of linguistic re-presentation which dogged the pan-European channels and which are discussed later.

A thirty-minute news feature on four distinct themes followed *La notte di San Lorenzo*. The UK's Central Television contributed a report (which assembled live action film, graphics and dance) on school truancy; the ARD contributed a commentary by a German expert on the South Atlantic war; RAI offered a compilation of monochrome archive footage on cinema stunts (much of the material from Universal Studios), and a report on international art thefts. The core of the final item was an interview with Kenneth Hoving, Director of the New York Metropolitan Museum, in English with two simultaneous voice-over interpretations, one in Italian and the second an English translation of the Italian.

Like *La notte di San Lorenzo* the news feature showed how difficult it was to organise and implement satisfactory systems of linguistic re-presentation. Doubtless the pressures of time under which Eurikon broadcasters worked were responsible for the absurd simultaneous transmission of a translation into English of an Italian translation of an original English language soundtrack. However the difficulty of devising programme content appropriate to a pan-European service was amply illustrated by the content of RAI's news and of its news feature. Both attempted to construct pan-European programming by adding 'a bit of this' to 'a bit of that' with the effect that the majority of the content of the programmes interested few viewers.

RAI's first evening of pan-European television closed with a report (lasting thirty minutes) on Hungarian cinema, followed by a five-minute foreshadowing of the main cultural events to take place in Europe the following day. The Hungarian cinema documentary was introduced by a female presenter, who was shown *reading* a script, whereas males had previously been shown as fluent – indeed intimidatingly verbose – experts without scripts, and included extracts from Sandor's 1976 *Baths of Herculanum*, Szabo's 1979 *Trust*, Gothar's 1981 *Imre* and Bacso's *Offeser*. RAI's round up of cultural events, in Athens, London, Rome, Nice, Montreux, Odense, Vienna, Barcelona and Catolica, reinforced the impression, established in its news and news feature, that to be European was to be here, there and everywhere.[14] It is difficult to imagine who the audience for the closing item of its first day's programme schedule might have been. What viewer would be interested in knowing about a single cultural event in each of nine European locations stretching from Athens in the East, Catania in the South to Barcelona in the West and Odense in the North?

Moreover RAI's ambitious attempts to offer a full palette of European content by drawing on the cornucopia of potential programming offered by Eurovision entailed numerous, unsolved, technical and presentational problems. The schedule was full of recurrent imperfect matches of sound and vision.[15] The penultimate item on the final day (Sunday) of RAI's schedule was a perfect example: the IBA noted (in an unpublished record) 'Montreux Jazz festival. Disastrous live link up with SSR. They failed to cue the anchorman so he sat before camera for fifteen minutes picking his nose . . . should have been drowned in the lake'.

More than 80 per cent of the programmes screened in the RAI week originated from the countries of the Eurikon consortium (see Table 5.3). Of the 46.1 per cent from Italy, 28.7 per cent had been made especially for Eurikon; 8.9 per cent came from the UK, 6.8 per cent from Austria, 3.1 per cent from Germany, 0.7 per cent from the Netherlands and 20.1 per cent were 'Eurocompilations' (EBU/OTS Operations Group 1983: 9).

### The ORF week. 27 September–3 October 1982

The first evening of ORF's Eurikon week both followed and broke with the precedents set by RAI and the IBA. Like them ORF began its contribution to Eurikon with a four-minute welcome from its chief. Gerd Bacher, the Intendant of the ORF, explained that satellite television offered broadcasters in small countries new opportunities to disseminate their programmes. Bacher's statement was re-presented to non-German speakers through voice-over simultaneous interpretation. However the ORF innovated later by using two presenters, a British woman, Susan Calland and an Austrian man, Hans-Friedrich Mayer, who addressed the audience in turn speaking English and German respectively. Calland and Mayer anchored the whole evening's programming (indeed the whole of the ORF's Eurikon week) and, as well as commenting in their mother tongues, also conversed bi-lingually.

The novel use of two presenters, each of whom addressed a separate audience language community, was time consuming (forty-five minutes of the first evening was taken up by the presenters; on other evenings the presenters were on screen for between sixteen and forty-five minutes); statements were first made in one language and then repeated in the other. Moreover, whereas English and German speaking viewers were able to identify with their co-linguist and to receive information in their native tongue, viewers who understood neither English nor German (and who audited a soundtrack of simultaneous translation of statements made in both English and German), were both denied identification with a co-linguist and subjected to a reiterated simultaneous translation of similar statements originally made by Calland in English and Mayer in German.

100

Table 5.3  Programme analysis. RAI week 19–25.7.82

| | UK | France | West Germany | Italy | Austria | Nether-lands | Spain | Ireland | Switzer-land | Other | Total |
|---|---|---|---|---|---|---|---|---|---|---|---|
| News | 32 | | 15 | 478 | 14 | | | 7 | 10 | | 556 |
| Documentary | | | 23 | 93 | | 20 | | 70 | | 10 | 216 |
| Drama | 50 | | 40 | 120 | | | 50 | | | | 260 |
| Arts | | | | 115 | 90 | | 65 | | | | 270 |
| Sports | | | | 150 | | | | | | | 150 |
| Light entertainment | 60 | 60 | | 120 | 25 | | | | 55 | | 320 |
| Children | 73 | | 25 | 28 | 25 | 25 | | | | | 176 |
| Adult education | | | | | | | | | | | |
| Feature films | | | | 110 | | | | | | | 110 |
| Religion | | | | | | | | | | | |
| Continuity | | | | 2 | | | | | | | 2 |
| Total | 215 | 60 | 103 | 1,216 | 154 | 45 | 115 | 77 | 65 | 10 | 2,060 |

*Note*: Programme times in minutes.

However ORF's use of the two presenters provided an important element of continuity which gave the ORF week a distinctive identity and character. Moreover the subdued flirtatiousness between, what the IBA described as 'attractive male and female presenters in their mid-30s', promised to foster audience identification. ORF also innovated through extensive use of teletext subtitles (in English, German and Italian) and of teletext to give information on the ratings, share and appreciation indices of each programme screened. However the problem of the simultaneous interpretation soundtrack conflicting with the original programme sound which had been so evident in previous weeks continued during the ORF week.

After Bacher's welcome, ORF's first Eurikon evening continued with a four-minute monochrome film about the first television satellite, Telstar (which went into service in 1962). Telstar was followed by a half hour pot pourri (a regular item in the ORF week's schedules) of ORF's version of the kaleidoscope format pioneered by RAI. The pot pourri always included a regular short film sequence (of three to five minutes) showing an Austrian landscape, the location of which viewers were invited to guess. The landscape quiz was followed by a short news roundup (five-minutes). On the first ORF day the news covered four items; political changes in West Germany, a bomb in Frankfurt, Mrs Thatcher's visit to Hong Kong and proposals for a European museum in Strasbourg, followed by a weather report for the whole of Europe. It was succeeded by a twenty-minute episode of a period costume children's drama serial *Der Verschwender* (The Cheat) which was acted entirely by children,[16] and teletext titled in English and Italian with the original German soundtrack.

Next came 'Eurohitparade'; the chief 'pan-European' innovation in ORF's programming. 'Eurohitparade' compiled current popular musical hits from around Europe – later ORF advocated it as a permanent Eurovision service. 'Eurohitparade' was presented in German but included songs sung in English, German and Italian. 'Eurohitparade's' format was somewhat similar to that pioneered by the IBA (with its 'Pop around Europe' formula), but in contrast to the IBA's largely English language programme, 'Eurohitparade' prioritised no single language.[17] After 'Eurohitparade' pop music gave way to high culture with a five-minute programme, 'Ars Electronica', transmitted from the Linz music festival. 'Ars Electronica' juxtaposed extracts from Mahler's *Fifth Symphony* with images of industrial production, and married electronic music with non-representational electronic images.

ORF committed twenty-minutes to the main evening news and a weather report which covered the whole of Europe. Its first night's news bulletin of nine items covered political developments in West Germany, inflation in the EEC, the opening of the British Labour Party conference, an explosion in Northern Ireland, a background informational on Strasbourg and the Council of Europe, Italian troops in Beirut, an explosion in a chemical warehouse in Manchester, skin cancer in Lippizaner horses and successes in the Prix Italia competition by the BBC and Danmarks Radio.[18]

The ORF news and weather was followed by three sports programmes. First, a forty-minute Dutch documentary 'Start in Finland, Finish in Friesland' (transmitted with English soundtrack) about long distance skate racing and made by AVRO (a principal Dutch broadcasting society) in 1980.[19] Second, a twenty-six minute compilation of European sports events from the previous week including World Cup soccer (Italy versus West Germany from RAI), gymnastics (from SRG), water skiing (from the UK) and an RTE report on the Cheltenham Gold Cup horse race.[20] Third, was a forty-seven minute ORF documentary 'Angst im Sport' which showed several dangerous sports (climbing, parachute free-fall, ski jumping, motor racing), and included testimony from participants (including Nikki Lauder and Reinhold Messner), and psychiatrists' elucidation of the motivation of participants in dangerous sports (the IBA referred to the psychiatrists as 'popping up every five minutes to explain').

Generally, ORF and RAI showed a very male and very white world,[21] but ORF's programme 'Was ist Europa?' (a seven-minute portrayal of the Vienna International School, which followed 'Angst im Sport'), redressed gender and ethnicity imbalances. School students from Australia, Bulgaria, Egypt, Japan, Lebanon, the Philippines, Sri Lanka, Turkey, Venezuela and the USA spoke in their mother tongue (without translation). After its portrayal of the Vienna International School, ORF screened an earnest think piece: 'Was ist Europa?' introduced by the Austrian Minister for Foreign Affairs, Dr Willibald Pahr. Pahr emphasised that Europe stretched from the Atlantic to the Urals and was thus greater than a Europe defined either by membership of the EEC or of the Council of Europe. For Pahr, Europe was a civilisation distinguished by its pluralist democracy and respect for human rights.

ORF closed with a fourteen-minute compilation of news stories gleaned from the main domestic news bulletins of the Eurikon partners (and SRG) and a ten-minute information film on Austrian teletext services (which revealed that Austrian teletext viewers are able to access Ceefax pages from the BBC). The news pot pourri included an ARD report on the election for the Land Government in Hessen, a report on a reduction in Swiss vehicle taxes from SRG, RAI's account of Andreotti's testimony given to the inquest on the murder of Aldo Moro, ITN's report on Margaret Thatcher in Hong Kong, ORF's own report on an environmental protection summit in Prague and a report from NOS on the risks of flooding due to under-investment in dikes. Though novel, ORF's compilation format for television news (a format analogous to that RAI used for a round up of European cultural events), seemed an unpromising model for pan-European television. Just as few viewers of RAI's arts roundup were likely to be interested in events in both Odense and Barcelona, so few viewers outside Switzerland were likely to be interested in changes to Swiss vehicle taxes.

The Operations Group Report (EBU/OTS Operations Group 1983: 4) described the ORF's programming as having 'a general pattern of programmes each evening, based around a different theme each day for the main programme'. However the ORF day sampled seemed to represent a mixed, rather than a thematic, programme schedule albeit there were a solid two hours of sports programmes in the schedule (see Table 5.4).

A very high proportion of the ORF week came from members of the Eurikon consortium – 69.4 per cent were made in Austria (of which 27.5 per cent were made especially for Eurikon including 11 per cent presentation), 7.8 per cent were made in Italy, 7.3 per cent in the UK, 6 per cent in the Netherlands and 4.8 per cent in Germany (EBU/OTS Operations Group 1983: 4 and 9).

### The NOS week. 25–31 October 1982

In the primetime of television programmes we will try to experiment with programmes and information for minority groups, because there is no information for these groups on primetime television throughout Europe. And there are no primetime sports broadcasts on a Monday, or Tuesday night. Mostly these are found on Saturday, Sunday and Wednesday nights. So contrasting airing times and contrasting formulae of information and news will be the back bone of our programme schedule. . . . Another thing is that we will not use presenters on the screen as the Italians and the Austrians did. We will follow the recipe of the British week – trying to do without and have our commentary off camera.

(Speech by Klaas-Jan Hindriks in *Connexions*, Eurikon presentation,
Strasbourg 13.10.82)

Analysing the first day of NOS' Eurikon programming was particularly difficult.[22] My analysis of the first hour of output is based on the IBA's record of the week which records that NOS opened with two-minutes of display of the 'Eurikon Programme Guide with two languages on screen', three-minutes of 'Euroka – Koot en Bie. Satirical comedy show – this is a clever send up of Europrog TV', six-minutes of news[23] and weather for children, fifteen-minutes of *The Stolen Scarf* (a children's puppet show screened for the first three days of the NOS week), a further seven-minutes of news and information,[24] followed by a seventy-minute sports compilation programme.

However the IBA's record of programmes transmitted by NOS is of uncertain reliability. The IBA stated that the theme of the sports programme screened by NOS was soccer. However the first intelligible item viewed was a report of steeplechasing (screened with a Dutch voice-over commentary), which was followed by two programmes on soccer: a RAI report on the impact of the World Cup on Italian soccer (with English voice-over the original Italian sound-track and with Dutch subtitles), and a Thames Television *TV Eye* programme on

*Table 5.4* Programme analysis. ORF week 27.9.82–3.10.82

| | UK | West Germany | Italy | Austria | Nether-lands | Spain | Ireland | Switzer-land | Total |
|---|---|---|---|---|---|---|---|---|---|
| News | 5 | | 49 | 319 | | 2 | | 6 | 376 |
| Documentary | 62 | 9 | 14 | 165 | | 8 | 35 | 8 | 244 |
| Drama | | 38 | 17 | 41 | 10 | | 20 | | 188 |
| Arts | 6 | | | 264 | 16 | | | 6 | 292 |
| Sports | 34 | | 4 | 11 | | | 6 | 3 | 58 |
| Light entertainment | 10 | 34 | 30 | 103 | 10 | | | 5 | 192 |
| Children | 20 | | 25 | 117 | 23 | | | | 185 |
| Adult education | | | | | | | | | |
| Feature films | | | | | | | | | |
| Religion | | | | | | | | | |
| Continuity | | | | 221 | | | | | 221 |
| Total | 137 | 81 | 139 | 1,241 | 59 | 10 | 61 | 28 | 1,756 |

*Notes*: Programme times in minutes.

The ORF week illustrated some recurrent problems in classification of programme content. As a result of the difficulties in differentiating the programme forms of current affairs and news and information programmes, both these types were classified under news. There were problems too in classifying different kinds of music. I placed brass band music under the category 'arts' whereas I classified pop music (and light opera) as 'light entertainment'.

the economics of soccer in the UK. The *TV Eye* documentary lost sound for several minutes. It was followed by two-minutes of Dutch public service announcements (on energy saving in the home and safety with bottled gas).

Next was a thirty-five minute TROS[25] documentary on the Dutch vessel 'Flyer' and its part in the 1977 Round the World Yacht Race which was transmitted with an English language soundtrack. It was followed by a twenty-three minute ARD compilation: 'On the Road in Europe' which assembled bland tourist promotional coverage of snuff manufacture in Ratisbon (English voice-over), windmills in Schiedam (English subtitles) and alpine farming in Austria (English voice-over). ARD's European peregrinations were followed by a NOS documentary on a German old people's colony – Altersheim – lasting for twenty-nine minutes.[26] The documentary on Altersheim was interrupted by a teletext flash concerning the New York stock exchange crash of that day.

As well as experimenting with a full repertoire of established re-languaging techniques NOS innovated with the Altersheim programme: the programme began with German subtitles and an English voice-over a Dutch soundtrack, which were followed by Italian subtitles and a German voice-over the Dutch soundtrack. As with RAI's pan-European cultural pot pourri and ORF's pan-European news (made up of items each of which had relevance to a section of a notional pan-European audience but none of which had relevance to the whole of the target audience), so NOS' experiment in linguistic re-presentation could be comprehended only by a polyglot audience. In seeking to address many Europeans it succeeded in addressing very few.

NOS closed the first evening of its Eurikon week with a thirty-minute news bulletin, the first item of which reported the Eurikon experiment. It stressed that Eurikon would enable broadcasters to prepare for the coming satellite era by experimenting with different forms of linguistic representation. Rather risibly the bulletin emphasised that the loan of the European Parliament's outside broadcast van was a vital element of the enterprise![27]

NOS strove to adopt different news and programme values to those of its Eurikon partners whose programmes and schedules retained a national character, and often smacked of political incorrectness. NOS screened considerably more material concerned with the role and place of women and ethnic minorities than did other Eurikon broadcasters. And the NOS sought to give its programming a genuinely pan-European dimension. Thus NOS' schedule contained documentaries made by Granada (UK) and NOS itself (screened 29.10.82) on European political institutions with a documentary about the European Parliament (screened 27.10.82). Moreover the news screened by NOS was notable for eschewing nationally specific locations and issues: NOS reported Amnesty International's judgements on the quality of international human rights (two items), the European Erasmus awards (one item), the consequences of use of lead-free petrol (two items), new initiatives in Europe and European sport round ups (two items), European inflation (one item),

USA–USSR contacts (one item) and a comic representation of the OTS/Eurikon experiment (one item).

NOS made strenuous efforts to ensure that it received programmes well before transmission so that comprehensive translation and linguistic re-presentation work could be done. This meant that (unlike the other contributors to Eurikon), NOS made little use of the Eurovision permanent circuits or of the programmes available through Eurovision (EBU/OTS Operations Group 1983: 6).

As shown in Table 5.5, about 70 per cent of NOS' programmes were made in the Netherlands (of which a fifth were made especially for Eurikon), 16.5 per cent were 'Eurocompilations', 11 per cent came from the UK, 3 per cent from Germany 1 per cent from Italy but none came from Austria (EBU/OTS Operations Group 1983: 9).

### The ARD week. 22–8 November 1982

Like the IBA, RAI and ORF the ARD began its Eurikon programming with an extensive (twenty-minute) introduction and welcome. Reinhold Voeth, the Chairman of the ARD, and Willibald Hilf, the Intendant (Director General) of Sud West Funk – the host broadcaster for the ARD week – spoke in German (with an English simultaneous interpretation laid over the German sound), and emphasised that Eurikon had discovered that 'Language problems are the greatest barrier' to pan-European television. The ARD welcomed viewers in Europe and the Arab world to Eurikon. Its Eurikon transmissions were received by Arab members of the EBU (in the Magreb), and the ARD week coincided with a visit by members of the ASBU to the EBU and to Sud West Funk.[28]

The ASBU visit and ARD's decision to transmit Algerian programmes and to screen a UK documentary about Qatar during its week of Eurikon programming, responded to North African broadcasters' dissatisfaction about the Eurovision News Exchange, expressed at a meeting between Eurovision news co-ordinators and North African broadcasters (see SPG 1974 of September 1982), and demonstrated an EBU commitment to the principles embodied in a contemporary UNESCO initiative to foster the exchange of television news between regional associations of broadcasters.[29]

The ARD's introduction foreshadowed highlights of the programmes which were to be screened later and included a brief history of the European OTS, the satellite from which Eurikon signals were relayed. The first ARD news bulletin followed using two formats neither of which had formerly been used in Eurikon. The news began with a preamble which headlined items to follow, and included teletext news flashes (in German and English) overlaid onto the images of the news bulletin proper.[30] Like NOS, ARD attempted to schedule non country specific news. On 27 November 1982, for example, it transmitted items on chauvinism in different European countries, on NATO, the GATT meeting, on the health hazard posed by asbestos and on Franco-German collaboration in the Super Phoenix nuclear reactor project.[31]

*Table 5.5*  Programme analysis. NOS week 25–31.10.82

| | UK | West Germany | Italy | Nether-lands | Ireland | Norway | Greece | European Institutions | Belgium | Portugal | Total |
|---|---|---|---|---|---|---|---|---|---|---|---|
| News | 10 | 10 | | 367 | | | 10 | | | | 397 |
| Documentary | 79 | 23 | | 274 | | | | 29 | 50 | | 455 |
| Drama | | | | 31 | 55 | | | | | | 86 |
| Arts | | | | 77 | | | | | | | 77 |
| Sports | 23 | | 23 | 36 | | | | | | | 82 |
| Light entertainment | 50 | | | 98 | 23 | | | | | 23 | 194 |
| Children | 6 | 18 | | 84 | 24 | 6 | | | | | 138 |
| Adult education | | | | | | | | | | | |
| Feature films | | | | 90 | | | | | | | 90 |
| Religion | | | | | | | | | | | |
| Total | 168 | 51 | 23 | 1,057 | 102 | 6 | 10 | 29 | 50 | 23 | 1,519 |

*Note:* Programme times in minutes.

Following the news the ARD screened a thirty-five minute current affairs programme, 'Europe 2000', made up of five items, each item drawn from a different European state. The programme began with a report on the German Reinheitsgebot,[32] and continued on French agricultural policy. Next came a report on the Eurikon experiment itself (which showed Wilhelm Hahn and screened extracts from programming shown in earlier weeks – notably the RTE programme screened on James Joyce and his wife Nora Barnacle and the multiple performances of Macbeth which had been screened during the RAI week), then a Swiss film on Italian terrorism and a BBC film about the British spy Greville Wynn. During 'Europe 2000' a teletext flash in English and Dutch reported (the newly appointed Soviet President) Yuri Andropov's statement on détente.

'Europe 2000' gave way to 'Your Country, Our Country' a thirty-minute compilation programme addressed to Greek migrants living in Europe which was introduced in German (with English simultaneous interpretation voice-over), but quickly changed to a Greek soundtrack. It covered the island of Santorini, the economy and economic problems of the Greek press (this item had a short English language voice-over introduction but most was screened in Greek without translation), pollution in Ithaca, new laws in Germany concerning loans and marriage bureaux and, finally, a Greek song sung to music by Mikis Theodorakis. A teletext flash (in German and English) indicated that France had blocked negotiations over Portugal's accession to the European Community.

The keystone of ARD's first evening was the eighty-seven minute 'Eurosport' (transmitted in German with English voice-over simultaneous interpretation). 'Eurosport' assembled a variety of items on current and past sports events with a strong emphasis on European soccer. Germany contributed material on the safety of ski equipment and a soccer match between FC Kaiserslautern and Bayern München; RAI, a soccer match between AG Roma and AC Firenze; ORF, a frisbee championship; RTVE, a soccer match between Real Madrid and Real Sociedad; Japan, film of the Tokyo Olympics; and Mexico, film of the 1968 Olympics in Mexico City. 'Eurosport' continued with Jazzgymnastics from the USA, soccer between Aston Villa and Manchester United from the UK and closed with six short items on show jumping and soccer in the Netherlands, a car rally in the UK, table tennis in Yugoslavia, ice hockey between Switzerland and Yugoslavia and rugby between Argentina and France. Eurosport also included an extraordinary animated film from the USA of animals playing a game combining elements of soccer and basketball! Two teletext news items were inserted into 'Eurosport'; news that Gunter Grass had received the Feltrinelli award and that the President of the USA had authorised the siting of 100 new MX missiles.

A thirty-minute RAI art documentary on Venice and its byways and backwaters 'Ritorno' followed. Like the film, 'Historia senza parole', shown by the IBA 'Ritorno' had no speech track but effectively orchestrated natural sounds for signifying effect. Indeed the only natural language used in the film was a paragraph of Hoffmanstahl (in Italian) overlaid onto the film's final image. 'Ritorno' was followed by a thirty-minute Saarlandischer Rundfunk programme on modern music, 'Musica Viva' which began with a lecture on Gandhi: a curious introduction to an extract from a performance by the Stuttgart Opera and an interview with the opera director, Armin Freyer. Most of the programme juxtaposed sounds and images of modern German cities, it showed *al fresco* musical performances (glossed by recurrent use of terms like 'stress' on the soundtrack which emphasised the generally alienated and disconnected character of modern life). 'Musica Viva' closed with a report from the Metz contemporary music festival. Teletext news flashes – in German and English – were screened during 'Musica Viva'.

ARD closed the first day of its week with a thirty-minute news programme 'Weltspiegel' (NDR's contribution to the ARD's terrestrial network service of the same day). 'Weltspiegel' included three reports (all originated by German television), on the successful testing of the Pershing 2 missile at the USA's White Sands missile base in New Mexico, and two reports on events in Afghanistan. The first, on the land reform programmes of the government, reported positively on the policies of the Marxist government (though the reporter emphasised that the policies had not been initiated by the Marxist government which was implementing them), the second reported on victims of the land reform policies who had fled to refugee camps in Pakistan.

For its contribution to Eurikon the ARD stated that it intended to 'offer a complementary service to national television channels using a fixed structure so that the viewer would know what to expect' (EBU/OTS Operations Group 1983: 6). It established a consistent structure to its programme schedule, although its in-vision programme and presentational formats differed from day to day. For example, the ARD week began with an anchorman speaking in German directly to camera, but other nights used voice-over with no presenter on-screen, and an on-screen presenter speaking several different languages. The ARD schedule comprised five programme elements; news, minority interest programmes, a magazine programme on a particular European theme, a collection of programmes on a theme to complement the schedules of terrestrial services (e.g. the ARD Eurikon week scheduled sport on Monday and current affairs on Saturday), and late evening experimental programmes (EBU/OTS Operations Group 1983: 6–7). The 'collection of programmes on a theme' constituted the first manifestation of the ARD's commitment to 'vertical scheduling' on satellite television.

The analysis of the ARD schedule was constructed from the IBA listing (in the same way as the analysis for other Eurikon weeks) and, for a section missing from the IBA listing (the schedule for late Saturday night and all day Sunday) an ARD schedule listing (Table 5.6).

Of the programmes screened by the ARD, 53.8 per cent were made in Germany (21.8 per cent of these were made especially for Eurikon), 10.4 per

Table 5.6 Programme analysis. ARD week 22–28.11.82

| | UK | France | West Germany | Italy | Netherlands | Spain | Ireland | Norway | European Institutions | Switzerland | Other | Total |
|---|---|---|---|---|---|---|---|---|---|---|---|---|
| News | 30 | | 581 | | | | | | 87 | | | 698 |
| Documentary | 90 | | 195 | 30 | | | | | | | 45 | 360 |
| Drama | | 20 | | | | | | | | | | 20 |
| Arts | | | 51 | | | | | 66 | | 30 | | 147 |
| Sports | | | 147 | | | | | | | | | 147 |
| Light entertainment | 35 | | 27 | 46 | | | | | | | 46 | 154 |
| Childrens | 30 | | | | 30 | | 30 | | | | | 90 |
| Adult education | 40 | | 60 | | | 30 | | 30 | | | | 160 |
| Feature films | | | 97 | | | | | | | | | 97 |
| Religion | | | 15 | | | | | | | | | 15 |
| Continuity | | | 20 | | | | | | | | | 20 |
| Total | 225 | 20 | 1,193 | 76 | 30 | 30 | 30 | 96 | 87 | 30 | 91 | 1,908 |

Note: Programme times in minutes.

cent were 'Eurocompilations', 8.9 per cent came from the UK, 4.4 per cent from Austria, 35 from Italy and 1.3 per cent from the Netherlands (EBU/OTS Operations Group 1983: 9).

## The influence of Eurikon on subsequent satellite television programming

Several elements in Eurikon programming foreshadowed later initiatives. The ARD's 'vertical scheduling' of its week was used by Europa and ARTE, and the title of its sports programme, 'Eurosport' was adopted for the EBU's satellite television sports channel. The presenter-less news format pioneered by the IBA, and also used by NOS, has been adopted by Euronews. However the most important innovation in news was ORF's attempt to create a new form of European television news, the 'domestic top news'. ORF's innovation influenced the news format adopted by Europa and, later, by Euronews. ORF recommended that the EBU establish a 'European top news' show as a regular EBU programme service which would make 'considerable use of the EBU Permanent Network to meet the daily deadline' (EBU/OTS Operations Group 1983: 5). The ORF described the domestic top news:

> During the test week of the OTS within the scope of the OTS trials of the EBU it was attempted to create a new form of European news, the domestic top news.
>
> It should be attempted to receive recordings of their respective top items of their main news broadcasts from each of the stations participating in the experiment. Those top items should be broadcast at the end, circa 2200 hours ... through the presentation of the various national top happenings in the main news, namely through the presentation of topics which are of high level interest in the various European countries on a given day in comparison with other national priority topics the relativity of the national happenings could be attained. It was apparent that, aside from big happenings such as elections and changes of government and happenings of interest to both sides of the borders, an uncommonly varied consideration of problems is created. The emphasis on special presentation of the domestic top news additionally allows insight into the special characteristic of the respective country. ... The development of the domestic top news in the ORF-OTS week worked without complaint. Six stations delivered regularly and timely the required contributions. ... On Friday, October 1, 1982 the ORT-OTS [*sic*] editors decided to dedicate the domestic top news to only one topic, because it could be assumed that this topic would have general appeal all over Europe. ... The respective editors were asked to report the contents of their news via teletex to the ORF-OTS editors in writing. The reports themselves were broadcast in the orig-

inal language. They were then translated by a simultaneous interpreter into other European languages. The problem of language is an unsolved point in this case. But since the broadcast addresses a multiple audience at a relatively late hour it can be assumed that a) the foreign language knowledge of the viewer will be relatively better and b) their tolerance towards aides such as teletex and printing computer would be markedly higher than with a normal audience. . . . The broadcast form of the domestic top news is excellently suited as a model of a very specific and very typical European news broadcast.

(Attachment to EBU Com. Pro. TV. SPG 2001)

Charles Barrand, a UK journalist who later became head of news at Europa, shared ORF's enthusiasm. The European top news was, Barrand observed, 'an interesting concept, poorly executed, needing more than a scissors and paste job. The words of introduction were missing. But given that and the NOS translation treatment, something could be made of this concept as a late-night news review' (Barrand 1983a: 6). ORF's innovation in news was paralleled by its innovative music show. 'Eurohitparade' adopted a similar format to the pan-European news pioneered by ORF. Instead of taking the top news item from each European country 'Eurohitparade' took the 'five best and most successful hits' (as defined by an average of the national hit parade ratings of particular songs in different European markets), thus ORF created a hitparade of hitparades.

## The vantage point of hindsight

History, it is said, is written by the winners, for it is they who leave most traces. My account of the development and management of Eurikon therefore reflects the point of view of those who, if not necessarily winners, documented its birth, life and demise and, like all parents, are likely to have been indulgent to their offspring. However, as with family history, not all the photographs in the family album were taken by the family. Other viewpoints were recorded and it is the scepticism of Jean Autin (the President of the EBU in the early 1980s), – see, interalia, Autin's statement to the EBU Administrative Council in 1984 (CA 1704 SPG 2653 May 1984) – and Michael Johnson (representing one of the EBU's largest and most influential members, the BBC), whose analyses appear particularly prescient. Johnson stated:

The EBU's ability to bring together an acceptable European schedule is totally dependent at present on the willingness of its members to contribute to it. Those contributions have their price, and whether members will wish to subscribe to a competitor to their own outlets probably depends on what other European services might emerge. For

113

the EBU to provide the 'least damaging' European service is hardly a
recipe for startling success.
(Unpublished letter to Henri Perez in connection with the EBU working
group [the Perez Group] on public service broadcasting dated 26.7.82)

Johnson's scepticism about the service which the EBU were considering for
the L-Sat doubtless reflected the BBC's self-interested concern to ensure that its
DBS service would have as little competition as possible.[33] But doubts were not
voiced exclusively by representatives of the BBC. A prominent Irish broadcaster,
Muiris MacConghail, argued that Eurikon programming reflected the *amour
propre* and institutional interests of the organisations which formed the Eurikon
Consortium (rather than the needs and interests of the target audience),[34] and
that the reception contexts of the pan-European services were sufficiently
different to make a successful service close to impossible.[35]

Yet, intimidating though the financial and organisational difficulties of establishing and maintaining a pan-European service had been shown to be by the
Eurikon experiment these difficulties were, as another Irish broadcaster recognised, not as challenging as the difficulties of programming a pan-European
television service:

> Within a measurable time, broadcasters will find themselves in an era in
> which national frontiers may be made irrelevant, and network to
> network links may be superseded by the direct broadcast satellite. The
> technical experts will be ready for it. I am not so sure that the
> programme makers will be ready.
>
> (White 1980: 60)

The pan-European satellite television services pioneered by Eurikon were
directed at the European viewer, a grammatically unexceptionable concept, but
an abstraction which had no empirical reality. There were no 'European viewers'
interested in Europe-wide weather, or Europe-wide news. Rather there were
different groups of viewers interested in what touched them concretely, but not
the abstract and rather anaemic, Europeanism represented by Eurikon and its
epigones. As White had foreseen in 1980 the challenge of programming satellite
television was much more formidable than the technological and engineering
challenge it presented.

The programming and scheduling decisions made by the broadcasters who
launched the Eurikon experiment (and the Europa operational service) were the
most important determinants of the success or failure of the ventures. Of course
these decisions were shaped by all manner of constraints. An official of the
Council of Europe who had been intimately connected with the life and death
of Eurikon confirmed that funding, translation and programming difficulties
were certainly important (personal interview 17.12.91). And, he added,
Eurikon had further problems (problems which persisted into the next stage of

the EBU's satellite venture, Europa). Eurikon programmers were sometimes unable to secure their first choice of programme material (because of the impediments presented by rights holders), and the advertisers (from whom Europa's funding was planned to have come), 'just weren't there'. These judgements touched on sensitive issues: how far were Eurikon's sponsors committed to the success of the initiative and how far could *any* advertising funded European satellite television service ever be viable? Hindsight enables us to see that Autin's and Johnson's concerns were well judged, as MacConghail also recognised shortly after the end of the Eurikon experiment. Yet Eurikon was followed by an operational pan-European public service satellite television channel. Why? To answer this vexing question we must consider the institutional and ideological imperatives which influenced the EBU and provided the context which shaped its decisions.

# 6

# FROM EURIKON TO EUROPA

Television is certainly the most effective vehicle of information. Information portrayal on television represents, in turn, the mirror of political and cultural choices. . . . In the past, attempts to coordinate efforts for the organization of a European television information service were unsuccessful. The most important was developed within the Europa TV experience between 1986 and 1987.

(Maggiore 1990: 70–1)[1]

## The Baden-Baden meeting of the Operations Group

The final meeting of the Eurikon Operations Group, at Baden-Baden on 2 November 1982, looked forward to the closing week of Eurikon transmissions later that month and to the next stage of the EBU's pan-European satellite television initiative. No minutes of the meeting are available but other evidence (notably the unpublished paper Neville Clarke produced for the meeting) suggests that the Operations Group's principal concern had become the promotion, planning and programming of the service which it was confident would follow Eurikon. Clarke's paper ended with the statement 'The turtle is flying. It requires but a short burst of the motor to put it in orbit' (Discussion paper for the Baden-Baden meeting of the Operations Group 2.11.82: 5).

The problems considered by the Operations Group show that new technologies may create potentialities for new services, and for the construction of new social relationships but successful realisation of such novel potentialities by no means follows automatically. The Operations Group considered long and hard how best to build the new service they sought and which would, they believed, as well as providing them with seductive advances in their own careers, help the cohesion of the new Europe. Should the new channel be a thematic or mixed programme channel? If thematic should it be sport or news led? Should it be a high culture channel? All these possibilities considered by the Operations Group were later implemented. The mixed channel was implemented as Europa; the thematic sport channel as Eurosport; the news channel as Euronews; and the culture channel as ARTE.

116

Before the Eurikon experiment ended, the Eurikon Operations Group led by Clarke began to campaign for the establishment of an operational pan-European satellite-delivered public service television service. Naturally, the Operations Group interpreted the history of Eurikon as a major success for European public service broadcasting. Thanks to its members creating a climate of opinion within the EBU, and among key European broadcasters who favoured the development of an operational service, the EBU decided to support a second stage of the satellite television partnership between its members and the ESA. The service built on Eurikon's foundations came to be known as Europa but was first known as the 'L-Sat' service and later as Olympus. It finally entered service on 5 October 1985 as Europa.[2]

The Operations Group painted its achievement in glowing colours in an extensive report and retrospect on Eurikon (EBU/OTS Operations Group 1983) and recommended that an operational pan-European service be established. Discussions in the EBU, informed by the Operations Group report, centred on two themes. Should there be an operational public service pan-European satellite television service? And, if so, how should it be programmed? The Operations Group began to set the agenda for these discussions in the final week of the Eurikon service.

## Eurikon's retrospect on itself

On Friday 26 November 1982, the last weekday of Eurikon transmissions and two days before the end of the experiment, the ARD scheduled an eighty-three minute symposium discussion 'Possibilities for a Pan-European DBS Channel' which was televised on Eurikon. Nine participants, from the EBU, from the Eurikon Operations Group and from the European Community, reviewed Eurikon experiment and considered European satellite broadcasting's future. Jean Autin and Albert Scharf (the outgoing and incoming EBU Presidents), Neville Clarke, Carel Enkelaar, Vittorio Boni and Dietrich Schwarzkopf from Eurikon, Wilhelm Hahn (European Parliament) and Franz Froschmaier (Director General, Information Commission of the European Communities) were joined in discussion by Abdul Chakroun, the President of the Arab States Broadcasting Union.

The ARD's programme was introduced by trilingual titles and the discussion was mediated to viewers by simultaneous interpretation bespeaking the considerable progress that had been made in linguistic re-presentation on Eurikon. However, even after five weeks of collective experience, mistakes were made. For example, the German language introduction by the ARD presenter, Franz Wordemann, was not interpreted for the first five minutes (and nor were long sections later in the discussion). The complex task of simultaneous interpretation in several languages and simultaneous transmission of a variety of soundtracks defeated even broadcasters with the ARD's unparalleled competence.

The discussants were very positive about Eurikon; Neville Clarke stated that more than two hundred hours of programming had been transmitted to fifteen EBU Member States from Finland to Tunisia. Research showed, he said, that 10 per cent to 15 per cent of the EBU audience of 300 to 350 million viewers would watch a service like Eurikon once a night. Clarke envisaged development of a 'mixed wide ranging service of quality' which would show Europe to the rest of the world and the rest of the world to Europe and 'would enable us to look into our neighbours' gardens'. Vittorio Boni was no less enthusiastic and stated that audience research, based on panels which exemplified a 'representative audience of a certain European possibility', had shown that a service such as Eurikon carries a very high degree of interest, much more than we expected in the beginning'. Both Clarke's and Boni's endorsement of a positive prognosis for pan-European television appeared at best Panglossian, at worst mendacious, in light of the research findings which the IBA published the following month. IBA researchers found that:

> the current experiments do not unfortunately offer much encouragement. Many more people from both panels who took part in these studies considered *Eurikon* in unfavourable terms than who looked upon it favourably. . . . It also needs to be borne in mind that . . . the samples were not representative. Instead both panels were heavily weighted towards better educated ABC1 people. Given that it is this section of the population at which Eurikon is primarily targeted, the fact that so few said they would be likely to watch, or said that they liked what they saw offers even less encouragement.
>
> (Gunter 1982: 15)

However both Scharf and Hahn echoed the Operations Group's enthusiastic endorsement of the experiment and testified to Eurikon's demonstration of the potential satellite television offered to unify European viewers. Scharf stated that 'satellites should be regarded as a natural instrument for European co-operation'. Hahn echoed him; satellites, he said, offered an 'opportunity to reach all Europeans with a common programme', a programme which recognises that Europeans 'have a common culture'. For Hahn satellite television offered the means to realise a European unity which hitherto had existed only in a latent state. 'We can', Hahn said 'agree on a political or economic level, but do Europeans realise that we have this common culture, do Europeans realise their unity?'[3] Eurikon had, he thought, conveyed to Europeans not only their shared high culture but their shared technological culture too. And Autin (perhaps ill advisedly, given Chakroun's presence and the stress which Scharf had placed on the extent of the EBU's reach from Iceland to Jordan – further than any other European institutional or political union), emphasised that Eurikon had demonstrated the possibility of creating a European television service to express a common European policy and culture which emanated from a common Christian civilisation.

Clarke argued that Eurikon was firmly rooted in the traditions of European public service broadcasting – committed to serve viewers of all income groups, all ages and all religions with wide ranging interests in the European and Mediterranean regions. Boni supported him and advocated a European programme which should not be 'a programme of uniformity' but one 'that will not kill the imagination of the various European countries, that will not kill the variety in little European countries and that will not discourage talent from joining and participating'. In contrast, Schwarzkopf argued for a strongly 'branded' channel. 'Any satellite television channel' he stated 'must be given a definite identity, 'multi channel television was a television of confusion'. Moreover (an interesting argument in respect of his later senior role in the Franco–German high culture channel ARTE) Schwarzkopf argued strongly for entertainment programming and against the temptations of worthiness. Public service satellite television should not, he said, programme culture and education exclusively but also entertainment and information.

Responding to Schwarzkopf, Clarke argued for a news-led service. He stressed the difficulties of simultaneous translation, and the consequential need for a new kind of interpreter (one able to do simultaneous translation in such a way as to sound interesting to viewers). Autin placed the emphasis differently. Satellite television was not the most important policy issue confronting European broadcasters. Rather, Autin emphasised the growing disparity between the volume of European television programme production and the number of hours in the schedules of European television channels which required to be filled. For him the chief challenge facing European television, and public service broadcasting in particular, was a challenge of production rather than distribution. From Autin's point of view therefore, establishing a new channel would exacerbate, not mitigate, the fundamental problem facing European public service broadcasters.

Both Enkelaar and Schwarzkopf challenged Autin. They pointed out that EBU members were unable to exploit all the programme rights which they had acquired. Enkelaar stressed that broadcasters had no space in their schedules for major cultural and sporting events which, he proposed, should be the mainstay of any successor to Eurikon. Schwarzkopf concurred: rights were often under-exploited by terrestrial broadcasters. It followed therefore that, contrary to Autin, there *was* a problem of distribution and not only one of production.

Schwarzkopf argued that future pan-European services should adopt the arrangements pioneered in Eurikon – which were similar to those used by the ARD for its services in Germany. There should be a small co-ordinating unit charged with assembling and scheduling programming produced by a network of members. As might have been expected participants beat their own drums but united, Autin excepted, in advocating a new operational service.

As discussion in the ARD retrospect on Eurikon, in its final week of trans-missions showed, there was, as yet, no solid consensus on how the future of pan-European public service satellite television should be built. Members of the Operations Group discussed how the channel's schedule was to be organised, proposals for specific programme concepts, how the channel was to be funded (including the role of advertising and sponsorship) and so on.

Four models for a thematic channel were considered:

> Euro-sports channel
> Euro-culture channel
> Euro-live events channel
> Euro-information; weather, road conditions, health information, immi-grants/guest workers, social problems, children, senior citizens.

And three specific programme proposals for a mixed programming channel:

> Euro-Hit Parade
> Euro Top News
> Good Morning Europa.
>
> (Memo from Neville Clarke 29.10.82)

After reviewing these options the Operations Group decided to recommend a mixed, not thematic, channel. They turned next to considering the character of the programme schedule to be adopted for the channel. Klaas-Jan Hindriks (an NOS broadcaster and founder member of the Eurikon Operations Group who subsequently became Director of Programmes of Europa) undertook detailed planning and proposed the following parameters for the new service:

- a pan-national DBS service to viewers in the countries of EBU Active Members;
- complementary to established national services;
- offer a public service programme mix of a 'wide range of informational, educational and entertainment programmes of high quality' and 'contain programmes of interest and relevance to the widest possible audience in the countries of the participating broadcasters';
- balanced in terms of programme type and geographical and linguistic origin and a 'substantial proportion' of them should originate from partici-pating broadcasters;
- where possible programmes should be comprehensible to the entire audi-ence in the reception area of the signals;
- the service 'should aim to reflect the characters and cultures of the indi-vidual participating countries to a wider audience', take into account 'the

totality of other national, regional and international services' and 'aim to establish a distinctive flavour and character of its own';

- 'the service should be self-financing and produced [*sic*] revenue for programme production';
- signals should be controlled in each national territory by the 'participating broadcaster' and content should conform to existing legislation.

(Derived from an undated, probably 1982, typescript working paper by Hindriks: 3 and 4)

Hindriks estimated that a staff of more than 200 people, 'a substantial initial investment in technical equipment and services', a transmission studio, a post-production studio, sound production, teletext production and translation facilities would be required for the new service. He and Charles Barrand developed detailed proposals for the mixed programme schedule which would have a strongly 'horizontal' character.[4] They proposed a schedule made up of seven 'building blocks':

Good Morning Europa. 06:45–09:15 CET

A rolling programme concept: a magic carpet which 'follows the sun' from 40 East to 40 West as dawn travels across the European Broadcasting Zone.

Follow the Sun (or Connexions). 09:15–12:00 CET

Regional and minority interests are explored and 'Connexions' sought between them. From the Tundra to the Sahara, from the Atlantic to the Urals – the roots of Western civilisation are presented to an audience until now accustomed only to national and transatlantic messages.

Festival. 12:00–14:00 CET

A permanent 'Festival of the Arts' drawing on the best in the performing and plastic arts: performances from the great theatres of Europe, commissions from the best of contemporary composers and artistes, explanations and explorations of the cultural heritage shared by the countries of the European Broadcasting Zone.

Stadium. 14:00–16:00 CET

The (as yet) unseen triumphs and disasters of athletic achievement – sports unique to their own country, Performances that go beyond national teams or champions, sporting events of Eurovision that never reach the national television screen.

121

Telecine. 16:00–18:00 CET

A showcase for the cinematic talent in the European Broadcasting Zone from cartoon to tragedy – the talent that fails to find an outlet.

Netherlands (i.e. the Dutch terrestrial service). 18:00–23:00 CET

Midnight in Europe. 23:00–24:00 CET

A look back at the day that has passed and a look forward to the day ahead.

(Source: Neville Clarke files, Working Paper 16.3.83)

Hindriks' proposals for Olympus/Europa echoed the Eurikon schedule, particularly in his emphasis on news and arts.[5] But the recommendations were conditioned by two constraints. The EBU members who, it was hoped, would sponsor the new service had to be assured that the new service would complement, but not compete with, their established terrestrial services. Moreover, the new channel had to enable the EBU to realise more fully the value of the Eurovision network itself, and the rights – particularly the sports rights – which the EBU acquired on behalf of its members but which were not fully exploited. In these respects Hindriks' proposals foreshadowed the EBU's Eurosport channel which was introduced in 1989 and borrowed from the ZDF's concurrent proposals for a satellite sports channel.

If the mixed programming character of the service Hindriks and Barrand proposed echoed Eurikon its consistent programme junctions, and consequential 'horizontal' stripping of similar programme types across the schedules (so that each weekday had a common structure) , then this reflected a new concern for viewers' preferences. A 'horizontal' schedule enables viewers to know what type of programme is available at any particular time.

## Deliberations in the EBU

The Operations Group's pre-planning of the new channel and its campaign for its establishment were manifest in the televised discussion on the final Friday of the Eurikon experiment and in the Operations Group's own discussions. The next stage in their campaign centred around its report and retrospect on Eurikon (EBU/OTS Operations Group 1983). The report drew out the lessons the Operations Group claimed had been learned from Eurikon and described Eurikon as a resounding success. So indeed, in some sense, it was. However the striking positive achievements of Eurikon were not a good guide to the likely future of any potential service. The staggering achievement of getting Eurikon 'on stream' at very short notice eloquently testified to the strength of the working relationships and procedures of the EBU. No less remarkable was the energy, idealism and professional commitment of the members of the Operations Group and their colleagues who worked hard to ensure that a rapidly extemporised experiment was brought to a successful conclusion. But this achievement did not testify convincingly to the future viability of an operational service.

Unfortunately the difficulties which had been encountered – cost, relanguaging, programming, audience rejection – and which were not foregrounded in the Operations Group's report, persisted and dogged Eurikon's successor, Europa. Since the Operations Group wrote the history of its own creation it is not surprising that it presented its work in a favourable light. The report (EBU/OTS Operations Group 1983) was written by enthusiasts who, as one might expect, wanted to see their achievements grow and not fade away. The report glossed over three important issues which threatened the viability of similar future services: the response of viewers to the Eurikon programme mix, the difficulties of establishing a satisfactory means of re-presenting programmes made in one language to viewers from other language communities, and the costs of establishing and running a satellite television service.

Eurikon had been established in a remarkably short time, it used an innovatory technology and assembled and transmitted a complicated series of programme schedules for viewers in four different language communities. Such a service would have been inconceivable without the technical infrastructure, the administrative apparatus, the established working practices of the EBU and, above all, the commitment of participating broadcasters and journalists. But the *esprit de corps* and bricolage which conjured into existence at short notice a provocative and illuminating experiment could not be the basis for an operational service and thus the precedent of Eurikon had only a limited applicability to its successor, Olympus/Europa.

## The Administrative Council: for and against

The EBU's Administrative Council, at its seventieth meeting in May 1983, decided to build on the Eurikon experiment and launch a new channel. Its decision was informed by reports from the Eurikon Operations Group's on the OTS experiment (EBU/OTS Operations Group 1983) and from a special meeting of EBU members, convened to consider the ESA's offer of the L-Sat for television broadcasting (see SG/1357 3.3.83). The special meeting was attended by the big guns of the EBU, including both Albert Scharf (the EBU President) and Régis de Kalbermatten (the EBU Secretary General).[6] It concluded that satellite television offered the potential to revivify an imperilled European public service broadcasting:

> with the introduction of direct satellites and L-Sat in particular, the broadcaster will be in possession of an entirely new technology, of a privileged instrument because it has been designed specially for

broadcasting, an instrument which will in the medium term enable him
to revive his first public service function which was being threatened.

(SG/1357 3.3.83: 5)

Following the special meeting de Kalbermatten wrote to EBU members to
build support for the proposed pan-European service – then still known as the
L-Sat service. He argued that 'in order to assume their responsibilities to their
public, broadcasters had to enter this [satellite television] market and they could
no longer afford to maintain a purely defensive attitude' (EBU 1983: 4). De
Kalbermatten further emphasised that 'for the public service broadcaster, to
maintain his rightful place on the audiovisual scene' the EBU had to actively
investigate satellite television (EBU 1983: 4). Eight EBU members, ORF,
BRT/RTBF, ERT, RTE, RAI, NOS, RTVE and SSR responded positively to
the Secretary General's proposals and committed to participating in the L-Sat
service. However, although the commitment of eight EBU members to the L-
Sat programme might seem impressive, none of the largest members of the
EBU, RAI excepted, had supported the proposal.[7]

Alan Protheroe, Assistant Director General of the BBC, categorically
opposed Europa; 'in the question of the need for a programme for the
European direct broadcast satellite, Mr Protheroe simply advised the EBU
against the use of this new vehicle' (Com.Pro.TV/GT TV News SPG 2663
September 1984: 23). The UK's commercial sector, the IBA and ITCA, which
had actively supported Eurikon proved hardly more supportive. The BBC, as
explained above had its own projects and the IBA, in spite of Clarke's valiant
attempts to persuade it otherwise, had learned at first hand the costs of participation in a pan-European venture, had seen the reports of its own researchers
on audience response to the Eurikon programme schedule and, like the BBC,
had other projects in the pipeline.

The Administrative Council's decision to follow Eurikon with an operational
satellite television service reflected a familiar dynamic in EBU decision making.
Small EBU members had most to gain and least to lose from new initiatives,
whereas for the large members the reverse was true. The small members of the
EBU were likely to be both more vulnerable than large members to commercial
satellite television competitors and have more to gain from collaborative
projects from which the EBU's French, German and UK broadcasting companies were conspicuous by their absence. However those who supported the
L-Sat service did not only do so out of cold eyed self interest.

Many of those who developed Eurikon and Europa were also motivated by
desires to use the unique technological characteristics of satellite television to
contribute to European integration. Neville Clarke captured this aspiration,
stating that 'the more romantic will recall the historic first words spoken by man
on the moon: "One small step . . . " and dream of uniting the peoples of
Europe (if only in front of their tv sets)' (Clarke 1982: 44).

George Waters, formerly Director General of RTE who became Vice

President of the EBU in 1982 (in turn, part-time Chief Executive on Europa and then head of the EBU Technical Department), stated that RTE's motivation for participating in Europa was to 'do something for Europe' (personal interview 24.2.92; see also Waters 1986). Jeremy Taylor (a UK broadcaster – and therefore likely to view Europa from a 'big country' perspective – who became Head of Press and Publicity for Europa and later for Channel 4) echoed Waters (personal interview 9.7.92). He also described the Europa Consortium as altruists. Taylor argued that the proponents of Europa were high minded Europeans of a generation who had been formed by their personal experience of the Second World War. They, like Waters, sought to do 'something for Europe'. Richard Dill (of the ARD, later Deputy Chief Executive of Europa and a member of the Eurikon Operations Group) was one such altruistic European unionist. He stated:

> the number of people whose lives go beyond national boundaries and who no longer regard themselves, culturally and economically speaking as citizens of a single country is growing constantly. Television and the media no longer have to encourage the European idea but to illustrate how Europe has long become a reality for an increasing number of people in more and more areas,

and lauded Wilhelm Hahn's statement, 'If Europe exists, then we also need European television' (Dill 1986). The choice of a white dove as the Europa emblem signalled the ethical commitment of Dill and his colleagues. Carel Enkelaar too emphasised that the programme content of the pan-European service (to which he referred as the 'European Programme'), was to be distinctively European; it was:

> to be different from everything that is already there . . . this difference is particularly the need for the European channel to cover Europe, not only in the technical sense but especially in a psychological-cultural sense.
> (Enkelaar interviewed in *Broadcasting News from the Netherlands*
> 1984, 2: 2)

However, in Taylor's eyes, the very qualities of disinterested commitment to European fraternity, so evident in those who brought Europa to fruition, was the measure of them being 'out of touch with ordinary folk everywhere'. Europa was, Taylor stated, run by multilinguists who didn't realise how unrepresentative of most Europeans they actually were.

Taylor was echoed by others. For example, a German commentator chose as a title for an article on Europa: 'Kennen Sie Europa TV? Ein Programme mit hohem Anspruch und wenig Zuschauern' – 'Ever heard of Europa TV? A programme with big ambitions but few viewers' (Wankell 1986). However, in spite of the scepticism of the big EBU members, the commitment of the EBU's big guns and eight member broadcasters combined with the Eurikon Operations Group's very positive (albeit somewhat misleading) account of the Eurikon experiment (EBU/OTS Operations Group 1983) were sufficient to persuade the Administrative Council to forge ahead on the next stage in the EBU's satellite television odyssey.

## Implementation of the Europa project

Accordingly, the Administrative Council established a group headed by two Eurikon veterans, Carel Enkelaar (Head of NOS television) as chair and Neville Clarke as rapporteur, to progress the project. Enkelaar and Clarke's group, though formally charged only with assessing the European market for satellite television programming, interpreted its remit more widely. It made development of the next stage of the EBU's transnational satellite television programme its vocation (CA 1655 SPG 2258 13.5.83). In doing so, the Enkelaar group (as it had come to be called) drew on discussions and planning which had already begun in the EBU's Television Programme Committee (of which the Eurikon Operations Group had formally remained a sub-committee) and in NOS, where Enkelaar was Director of Television.

But, although the L-Sat pan-European service was born out of EBU members' fear of commercial competition, nowhere in the reviews which the EBU and its committees undertook at this time (and which surveyed the development of cable networks, possible national DBS from the UK, France and West Germany as well as the EBU's own proposals for L-Sat services) were commercial DBS initiatives, such as Luxembourg's Astra, contemplated. The EBU seems to have believed that if it got into DBS quickly it would have the field to itself and would be able to defeat the nascent commercial competition represented by Brian Haynes' Sky Channel with a knockout blow.

## 'Project A' versus 'Project B'

Perhaps the most important task of the Enkelaar Group was to evaluate rival programme formats for the new pan-European satellite service. Two principal proposals, known as 'Project A' – a diversified, but costly, programme stream, and 'Project B' – a cheaper live event (principally sport) based format, were considered by the Enkelaar working group (and by the EBU's Administrative Council in 1983). Supporters of Project A argued that it offered 'the only innovative step forward in European culture'. Proponents of Project B argued that 'the programme was too expensive for what it offered and [was] not expensive enough for what it ought to be'.

Project A was sponsored by the NOS (the detailed development of the concept came from a group led by Clarke drawing on the Eurikon Operations Group's preferences for a mixed channel format). The ARD, ERT, RTE, RTVE and SSR supported this concept. Project A was conceived as a 'public service channel (i.e. including news and sports programmes, documentaries, educational and cultural programmes and those for minorities, etc.) but with a European outlook' (CA 1680 SPG 2450 17.11.83: 1). It was costed at 60 million Sfr per annum.

Project B was sponsored by ZDF (drafted by Werner Schwaderlapp of ZDF) supported by eight other backers, as an embodiment of pre-existing (and therefore widely supported) EBU policies – as the so-called 'zero-plus' option. Its proponents argued that Project B would enable the EBU to exploit its programme rights, and in particular sports rights (sport was to constitute 70–80 per cent of the programming of the pan-European channel), more effectively. Project B was estimated to cost 12–15 million Sfr per annum.

Europa was modelled on the NOS 'Project A' model. Its failure cleared the way for adoption of the Project B model for the EBU's Eurosport channel launched in 1989. After the Project A mixed programming model was adopted for Europa, discussions centred on 'vertical' or 'horizontal' scheduling for the channel. Whilst the Eurikon veterans and their allies had 'won' the battle for a Project A mixed programme format, like that thrashed out at the Baden-Baden meeting of the Operations Group, they lost the battle for horizontal scheduling. Their well developed plans were quickly discarded in the face of the institutional imperatives of the broadcasters which eventually sponsored Eurikon's successor. As described above, the Eurikon veterans had proposed a morning news service, yet the pan-European service (Europa) which succeeded Eurikon began as an evening, rather than all day, service.

Instead of the clear horizontal programming and schedule envisaged by Hindriks and Barrand the pan-European service proposed was a 'pattern of daily vertical streaming by programme type' (Clarke 1983: 34).[8] None of the three specific programme proposals considered by the Operations Group; Eurohitparade and Euro Top News (programmes which had been introduced in the ORF's Eurikon week and proposed by the ORF as a permanent part of Eurovision services), and Good Morning Europa (the 4.5 hour breakfast television news show devised by Charles Barrand and Klaas-Jan Hindriks) was adopted for the pan-European channel Olympus/Europa.

Moreover, the goal of establishing a European programming channel proved more difficult than had been anticipated. Although Eurikon had drawn its programming predominantly from its five active partners; Austria contributed 18.5 per cent, the Netherlands 15.8 per cent, Germany 15 per cent, Italy 13.6 per cent and the UK 12.7 per cent, it also drew on the European Parliament, the European Space Agency and on eleven other states (including Mexico and Algeria but not the USA), for programmes. The absence of the USA from the list of sources of Eurikon programmes may seem to signify successful achievement of the intention that 'content was to be European' (Barrand 1982: 2). But this success was more apparent than real. Not only were many American elements embedded in European programmes,[9] but the USA was an important source of, and location for, news. Indeed, the US accounted for 10.5 per cent of the Eurikon news items and the Operations Group stated that, 'the "European Perspective" often went by the board because there was no way of illustrating it' (EBU/OTS Operations Group 1983: 13).

On Eurikon, Barrand and Hindriks had found how difficult it was not to cover world news from a North Atlantic, Anglo-American, perspective. They concluded that there was simply no economic alternative. Making a virtue of necessity they borrowed the title 'Good Morning America' and proposed a 'Good Morning Europa'. 'Good Morning Europa' was to use well established news sources and supply channels even though many of these were centred on and in the USA. Sourcing and routing news from other world locations presented formidable difficulties. Indeed the Eurovision news exchange itself depended on US sources as Barrand observed in his private letter to Clarke, 'EVNs have proved an inadequate source of European material . . . EVN-O derives much of its content from the USA' (Barrand 1983a: 5).[10] Thus Barrand foresaw a morning news service using the '15 minute digest of ABC and UPITN material (plus some CBS stories)'.[11]

The new service would rely on the USA for its coverage of the Americas: 'the bulk of news material from this region [Central/South America and the Caribbean] would be received through Newyork [*sic*] in co-operation with the U.S. networks' (Barrand 1983). And although Barrand foresaw few problems in gathering news from Asia and Australasia independently of the USA he feared that 'Since breakfast in Europe represents mid-afternoon in Asia . . . there may be some obstacles to accessing some stories within the European breakfast deadline'. Moreover 'West, Central and Southern Africa will remain problem news areas for the foreseeable future for a variety of reasons . . . in many areas television news coverage hardly exists and where it does, relies mostly on air freight to reach Europe the next day. South Africa and (sometimes) Kenya are currently the only exceptions. Yet, even from Johannesburg, it will not be possible to transmit by satellite in time for European breakfast programme deadlines' (Barrand 1983).

## NOS' vision for Europa

In April 1983 the EBU's Television Programmes Committee met in Cannes (concurrently with the MIP Conference and Trade Fair) and reviewed a proposal (including draft morning and afternoon programme schedules) tabled by NOS for a pan-European satellite television service using an 'A'-type programme format. NOS proposed that the morning service would be news and information led and would aim 'to provide continuous programme material of interest, relevance and entertainment to the range of languages and cultures across the European time zones'. The afternoon service promised 'The best of the European arts (concerts, ballet, theatre) live events (sports, actualities), European cinema (movies, documentaries)'. NOS argued that the morning schedule was most important because, with the exception of the UK, Spain and

Portugal, no breakfast time television services were offered by European broadcasters. There was therefore, it believed, a window of opportunity for the
EBU's pan-European service.

## The role of the NOS

In the mid 1980s the NOS had become the centre of the European public
broadcasters' satellite television initiatives.[12] At the time, Dutch cultural and
broadcasting policy was in transition. A new Dutch media law was enacted in
1987 following fierce debates in the Netherlands during the mid 1980s. These
concerned the possible introduction of a third terrestrial television channel;
whether the new channel should be a commercial or public service channel;
and, whether the NOS should be broken up by separating its production and
technical facilities from its programming and organisational activities. There
were, therefore, strong incentives for the NOS to be seen to be actively moving
into a new medium, satellite television, of which much was expected and
thereby demonstrating that it, as well as commercial broadcasters, could inno-
vate. Like the IBA's decisions, first to enter the EBU initiative and then to
withdraw, NOS' commitment to pan-European television was principally driven
by domestic considerations.

In 1984 Eric Jurgens (Voorzitter of NOS), had pressed the EBU's
Administrative Council to move forward with the pan-European service
declaring that 'it was essential to find a place on the market to test the
European audience as soon as possible. A joint experiment therefore appeared
necessary and urgent' (CA 1704 SPG 2653 May 1984: 72). Jurgens was
supported by George Waters, then Director General of RTE (who, after his
retirement from RTE, became the part-time Chief Executive of Europa), who
affirmed the importance of broadcasters taking 'their place sufficiently early . . .
so as not to lose their chances to obtain the necessary channels and to take a
leading part in the action' (CA 1704 SPG 2653 May 1984: 73).

By the early part of 1984 the NOS, not the EBU/OTS Operations Group,
had become the locomotive of the pan-European service. In consequence
Clarke's influence declined as, of course, did that of the IBA. Although Clarke
and Hindriks had claimed that there was 'considerable interest in and support
for' the Pan-European Television Service from ITV, [13] it is a matter of record
that neither the IBA nor the ITCA contributed to Europa initiative (beyond the
IBA's contribution of Clarke's salary until his return to the IBA in 1985).

The ITV companies were committed to establishing their own European
television channel (with the notable exception of Thames Television which
chose instead to take a 10 per cent holding in SES, the company which operated the Astra satellites). This initiative, Super Channel, was based on the Music
Box channel previously launched by two ITV companies, Granada Television
and Yorkshire Television, in conjunction with Virgin. In 1986 the remaining
ITV companies (with the exception of Thames) took holdings in Music Box

which was relaunched in 1987 as Super Channel. By 1988 Super Channel had become effectively bankrupt and the ITV companies ceded their holdings to Virgin. A UK source, who had played a leading role in Super Channel judged that Super Channel had failed because it mistakenly targeted 'Euro yuppies' as its core audience rather than a mass market, 'the lowest common denominator programming is easiest to do across language barriers in Europe' (personal interview 9.7.92). This suggests that there were further grounds to doubt the suitability of the 'elitist' programme mix chosen for the Eurikon and Europa.

The NOS proposals drew on the detailed plans which Klaas-Jan Hindriks put forward in a Working Paper (dated 16.3.83), and circulated at the Cannes meeting. However the NOS made several novel proposals including a new method of service delivery. NOS proposed that the morning service be retransmitted from terrestrial transmitters fed from the satellite (first the ECS and then L-Sat). The absence of established terrestrial morning television services in most European countries meant that terrestrial frequencies (used only for afternoon and evening transmissions), were vacant in the morning. But using these spare frequencies would also mean that the pan-European afternoon programme could not be transmitted by terrestrial means and would have to be transmitted by satellite, either directly to homes or relayed via cable. This meant that the Europa service would be on different channels at different times in the day. But NOS believed that the advantages of establishing a terrestrial morning service outweighed the disadvantages of split frequencies, and the consequential viewer-confusion and loss of channel identity. Here was a clear indication of the subordination of the proposed new service to the established terrestrial services of EBU members.

The morning schedule was to be funded by payments from terrestrial re-broadcasters and by advertising and the afternoon schedule by subscription (NOS memo to the EBU Television Programme Committee meeting on 19–22 April 1983). The pan-European service was planned to tap into what its proponents believed was a vast, unexploited, transnational European television advertising market which was estimated to amount to 3 billion Dutch guilders (hfl) per annum (Verveld 1986: 2). NOS estimated that the cost of the first full year of Europa transmissions, 1986, would be approximately 50–60 million hfl and therefore it was easy to believe, if both these assumptions were granted, that the pan-European service could be financially viable.

NOS' support for a mixed programme format, and the perceived success of Eurikon using such programme, meant that the rival thematic format for the pan-European channel (canvassed by ZDF), was rejected. (This perception was based on the partisan report and recommendations of the Eurikon Operations Group.) Accordingly, the project team formed to progress the EBU's satellite venture was charged with developing a Project A type service. The project team's report 'Pan-European Television Service via ECS. A Feasibility Study' (Clarke 1983),[14] proposed a self-financing service for a 'new multinational audience that will attract new sources of advertising revenue' and which would 'complement and not compete with existing national programmes'; it was planned to break even in 3 to 5 years (Clarke 1983: 3).

## The Clarke report

The feasibility study (Clarke 1983), sometimes known as the 'Clarke report' (though drafted by Clarke, Dill and Hindriks) recommended that Europa (although the proposed service had not then been so named), should be established via a consortium of EBU members, should be located at Hilversum and should use English as its working language. It proposed a service designed for direct reception and/or cable redistribution to consortium members which was to be transmitted for between two and five hours daily in scrambled form. Programming was to 'correspond to the specific character of high level European public service television programmes' (Clarke 1983: 14).

Clarke, Dill and Hindriks envisioned the 'European Programme' being transmitted with multiple sound tracks in different languages with no presenters in shot – a presentational format subsequently adopted by Euronews. Of its programming, 35 per cent was to be produced by the broadcasters who formed the Consortium providing the pan-European service, 10 per cent would be purchased or commissioned, 40 per cent would be archive material from consortium members, 10 per cent would be new material from Eurovision and Consortium members and 5 per cent was to be advertising (Clarke 1983: 43). Clarke, Hindriks and Dill proposed a four-hour evening schedule in which news was planned to account for 25 per cent, advertising 5 per cent (i.e. three minutes per hour), current affairs 9.8 per cent, documentary and education 14.7 per cent, sport 7 per cent, cinema 7 per cent, drama and arts 15.5 per cent, children and youth 7 per cent and entertainment 7 per cent. Continuity and presentation was to account for the remaining 2 per cent of transmission time.

The schedules reflected the 'vertical' presumptions of the ARD advocated by Dill. Different nights were to be given clearly different characters accentuating the 'vertical' differentiation of programming on different days: Mondays – sports, Tuesdays – arts, Wednesdays – 'Europe at home' (a pot pourri of different entertainment genres), Thursdays – 'Neighbours' (documentaries and education programmes on Europe which 'tackle the serious issues of the day'), Friday – youth, Saturday – theatre, and Sunday – cinema (from Clarke 1983: 38–9).

Rather than a distinctive, well-planned schedule based on a breakfast show (which did not compete with established daytime programming of the majority of its potential public service broadcasting sponsors) and a well planned horizontal schedule, the pan-European service (Europa) which was actually established had a programme mix and schedule which reflected 'political' priorities; notably those of the broadcasters which sponsored the channel but also the interests of the rump of the Operations Group itself. Those who had invested much in Eurikon understandably saw the future of pan-European television and their own careers as closely intertwined. Understandably the Operations Group's proposals for the new service were formulated in the light of what was judged politically possible. Unfortunately what was politically possible was not always what the lessons learned from the Eurikon experiment had taught should be done.

For example, Clarke, Dill and Hindriks invested (what was to become Europa) with the mission of providing 'a European perspective of the world which does not replace but supplements the mainstream of national news programmes' (Clarke 1983: 35). This formulation suggests both the subordination of the identity and possible success of the new service to existing services but also a Nelsonian attitude towards the finding of the Eurikon news teams that a European perspective was not only close to impossible to achieve organisationally but that (as Barrand stated in his report on Eurikon news services) 'there is no absolute European perspective' (Barrand 1982: 11).

The feasibility study envisaged majority ownership (51 per cent) of the channel by participating broadcasters and minority ownership of 49 per cent, by investors: broadcasters would divide their share of investment and liability using the EBU's basic units formula. This meant that participation by the UKIBA (the feasibility study assumed the participation of the UK's ITV system), would commit the UK's ITV system to a contribution more than double that of NOS and four times the Irish contribution. Under the ownership and funding proposals outlined in the Clarke report the UK's commitment to the pan-European service would be exceeded only by the ARD's. Such a financial structure underscores the relatively greater attractiveness of the pan-European ventures to small broadcasters.

File papers show that the Clarke group did a considerable amount of juggling with budgeted costs in preparing their report. For example start-up costs budgeted on different assumptions ranged from an anticipated 37.4 to 50 million Sfr (these sums did not include an estimated capital sum of 1.1 million Sfr required for the establishment of a news service). Moreover the feasibility study stated that 'in addition to their contribution to the central budget, members of the consortium will incur expenditure on their own territory. The cost estimates . . . do not include provision for the down link from the satellite'. The downlink costs were estimated to be 90,500 Sfr per annum (Clarke 1983: 89).

Evidently, even after extensive massaging, the cost estimates troubled potential participants. The RTE telexed Clarke asking for assurances that anticipated revenue flows had been properly researched and questioning the estimated cost of the L-Sat/Europa service. 'What', Finn of RTE asked, 'is the estimate of television homes capable of receiving the service in each of the three years and has any estimate been made of the amount of advertising which would be generated, by sector, from various target categories of international products and services?' Finn commented both that 'the initial investment required seems very large to us' and that 'to us, given the service envisaged, and the programme/facilities input expected from the various partners, the total costs of 40 million Swiss Francs seem high' (Telex from Vincent Finn Deputy Director General RTE,[15] to Clarke 14.12.83).

In response to the caution expressed by RTE and other sceptics, Clarke and Hindriks wrote to Enkelaar (16.1.84) affirming their view that the pan-European Television Service remained 'both feasible and viable'. They attested to the support by European political institutions, by the NOS, ARD, RTE and ITV (even though RTE had, as Finn's telex attests, expressed its concern about the likely viability of the Pan-European service), and from 'independent suppliers of services and finance'. Clarke and Hindriks claimed that the service would require 360 staff at an annual cost of 22,745,000 Sfr; a considerable reduction on even the lowest estimated cost of service envisaged in the feasibility study (though significantly more costly than Hindriks had estimated in 1983). Clarke and Hindriks acknowledged that additional 'technical transmission facilities staff . . . maintenance and cleaning staff provided by NOS' would be required. However, the chief advocates of the new service, Clarke and Hindriks, affirmed that they were 'confident that the project as outlined in the Feasibility Study and Proposal is not only feasible and viable but also realisable in terms of its initial financing' (Europa file 16.1.84).

Proponents of the pan-European service were clearly caught between the need to calm the apprehensions of the broadcasters whom they hoped would sponsor the initiative (and who feared that estimated costs were too high for the service to be sustained), and their own knowledge (based on their direct experience of running Eurikon), of how complicated and costly a multi-lingual pan-European satellite service would be. The 'independent suppliers of services and finance' costings which Clarke and Hindriks adduced in support of their budgetary estimates were not as reassuring as Clarke and Hindriks led others to believe.

## Finance

The EBU Finance Group independently assessed revenues and costs for the proposed pan-European service. The Finance Group assumed a service delivered by satellite to cable (with possible terrestrial rebroadcasting), with a four hour evening schedule complementing (rather than competing with) terrestrial services. The pan-European service would use teletext titling or multiple channel sound and would devote 50 per cent of its programming to news (rather than the 25 per cent of news programming envisaged in the feasibility study). The Finance Group adopted more generous assumptions than had the authors of the Feasibility Study in their estimates of the amount of time (and therefore revenues which might accrue) dedicated to advertising on the channel. The Finance Group assumed that twenty minutes of advertising per day would be scheduled rather than either the twelve minutes initially envisaged in the feasibility study, or the 5 per cent of total transmission time (about eighteen minutes) which Clarke had later envisaged.

The EBU Finance group assumed that the L-Sat channel would attract more viewers in its target universe than the average share (15–30 per cent) which had actually been achieved by foreign terrestrial television channels in the European television markets. They did so on the grounds that the L-Sat channel would be translated into the native languages of the target viewers and would not be perceived as a foreign channel. The Finance Group believed that c.20 million television homes (10 million cable/MATV subscribers, 10 million DBS homes), would receive the L-Sat channel in its first year of operation. Overall, it estimated, 2 per cent of European television homes would watch the L-Sat channel (i.e. 400,000 homes) in the first year, yielding a potential income of 50 million Sfr. The Finance Group foresaw a remarkably short period of losses for the new service. Europa was expected to be 'successful and profitable within the 3 year period' (EBU 1984: 13).

The Finance Group assumed that the L-Sat channel would stimulate demand for advertising and would not rob terrestrial channels (EBU 1984: 10). Indeed a categorical undertaking was given that 'the proposed European service would not be a threat to the advertisement revenue of the national broadcasting services' (EBU 1984: 12). It is hard to reconcile this claim with other assertions that Europa would contribute to EBU members' revenues and would act as an effective spoiler to commercial satellite broadcasting. The service could not simultaneously be part of satellite television, a sector which threatened public national broadcasting, and not be a threat to the advertising revenue of the national public broadcasters. Here the political considerations which led proponents of the pan-European service to plan and present it as non-threatening to the services and interests of EBU members' terrestrial services led to misleading cost and revenue assumptions. These optimistic estimates did not serve the channel well once it had been established.

Rather than dispassionately assessing the economics of the proposed new pan-European channel, the EBU Finance Group acted as an advocate for it. It warned, should the EBU not seize the initiative, that commercial interests would do so to the ultimate detriment of public sector broadcasters throughout Europe:

> if it doesn't happen through the EBU, an opportunity is being provided for commercial exploitation without any reciprocal benefit to the members of the EBU. Future development of electronic media, including cable origination, satellite programmes, trans-Border reception etc., will and must affect national audiences and increase fragmentation of shares. It is important, therefore, national broadcasting organisations do everything possible to maintain audiences through being a part of the new media mixture.
>
> (EBU 1984: 12)

However there was at least one sceptic in the Finance Group. Jean-Bernard Münch (then Director of Finance and Administration of Swiss Broadcasting and later Secretary General of the EBU) argued that the audience levels for Europa which the Finance Group anticipated were not achievable with programming budgets of the kind specified by the Finance Group. Münch's attachment to the report, dated 19.6.84, states: 'le taux d'audience supputé n'est à mon avis atteignable qu'avec un programme très attractif. Un tel programme me semble devoir couter beaucoup plus que les Frs. 40 Mio. que pourrait rapporter la publicité' ['in my judgement the audience size envisaged isn't attainable except with a very attractive programme schedule. Such a schedule, I believe, would cost much more than the advertising income of 40 million francs envisaged'].

Münch further challenged the predicted levels of market penetration assumed for Europa, the relative attractiveness of Europa *vis à vis* alternative viewing opportunities, the anticipated viewing share of Europa, the amount of advertising time likely to be sold and, in consequence, the likelihood of Europa achieving financial viability. He judged the Finance Group's conclusion 'this European service could meet its full cost from advertising and be a positive contribution to the funds of the EBU', 'à la fois trop optimiste et surtout trop hâtive: il est impossible de connaître le degré de couverture financière avant de connaître le coût du programme. Les programmes cités en p.2 ne me semblent pas pouvoir être couverts avec un montant de 40 Mio' ['both too optimistic and above all too speculative: it's not possible to know how far costs will be covered before knowing the cost of the service. The schedule cited on page 2 cannot, I believe, be covered by a sum of 40 million'].

The sceptics' vision was vindicated by events.[16] But, despite Münch's caution, the Finance Group recommended that the pan-European service should go ahead.

## EPS: Europees Programma via Satelliet

To progress its policy of establishing (and ensuring it was located at Hilversum) the new pan-European service, NOS circulated a paper (written in English) in October 1984 entitled 'Europees Programma via Satelliet' (EPS) which stated: 'the NOS is holding the key to a realization of the European Programme' (NOS 1984: 4). NOS' contention was borne out by events. In the EPS paper the NOS rehearsed a familiar economic case for some form of transnationalisation of television. It stated, 'the relatively high cost of television programmes should make their spreading on a larger than national scale an obvious matter' (NOS 1984: 1). However NOS also argued for a public broadcasting presence in the European satellite television market (the chosen route to internationalisation), both because of the intrinsic worth of such a service and as a defence against new commercial initiatives.

The public system which has been regulated in the interest of a pluri-form freedom of speech and on the basis of cultural policies, will meet with strong competition from international commercial television programmes spread via satellite. . . . If the public broadcasting system should fail to act, it will particularly be in danger of eventually losing access to the (sports) programme rights that are as a rule obtained on an international scale.

(NOS 1984: 1 and 2)

NOS further argued for a pan-European service which would:

be capable of expressing a pluriform European television culture and of stimulating the European audio-visual industry, thus counter-balancing the inflow of American programmes brought about by the price–popu-larity ratio.

(NOS 1984: 2)[17]

In EPS, NOS emphatically rejected the notion of a thematic channel (whether the sports channel consistently advocated in the EBU by ZDF or a news channel), for reasons of public service principle. It strongly advocated a vertically streamed mixed public service channel as:

- a complement to the programmes of national broadcasting organisations;
- different in character;
- of an obviously European nature; the American serial entertainment product will not occupy a place of any significance in it;
- independent of any national or international government influence and of any influence from (advertising) trade and industry, in accordance with the traditions of public broadcasting in Europe;
- the Programme's set-up leaves no room for excessive attention to 'events' which could soon turn it into a sports channel.

(NOS 1984: 7)

NOS made its case for locating the pan-European service in the Netherlands on the grounds that the Netherlands could 'act as a pioneer, the concentration of organisational and distributional activities on Dutch territory would have rather an attractive secondary effect as regards employment' (NOS 1984: 4). In order to secure these benefits the NOS guaranteed 6.72 million Sfr to 'a European Programme during a pre-operational phase over a limited period and to test it under realistic circumstances' (NOS 1984: 6). The limited period was defined as six months – long enough to obtain reliable data on the programme's financial viability and short enough to reduce risk.

For the operational period following the limited, experimental period, financing was planned to come 51 per cent from participating public broadcasters and 49 per cent from European Institutions and commercial interests. The annual cost of the operational service was projected as 33 million hfl per year (there is no explanation of the basis on which this estimate was made in NOS 1984), of which the NOS was able to commit 14 million hfl for 1983 and 1984 thanks to a special appropriation from the Netherlands Ministry of Culture. The total annual cost share to be shouldered by broadcasters was to be 17 million hfl leaving 12.5 million hfl to be raised from commercial sources (after an anticipated 3.5 million hfl participation of the European Institutions). All these assumptions proved to be optimistic.

Following the Operations Group's rosy retrospect on Eurikon, the EBU Finance Group's optimistic estimates of the revenues which would accrue to the Pan-European service, NOS' advocacy, coupled with the widespread anxiety among EBU members about the threat to their services posed by commercial satellite television, the EBU firmly committed itself to a pan-European channel. Albert Scharf, the President of the EBU, told the General Assembly in summer 1984 that 'it was the Union's duty and in a way a moral obligation, to promote a European programme, and this was a duty of solidarity towards all members'. The Secretary General supported Scharf and referred to the European Parliament's Arfé Resolution (European Parliament 1984) of the same year which proposed a pan-European satellite service and which, he stated, 'simply reiterated the Union's idea'. Moreover, the Secretary General argued, if 'the EBU was incapable of carrying through a European Programme, its image would be diminished' (EBU 1984a: 69). A consortium to deliver the pan-European service was therefore established by four founding partners, the ARD, NOS, RAI and RTE, under the aegis of the EBU.

## The Europa Consortium

The Consortium agreement on which the new pan-European service was founded provided that the Consortium should last for six years from 1 January 1985, that other EBU members should be permitted to join the Consortium (on terms agreed unanimously by Consortium members) and that members' contributions should be set at: RTE 10 per cent proportion of total costs, ARD 25 per cent, RAI 43 per cent and NOS 22 per cent. The accession of RTP in 1985 (just before Portugal's accession to the European Community in 1986) changed the funding balance to RTE 9 per cent, RTP 12 per cent, RAI 38 per cent, ARD 22 per cent, NOS 19 per cent.

The partners envisioned 40 per cent of the programming of the pan-European service would be live sports events via Eurovision, 20 per cent other live events (including news), via Eurovision, 20 per cent existing programmes from members and 20 per cent new programmes produced by members (source Consortium Agreement). The estimated cost of establishing and running the pan-European service at the time the Consortium Agreement was drafted was 64 million Sfr (CA 1728 SPG 2795 22.11.84: 1). The channel would require expenditure by the consortium members of 30.2 million Sfr for three years from June 1985. The shortfall between costs and capitalisation from the Consortium members was to be made up by income from advertising and sponsorship, subventions from European institutions and investment from the new consortium members who, it was anticipated, would join.

During its passage through the committees of the EBU the pan-European service came to diverge strikingly from that initially envisaged. A channel which was initially conceived to pre-empt commercial competition and carry the champions of public service broadcasting into the space age was now to rely on advertising revenue. Whereas the channel had been planned to extend public service broadcasting into a new technological domain, a corporate structure for the channel with a 49 per cent share held by commercial investors was proposed. Because European public service broadcasters feared competition to their terrestrial services, the pan-European service had to be planned as a service complementing, rather than competing with, established terrestrial services. Rather than striking out into new territory the pan-European service was condemned to take what was left at the margins of the European television market.

An insider formerly employed at Europa (personal interview 9.7.92) characterised the Europa Consortium as 'half hearted' and 'for none was the first priority the successful running of a European channel'. The ARD wanted, this informant stated, 'to try everything – cable, satellite, pan-European television, and it had the money to do so'.[18] The NOS had an excess of facilities and capital resources ('the NOS at Hilversum makes the BBC at White City look like toytown'), an unused satellite transponder and the knowledge that the Dutch language prevented it from developing as a serious supplier of programmes to other broadcasters. Moreover Europa offered NOS the opportunity to play on a bigger stage. RAI wished to broaden its base of activities and pre-empt competition from commercial television, notably Berlusconi. RTP had a terrestrial channel which was unused and saw Europa as a source of low cost programming. RTE joined Europa for 'fun' (all quotations from interview with source 9.7.92). All of these speculations, except perhaps the last, are plausible at worst, convincing at best, accounts of the motivation of the participants in the Europa consortium. However, it seems unlikely that Irish broadcasters would move from Dublin to Hilversum for fun.

NOS became the most important influence in public service satellite television. It had played a major role in Eurikon and maintained its commitment to the development of the pan-European service from participation in Eurikon through commissioning and funding the feasibility study (Clarke 1983) to eventual establishment of Europa. Accordingly, the headquarters of the Europa pan-European service were established in the cradle of Dutch public service broadcasting, NOS' old headquarters building at number 2, Emmastraat, and the character of Europa came increasingly to be shaped by the priorities and viewpoint of the NOS.

# 7

# EUROPA: THE CASTLE IN THE AIR

Europa TV, that unfortunate venture which, inspired by Dutch television, was to become, as a first step, a showcase for Irish (RTE), Portuguese (RTP), Italian (RAI) and German (ARD) television. Its failure was undoubtedly commensurate with the project's premature ambition.

(Stephane 1988: 20)

Our only chances of survival and of being recognized as European lie in bringing together European television programmes adapted to the many different languages. The Eurikon experiment which expanded into the Olympus project might prove an alternative to the existing deadlock which must be broken if the public broadcaster isn't to sign its own death warrant.

(Hindriks n.d.: 3)

The EBU's Administrative Council (on 20 November 1985) recorded the beginning of service by Europa, the first operational public service pan-European satellite television service, thus:

Europa Television began broadcasting daily transmissions via the ECS-1 satellite on 5 October 1985. Europa Television is a programme service provided by the pan-European satellite broadcasting consortium, which was established by five European public service broadcasters (ARD/West Germany, NOS/Netherlands, RAI/Italy, RTE/Ireland and RTP/Portugal). The consortium is operating under the auspices of the European Broadcasting Union (EBU) and is open to all EBU members. Among broadcasters who are currently studying the possibilities to join, support or cooperate in this venture are BRT/Belgium, SRG/Switzerland, TVE/Spain, SVT/Sweden and TRT/Turkey.

(CA 1784 (dt) SPG 3167)

Europa was first transmitted from 18:00 to about 22:30 CET daily. As the service became established transmissions lengthened; by the end of the channel's life they usually ended about an hour later, and sometimes, particularly at weekends when additional sports programmes were screened, began earlier. The transmissions were scrambled and were designed for re-distribution by cable networks. Because of delays in launching and commissioning the Olympus satellite,[1] Europa was first transmitted from the ESA's ECS-1 satellite (and subsequently moved to Eutelsat's Eutelsat 1 F-1.4, rather than the ESA's Olympus/L-Sat satellite as had been envisaged).[2] Europa shared its satellites with its principal commercial rival, Sky Channel.

English was the main language used for Europa but Dutch, German and Portuguese soundtracks were also transmitted using sub-carrier frequencies. *New Media Markets* (18.2.86: 7) estimated that the annual cost of relanguaging a single channel was c.£1 million – a substantial cost in relation to the average programme budget for Europa planned as £13,000 per hour. The service was funded for the first year by the five members of the Europa consortium who committed 34 million Sfr in cash and 'contributions of personnel, programmes, production facilities and other infrastructural elements' (Europa Television mimeo April 1986: 3). Expenditure was budgeted at 42.9 million Sfr in 1986, 56 million Sfr in 1987 and 108 million Sfr in 1988 (Europa Television mimeo April 1986: 6).

Reception required Wegener Panda equipment (costing between £1,000 and £2,000 per receiver) so the cost of receiving equipment was beyond the reach of individual households and was a significant disincentive to cable relay-Europa signals. Whereas, Europa claimed to reach a potential audience of 6 million viewers, (of whom 5 million were in the Netherlands) a disinterested source, *Cable and Satellite Europe* (July 1986: 54), claimed that Europa's reach was considerably less; perhaps 2 million cable homes in the combined markets of the Netherlands, Denmark, Finland, Germany, Iceland, Luxembourg, Norway, Portugal and Sweden.[3] In May 1986 a further 1.5 million television homes (in Portugal) received three hours a day of Europa programming via terrestrial rebroadcasting.

Europa's revenues did not meet its sponsors' hopes and expectations (see, *inter alia, Cable and Satellite Europe* July 1986: 54). For six months of the channel's first year of operation advertising time was donated to advertisers free of charge, a signal that securing advertising for the channel was far more difficult than Europa's sponsors had anticipated. In common with other pan-European satellite television services, notably Sky Channel and Super Channel, Europa discovered that there were too few transnational brands and too many differences between viewer groups to make an advertising funded pan-European service viable. Taylor (personal interview 9.7.92) pointed out that identical products were differently positioned in different European markets. He gave a striking example of the differences in the British and Italian marketing of Volvo cars. In the UK Volvos are sold as solid, safe and rather boring cars, in Italy as sexy, high status and frivolous. Consequently no single Volvo advertisement or campaign was likely to succeed across Europe.

## The Europa schedule

And for all our broadcasting projects we need programmes. Programmes, indeed, which is [*sic*] usually easily forgotten, as they are the closing-entry in every budget, the final topic in any political discussion or when television is at stake.

(K.J. Hindriks Programme co-ordinator Europa,
Olympus TV press release, undated [c. January 1985] mimeo, EBU
Pan-European Satellite Broadcast Project, Hilversum)

In spite of the importance, Hindriks, the Europa programme controller, placed on programming, Europa was budgeted at a level appropriate to a sports channel rather than that required for its 'Project A' type mixed programme schedule,[4] which had been estimated to cost approximately four times as much as a 'Project B' type sports channel. The channel's sponsors (notably NOS) were wedded to the idea of a mixed 'public service' type programme schedule, yet were neither able to fund such a schedule, nor could they permit the channel to generate advertising revenues (even were such revenues to be available) sufficient to sustain a 'public service' programme mix as the sponsors' own terrestrial services would thereby be threatened. The discrepancy between Europa's resources and its ambitions was not the only difficulty under which it laboured.

Although the channel was committed to a mixed programme schedule there was no consensus as to how the schedule should be organised. By the time Europa began service in 1985 the 'vertical' programme schedule, advocated by the NOS and the ARD, had become diffused. Whilst particular evenings were associated with particular kinds of programming (and thus had a 'vertical' character) programmes (such as news), were stripped 'horizontally' across the week. The compromise was an uneasy one and was identified as one of Europa's many weaknesses by a UK broadcaster who worked on Europa who stated 'Europa never really had a proper schedule' (personal interview 9.7.92).

For this commentator, poor scheduling was one of Europa's most serious weaknesses. The senior broadcasters, who controlled Europa, lacked scheduling experience and, more damagingly, experience of the day to day running of a television station (still less of running a television station competing for viewers and revenue). In consequence, Europa's senior managers, this source argued, paid insufficient attention to audience tastes and to the characteristics of the broadcasting markets which Europa had entered. Charles Barrand (who, after running the UKIBA news inputs to Eurikon, became Europa's Head of News and Current Affairs) saw Europa in a similar way and acidly stated, 'It is possible to devise extra-ordinarily elegant programme schedules based on philosophies and concepts, ideals and ambitions. In concert with every emerging new broadcast entity, Europa Television has built castles in the air' (Barrand 1986: 12).

The first days of the Europa service (from 5–7 October 1985) show how the channel lacked a regular schedule. On the first day transmissions began at 18:00 (and ended at 22:10) the principal programme junctions were at 18:50 (when children's programmes gave way to sport), at 20:30 (when sport gave way to the weather report) and at 20:35 (when a music show began, ending at 22:02 shortly before close down at 22:10 after commercials and a preview of the next day's programmes). Commercials were scheduled in three short blocks between 20:27–20:30, 20:32–20:35 and 22:02–22:05. However, on the following day programme junctions were differently located: at 18:50, 19:42, 20:30 and at 21:00. On the following day, Monday 7 October, the principal programme junctions were at different times again: at 18:20, 20:30 and 21:25. Effectively there was only one stable junction, at 20:30, in the first few days' of the new channel's service. Moreover this irregular schedule persisted throughout the first week of Europa transmissions.

The schedule for the first week of Europa transmissions had a strong and consistent programme junction at 20:30 and consistent weekday junctions at 18:20 (when programmes for children gave way to programmes for adults), and a weaker one at 19:47 (when the first part of sports reports gave way to the second part of sports reports), but the latter half of the evening lacked consistent programme junctions.[5] By week 10 (7–13 December 1985), strong programme junctions at 19:20, 20:30 and at 20:40 had been established. But thereafter there was no consistent structure to the schedule (though there was a weak junction in the mid-evening period of 21:30–21:45).[6]

By the first weeks of 1986 (4–10 January) the Europa schedule had matured and was built around strong continuities in the early and mid-evening periods. The times 17:55–18:00, 18:25–18:20 and 19:20–19:25 were consistently used to begin programmes and 20:30 had become an inviolable centre point in the schedule. Not surprisingly the very late evening period displayed much less consistency in location of programme junctions for variations in programme length are likely to have a cumulative effect on schedules.

In mid 1986 (7–14 June) the schedule had strong junctions in the early evening but not in the mid and late evenings. However, Barrand recognised the positive effect of the changes and commented:

> Now the foundations are being dug and the building blocks of programmes set in. Horizontal and vertical streaming, however baffling such concepts may seem, are actually designed to assist the viewers by providing a regular theme of programmes for each day of the week and a regular pattern for each time of day. . . . The interim programme schedule practice of Europa Television – as opposed to the philosophy – has been devised with a symphonic structure of three

principal movements: programmes for children, which naturally start off the evening schedule at 18:00 CET; sports programmes, often derived from the live exchanges of Eurovision; and the evening's main programme, drama, film, opera, ballet, documentary or light entertainment. These three elements have provided the framework onto which other programmes can be built. It may not be the framework we would ask Santa Claus to bring, but it functions.

(Barrand 1986: 12 and 13)

## Europa programming

Although Barrand's symphonic metaphor smacks of special pleading there was no doubt that, although imperfect, Europa's schedule had been significantly improved by early 1986. But the halting start and constant changes to programming and scheduling had not helped the channel to establish a firm identity. Indeed the quality and character of its programming remained a troubling problem. In spite of the NOS' proclamation that 'a European Programme will be capable of expressing a pluriform European television culture and of stimulating the European audio-visual industry, thus counter-balancing the inflow of American programmes brought about by the price–popularity ratio' (NOS 1984: 2), Europa screened numerous American programmes. *Thunderbirds*, *Jason King* and *The Persuaders* appeared in its first months, but, even when programming was made in Europe little of it was genuinely pan-European. As Taylor stated, although many of Europa's programmes were made in Europe few of them were European; they were national programmes screened to a notionally pan-European audience (personal interview 9.7.92).

Although the schedule for Europa was, more or less, under the control of the channel, the programming it transmitted was not. The channel relied on Eurovision and above all on the members of the Europa Consortium for its programming. Programming decisions were therefore driven not by viewers' demands but by the values and priorities of Consortium members (for whom Europa was always secondary to their terrestrial services), and by what EBU members happened to contribute to the Eurovision programme pool. The ARD, for example, contributed about 3.5 hours of programmes per week to Europa and its Programmkonferenz (Programme Committee), chose which ARD programmes would be made available to Europa: the Europa Programme Controller had scant influence on what Europa was given (Schwarzkopf 1986: 80). Indeed Schwarzkopf (1986: 80) notes that the majority of programmes which were actually originated by Europa, rather than recycled gleanings from the terrestrial service offerings of consortium members, were news programmes. Jeremy Taylor underscored Schwarzkopf's judgement and stated that '99 per cent of the programmes made for Europa were news and weather' (personal interview 9.7.92).

Europa's programming priorities were, Taylor argued, news (reflecting the traditional NOS and EBU conception of news as the 'flagship' genre of public service broadcasting), sport (again reflecting a long-standing EBU commitment) and high culture (personal interview 9.7.92). The cultural emphasis of Europa programming was not surprising. The rules of NOS, a Dutch public law foundation, were subject to the approval of the Netherlands Ministry of Cultural Affairs which appointed one-third of the members of the NOS Board of Governors and a further one-third of the NOS Governors were appointed by representatives of Dutch cultural organisations. The constitutions and traditions of NOS' partners in Europa also required and encouraged transmission of cultural programming (see Shaughnessy and Fuente Cobo 1990).

## Schedule and programmes: out of control?

Europa was neither able to control its programming nor, because of disagreements between Consortium and staff members, did it project a clear identity and stable schedule. As Taylor stated, 'changes from the published schedule are a continual hazard to the appreciation of Europa by the viewer. It is really necessary to maintain consistent patterns in each of the time-bands across the transmission day' (in 'Press and Public Relations Policy for Europa Television – a proposal' presented to the Europa Consortium board meeting in September 1986 shortly before Taylor left Europa). Taylor's diagnosis was confirmed by the EBU Television Programme Committee which, after its post-mortem on Europa, concluded that 'differences of opinion on programme format' had been an important contributory cause of the failure of Europa (EBU 1987a: 2).

As the EBU Television Programme Committee had recognised, financial pressures made Europa's failure almost inevitable, and certainly made it impossible to deliver high quality culture programmes. The rival imperatives of fulfilling the high cultural vocation of European public service broadcasting and keeping programme expenditure down resulted in the screening of too many 'Bulgarian operas' (as Taylor put it). Taylor argued that the cultural preconceptions of European public service broadcasters inhibited Europa from reinforcing the genuine success it achieved with a pop music show, Countdown, produced for Europa by the Dutch independent producer Jon de Mol (personal interview 9.7.92).[7] Taylor described Countdown as 'the success' of Europa and a model of the kind of programme which could effectively cross language barriers.[8] However he pointed out that many of the sponsors of Europa were uncomfortable with Countdown's success. A pop music programme did not conform to the high culture, traditional public service, ethos of the most important members of the Europa Consortium (Taylor described both Europa and the EBU as 'old' institutions run by 'old' people).

## Service ends

On 27 November 1986 Europa was closed down by NOS. NOS expressed profound regret but argued that its assumption of 'a disproportional [*sic*] share in the total risk of this all the way along very uncertain enterprise' (NOS 1986: 1) had brought it 'very near' to a situation where it would not be able to pay the salaries of its own staff anymore. 'This forced us to summon ETV [Europa] demanding payment of hfl 7.3 million before 22.11.1986 and another hfl 4.3 million before 5.12.1986' (NOS 1986: 3). Belatedly, NOS stated that the financial projections on which Europa had been established were 'far too optimistic' (NOS 1986: 2). The combination of lower advertising revenues than had been anticipated and no growth in the membership of the Consortium made the financial burden too heavy to bear.

There were multiple causes of Europa's demise. Jeremy Taylor emphasised the problem posed by its 'worthy but rather dull' programming (in his Press and Public Relations Policy for Europa Television – a proposal, to the Europa Consortium board meeting in September 1986). The House of Lords Select Committee on the European Communities concurred but also emphasised management factors 'It is likely . . . that other factors such as management and programming contributed to the failure of Europa' (Great Britain. Parliament. House of Lords. 1987: 10). Richard Dill (Deputy Chief Executive of Europa) argued that the absence of a UK member in the consortium was very damaging. He stated 'We are an English speaking channel yet with no integrated relationship with a UK broadcasting company' (*Cable and Satellite Europe* July 1986: 54). Europa's financial and management difficulties were certainly important but were symptoms of more profound, and intractable, problems. Notably the unsolved (perhaps insoluble) problems of harnessing the resources and commitments of EBU members with different, often antagonistic, interests to a common project and in constructing a programme schedule that was both attractive to diverse audiences and which could be reconciled with the values of European public service broadcasters.

The close down of the EBU's flagship service came as a shock; few were prepared for NOS' drastic action. At the seventy-sixth meeting of the Administrative Council of the EBU in 1986, held a year after Europa's launch had been announced and only a couple of months before the channel's fade to black, the Chief Executive of Europa, Ernesto Braun, had given an upbeat report. He presented a rather rosy estimate of Europa's potential reach[9] and emphasised that the channel's reach would grow to about 4 million homes by the end of 1986 (with a possible further 900,000 in Belgium and Ireland if legislation there were to be changed to permit cable relay of the Europa signal). Braun reported that there were seventy-five Europa staff and that 'a new management took over the operation as from 1 December 1985, reorganizing the project, seeking broader internationalization of the staff and reforming commercial and financial policy'. He emphasised that 'very positive reactions to the project have been expressed by the European Parliament and the European Communities' Commission, the latter having allocated 2 million ECU to Europa TV, part of which, however, is subject to the final approval of the Commission's own budget'.[10]

But Braun also stated that 'future development [of Europa] is subject to strong support by the EBU . . . and by individual EBU members' (EBU 1986: 2). However, no EBU members had joined the five founding members of the Consortium. In consequence the conditions Braun specified for Europa's survival were not satisfied. EBU members had many reasons to be cautious about joining the new venture, not least among them the growing interdependence between Europa and the European Community's political institutions. EBU members believed that an axiom of public service broadcasting, independence of government, was in danger of being compromised by the increasingly close association between the EBU and its pan-European channel, and the Commission of the European Communities and the European Parliament. [11]

As Michael Johnson of the BBC (the UK member of the Perez Group) stated: 'It is possible that a European Parliament or a consortium of European advertisers might both be pleased to invest in a European service which had the potential authority which the EBU could bring to bear. Whether the strings attached to such money would be acceptable to the EBU and its members is another matter' (Letter to Henri Perez in connection with the Perez Group's enquiry into public service broadcasting 26.7.82).[12] Yet EBU members' reluctance to support Europa – whether for reasons of political rectitude, institutional self-interest, or financial prudence – led inexorably to a growth in the European Community's potential political influence in virtue of its increasingly important role as a patron of the pan-European channel.

## Television and politics

Johnson was not alone in his concern. In 1984, in the course of consideration of new areas for co-operation, the EBU's Television Programme Committee Working Party on Television News viewed a video cassette on the workings of the European Parliament which had been prepared by EBU members from Belgium, France and Italy. The programme was described by Rory O' Connor (of RTE, one of the EBU member broadcasters participating in the Europa Consortium), as 'the first time in his experience [he had] seen the Working Party presented with a concrete example of real propaganda'. O' Connor further objected to what he saw as the programme makers' 'desire and perhaps also . . . duty to defend a philosophy aimed at the unification of Europe . . . ', in Mr O' Connor's view it was clear that all activity of this type should be banned, no 'pan-European' editorial balance being possible on any major question such as the division of Germany, the situation in Cyprus, Northern Ireland, or indeed the internal affairs of Spain, Denmark or any other country in Europe.

O' Connor was strongly supported by at least one other member of the

Working Party who pointed out 'that EEC members represented a minority within the EBU and that even within EEC member countries a large majority of citizens, and hence of television viewers, had only a very limited interest in European matters – as the low turn out at the last European elections had shown' (Com.Pro.TV/GT TV News SPG 2663 September 1984: 21–2). However, not all agreed that Europa was dependent on Brussels. A UK broadcaster who worked on Europa said that 'although Ernesto Braun and Richard Dill were constantly going off to Brussels to get money the influence of the European Community was never translated into programming decisions and news values. It didn't come out at the Hilversum end' (personal interview 9.7.92).

What O' Connor saw as objectionably close links between European broadcasters and European political authorities might be seen, and were seen by many of those directly involved in developing Europa, differently. Not only were broadcasters working on Europa generally committed Europeans but pointed out that a principal rationale for the development of the channel was the under-representation of pan-European political institutions on European television. For example, Hindriks stated (in a speech advocating the establishment of the pan-European service – then called Olympus) that, 'European politicians in general favour a European programme, especially the politicians of the "ten" which is scantily represented on television' (Hindriks n.d.: 1).[13] And Hindriks specifically stated, 'it is no part of OTN's [Olympus Television News] brief to create an artificial European perspective where none such exists. The programme will reflect both harmony and discord among the nations and people of Europe', and that, 'the future Olympus Programme must *not* be a mouth-piece of European institutions or of national interests of the countries supporting this project' (Hindriks n.d.: 6).

The interdependence between pan-European television service and pan-European politics was apparent in the difficulties presented to pan-European television by the contemporary regulatory regime. The absence of a European 'Television without Frontiers' – a single market in broadcasting – profoundly disadvantaged Europa. Indeed, the European Parliament commented that 'one of the most significant factors in its [Europa's] failure was the existence of national legal restrictions preventing it from gaining access to cable networks; it could not reach a sufficient audience to generate advertising revenue' (European Parliament 1987: 8). Perversely, three (Germany, Ireland, the Netherlands) of the four states named by the Commission of the European Communities as countries which had excluded Europa signals from their cable networks were sponsors of Europa (Great Britain. Parliament. House of Lords. 1987 Evidence: 77).

## The viewers' response

Assessing viewers' reception of Europa is difficult. Taylor stated that Europa did little audience research and there is no evidence of any studies comparable to those undertaken by RAI and the IBA for Eurikon. In consequence, the channel lacked a clear sense of the behaviour and interests of viewers (the two most important being Dutch cable subscribers and Portuguese terrestrial viewers). The lack of information about reception meant that Europa's programmers were not able to match the channel's programme offer to audience demand nor provide potential advertisers with the data necessary to sell the channel as an effective advertising medium.

Bekkers (1987: 33) claims that in 1986 (when Europa closed down) Europa was available to only 28 per cent of Dutch television viewers. In contrast, Sky Channel was available to 50 per cent of Dutch viewers. This suggests that Dutch cable operators viewed Sky as more likely to appeal to their subscribers than Europa. This presumption is borne out by the viewing shares achieved by the rival pan-European channels. Europa achieved a 1 per cent share of viewing, whereas Sky Channel achieved a 5 per cent viewing share in Dutch homes with access to both channels (Bekkers 1987: 34).

However, Rato claims that Europa achieved a 14 per cent viewing share in the Netherlands and similar shares for some of its programmes in Portugal; notably 12 per cent for 'Eurosport' and 16 per cent for 'Countdown' (Rato 1987: 2). But Rato's estimate of the Europa share in the Dutch market cannot be reconciled with Bekkers' estimates or with data from other sources. Notably, Pan European Television Advertising Research's (PETAR) estimate of the 8 per cent share of Dutch viewing achieved by all satellite television channels (PETAR Spring 1987 Diary Survey).

In spite of Europa's lack of success in capturing audiences' attention it, like its predecessor Eurikon, kindled the enthusiasm of the broadcasters who worked on it. Several participants testified to the reinvigoration of public service broadcasting achieved by the EBU initiatives. Frank Tappolet, the Television Programme Co-ordinator of SRG, contrasted the *esprit de corps* of Eurikon with the customary day to day experience of television producers: 'I feel that we have recovered the pioneer spirit of the fifties and sixties (great enthusiasm and flexibility) which contrasts to the present sullenness of general broadcasting' (telex to Clarke 1.6.82). And, an otherwise sceptical Jeremy Taylor testified that Europa was, 'what setting up BBC Radio or working in BBC television in the early days must have been like' and emphasised the personal and ethical commitment of many of his Europa colleagues who were 'terribly idealistic and all highly committed Europeans, and very few broadcasters are now so committed to what they are doing' (personal interview 9.7.92).

However Taylor recognised that the very qualities which had made working relationships on Europa so productive, and the solidarity between colleagues so strong, also made Europa people unrepresentative of the viewers they sought to serve. Whereas the enthusiasm and linguistic skills of those working *in* Europa were sufficient to make a success of the production of pan-European television, similar skills and dedication were absent *outside* the channel. Whilst Europa was, Taylor said, 'tremendous fun' it was an 'Esperanto' channel that spoke to the central interests and identities of none of its viewers.

## The end of Europa

L' Europe devrait être beaucoup plus présente sur les écrans des foyers de nos pays sous la forme d' émissions d' information sur la réalité européenne, sur la vie quotidienne des européens, et des institutions. Les récentes difficultés d' Europa TV nous montrent que l' on est encore loin du compte. [Europe, in the form of news broadcasts about European events, institutions and the daily life of European people, must become much more visible on the living room screens in our countries. The recent difficulties of Europa television shows us that we've still got a long way to go.]

(Marcelino Oreja, Secretary General of the Council of Europe, in Council of Europe 1988a: 5)

The leading broadcasting trade journals, *Cable and Satellite Europe* and *Variety* had both published unpromising audits of Europa before its cessation of operations. *Cable and Satellite Europe* was the most comprehensive and documented Europa's disappointing achievements. Fewer cable homes than anticipated had been reached, advertising revenues was lower than anticipated ('For its first six months on-air Europa offered commercial spots free of charge' *Cable and Satellite Europe* July 1986: 54) and an Ariane launch failure put back the date anticipated for moving onto Olympus DBS service delivery from 1987 to 1988. *Variety* (9.10.85: 1) had underscored the high levels of expenditure incurred by the Consortium and estimated that Europa had cost $14 million in development and annual operating costs amounted to $42 million. These costs were borne by the five original members of the Consortium who, in spite of redoubled efforts to secure new members, remained wholly responsible for the costs of the channel. NOS identified the lack of success in recruiting new members to the Consortium as the 'main cause of the problem' resulting in the channel's demise (NOS press release 2.12.86).

The contrast between the optimistic forecasts of costs and revenues which had preceded (and made possible) the establishment of Europa and the paucity of advertising revenue actually won by the channel; the disparities between the costs of production (and in particular the costs of linguistic representation) and the resources available from consortium members; and the lack of viewers, led Europa into a crisis which became terminal in late 1986. The channel's managers had first explicitly acknowledged the crisis in March 1986 when Dill wrote to de Kalbermatten (the EBU Secretary General), requesting a 6 million Sfr loan to bridge what he envisaged would be 'an important cash flow gap in the 2nd half of 1986' (Dill to de Kalbermatten 14.3.86). De Kalbermatten replied on 8 April regretting that the EBU could not provide the loan and cited the EBU's commitments to fund satellite relay costs (the Mexico World Cup competition was particularly costly). However de Kalbermatten offered the EBU's assistance in negotiating a bank loan to be guaranteed by the five members of the Europa Consortium (de Kalbermatten to Dill 8.4.86). The Consortium did not take up this offer.

## Braun's business plan

The Consortium board meeting of July 1986 decided that Ernesto Braun, the Chief Executive of Europa, should prepare a Business Plan for Europa to the end of 1986. At the next Consortium board meeting in September 1986 the deficit for 1986 was estimated at 18 million Sfr of which 12 million Sfr was owed to NOS. A further 50 million Sfr of investment was required to capitalise the channel until 1989 when the board estimated that revenue would exceed expenditure. This estimate was conditional on the channel *not* establishing the direct to home service via the Olympus satellite for which it had been established.

Braun's business plan was tabled in November 1986 – it was dated 17.11.86 ten days before Europa ceased transmissions – and began: 'Europa TV has run into serious operational and financial problems'. Braun identified Europa's chief problem as undercapitalisation based on 'an irrealistic [*sic*] estimate' of the levels of capital investment necessary to start and operate the channel through protracted start-up losses. The channel's commercial income potential had been overestimated, Europa had suffered from a premature start to its operations and from unforseen media-political developments in Consortium member countries. Braun further stated that the Olympus launch delay, the reluctance of new members to join the Consortium and limited programme material had all damaged Europa's prospects. Braun regretted that the audience 'prepared to look beyond the frontiers set generally by the domestic approach of their national TV networks is restricted and of a particular middle-high class type'. He thereby euphemistically acknowledged that there was insufficient demand for Europa to be viable.

## *Die Lösung*

Braun's emphasis on viewers' deficiencies is a fine, if melancholy, example of the familiar 'transmission mentality' of European public service broadcasters. It is reminiscent of Brecht's poem *Die Lösung* (given the title 'The Solution' by its English translator): ... the people / Had forfeited the confidence of the government / And could win it back only / By redoubled efforts. Would it not be easier / In that case for the government / To dissolve the people / And elect another? (Brecht 1979: 440). Rather than the responsibility for Europa's failure lying with European television viewers Braun's report can plausibly be read as showing that Europa had been established with too small a potential audience for it to be viable, with too little potential advertising revenue to cover its costs[14] and without access to programming suited to its potential audience. In spite of the problems he catalogued, Braun expressed his confidence that 'a European Public Service Television Programme is feasible and has an audience'. Such a service would, he argued, 'be a vehicle for the diversity of European culture in all its aspects, it is to contribute to a wider understanding of such differences, their expressions and causes'. The demise of Europa came as an abrupt surprise to its viewers. Appropriately perhaps the final transmission was a videoclip of Peter Gabriel singing 'Don't give up'.

NOS, and the Netherlands, had not given up easily. Their commitment to Europa had been remarkable. The Dutch government had made very considerable direct financial subventions to Europa (variously estimated at 30 million hfl (*Variety* 3.12.86) and 42 million hfl (NOS press release 2.12.86)). NOS contributed twice as much to Europa as did either RAI or the ARD, each a broadcaster three times its size. Europa's close down followed the action initiated by a UK creditor, Good Morning Limited, a provider of news services, against RTE in the London Courts. Europa's liabilities were estimated to be 41,336,685 Sfr of which 38,933,653 were due to NOS, 1,156,000 to the EBU, 870,467 to the ARD, 201,565 to RTP and 175,000 to RAI (summary of meeting of Directors General 4.7.87).[15] NOS agreed to waive substantial parts of the debts it was owed and offered (at the meeting of Directors General chaired by the EBU President on 4.7.87) to reduce the total liabilities to be divided by the consortium partners to 12.1 million Sfr. The EBU subsequently discounted its dues from the consortium by 50 per cent. Neither of these gestures were sufficient to rescue the channel.

The EBU President, Albert Scharf, delivered the official obsequy for Europa at the meeting of the Union's Administrative Council in December 1986. Scharf said

> The problems encountered by Europa TV, whose causes were multiple, were to be regretted. In fact the operational basis of the enterprise was too limited due to the fact that EBU members, for various very understandable national reasons and due to divergences on the programme format, had not joined the hard core of committed organisations. The general impression was nevertheless largely a poor one.
>
> (CA 1850 SPG 3486 25.2.87: 78)

## The lessons learned – official and unofficial versions

NOS' public retrospect on the rise and fall of Europa recognised that some EBU members were constitutionally prohibited from participating in services outside their frontiers and that financial pressures inhibited others' participation (NOS press release 2.12.86). In consequence, the pool of EBU members who might have participated in Europa was considerably smaller than the total pool of the EBU. However the decision of the EBU's large members (ARD and RAI excepted) – those whose size and strength was a *sine qua non* of success – not to participate in Europa was crucial and particularly galling to NOS. NOS specifically mentioned German and French commitments to DreiSat and TV5 as lethal to Europa but UK broadcasters' commitment to Super Channel was also significant, particularly as it denied Europa access to UK programming. The Director of the EBU's Television Programme Department, Miro Vilcek, attributed Europa's demise to 'the hostility of certain member organisations which – legitimately no doubt – wished to promote their own transnational projects' (EBU 1987: 18).[16]

But, as well as being weakened by the non-participation of key EBU members who prioritised their own satellite services, it was also weakened by NOS' own refusal to allow Europa to survive as a potential rival to its own terrestrial services.[17] As Neville Clarke stated, EBU members' lack of commitment to the successor to Eurikon was partly due 'to differences in style and common language . . . but more importantly because of the national preoccupations and ambitions of the participating broadcasters' (Clarke and Riddell 1992: 219). ZDF's response to the Consortium's final appeal to EBU members for assistance offers an enlightening insight into the motivation of one of the most important of the non-participants. It also prefigures the character of the EBU's next ventures into pan-European satellite television.

ZDF (in a telex from Stolte (Intendant of ZDF) to Schwarzkopf (Chairman Europa board) 18.11.86) pointed out that it had developed a programming concept for the post-Eurikon stage of the EBU's satellite television initiative (i.e. for what became Europa). This sports based 'Project B' had been rejected by the majority of EBU members who preferred 'the more 'European' and more cultural 'Project A'. ZDF reminded Schwarzkopf that it had viewed 'formula A' as 'too ambitious, too expensive, and premature for the successful constitution of a European viewership'. As well as inculpating Europa for its mistaken programming strategy, ZDF attributed Europa's failure to its primary commitment to pleasing political authorities, rather than satisfying audience tastes and interests.

ZDF stated 'that the good will of European authorities is a good thing to have, but that it is much more important, in the crucial first three or four years, to look at the European viewer'. Indeed Stolte argued that the decision that Europa was to be a high cultural channel befitted the time honoured practices of monopoly public service broadcasters as well as gratifying the preferences of

Brussels, and thus Europa's failure and dependency on political subventions necessarily followed.

> [A] negative result of the experiment ought . . . to be referred back to a programme strategy disregarding the potential European audience, to optimistic and therefore inadmissible conjectures concerning the flow of advertising money on the basis of the given programme profile, to an unnecessary early start with a pre-operation phase on a satellite system entirely different from the final one, and to the temptation of paying tribute to the hopes of European politicians and to one's own cultural enthusiasm.
>
> (Stolte to Schwarzkopf 18.11.86)

There were grounds to believe ZDF's accusations were well founded. Europa had became dependent on European political institutions. Its budgetary crises led to a successful courtship of the Commission of the European Communities and, on 14 October 1986, Europa received 1 million ECU from the Commission of the European Communities (IP (86) 483) of which 80 per cent was actually paid. However Europa's closure embarrassed its sponsors in the Commission and occasioned an angry letter (dated 3.12.86) from Ripa di Meana, the Commissioner responsible for the subvention, to Schwarzkopf. Di Meana's letter was followed by a further letter (dated 15.12.86) from the Director General of DG X, Franz Froschmaier, to Schwarzkopf and to the Presidents and Directors General of the members of the Europa Consortium. Froschmaier complained that no reply to di Meana's had been received and demanded that the consortium either execute the contract it had concluded with the Commission or return the subvention and accrued interest.

Between March and May 1987, Danish, French and UK MEPs tabled questions in the European Parliament requesting information from the Commission on the circumstances in which the Commission had made its subvention to Europa and about the prospects for repayment (a UK MEP, Richard Cottrell, told the Parliament that the Commission had committed £750,000 to Europa). The Commissioner, Ripa di Meana, was able to answer only that the Commission was studying the matter and that its subvention had been made in accordance with policies established under the Hahn Resolutions of 1982 and 1984 and the Arfé Resolution of 1984. Di Meana stated that 'the participation of the Commission was placed within the framework of the Commission's audiovisual policy, aiming at promoting multinational and multilingual TV programmes receivable in most Community countries'. He affirmed that the 'first share' of the Commission's contribution was 800,000 ECU or £580,000 (not, as Cottrell had stated, £750,000) (OJ C 191 20.7.87: 27/8).[18] There is no evidence that the Commission was repaid.[19]

An influential member of the European Parliament, Gijs de Vries, stated (European Parliament 1989: 15) that Europa was 'poorly prepared and implemented'. A UK source supported de Vries' analysis and stated that some of the senior personalities in Europa had been 'dumped' on the channel by their employers and that too few of the Consortium members and senior personalities were really committed to making the channel a success. This source contrasted the single minded ruthless commitment of Rupert Murdoch to establish Sky as a viable service with the defensive and exploratory attitudes of the sponsors of Europa. On these differences depended the fates of Europa and Sky Television.

Europa had shown that there were formidable difficulties standing in the way of successful establishment of a pan-European public service television service. Differences of language and culture in the audiences for pan-European television showed that an actual pan-European audience was more elusive than European unionists imagined. That the separate interests of individual broadcasters in launching their own services were stronger than was their collective interest in collaboration on a joint channel. And that the programme mix demanded by traditional European public service broadcasters was ill fitted to the competitive broadcasting market into which Europa was launched.

In spite of the Europa debacle the European Parliament continued to advocate a multilingual transnational European television programme (see, *inter alia*, the Baget Bozzo Resolution; European Parliament 1987a). Whereas ZDF advocated that any future EBU satellite channel should adopt its Project B – sports channel – format (the EBU followed ZDF's counsel in its next satellite initiative, Eurosport). The failure of Europa persuaded the EBU that a mixed programming pan-European channel was not viable and accordingly it turned its attention to thematic channels. The EBU Television Programme Committee stated that 'the EBU cannot assist the consortium [i.e. Europa] either financially or operationally. The Union can however, continue to support the idea behind the venture . . . and reflect on new European programme formats which might be of interest to their respective organizations (for example, sports channel, Euro-events channel etc.)' (EBU 1987a: 2).

This response, discouraging though it was for supporters of Europa and particularly for the NOS, represented a minor triumph for the 'modernisers' over the 'traditionalists'. It was striking that none of the individuals who made up the Perez Group, the bastion of the 'modernisers', participated in Europa or Eurikon. The programming and scheduling of Eurikon and Europa expressed the values and practices of the 'traditionalists' (whose voice was heard through the Wangermée Group). True, RTE and NOS were represented on the Perez Group and in the Europa Consortium but the robust arguments advanced by Hans Kimmel of ZDF, Muiris MacConghail of RTE and Michael Johnson of the BBC demanding changes to the programming of public service broadcasting and a break with what Kimmel (1982: 7) had called 'a successful and exclusive club of monopolist (or almost monopolist) PSB', had not influenced the delivery of the EBU's flagship pan-European service. The 'profound change in the current balance of television systems' (Perez 1983: 3) which the Perez

Group had identified, and to which it urged the EBU to respond, had elicited imaginative and innovatory responses from the EBU in its pan-European channels. But too few of Eurikon and Europa's innovations were in their programming and scheduling – the EBU's first pan-European channels were innovatory in their technology, organisation and delivery but traditional in their programming.

The failure of its pan-European channel left the EBU, and pan-European public service television, significantly weakened. Louis Heinsmann characterised NOS as 'suffering from a hangover from Europa' which had led it to refuse to participate in subsequent pan-European initiatives (interview 5.11.92).[20] Since Europa the NOS had stayed out of Eurosport, ARTE and Euronews. And, Heinsmann believed, the EBU's shift to thematic channels has weakened public service broadcasting.[21] For controllers of terrestrial public service channels have been able to retreat from their former commitments to mixed programme schedules on the grounds that themed services in sport, news and arts are now available via satellite. They are therefore free (or perhaps compelled), to counterschedule a more competitive (but less diverse) service against the growing commercial sector unencumbered by the perceived need to schedule worthy, but unattractive, programming.

From the wreckage of Europa, the EBU established two further satellite television channels – Euronews and Eurosport – which offered thematic programme streams in the two areas identified by the Secretary General of the EBU as being 'most coveted by the newcomers . . . sports and news' (CA 1852 SPG 3612 25.2.87: 3). The choice of thematic sports and news channels suggests that Jean-Pierre Julien's melancholy judgement on Europa was correct. What Europa taught, Julien averred (personal interview 25.2.92) was a very expensive lesson in what not to do.

# 8

# EUROSPORT AND EURONEWS

Sport and news are the two pillars of cooperation between the Union's
Members in programme matters, and its [*sic*] important to strengthen
this cooperation in both of them and to render it more active.
(Report of the Study Group on the Future of Public Service Broadcasting
[the Wangermée Group] AG 551 SPG 2642 June 1984: 14)

Feature films and sport are the two most powerful weapons in the Sky
Barons' armouries.
(Clarke and Riddell 1992: 203)

After the demise of Europa, the EBU acted as midwife to two further pan-
European satellite television channels, the thematic channels, Eurosport and
Euronews (which entered service in 1989 and in 1993 respectively). The failure
of Europa finally led European public service broadcasters to play to their
strengths by drawing on the EBU's core resources in sport and news –
programming which the Wangermée Group stated were the EBU's most
notable strengths. Moreover, the burgeoning success of commercial thematic
channels and the failure of Europa's mixed programming format led public
service broadcasters to adopt a thematic format for their new European channels. Eurosport and Euronews represented further departures from established
public service broadcasting norms in that they were launched in partnership
with interests from which European public service broadcasting had formerly
maintained a scrupulous distance – commerce and the state, specifically News
International and the European Community, respectively.

## The genesis of Eurosport

The EBU first considered launching a thematic sport channel in 1981 when
Jean-Pierre Julien proposed a sports format for Eurikon.[1] The EBU's Sports
Working Party consistently advocated an EBU sports channel and its proposals
crystallised in ZDF's 1984 'Project B' which proposed a sports format for

Europa. After the decision to establish Europa as a mixed programming channel, the EBU Administrative Council mandated its Sports Working Party to consider whether an EBU sports channel should be established. In 1986 the Sports Working Party made a positive recommendation and advocated a sports channel which offered European public service broadcasters the potential to:

- make better use of rights already acquired by the EBU and individual members;
- form new relationships of cooperation with International Sports federations, which could ensure the EBU's future in the area of sport;
- preempt any initiative from competitors to establish a similar service.

(CA 1819. SPG 3336. 20.6.86: 1)

The Sports Working Party proposed that Europa (still in operation at the time) be used to test a pilot sports service screening a 'wide variety of sports events' which would complement members' national sports programming. The pilot service was to have soundtracks in English, Dutch, German and Portuguese, and would cost an estimated 1.8 million Sfr for the first six months of the experiment (CA 1819 SPG 3336 20.6.86: 3–4).[2] Final control of programming was to rest with Europa, which was to retain its own distinctive channel identity and was not to suffer by its advertising being bled away to the sports channel (SG/S/457 26.6.86: 2).

The emphasis on complementarity reflected many EBU members' suspicion of new services. But complementarity provided a convenient fig leaf for a service which would inevitably compete with EBU members' terrestrial services for viewers' attention. ZDF strongly supported the proposal and (on 31 June 1986) its Intendant, Dieter Stolte, wrote to the EBU President, Albert Scharf, and stated that ZDF was 'in favour of every step by EBU, bringing us back to the so-called "Project B"'. But Stolte noted that the budgeted figure of 1.8 million Sfr for the sports service projected by the Sports Working Party was 'very much lower than the earlier figures elaborated by ZDF'.[3]

## The changing rights balance

The EBU's sports channel was 'pulled' by the EBU's persistent desire for a presence in the growing satellite television market and 'pushed' by its recognition that its bargaining power, with both advertisers and the owners of sports rights, was weakening. At its meeting in January 1986 the Sports Working Party noted that 'it was becoming increasingly more difficult for member Organisations to schedule all the sports that were available under contracts concluded either by the EBU or by individual member organisations. In addition, the financial contribution of advertisers was of the greatest importance to most Federations, but advertisers were not prepared to invest in sport unless they had certain limited guarantees on the exposure' (SG/S/372 24.2.86: 2).

If EBU members did not fully exploit the sports rights they risked losing them to commercial sports channels able both to offer rights holders higher licence fees and advertisers better exposure to viewers.[4] The Secretary General recognised the problem in a statement to the Administrative Council:

> One of the areas where competition is becoming tougher is that of sporting events. It was felt severely during the first talks for purchase of the rights of the 1988 Olympic Games and recent negotiations for the future World Football Cups. For the moment it is still in the interest of the big Federations and the IOC to give preference to the EBU, which guarantees true professional coverage of the events and a wide distribution in Europe. . . . However this is no time for complacency: the competitors of the hitherto strongly placed public service organisations, are awaiting their opportunity. The financial offers they are capable of making are enticing. They can act swiftly to amass the necessary funds – which is still not the case for EBU – and furthermore they have no problem in accepting the kind of advertising which the existing EBU rules forbid.
>
> (CA 1789 SPG 3292 14.5.86: 3)

A satellite sports channel would enable the EBU to use rights more fully and maintain access to leading sports events (which European public service broadcasters and their audiences traditionally enjoyed). Not only would a satellite sports channel make the EBU a more attractive partner in the eyes of sports federations but the sports channel's revenues from advertising would help defray the increasing costs of sports rights. Stolte noted that 'ZDF's transmission rights payments for the Winter [Olympic] Games rose by 538 per cent and for the Summer Games the figure was 875 per cent' (Stolte 1993: 4). Although EBU members might fear the competition posed by an EBU satellite sports channel they preferred competition to come from within the European public service broadcasting 'family' rather than from a commercial sports channel. As members of the Sports Working Party recognised, 'it was better for competition on sport to be controlled internally than to be left to external activities such as those of Mr Berlusconi' (SG/S/372 24.2.86: 3).

The sudden closure of Europa meant both that Eurosport was not piloted on Europa and made possible an accelerated development of a dedicated sports channel. It left a clear field for EBU members – notably the BBC and ZDF – which had opposed the mixed programme format pan-European services and were adamantly opposed to the resurrection of Europa (SG/S/653 18.6.87: 3). A measure of the shock created by the death of Europa was RAI's insistence that the new sports channel be launched in conjunction with a commercial partner. Vittorio Boni's (the Chairman of the EBU Television Programme Committee) consistent support for Eurikon and Europa made his insistence on a commercial partner 'to take the major financial risk' (SG/S/653 18.6.87: 2) particularly telling.[5] Accordingly, the EBU negotiated throughout 1987 with possible commercial partners including Sky Channel, Super Channel, Visnews and the Dutch company Proclama. Eventually the EBU's 'Hart Group',[6] which was responsible for these negotiations, recommended News International as the EBU's partner. News had, it judged, 'the necessary finance, and through its subsidiary Sky Channel, the expertise, experience and capability in the areas of sales, marketing and accessing cable systems' (Report of the Hart Group 30.11.87: 2).

## Supper with the devil

The Hart Group's recommendation was a devastating indictment of European public service broadcasting. After five years of first hand experience of pan-European satellite television EBU members recognised that they needed a commercial partner to launch a viable satellite service. Moreover, their preferred partner was the very commercial rival whose innovative service on the OTS had tipped the EBU and its members into launching Eurikon and Europa. Far from its position in 1982 when the EBU urged members to 'take the utmost caution if they are contacted by any enterprise such as Satellite Television Ltd' (Decisions of the Administrative Council 18.1.82 SPG 1801 inf) the EBU now underwrote a partnership between Rupert Murdoch and European public service broadcasting. The piquancy of this reversal was increased by the match making role played by Europe's flagship public service broadcaster the BBC.[7] The EBU's alliance with News International perfectly illustrated the extent to which time honoured values and allegiances had been overturned and the wall between commercial and public broadcasters had been breached. Whereas, in 1984, the Voorzitter of NOS could confidently invoke the BBC and its history as a touchstone of public service values,[8] in 1987 the BBC was organising a supper with the devil without the benefit of long spoons.[9] The EBU's alliance with News International in Eurosport amplified the uncomfortable inconsistency between the EBU's overt theoretical commitment to a pure vision of public service broadcasting, manifested in its continued refusal to admit commercial broadcasters to membership, and its actual practice of close links with some commercial broadcasters – not least the admission of some, such as RTL and Télé Monte-Carlo, to membership. This contradiction subsequently proved to be the EBU's Achilles heel and provided much ammunition for those, such as the Commission of the European Communities' Competition Directorate, which believed European public service broadcasters were abusing a dominant position under a rhetorical umbrella of public service.

The need to preserve public service broadcasters' access to sports events, coupled with EBU members' inability to capitalise the development of a new television channel, meant that a partnership with a private broadcaster was unavoidable. In consequence, the control of the new sports channel had to be decoupled from the public service broadcasters in whose interests it had been developed: 'It was clear that since the interests of any partner were to make the channel a profit-making venture, thereby justifying the initial financial risk, freedom should be given to the channel to run its own affairs' (SG/S/738 21.10.87: 3).

Partnership contracts were signed by an EBU consortium (numbering sixteen EBU members from fourteen countries)[10] and News International on 23 December 1988. They provided for joint ownership of the Eurosport channel by the EBU Consortium and News International. News International was to capitalise the anticipated four or five years of initial losses, EBU members were to acquire programme rights for the channel. The deal was attractive to both parties. The EBU was to charge Eurosport high fees for access to its pool of sports rights and, because of these high fees, Eurosport would make losses which News International would set off against profits made elsewhere. News International would thus reduce its overall liability to corporation taxes. Profits were to be divided equally between the Consortium and News International. Eurosport thus secured public funding, via the tax which would otherwise have accrued to the national exchequers of the countries in which News International's operations were domiciled, for a joint public–private broadcasting venture. This inventive form of public funding for broadcasting was enigmatically recorded by the Hart Group on 5 October 1987: 'it was accepted that the value of the programmes should be fixed as high as possible, which could be an advantage to the fiscal position of the channel' (SG/S/738 21.10.87: 3).

This financial structure, which enabled the EBU to load a substantial portion of the costs of its sports rights on to the taxpayers, was accepted by the EBU early in 1988 (SPG 3951 SG/S/781 4.2.88: 4). The complex corporate structure necessary for these arrangements was achieved by dividing Eurosport into a sales company wholly owned by Sky Channel (Satellite Sports Sales) and a production company owned 50/50 by the EBU Consortium and Sky Channel (Satellite Sports Services).[11] Eurosport began transmissions on 5 February 1989 for six hours daily from the Astra and ECS satellites in English, German and Dutch. Between 75 per cent and 80 per cent of its programming came from EBU members.

The EBU's partnership with Sky Television in Eurosport was particularly surprising in that Sky had formerly complained to the Commission of the European Communities, in 1986, that the EBU had denied it access to coverage of the Mexico World Cup and had thus offended against Articles 85 and 86 of the EEC Treaty. Sky's complaint foreshadowed a later, and better known complaint by Screensport to the Competition Directorate of the Commission of the European Communities, DG IV. The Commission investigated and made clear that its concern

> was not so much with the concrete Sky Channel case but with the
> future attitude of the EBU in the field of acquisition and sharing of

sports rights. For the Commission it is unacceptable for the EBU to act as a central agency for rights acquisition, but to assign responsibility to the national level ... when it comes to sublicensing of rights. ... What mattered for the Commission ... was that for broadcasting purposes the EEC constituted one single market.

(CA 1860 SPG 3619 13.5.87: 3)

This was the first shot in DG IV's campaign against the EBU and European public service broadcasters' established working arrangements.

The Competition Directorate was to haunt the EBU for the next five years. DG IV posed so significant a threat to the EBU that the EBU President stated (to the Administrative Council at its meeting in May 1987) that on the outcome of the Union's struggles with DG IV 'depended the policy and strength of the Union' (CA 1882 SPG 3697 9.10.87: 40). Five years later, in 1992, the Secretary General of the EBU was even more emphatic and described the conflict between the EBU and DG IV as 'potentially fatal'. The second shot in the campaign against the EBU's notional anti-competitive working arrangements was fired by Screensport (then a subsidiary of W.H. Smith Television and later of ETN – European Television Networks)[12] which complained that the 'rules of EBU membership violated antitrust legislation and that Eurosport would threaten Screensport's future survival' (SPG 3951 SG/S/781 4.2.88: 2). The Commission was as sympathetic to Screensport's contention as it had been to Sky's. As the Director of the EBU's Legal Department, Werner Rumphorst, stated that the Commission's objections went beyond the Eurosport project and concerned 'the very nature of the EBU, its membership conditions, rights acquisition practices, exclusivity policy, long term contracts etc.' (SPG 4056 27.5.88: 3).

## EBU versus DG IV

DG IV, the Directorate for Competition Policy, the EBU's chief adversary in the Commission of the European Communities, is often described as the most powerful section of the Commission. When DG IV was under the direction of the senior Commissioner nominated by the UK, Sir Leon Brittan,[13] the Competition Directorate initiated a number of raids against the EBU. DG IV's most celebrated foray followed a complaint by the UK company W.H. Smith Television. W.H. Smith Television was the principal investor in the satellite television channel Screensport which competed against the sports channel Eurosport.

W.H. Smith Television's case enabled DG IV to address what it regarded as the fundamentally anti-competitive practices of the European public service broadcasters. W.H. Smith Television argued that its sports channel, Screensport, was improperly disadvantaged because its principal competitor, the Eurosport satellite television sports channel, enjoyed competitive advantages denied to

Screensport which derived from Eurosport's privileged relationship to the EBU. Eurosport, W.H. Smith claimed, benefited from its access to sports rights which the EBU had acquired on behalf of its members. These rights were either exclusively made available to Eurosport or were made available at lower cost than to competing services – notably to Screensport.

The Commission upheld Screensport's complaint. It judged that the EBU's 'joint venture agreements and all related contractual provisions . . . constitute an infringement of Article 85(1) of the EEC treaty' (Decision 19.2.91 in OJ L 63/32–44 9.3.91). It rejected arguments made by the EBU that Eurosport had 'a public service character' and that because 'Eurosport enjoys the rights of an EBU member' the channel was a public service channel. Rather, the Commission found that the 'viewing public has tended to associate Eurosport more closely with Sky' and rejected the proposition that Eurosport was a public service channel. The Commission's judgement led to the termination of the Eurosport agreement and to Eurosport going off air between 6–22 May 1991. Subsequently, a new partnership was concluded between the Eurosport Consortium and the French channel TF1 and transmission recommenced. In January 1993 Eurosport merged with its principal commercial rival, the Screensport Channel (owned by ESPN, a subsidiary of the largest US television company Capital Cities/ABC).

The Screensport case was certainly the most important of the Commission's challenges to the EBU and its practices but it was neither the first nor the last. In 1988, prior to the Eurosport judgement, the Commission attacked the heart of the EBU's activities and formally requested information on Eurovision. It stated that 'the Commission considers that there are grounds for finding that the joint acquisition of exclusive television rights for sports events by the members of the EBU and the members' refusal to sublicence those rights to non-members infringe the EEC competition rules' (Letter from Overbury to EBU 26.7.88).

However, it was acknowledged that 'the Commission considers that the joint acquiring of television rights for sports events as well as the Eurovision system produce advantages which can be passed on to consumers and are able to outweigh the restrictions of competition' (Letter from Overbury to EBU 26.7.88). The Commission signalled that established arrangements could only continue if the 'EBU and its members submit an undertaking to grant sublicences [i.e. to commercial competitors] on reasonable terms at least for deferred transmissions and extracts and for live and first transmissions with regard to those events which EBU members do not transmit themselves' (Letter from Overbury to EBU 26.7.88). In 1989 the Commission complained again about Eurosport and what it saw as the EBU's anti-competitive working practices (European Report 1463/111/3–4 14.1.89) and accordingly it required the EBU to sub-license programme rights to non EBU broadcasters (OJ C 251 p.2. 5.10.90) to break what it perceived as anti competitive behaviour.

Commission officials (interviewed by the author 11.11.91) emphasised that in their view the EBU's established arrangements, notably the exclusive acquisition of sports rights, constitute a barrier to entry to European television markets. They stated that 'new operators find it difficult to get access to attractive programmes'. Consequently, DG IV was determined to ensure that 'the foreclosure effects of exclusive contracts are limited' a stance which directly challenged one of the chief reasons for the EBU's existence – its collective exclusive acquisition of sports rights for its members.

After the Eurosport judgement, a related case was brought by the French commercial channel La Cinq. It was heard in the European Court of the First Instance in January 1992 (before the bankruptcy and closure of La Cinq led to the cessation of the case). Like Screensport, La Cinq complained that the EBU denied it access to programming available to EBU members and had refused to admit La Cinq to EBU membership.[14] The Court of First Instance's ruling confirmed the judgement handed down in the Screensport case and found that 'the EBU's collective purchasing practices for sports events are likely to materially reduce attempts by rival channels seeking events rights which interest a large number of spectators' (*Cable and Satellite Express* 7.2.92).

In 1993 the EBU was permitted to continue to acquire sports rights on behalf of its members, a practice which otherwise would have fallen foul of competition provisions of the Treaty of Rome (Article 85), for two reasons. First, because it was recognised that consumers 'benefit from the Eurovision system in that the system enables the members to show more, and higher quality sports programmes . . . than they would be able to without the benefits of Eurovision' (para 68 Commission decision of 11 June 1993 relating to a proceeding pursuant to Article 85 of the EEC Treaty (IV/32 150 – ebu/euro-vision system) OJ L 179, 22/7/93: 23). And, second, because the EBU agreed to sublicense sports rights to commercial broadcasters – that is to provide 'access to non-members on reasonable terms' (para 71 Commission decision of 11 June 1993 relating to a proceeding pursuant to Article 85 of the EEC Treaty (IV/32 150 – ebu/eurovision system) OJ L 179, 22/7/93: 23).

Notwithstanding the EBU's stated willingness to sub-license programme rights to non-members and to carry commercial broadcasters' signals on the Eurovision network, DG IV remained hostile. It perceived the EBU's collective acquisition of rights on behalf of its members to be an abuse of a dominant position which improperly denied non-members of the EBU the competitive advantages enjoyed by EBU members. Accordingly, in June 1992 DG IV required the EBU to grant the commercial sports channel Screensport comparable access to the Barcelona Olympics to that enjoyed by the EBU linked channel Eurosport – in spite of the EBU having acquired exclusive European rights to the Games (*Financial Times* 27.6.92: 2). However, antagonism subsided after the EBU stated that it proposed to appeal to the Court of First Instance against DG IV's requirements. In 1993, after Sir Leon Brittan ceased to hold the office of Commissioner responsible for DG IV, the new

Commissioner responsible for competition policy, Karel van Miert, authorised the EBU to continue its established arrangements for Eurovision (Commission Decision 93/403/EEC of 11 June 1993).[15] But a further turn in this complicated history saw the European Court of the First Instance respond in July 1996 to complaints from several Italian commercial broadcasters and rule against public broadcasters combining (i.e. through the EBU) to acquire sports rights (Court of Justice of the European Communities. Case T-528/93 11 July 1996).

DG IV's actions against the EBU in the late 1980s and early 1990s contrast with the early 1980s when the European Community saw the EBU as a major ally and a powerful instrument for the achievement of the Community goal of European union. The Commission's contradictory dealings with the EBU reflect fundamental divisions within the Community – between European unionists and European free traders. For unionists the EBU offered, and potentially offers, a powerful instrument for the prosecution of 'ever closer union'. For free traders the EBU's closed membership (and anomalous membership rules), access to programme exchanges and exclusive acquisition of programming for the benefit of members only, were and will always be troubling. DG IV's interest in the working arrangements of the EBU and Eurovision was perceived in Geneva as profoundly threatening. Nor could it be otherwise, for the values of the EBU and DG IV were mutually hostile.

## Universal access via monopsony versus restricted access via competition

The EBU used its monopsony powers to acquire rights (particularly sports rights) at a lower price than a competitive market would permit. These rights were made available, to viewers of EBU member broadcasters' television services, more widely than a competitive rights market would have done. Commercial broadcasters are best able to realise value from the rights they have acquired by *excluding* viewers from consumption and requiring those who wish to watch to pay.

The EBU has improved the bargaining power of broadcasters, relative to rights holders, by establishing a monopsony. Until commercial broadcasters were excluded from EBU membership, and the benefits available to members, few complained about these arrangements. Viewers and listeners benefited and only rights owners – mostly sports rights' owners – lost. But once competition in European broadcasting was established those outside the charmed circle of EBU membership were disadvantaged. Therein lie the grounds for the Commission's concerns about the EBU's exercise of illegitimate market power.[16] The Commission attempted to make the imperfect markets in information and broadcasting services (which are public goods in the sense that they are not exhausted in consumption) conform more closely to the classical character of competitive markets. Whereas the EBU and public service broadcasting have sought to exploit the economic imperfections of broadcasting markets, to maximise viewer and listener welfare, by bringing them access to information content that they would otherwise have been denied. As the Secretary General of the EBU stated, the EBU is a re-distribution agency. It is a 'unique example of European collaboration constituted by Eurovision and by its basic principles of solidarity in favour of the smallest or least well endowed members of our Union' (Münch in *Espace* No. 14 September [1992]: 1).

The conflict between DG IV and the EBU is a fundamental conflict between rival principles for the organisation of European broadcasting. Between a public service principle underpinned by a conception of broadcasting markets as inevitably and unredeemably failed markets and a competitive market principle based on the proposition that broadcasting markets can be made reasonably, if not perfectly, competitive. It is not clear whether the Commission or the EBU has most effectively maximised the welfare of consumers of broadcasting services or whether DG IV acts even-handedly in respect of private and public broadcasters.

Reino Paasilinna (when Secretary General of the Finnish Broadcasting Company, YLE) stated that 'In the media field, Brussels tends to help private entrepreneurs much more . . . if the EBU buys sports rights it is often considered a cartel. But if an individual, a speculator, does the same he is not viewed in the same light. The tendency in Brussels is quite problematic for us' (cited in *World Broadcast News* Vol. 15 No. 1 [1992]: 35).[17] Porter and Hasselbach have made similar claims (Porter and Hasselbach [1991: 159]).

The EBU's restrictive membership policies certainly gave EBU members access to programmes denied to non members. Yet the advantages which EBU membership afforded to its small public service members may have promoted competition and diversity rather than harmed it. If small public service broadcasters were unable to survive if denied the advantages of EBU membership competition would be reduced and the ends to which the efforts of the Competition Directorate were notionally directed negated. After van Miert's appointment as Commissioner responsible for DG IV it seems the Commission has accepted this argument. The Secretary General of the EBU, Jean-Bernard Münch, stated that: 'it is the viewer who has won . . . to him, wherever he may be . . . the EBU guarantees access to all the major events. This is particularly true of the smaller countries, which without the EBU would have difficulty acquiring the rights. . . . These plus points were recognised . . . by the Commission' (in *Espace* No. 20 July [1993]: 1).

But, whatever the judgement on the balance of consumer advantage and the fairness of DG IV's interventions, it is clear that such conflicts are likely to recur. The geographical area in which European Community competition regulations apply has been extended with the creation of the European Economic Area (EEA) – European Community competition regulations, and thus the jurisdiction of DG IV, now extends to the whole of the EEA and not just to the EC. There is also an unresolvable theoretical contradiction underpinning the conflict between advocates of competition and of public service. Broadcasting does not exhibit the characteristics which neo-classical economists demand in well functioning markets. Resolution of the conflicts between the EBU (and public service broadcasters) and re-regulatory advocates of competitive markets are therefore more likely to depend on the relative strengths of the rivals' political connections than on the quality of their arguments.

The rapprochement between the Commission and the EBU can neither be completely explained by reference to the changing of the guard at the highest level of DG IV nor by the EBU's successful diplomacy in Brussels, however important these initiatives may have been. The EBU has itself retreated from the positions it took at its Marino Conference in 1990. Its intransigent rejection of commercial broadcasters at Marino, whilst thoroughly in keeping with the recommendations of the Wangermée Group, was recognised by senior EBU officials to be irreconcilable with the Commission's prescriptions on competition and commercial broadcasters' access to markets. Accordingly, the EBU has opened doors to commercial broadcasters. It has sublicensed sports rights and has opened the Eurovision network to commercial broadcasters as a quasi common carrier. Moreover: the commercial decisions which resulted in Sky's merger with BSB to form the main UK DBS service provider, BSkyB, in November 1990; Sky's withdrawal from Eurosport;[18] and the merger between the EBU's sports channel, Eurosport, and Screensport (the Competition Directorate's principal stalking horse), did much to transform the regulatory environment.

Between 1982, when Eurikon was launched to challenge commercial broadcasters and advance the ends of European union, and 1993, when EBU members entered a partnership with an American-owned commercial broadcaster, European public service broadcasting lost its dominant position and experienced a remorseless exposure of the weaknesses which had been hidden through decades of monopoly. If Eurosport made evident European public service broadcasters' diminished ability to remain independent of commercial interests, the second of the EBU's thematic satellite television channels, Euronews, demonstrated equally eloquently public service broadcasters' diminished ability to remain independent of political interests.

## Euronews

We don't want to leave international news to CNN.

Mariano Maggiore's statement (interviewed by the author when he was a senior official in DG X. 11.11.91), is representative of the sentiments of European political elites following Operation Desert Storm. Maggiore's views were echoed by his colleague in DG X, Saturnino Munoz Gomez (personal interview 8.11.91), by Roberto Barzanti MEP, Chairman of the European Parliament's

Committee on Youth, Culture, Education, the Media and Sport (personal interview 7.11.91) and by a UK MEP, Michael Elliott, a member of the aforementioned Committee (personal interview 1.11.91). All four stated that CNN's coverage of the Gulf War of 1991 had sparked a widespread commitment to establishing a pan-European television news service in European political circles. Whether or not CNN had set the news agenda during Operation Desert Storm is not the point. What counts is that the Community's political elites generally believed that it had done so, and that, in consequence, what they believed to be the 'European view' of the war had gone by default. CNN's coverage of the Gulf War thus amplified the intense anxiety among the European Community's audio-visual policy community about the US presence in the European audio-visual market.[19]

The EBU had considered establishing a European news channel in the early 1980s but, chastened by Europa's failure, had not done so. But widespread concern in European political circles about the under-representation of 'the European point of view' during the Gulf War gave the EBU an opportunity to rebuild its troubled relationship with Brussels – poisoned by its recurrent confrontations with DG IV – by exploiting its undoubted strengths in news. Euronews offered what the Secretary General described as, 'a project which could serve to demonstrate the vitality of public service broadcasting' (SG/2975 8.6.90: 1). Immediately after the Gulf War the Secretary General prioritised development of Euronews and stated explicitly that political imperatives required the EBU to do so: 'the Euronews file, the file par excellence to be undertaken without delay, was a political file not a commercial one ... EBU's image with the European institutions was at stake' (CA 2116 SPG 5254 18.2.91: 17).

The political forces which sought to establish Euronews were not confined to the European Community. Hjarvard cites a speaker at the EBU Administrative Council's meeting in 1989 who urged that the EBU actively support Euronews because: 'political and professional expectations were very strong. The project would be one of the important points of the Paris Conclave [i.e. the Assises européens de l'audiovisuel] and it was essential to be able to announce that progress had been made' (SPG 4457 May 26–8 1989 cited in Hjarvard 1991: 16). So it proved, the President of France, François Mitterand, advised the Assises européennes de l'audiovisuel that he had taken a 'great interest in the 'Euronews' multilingual news channel project' (Assises 1989: 19).

## Dependence or independence? Public service broadcasting and the European Union

Important though the Gulf War was, Euronews had began to change from vague possibility to a specific programme before the onset of the War. In May 1989 the Administrative Council of the EBU received a feasibility study (CA

2014 SPG 4453 18.5.89) from the Euronews Study Group which makes clear the central importance of political considerations in Euronews' development. It stated nakedly that 'It is in the interest of European public service broadcasters to create Euronews as a response to political demands' (CA 2014 SPG 4453 18.5.89: 2). Earlier, on 22 November 1987, Werner Rumphorst (the Director of the EBU Legal Department) wrote to the Chairman of the EBU TV News Working Party (Vandersichel) and stressed the importance the Commission of the European Communities attached to development of a European News Channel.

Rumphorst asked Vandersichel if a 'final attempt could be made by the news experts to launch their own project for a European News Channel' and explained 'Three days ago I attended a meeting of the European Institute for the Media in Brussels. EEC Commissioner Ripa di Meana mentioned in the course of his speech . . . that he had just met with Mr Ross of CNN who explained to him CNN's plans for a European News Channel.[20] As on earlier occasions, the EEC Commissioner deplored once again the apparent incapacity of established European broadcasters to join together and provide their own European News Channel rather than leaving this important field to non-Europeans'. Vandersichel's reply testified to the gulf between the EBU's diplomats (as a former UK broadcaster employed at the EBU had described members of the EBU staff) and European public service broadcasters committed to the political independence of public service broadcasting.

Vandersichel replied, on 1 December 1987, to Rumphorst stating 'EBU has been operating a European Newschannel since the 6 October 1958. And a very rich and varied channel indeed, since it has some thirty-two different outlets, adopted [sic] to the local needs of the European audiences. A standardized, so-called European channel can only be a poor substitute and hardly a complement [sic]'. He continued 'there is no such thing as a common European interest in news, like there might be with a portion of the audience in sports and culture. And even then a possible Sportschannel will be faced with difficult choices, unless it can simultaneously send ice hockey to Finland, cycling to Italy and cricket to Britain'.

The exchange between Rumphorst and Vandersichel encapsulates the issues that were at stake. Rumphorst urged the political utility of the channel and pointed out how it would serve the EBU's interests. Vandersichel emphasised the futility of the project because of the impossibility of creating the programming necessary to attract European viewers on whom the success of the channel, and its underlying rationale of European integration, depended. Rumphorst represented those who wished to use the mass media to build a collective European consciousness and character, Vandersichel those who wished public service broadcasting to remain independent of politics. As Vandersichel eloquently stated: 'That politicians of the European commission [sic] wish to promote a news channel is another cause for concern. Let us be grateful that in most West-European countries the TV News departments are not operated by missionaries or politicians' (Letter to Rumphorst 1.12.87).[21] But EBU news professionals' opposition to the EBU's growing dependence on the Commission of the European Communities was outweighed by EBU diplomats' judgement that the EBU needed to cultivate links to the Commission if it was to survive.

However, although Euronews may appear to have been launched to advance the EBU's political interests in Brussels and to be vulnerable to influence exerted by its funders, both Massimo Fichera (founding Chairman of Euronews) and Pierre Brunel-Lantenac (founding Secretary General of Euronews) forcefully asserted Euronews' independence. Fichera stated that 'The programmes produced by Europeans for Europeans are free from any influence or political interest of any country. Information is currently controlled at national level. We believe that the launch of Euronews can break this mould' (in *16/9* No. 7 March 1993: 18). Equally firmly Brunel-Lantenac insisted that Euronews has 'eleven television companies as our boss and it is easier to be independent with eleven bosses than with one' and that the Euronews charter (to which all sponsoring broadcasters are signatories) prohibits the exercise of political pressure on Euronews (in *16/9* No. 7 March 1993: 18).

## Euronews: from birth to troubled youth and uncertain future

Euronews began to take shape in 1990. In December of that year Massimo Fichera (then Vice President of RAI and later Chairman and Director General of Euronews) presented a proposal to establish Euronews to the Administrative Council based on:

- the availability of members' news and current affairs material free of embargoes;
- ten members, including four large members, joining the project;
- subsidy during the first years of operation 'to a large extent from European public funds'.

(CA 2104 SPG 5254 14.11.90)

In spite of senior members of the EBU's testimony to the critical importance of Euronews in building relationships between the EBU and the European Community the Commission remained sceptical about public service broadcasters' commitment to Euronews.[22] Mariano Maggiore (personal interview 11.11.91) observed that the EBU had sought an annual subvention of 10 million ECU from the Commission for Euronews but that its own (i.e. its members'), commitment was in doubt.[23] There was much to support Maggiore's scepticism for only a minority of the EBU's members had joined the Euronews consortium. RTBF (Belgium), ERTU (Egypt), YLE (Finland), Antenne 2 and FR3 (France), the ARD and ZDF (Germany), ERT (Greece),

169

RAI (Italy), TMC (Monaco), RTVE (Spain) and JRT (Yugoslavia) initially supported the nascent Euronews. But in 1992 both the ARD and ZDF withdrew and, in September 1992, established a joint working party to progress development of a rival German (strictly German language) twenty-four hour satellite television news service.

Ironically, in view of Euronews' putative role as a European alternative to CNN, ZDF withdrew from Euronews to consolidate its own relationship with CNN (*World Broadcast News* November [1992]: 18). The withdrawal of the ARD and ZDF meant not only that the Euronews consortium was very seriously weakened but also that it would have an unanticipated, and potentially powerful, German language competitor. Euronews' counter proposal, to establish a Euronews Deutschland with a subsidiary of Hessischer Rundfunk – a member of the ARD, led the ZDF to threaten cessation of its contributions to the EBU's Eurovision news exchanges on which Euronews, and thus the proposed Euronews Deutschland, depended. A similar conflict of interest between Euronews and other large and powerful members of the EBU was evident in France where TF1 refused to contribute to the establishment of a Euronews France because of its commitment to its own news channel 'La Chaîne Info'.

The BBC too maintained its customary distance (Eurosport only excepted) from the EBU's satellite initiatives. In spite of the Administrative Council's testimony to the important role which UK broadcasters could play in Euronews,[24] neither it nor ITV/IBA has joined Euronews.[25] The BBC had stated that it would 'support the project by providing its material in as far as the question of rights had been resolved. But it was not prepared to invest. It had reservations on the estimates of the advertising receipts, which seemed too optimistic, and wondered whether it was realistic to count on obtaining sponsorship and advertising for the new channel' (CA 2116 SPG 5254 18.2.91: 17). So too with UK commercial television. The 'UKIB/ITV was not in favour of the project which had too many financial uncertainties. Euronews would depend on sponsorship, on certain governments and would be at the mercy of the EC budget. In these circumstances what guarantees of independence and reliability would it offer?' (CA 2116 SPG 5254 18.2.91: 17). At the Administrative Council meeting in February 1991 other member broadcasters, notably SSR, echoed the UK and German broadcasters' scepticism about Euronews' viability.

Development of a competing German language news service, coupled with the BBC's establishment of its own English language twenty-four hour satellite television news service, suggests that Euronews can neither act as a public service champion against commercial twenty-four hour television news services nor achieve the share of viewing among German and English language speakers necessary for it to realise the objectives of its political sponsors. Indeed, services such as the BBC's World Service Television news service (although founded to 'challenge the US owned Cable News Network International as the primary source of international news' [BBC 1992: 39]) was, because a unilingual service originating from one European state, hardly more acceptable to Community elites than CNN.

In the spring of 1991 the EBU briefed the Commission of the European Communities and the European Parliament on Euronews' progress and was received at the highest level of both organisations (*Espace* No. 1 [1991]: 4–5). On 8 May 1991 it formally established Euronews Development as a separate legal entity. Euronews Development, and Euronews itself, were established as distinct entities because of provisions in the EBU statutes which define the Union's objectives as 'to promote co-operation and in particular programme exchanges between its members, and to support members' interests in every domain, but not to assume the role of a broadcaster itself' (Note from Rumphorst to Brunel-Lantenac 21.9.89). Thus, because broadcasting is not an objective of the EBU, it would require 'virtual unanimity of all active members' (note from Rumphorst to Brunel Lantenac 21.9.89) for the EBU to run Euronews directly. In July 1991 Pierre Brunel-Lantenac was appointed Executive Secretary of Euronews and Ernesto Braun (formerly Chief Executive of Europa and charged with negotiating the Eurosport contract for transponder rental) was appointed Head of the Euronews Task Force. Braun later became Chief Executive of Euronews and was succeeded by Massimo Fichera in 1992.

The Secretary General of the EBU made it clear that even though Euronews was not conceived as a commercially profitable channel (SPG 5424 5.4.91: 2) it required an annual subvention of 10 million ECU for six years (SPG 5424 5.4.91: 1) based on anticipated annual operating costs of Euronews of c.21–5 million ECU, in addition to a start up cost of 11.6 million ECU.[26] Subsequent projections (Euronews brochure n.d.: 9) foresaw annual operating costs of between 49 and 50 million ECU. Over the first six years of operations Euronews planned for 54 per cent of revenue to come from EBU members (mostly in contributions in kind), 22 per cent from European public funds and 22 per cent from sponsorship and advertising (Euronews brochure n.d.: 8). The 1993 budget of 50 million ECU planned for 55 per cent of the budget to come from participating broadcasters, 20 per cent from public sector funders, notably the Commission of the European Communities, the Audiovisual Eureka and the city of Lyons, and 25 per cent from advertisers[27] (Media Policy Review No. 11: 5; and *16/9* No. 7 March 1993: 19). Clearly, Euronews was recognised to be financially dependent on European political bodies.[28]

Euronews began transmission on 1 January 1993 supported by France Télévision (16,000 shares), RAI (13,000 shares), RTVE (12,000 shares), Télé Monte-Carlo (7,000 shares), RTBF (6,700 shares), ERT (5,600 shares), ERTU – Egypt (5,300 shares), YLE (5,000 shares), RTP (5,000 shares) and CYBC – Cyprus (1,000 shares). However, in spite of European institutions' support, the future of Euronews remained, and remains, uncertain – in spite of ITN's acquisition of a controlling 49 per cent of its share capital in November 1997.

In contrast to the establishment of Eurikon and Europa by EBU members, the genesis of Eurosport, in conjunction with News International, and

Euronews, in close association with the European Community, demonstrates the very limited extent to which the EBU and its members were able to shape their own destinies and thus how far the strength and confidence of public service broadcasters had declined between 1982 and 1993. Whereas, in 1982 the majority of the EBU's members enjoyed a monopoly and were rapidly able to establish an experimental service, by 1993 in response to the pinprick threat posed by Sky Channel the EBU was dependent on a commercial partner for its sports channel (itself established to consolidate the EBU's threatened position in respect of sports rights) and on the patronage of the European Commission and the European Parliament for its news channel. Perversely, the news channel was itself spawned by the need to restore good relations with the Commission of the European Communities which had been damaged by what the Competition Directorate perceived to be the EBU's abuse of its dominant position in European broadcasting.

The hegemony of public service broadcasters had been so much eroded that measures taken to improve the commercial position of EBU members in the European broadcasting market compromised public service broadcasters' relations with political authorities. Attempts to restore those damaged relations risked compromising European public service broadcasters cherished political independence. Unlike the early 1980s, when the EBU first ventured into satellite television, European public service broadcasters in the 1990s were competing in an increasingly crowded market place and were no longer uniquely endowed with the ability (thanks to Eurovision) to provide pan-European and global news and sports coverage.

Indeed, Neville Clarke – the animator *par excellence* of the EBU's first satellite ventures – testified to the superior competitive position of the EBU's chief commercial rival. Clarke quoted Rupert Murdoch to show how powerful the EBU's rival and erstwhile partner had become: 'Sky News, the Fox [his US television network] news service and the News Corporation's combined reach – which have together over three thousand journalists spread over every continent and very country – leave us with an army of newsgatherers second to none' (Clarke and Riddell 1992: 43).

In contrast, the *European*'s obsequies on the sale of a controlling 49 per cent of Euronews to a commercial television news organisation, the UK's Independent Television News (ITN), stressed Euronews' deficiencies:

> A European journalistic paradigm, it had no presenters, poor quality film dubbed into five languages and latterly no viewers. Last week it was sold to Britain's ITN for a mere $8.5 million. . . . As a metaphor for Europe, Euronews is a grim one: its origins lie in the ideal of a united Europe, its revenues came from subsidies, and its editorial board from a nightmarish conglomerate of public service broadcasters from 18 different countries. Good luck, ITN.
>
> (*European* 4–10.12.97: 23)

Euronews and Eurosport stand in a direct line of continuity with the EBU's first satellite television channels – Eurikon and Europa. Key personnel who developed the EBU's first ventures in satellite television also developed and managed its later initiatives. The format of the thematic channels was strongly influenced by the lessons learned through the failure of the earlier mixed programme channels. For example, Euronews uses teams of journalists of different nationalities to develop stories; a practice which clearly responds to some of the difficulties experienced in the earlier channels. But, whilst developed as public service channels, both Eurosport and Euronews challenged established identities and historical vocations of European public service broadcasting. Not least in both channels embracing a commercial identity at odds with their origins.

Eurosport was established and ran in partnership with commercial broadcasters – notably Rupert Murdoch's Sky Channel which perfectly exemplified the forces which the EBU established its first satellite ventures to combat. Euronews has been closely dependent on the European political authorities from which the EBU, an organisation of public service broadcasters committed to political autonomy, formerly sought to remain independent – as the *European* noted following ITN's acquisition of Euronews: 'Shortly after CNN's triumphal coverage of the Gulf War (remember how they won it single handed?), public service broadcasters in Europe, with the help of heavy EU subsidies, decided to set up their own competing channel' (*European* 4–10.12.97: 23). Eurosport and Euronews thus represent dramatic departures from the EBU's historical mission and policies, and testify to the striking loss of power experienced by Europe's public service broadcasters and their collective embodiment – the EBU – in the first decade of satellite television in Europe. In a decade the Sky barons had come to rule the skies and Neville Clarke's role changed from challenging them to recording their exploits.

# 9

# THE LANGUAGE FACTOR

> The limit of the limitations which internationalism imposes is best seen
> in such films of Frederico Fellini as *Casanova*. . . . There was no dialogue
> for this film. The international cast merely counted, each in his or her
> native language, the cardinal numbers. Fellini would say: 'Go back to
> number twenty-seven – or siebenundzwanzig – or ventisette' like an
> orchestral conductor. Words fitting the mouth and tongue positions
> were added later. That is international art.
>
> (Burgess 1990: 19)

> A comparative analysis of Italian and British TV news has shown differ-
> ences both in televisual syntax and in political semantics. Formal analysis
> reveals that similar elements are combined in different ways, with effects
> at the level of framing and continuity. British news is more strongly
> framed, the role of the newscaster is more dominant, and there is a high
> degree of formal narrative continuity. Pursuing the linguistic metaphor,
> the televisual grammars of British and Italian news include different
> rules, and hence the national news broadcasts can be said to use different
> dialects of the same underlying language
>
> (Jones and Cere 1991: 42)

Terms such as 'Europe', the 'single market', 'unification', 'the European
Community' are all grammatically singular but they nominate a plural, diverse
and contradictory European reality and obscure important linguistic and
cultural fissures which divide Europe. The European Community has nine official languages,[1] and many further language communities living within its
boundaries. If Europe is defined more widely, e.g. in terms of membership of
the Council of Europe or the EBU, then the number of its official languages
swells further.[2]

The Commission of the European Communities recognised that monoglot
television would not enable European viewers and broadcasters to participate in
a fully European television culture because: 'Initiatives based on language, like
the common French-language proposal, launched jointly by France, Belgium

and Switzerland [i.e. TV 5], only confirm and reinforce a cultural reality which has existed for a long time. By their very nature, they cannot come to grips with this new multilingual European reality' (Commission of the European Communities 1983: 22). Hence the importance of the polyglot pan-European channels developed under the EBU's sponsorship and their experiments in re-languaging and re-presenting programmes for viewers in different European linguistic and cultural communities.

Thus, although technological change and re-regulation during the decade between 1982 and 1992 established some of the necessary conditions for a European broadcasting market, the essential linguistic (and cultural) unity required for a genuinely integrated European broadcasting and audio-visual market is conspicuous by its absence. As Burgess, Jones and Cere indicate, linguistic and rhetorical differences limit the circulation of programmes beyond their cultural and linguistic place of origin. In consequence, the effectiveness and acceptability of the re-languaging used in film and television is a key variable on which a genuine European single market in television depends.[3] As Charles Barrand (UK news editor on Eurikon and Head of News on Europa), stated 'Language was then and remains now the central issue of pan-European television' (Barrand 1986: 11).

## Re-languaging and cultural discount

If television programmes are to circulate from country to country within Europe, then more and more programmes will require re-languaging. Dubbing and subtitling are the principal means used to re-language programmes and reduce what Hoskins and Mirus (1988) called 'cultural discount' in pan-European television. But reducing 'cultural discount' does not come cheap. Clarke estimated that 40 per cent of Eurikon's budget was spent on re-languaging (telex to Froschmaier 3.12.82).[4] Eurikon was not exceptional.[5] Burnett reported that Europa spent 50 per cent of its budget on re-languaging (Burnett 1989: 38).

Helen Reid (a translator for NOS) points out that in subtitling a programme three kinds of linguistic change are necessary. Change is necessary 'from longer units into shorter ones, from one language into another, from spoken language into written text' (Reid 1987: 28). Satisfactory translation depends on the knowledge of the receiving audience as well as on its comprehension of the source text. Thus, Reid observed

> The meaning of a phrase . . . depends on what the speaker *feels* about the subject and what the hearer *knows* about the subject. The phrase itself seems to be the empty, meaningless bit in the middle. This explains why . . . the French subtitles of an American film must be different from the Dutch subtitles. The general knowledge about the USA is greater in the Netherlands than it is in France, and institutions

and concepts that needed to be described for the French viewer could be left untranslated for the Dutch audience. Subtitles are directed at one particular audience and to retranslate them for an audience with a different mother tongue and culture will never do.

(Reid 1987: 30)

Dubbing involves different but no less demanding transformations. Jean Yvane (Head of Dubbing, Société Française de Production) stated (in a comprehensive discussion of the difficulties of dubbing), that 'In many cases the intonation of the original cannot be slavishly reproduced . . . without the melodic base of the target language being spoilt. Thus, Italian's expressiveness creates some problems in French, as the latter does not contain any tonic accents. Recreating Italian expressiveness would run counter to the phonetic status of the French language which . . . is based on phrases and not words' (Yvane 1987: 19). Moreover Herbst has argued that dubbing (and his argument clearly also applies to other forms of re-languaging) involves 'such factors as equivalence of *genre*, equivalence of *text quality*, equivalence of *meaning* in a way that plot-carrying meaning elements must be translated and atmospheric meaning elements must be expressed in some form or another in the translation, equivalence of *character* (including regional and social status), equivalence of *cultural context*' (Herbst 1987: 23).

The intrinsic difficulties of re-languaging, forbidding enough whether dubbing or subtitling is used, are amplified because neither system is acceptable to all European viewers. Some European states are accustomed to dubbing and others to subtitling; 'The Scandinavian countries and the Netherlands are resolutely fixed on subtitling; France, Germany, Italy, Austria, and Spain have a long tradition of dubbing. In the UK, people are starting to accept subtitles' (Anonymous 1987: 10).[6] Large European countries (France, Italy, Germany, Spain) broadly prefer dubbing whereas small countries (Belgium, Denmark, Finland, Greece, Netherlands, Norway, Portugal, Sweden) prefer subtitling (see British Screen Advisory Council 1992: 20–1). As the Eurikon Operations Group stated 'subtitling was not popular in Germany and Austria, whereas Dutch audiences were used to it' (Minutes of the EBU/OTS Operations Group Meeting held in Rome 26.7.82: 5).

Moreover, some programmes require more extensive re-presentation if they are to circulate successfully outside the cultural and linguistic community of their origin. Patrick Dromgoole (when Assistant Managing Director of HTV), testified to how European viewers had become accustomed to very high standards of re-presentation – which were commensurately costly.[7] In response to a call from Mariano Maggiore (the European Commission's observer at the meetings of the Eurikon Operations Group) who sought 'a film with five or six soundtracks in different languages' for Eurikon (OTS Operations Group Rome Meeting 26.7.82 Minutes: 5), Dromgoole explained:

you are probably aware that when dubbing, it is sometimes necessary to 'nip' a film in order to exactly match the mouth movements to carefully selected verbiage. . . . Quite a few nips were involved when *Kidnapped* went out in Germany, where it went out as four ninety minute dramas. the French ran it as six hours, while in the UK we ran it as thirteen half-hours. You can imagine what a fun time you would have trying to match up their dubbed tracks to the English film version.

(Letter to Marc Wright 6.8.82)

Moreover Dromgoole pointed out that foreign language scripts were usually owned by the broadcasters who had acquired rights to particular geographical markets and had, in consequence, translated a script for those markets. Thus (to cite Dromgoole's example), the rights to *Kidnapped* had been sold to ZDF for Germany, Antenne 2 for France and RAI for Italy. Each of these broadcasters had rights in the language versions of the scripts they had prepared. Thus, securing a range of foreign language scripts and clearing the rights for transmission to several language markets would involve a complex series of negotiations with different companies each of which would have a veto over a pan-European broadcaster's use of a script.[8]

Further, as Jones and Cere's (1991) comparison of television news in Italy and the UK suggests, problems of re-presentation are not confined to natural language. There are significant cultural, as well as linguistic, obstacles to transnational television as evidenced by the rhetorical differences in UK and Italian television news identified by Jones and Cere:

The technique found on RAI news of enchaining free-floating items can lead to difficulties of orientation for the British viewer, accustomed to being metaphorically led by the hand by the newscaster from the studio to the scene of the next report. In one case, on TG2 [in their paper Jones and Cere do not explain the meaning of TG2, but it presumably means 'Tele Giornale 2'], we registered three filmed reports broadcast consecutively with no intervening return to the studio. This is not intended as a criticism of Italian news: it is also true to say that Italian viewers of British news find its pedantic concentration on factual detail somewhat puzzling: so much information on type of weaponry in the Gulf! But it does signal a different approach to the construction of a news report, and perhaps reflects different assumptions about the audience's ability to 'read' the news.

(Jones and Cere 1991: 21)

Jones and Cere refer (1991: 42) to the greater dominance of the news presenter on UK television relative to Italian television.[9] Finding a visual rhetoric for a transnational service acceptable to more than one target audience

177

will be intimidatingly difficult (even if the greater problems specific to the re-presentation of natural language can be solved). Indeed Desgraupes (1985) specifically chose television news to exemplify the *differences* rather than the similarities between European television services.[10]

Desgraupes' and Jones and Cere's view, that television news is *particularly* nationally distinct and that a *particularly* high level of 'cultural discount' attaches to news, suggests that the political aspirations which led to the estab-lishment in Euronews are not likely to be realised. For pan-European television news competes for viewers' attention with established national news services which are cast in a rhetorical mould familiar, and thus attractive, to viewers. Whereas new, pan-European services, can only transmit using a presentational rhetoric that is unfamiliar to some or all of its target audiences. At the very least it will take time for viewers to become accustomed to, and tolerant of, the new service. Unfamiliar presentational protocols require considerable marketing and promotional efforts, and resources sufficient for the service to survive during a (perhaps long) period in which audiences become familiar with its novel presen-tational strategies, if the new service is to succeed. As the ARD emphasised, pan-European services were 'battling against the deeply-rooted habits of viewers' and their success required viewers to 'change listening habits when we listen to a foreign language' it is a case of 'accepting the unfamiliar' (Minutes of Rome meeting of the Eurikon Operations Group 14.6.82: 2). The evidence provided by the EBU's pan-European channels was that European viewers were and are insufficiently ready to change their habits for pan-European television to succeed.

## Re-languaging in Eurikon

The Eurikon Operations Group reported that 'The methods employed to arrive at a solution [to the problems of re-languaging] were complex and in a state of constant flux. The conclusions reached will indeed require further experiments and refinements yet they constitute a considerable amount of progress in this field' (EBU/OTS Operations Group 1983: 18). Eurikon programmes were transmitted with up to six soundtracks. Dutch, English, French, German and Italian language tracks were transmitted regularly and the remaining, sixth, channel was used for a variety of other languages. The key technological constraint was the six sound channel capacity of the scrambling equipment used. But even the six channel sound system posed numerous problems to the Eurikon partners; Barrand described it as 'very complex, rather temperamental and expertly handled by the sound engineers' (Barrand 1982: 8).

The requirement for multiple soundtracks had implications for the visual characteristics of Eurikon's pan-European television programming. Because it was difficult to marry images to the different lengths of time required for speech in different languages Eurikon developed a visual rhetoric which minimised the amount of time speakers were shown in shot. Many programmes were screened without speakers in shot including the news shown during the UK week of the Eurikon experiment. UPITN's bid for the Europa news contract (UPITN 1983 para 6.1) stipulated that 'the need to supply multiple language tracks simultaneously with the programme picture dictates that Eurikon News must be presented without on-camera newscasters'. This, presenter-less, news format was adopted by both Europa and Euronews but clearly denied viewers a point of identification to which they had become accustomed in their domestic news programmes and denied the pan-European channels a key factor of competitive advantage.[11]

Several re-languaging methods – ranging from voice-over, dubbing and subtitling, to innovative use of broadcast teletext – were evaluated during the Eurikon experiment.[12] The first, IBA, week of Eurikon transmissions used the simplest of methods: interpreters were placed in standard interpreters' booths from which they watched transmissions on 15 inch monitors and listened to the original soundtracks on headphones. Their simultaneous interpretations were transmitted together with the original track. Several difficulties became apparent. Not only did the interpreters' booths require to be adapted for the broadcasters' technical requirements (and thus diverge from the International Standard to which the interpreters were accustomed) but there was a confusing combination of original sound and voice-overs. Richard Fleming, of the European Commission's Interpretation Service, judged the result 'bewildering' (Fleming 1982: 3).[13] Programmes were also subtitled in one of the languages of the imagined viewer population and transmitted with subtitles. Some programmes therefore reached viewers with the original sound, the interpretation and the subtitles each in a different language.

### Lessons from the ITN week

Fleming concluded that 'genuinely satisfactory results could only be achieved if the interpreters were associated upstream in the early stages of news preparation, possibly even helping to conceive and prepare the news in the various languages right from the outset' (Fleming 1982: 5). Fleming recommended:

1 Greater up-stream integration of the interpreters in programme preparation.
2 Advance preparation, co-ordination and rehearsals at booth level.
3 A more active 'casting' policy with greater attention given to voice quality, delivery, acting ability etc.
4 Greater integration and variation of different language techniques – interpretation, dubbing, sub-titling, etc.

(Fleming 1982: 7)

But to implement Fleming's recommendation both broadcasters' and interpreters' established working practices had to change. Fleming's insistence on fundamental changes were echoed by other commentators. Barrand (1982), Daly (1982) and Reiler (1982) reached similar conclusions. Albert Daly (President of the International Association of Conference Interpreters, an interpreter regularly used by the EBU and the chief interpreter employed on the Eurikon experiment) concurred and stressed 'the need for 'integration' of the linguists into the production and programming phase' (Daly 1982: 2). Daly showed quite how comprehensive the shift in professional cultures and practices would have to be:

- the news can only be handled by first translating and typing the foreign version to be delivered. Even then, there are difficulties of synchronisation, but these can presumably be overcome with experience, although, there too one feels that certain natural aptitudes will be required.
- sound on film must be pre-viewed, transcribed and where necessary translated at the editing stage, to overcome the problem of sudden changes in sound level.
- all scripted material should be previewed with script.
- 'specialized' programmes (this is the case with *all* sports) should be done by specialists.

(Daly 1982: 2)

Not only did Daly's recommendations conflict with one of journalists' core values – news should be up to date and fast breaking – but they posed major organisational and cost challenges. They point to the difficulty of establishing a successful pan-European service which either 're-cycled' existing programmes or originated new works. Moreover Daly's insistence on the importance of changed professional practices (and therefore a changed professional culture) suggests that there would be serious obstacles to launching and successfully establishing such a service from within an established broadcasting organisation with a well established professional culture and working practices. In short, for pan-European television to succeed a new institutional culture and new professional practices were required as well as considerable resources.

### Alternative strategies: the ORF

The ORF, in the third week of Eurikon transmissions, attempted to redress some of the problems which had become apparent in the IBA and RAI weeks. ORF had two professional broadcasters, a German male and an English female native speaker, to introduce its programmes. They mediated between viewers and programmes and acted as rapporteurs. The explanations they gave to viewers successfully gave 'a human face to two different languages' at the 'level of accepted broadcast quality' (EBU/OTS Operations Group 1983: 19). But the system was very time consuming. This presentational device accounted for approximately 10 per cent of the total time of transmissions during the ORF week. Moreover, viewers who spoke neither English nor German were doubly alienated. Not only were they subjected to the lengthy addresses directed to English and German speaking viewers but the voice-over interpretation of both the English and German statements deluged them with redundant information.

ORF's decision to sideline languages other than English and German offended speakers of other languages. At the Rome meeting of the Operations Group, Clarke reminded ORF that 'one of the general principles set by the Operations Group was that the programmes should be understandable to as many people as possible'. The Operations Group established the principle that from 'an EEC point of view that all the Community languages should receive equal treatment' (Minutes of the EBU/OTS Operations Group Meeting held in Rome 26.7.82: 7). The Operations Group's commitment is a reminder of the difficulties of implementing a service based on linguistic parity (albeit there were only six official Community languages in 1982) and of the importance of the European Community as a sponsor and supporter of the pan-European service.

But other ORF innovations in re-languaging were less controversial; notably its use of teletext. ORF offered these teletext services:

- news headlines in German and English
- weather maps
- subtitling (e.g. *Falstaff* from Salzburg – broadcast in the original Italian with German/English subtitles)
- newsflashes
- road reports from around Europe.

ORF also screened text to accompany speech in the news and some other programmes. The children's programme *Der Verschwender* (The Spendthrift) and the opera *Falstaff* were given teletext titles: *Der Verschwender* in Italian and English and *Falstaff* in German and English. Thus German-speaking viewers of *Der Verschwender* was able to watch in their native language uninterrupted by subtitles, whereas an English- or Italian-speaker (endowed with a suitable tele- text decoder) was able to select teletext titles. An Italian-speaker would have been able to listen to *Falstaff* in Italian whereas English- and German-speakers could retrieve teletext titles in their own languages. But, the benefits conferred by teletext came with a cost. ORF found that teletext titling (not including translation) required up to eight hours of titling work for each programme hour. It estimated that 'If there are no special dialogues one hour of programme can be subtitled within two days' (Zurek letter 7.10.82). The IBA was less optimistic.

An IBA official estimated, in the planning stages for Eurikon, that '20 hours of effort would be required to provide just 1 hours programme with an English subtitle (prepared, not instantaneous). Dubbing of programmes, especially drama or light entertainment, could take just as long' (Waddington to Clarke

23.3.82). Nonetheless, in spite of its formidable cost, the Operations Group judged ORF's innovations in teletext 'very successful – the original language was left uninterrupted, and the choice of subtitles was optional. Also more than six languages could be transmitted simultaneously as an extra language would only require an extra page for transmission' (EBU/OTS Operations Group 1983: 20).

### Alternative strategies: NOS and ARD

The fourth and fifth, NOS and ARD, weeks of the Eurikon experiment explored another approach to re-languaging. Instead of *interpreting* programmes NOS and ARD attempted to *translate* programmes to viewers in different language communities. NOS dubbed voice-overs using professional actors and actresses (and a variety of voices), attributing female voice-overs to females shown in vision and male voices to males shown (whereas the IBA and RAI weeks had not matched the sex of the interpreter to that of the person on screen). Or, alternatively, followed ORF's precedent providing comprehensive and accurate teletext titles. Wim Hohage – the Head of Translation at NOS (telex to Wright 9.3.83: 1), estimated that 'approximately 50 per cent of all programmes were prepared in advance in this way'.[14]

NOS transmitted an average of five pages of teletext (in addition to the normal teletext service on the NOS terrestrial service) especially for Eurikon. Wim Hohage (in an undated note to the Operations Group which internal evidence suggests was written in late summer 1982) argued for titling rather than dubbing as a standard for re-languaging. 'If the EBU wishes to produce a European satellite programme to compete with the commercial stations a deci-sion about dubbing versus sub-titling will have to be made. One relevant factor is that the cost of dubbing – necessitating the use of actors and recording studios – is 6 to 8 times the cost of sub-titling. . . . Also, translations for sub-titles can be produced many times faster than those needed for post-synching'.

Hohage argued (perhaps with a touch of special pleading) that subtitling would promote European integration better than dubbing. 'Sub-titling offers the viewer the possibility of hearing and absorbing the language of the original while reading the translation . . . Dutch viewers appreciate the educational value of sub-titling. Being able to hear the original increases their linguistic awareness and may lead to further language learning and, eventually, to greater European integration'. Yet, in spite of Hohage's enthusiasm for teletext, the NOS based Europa service did not use teletext.[15]

About fifty of the programmes screened in the NOS week were re-languaged before transmission, thus leaving time and human resources available to deal with late arriving pre-recorded programmes and live programmes. None the less, the NOS system also had conspicuous disadvantages. Rob Golding's report,[16] to the Board of Central Television (Golding 1982) stressed the intractable difficulties of re-languaging. He paid tribute to NOS' elaborate methods but recognised the melancholy trade-off between successful re-languaging and news values: what the 'programme gained in translation it lost in topicality' (EBU/OTS Operations Group 1983: 20). Golding also identified another intractable problem of pan-European television. He wrote 'A preview of Spanish elections on the eve of polling probably broke Spanish law, which demands a day's grace from campaigning, reporting and general politicking. Equally American reportage of the Cheltenham secrets case couldn't legally be taken and rebroadcast because it would have constituted contempt of court in Britain' (Golding 1982: 6–7).

Hohage summarised the Operations Group's evolving understanding of re-languaging:

> England bore the brunt of the OTS experiment. Experience then proved that they had underestimated the matter of translations . . . each programme that is produced for a pan-European broadcasting [sic], necessarily bears the mark of its makers, of the country of origin. The 'mother' tongue, for the greater part, determines the atmosphere, the character of the programme. By dubbing a programme, it loses a lot of its animation. When using voice over texts to translate emotional dialogues, you create a sobering analysis of what's going on which makes the whole picture worthless. Nature films or observations and contemplations, for instance, can stand voice over. In this respect news programmes, which are factual topics, are very suitable for voice over because of their very to-the-point nature and therefore necessarily impersonal note. In live broadcasting, voice over or simultaneous translations would fit very well. England has experienced that inter-preters are not trained in simultaneously translating plays, let alone difficult to understand dialects. Voice over in these cases is in principle totally unacceptable and dubbing, even when done by actors trained for this purpose, is out of the question for the reasons already mentioned. Undertitles, on the other hand, do not impair the produc-tion in any sense and also have an educational value: by watching a 'foreign' production and hearing that language, whilst being able to read what is being said, foreign languages become familiar and thus a piece of culture. . . . Finally the expense: dubbing a one-hour feature film costs in the range of 25,000 to 30,000 guilders, undertitles cost about 6,000! When using compatible equipment, including teletext, a truly pan-European broadcasting company is possible in optimal form.
> (Hohage in *Eurikon Pan European Experiment* Televizier AVRObode 25–31 October 1982: 22)

Barrand wrote privately to Clarke on 22 January 1983 to review Eurikon's news output (Barrand 1983a). He argued that in-shot presenters not only gave rise to intractable problems in marrying sound and image but also signalled an inequality in status between viewers of different language communities. 'The on screen presence of any kind of moderator, whether for news or continuity, imposes a "dominant language." But that "dual language" presentation [as in the ORF experiment] appears to slow down the system, by presenting the same information twice . . . applying culture shock to other nationals, or boredom, or even insult' (Barrand 1983a: 1). Barrand went on to assert that 'The lesson of the NOS week was: it is possible to deliver a good news programme with a selection of different language channels, each an authoritative rendering of the day's news. . . . For me at least after the NOS week, translation is the key, rather than interpretation . . . all the interpreters employed during the experiment found it impossible at one time or another to render accurately what they heard. Mistakes were bound to happen: mistakes of the kind which, projected into the future, could lead a development of Eurikon News into legal trouble. . . . We have proved that interpretation lacks the control and discipline of a news programme; it is in fact beyond control' (Barrand 1983a: 1–2). But he continued: 'I have seen no serious graphics input since the London week. There is serious confusion about how to design maps and what written information should appear on them and in what language' (Barrand 1983a: 3).

The ARD followed the re-languaging precedents of its Eurikon partners (see Reiler 1983; and Hohage, telex to Wright 9.3.83). The ARD host broadcaster, Sud West Funk, used simultaneous translation,[17] and transmitted programmes re-languaged in German, English, French, Italian, Dutch, Spanish and, on one evening, Arabic.[18] Sud West Funk also translated programmes into English, Dutch and Italian using 'additional translators and professional voices'. The ARD therefore used 'a mixture of the ORF/OTS week (exclusively interpreters) and of the NOS/OTS week (exclusively translators and professional voices)' (Reiler 1983: 1).

Hohage judged Sud West Funk's re-languaging inferior to NOS'. In fact, the ARD had returned to something close to the IBA/RAI system with all its disadvantages. Local translators worked straight from scripts which were 'Translated at very short notice, just before the actual broadcast' (telex to Wright 9.3.83: 2). Moreover the physical separation of news editors (in Hamburg) from programme and translation staff (in Baden-Baden) made for great difficulties. Hohage commented 'A large number of news items and interviews were not accompanied by a typed-out text and had to be interpreted live during transmission. The difference in quality between these and the translations made in advance was remarkable. (A more persuasive plea for the translation methods chosen in Holland cannot be given). A number of programmes could not be translated at all due to lack of time, and the organising editors considered them unsuitable for simultaneous translation. They were transmitted as they were' (Telex to Wright 9.3.83: 2).

## The language lessons of the Eurikon experiment

Hohage concluded that successful re-languaging required:

1   Pre-production was a must, since advance preparation made it possible to pay proper attention to news items and current affairs programmes as they arrived.
2   Only professional translations and professional broadcasting voices can guarantee good quality and ensure that the viewer realises that care has gone into the programme.
3   It is essential that all the material (word-perfect scripts, film or video-tape) is supplied as early as possible.
4   Employing free-lance translators and voices increases flexibility.
5   Interpreters are unsuitable for doing simultaneous translations of television programmes (see point 2). An exception may be made in the case of live interviews and live panel discussions.

(Hohage, telex to Wright 9.3.83: 1–2)

His conclusions were widely shared, [19] the Eurikon team concluded that:

1   Conference interpreters cannot offer a standard of voice-over tolerable to a television public.
2   The original sound of a programme should be respected and preserved as much as possible.
3   Translation and interpretation cannot be tacked on at the end of the production line; pre-production is essential for all but news and current affairs programmes.
4   A special production team under a translation manager should be recruited with experience in translation and television. Translators and editors should be in the same building.
5   Teletext subtitling works but is often slow.
6   Production staff require continuous access to expertise in translation and interpretation.
7   Programmes with a high visual content are easier to handle than those with a high talk content.

(summarised from EBU/OTS Operations Group 1983: 21)

Barrand, Daly, Fleming and Reiler had all recognised that pan-European television required fundamental changes in working practice, new combinations of skills and substantially higher levels of resourcing than was required for single language, 'national' television. Moreover, Eurikon showed that pan-European television entailed development of programme forms and presentational styles unfamiliar to viewers (e.g. presenter-less news). Such novelties were likely to be less attractive to viewers than the forms and styles to which they were accustomed. Only certain kinds of programmes lent themselves to pan-European television services. Hohage mentioned nature documentaries and contemplative or observational programmes because they lent themselves to successful re-languaging. Fleming also concluded that some programmes were better suited to a multi-lingual viewer population: 'Documentaries, very often including interviews, appeared to lend themselves quite well to an interpreting mode' (Fleming 1982: 6).

But entertainment programmes, the staple of European television viewing, were more difficult to represent to viewers in different language communities. Fleming stated 'I have the impression that the essential mood of many of these programmes, characterised by snappy dialogue and pithy language, is practically impossible to convey in other languages and that some of them may not in any case arouse much interest in countries where a different language is spoken' (Fleming 1982: 7).

During the Eurikon experiment considerable resources were devoted to translation, interpretation and novel combinations of written text, sound and vision signals. Yet, in spite of the importance of the problem and the inventiveness of some solutions finding what Dill described 'as the key to the acceptability of the service' (Minutes of the EBU/OTS Operations Group meeting 26.7.82) defeated the Eurikon broadcasters. Subsequent pan-European television services were no more successful.

Eurikon revealed serious technical problems when original sound was combined with voice-overs, especially when original sound on film/video was mixed with translated speech in different languages on multiple soundtracks. Viewers were subjected to a confusing miscellany of sounds, some of which (e.g. natural 'background' sound and voice-over translation) they sought to hear but some of which they sought to filter out (e.g. original speech uttered in an incomprehensible language). The EBU commented (R3/TEST 34 GT V4 123. August 1982: 4) that 'the solution adopted for the provision of audio channels is not suitable for the European programme'. The EBU Technical Centre stated that changes in receiver design and circuitry (so that mixing of original sound and commentary track took place at the point of reception) were required if a satisfactory solution was to be found. 'It is clearly apparent from the above considerations, that the production of a European programme in a relatively large number of languages (more than three or four) and including programme material for which there is no "international sound" available will be severely compromised, or even rendered totally impossible, if an automatic mixing facility is not available within every receiver (R3/TEST 34 GT V4 123. August 1982: 4).

Thus, it became clear, that if pan-European television was to provide programming with synchronous sound and image changes in broadcasters' working practices were required and the enormous installed population of television receivers in European homes required costly change. But, the palpable difficulties of re-languaging, devising an attractive programme mix, and surmounting the diversity of preferences and modes of behaviour of European television viewers experienced with Eurikon did not dissuade the EBU and leading European public service broadcasters from progressing to the next stage in pan-European public service satellite television. That this service, Europa, was launched (and that other comparable services continue to be put into operation), suggests that political 'push' by European unionists and European public service broadcasters to advance their institutional and ideological interests was, and is, more important in determining outcomes than was and is the 'pull' exerted by European television viewers.

# 10

# THE AUDIENCE FOR PAN-EUROPEAN TELEVISION

It is clear that the pattern of change in the amount and distribution of television viewing across different countries in Europe is a variable and complex one. Not all European domestic audiences, especially in the west, have exhibited the same response to the introduction of new television channels made available through cable systems or direct broadcasting by satellite. Thus, even with the increasing internationalisation of television systems, there is no emerging, overwhelming commonality of viewing behaviour.

(Gunter 1991: 20)

The Eurikon and Europa experiments clarified two vexed questions. They showed how far the traditions and established values of public service broadcasting were viable in European broadcasting's new circumstances; and, whether the technological potentiality of satellite television to deliver a pan-European television service could be successfully realised. Eurikon can be considered a successful experiment, in that the experience it conferred provided a sound basis for assessment of implementing an operational service. That the progenitors of Eurikon chose not to learn the lessons it taught is another matter. However, Europa must be judged a botched experiment for it only reinforced lessons which Eurikon had already taught. Why did European public service broadcasters require the agonising lessons of Europa to re-experience what Eurikon had foreshadowed?

Eurikon showed that there were no serious technological obstacles to pan-European television, that the established working relationships between public service broadcasters within the EBU (and the significant reservoirs of trust and mutual confidence that decades of collaboration within the EBU had conferred) were more than equal to the challenging task of rapidly commissioning an unprecedentedly new service. However, Eurikon also showed that the costs of establishing pan-European satellite television services were considerably higher than had been envisaged, that re-languaging programmes was not only expensive but intimidatingly difficult, and that when exposed to mixed programming pan-European public service television European viewers did not like it.

Europa taught further uncomfortable lessons. True, some were new. Europa showed that vertical schedules were unsuitable for the new European television markets, that the priorities of European public service broadcasters were, when push came to shove, with their terrestrial services and a pan-European service came a poor second, that better management and marketing were required, and that the size of the pan-European advertising market had been overestimated. But most of the lessons of Europa were old lessons. What Eurikon had already taught was relearned in the most painful fashion: the costs of a service which conformed to the stipulations of public service broadcasters far outweighed the resources that could be won from viewers; viewers' demand for more sport and/or entertainment were the antithesis of the demands of European political elites and European public broadcasters; and, above all, viewers' tastes and interests were resolutely national.

Eurosport showed that the EBU had drawn appropriate conclusions from its two prior experiments. Eurosport was established as a strongly branded thematic channel. As proponents of a themed channel had insisted, this configuration enabled viewers to develop firm expectations about the service – and to have them satisfied. It launched Eurosport in partnership with a commercial partner endowed with a track record of successful marketing and management. And it drew on a hitherto poorly exploited EBU asset – its sports programme resources. The EBU built Eurosport around one of public service broadcasting's most notable strengths and competitive advantages and was thus able to draw into its third satellite ventures the two hardest nosed sceptics among its members – the BBC and ZDF. However, Eurosport's business strategy could not easily be reconciled either with the historical vocation of European public service broadcasting or with DG IV's stipulations.

With Euronews the EBU returned, at least in part, to strategies shown by Eurikon and Europa to be likely to fail. Like Eurosport, Euronews has a strong brand identity and drew on solid EBU strengths; but, like Eurikon and Europa, Euronews addressed an imagined entity – the pan-European interested in news, events, weather and the like across the whole of Europe. Namely, a viewer prepared to accept programming tailored not to her or his specific national context, language and expectations but to a chimerical 'European' identity. However, like Eurikon and Europa, Euronews' programming seemed eminently compatible with public service broadcasting's unique mission to inform and educate viewers so that they were able to participate fully in political life. With Euronews, unlike Eurikon and Europa, the EBU was able to draw on funding from European (and national) political sources to sustain the service (although public service broadcasting's consequential dependency on governments offended many). But Euronews' viability and value to viewers remain to be demonstrated.

Gunter's statement that there is 'no emerging, overwhelming communality of viewing behaviour' (Gunter 1991: 20),[1] attests to the most important finding of research on European television viewing in the 1980s. The EBU (and commercial) pan-European satellite channels constituted an empirical test of the hypothesis, or hope, that there was a transnational European community of television viewers bound by a common culture. Gunter's social scientific audience studies spelt out the findings and sounded a death knell for the hope that television would be a powerful instrument to foster European union. European television viewers seemed neither to possess the latent collective European identity (which lacked only a medium of expression – which pan-European television would provide – for its realisation), nor to represent a kind of identity vacuum (which pan-European television would fill and endow viewers with the collective identity they had hitherto lacked). Research revealed strongly marked national patterns of collective viewing behaviour. Patterns, or identities, which had to be overcome if pan-European television was to work – either commercially (by attracting audiences and revenues sufficient to make pan-European services profitable) or politically and culturally (by developing a pan-European collective identity in viewers). The strength of established national broadcasting services and of the national languages and cultures of the communities they served meant that pan-European television was too weak to overcome national viewing preferences and behaviour.

Eurikon was defined by the EBU's Group of Programme Experts as an experiment with the goal of 'carrying out research designed to assess possible audience reaction to such a service and its impact on existing national services' (Minutes of Meeting of Programme Experts in Geneva 21.1.82 SPG 1806). An extensive programme of audience research, almost certainly the first research conducted on the reception of satellite television in Europe and an extensive programme by any standards, accompanied Eurikon. This research provided the first evidence of viewers' responses to an actual, rather than a hypothetical, satellite television service and extended and deepened broadcasters' understanding of European television audiences and was undertaken in a representative set of European broadcasting markets.[2]

## Eurikon audience research

The Eurikon Operations Group recognised the importance of audience research in testing the viability of an operational pan-European satellite television service.[3] It identified five research questions:

- Does the audience perceive the Eurikon programme schedule to be more internationally European orientated than the national television channels?

- Does the audience perceive the Eurikon programme schedule to be complementary to the national television channels, offering something additional rather than more of the national same?

- What does the audience consider particularly strong points and particularly weak points in the Eurikon programme schedule and what is the audience appreciation of a full evening's programme schedule as a whole (rather than of the individual programmes)?

- What is the audience appreciation of the Eurikon programme schedule's language accessibility through voice-over and/or (teletext) subtitling techniques in about seven languages simultaneously?

- Finally, what might be the future audience interest in watching such a Eurikon programme?

(EBU/OTS Operations Group 1983: 23)

Researchers from the participating broadcasters met in Geneva on 9 March 1982 to assess 'possible audience reaction to such a service and its impact on existing national services' (EBU/OTS Operations Group 1983: 22). They defined the main objective of their study as testing 'the comprehensibility of the programmes' (Conclusions of the Research Group. Note of meeting). Four of the participating broadcasters (IBA, NOS, RAI, RTE) adopted a common research design.[4]

> The research design involved about fifty test persons per country watching a sixty-minute tape compilation of four hours of a 'typical' Eurikon evening programme schedule. Test persons were males and females, age 18–55, from upper as well as lower social classes and living in an urban setting. While watching the compilation, test persons had at their disposal a programme guide showing title and real time of each programme in the compilation. After watching this tape – containing mainly voice-over translations – as well as a ten-minute tape containing subtitled clips, test persons recorded their appreciation of Eurikon in questionnaires where spontaneous reactions could be written in.
>
> (de Bock 1983: 1)[5]

### UK research

UK research on viewer responses to Eurikon programming was directed by Dr Barrie Gunter (a research officer at the IBA and later head of research at the ITC) using the common research design. The IBA sought viewer reactions to a compilation of programme extracts representative of a Eurikon evening. Preliminary findings (Gunter 1982a, 1982b) were made available to the Operations Group in July 1982 and considered at its meeting in Strasbourg in October 1982. These findings were revised and published in December 1982 (Gunter 1982) and January 1983 (Gunter 1983).

The UK research was undertaken in two stages. Respondents were first exposed to a selection of programming taken from the first, IBA, and second, RAI, weeks of the Eurikon experiment.[6] These selections were designed 'to give respondents an opportunity to form a general impression about Eurikon' (Gunter 1982: 3). They were then asked to rate Eurikon programmes in comparison to UK terrestrial television programming using seventeen variables through multiple-choice questions. Their responses are given in Table 10.1.

UK viewers did not view Eurikon as a distinctive channel. Numerical values (which express the sum of viewer responses) tend to cluster around the mid point of the five point scale used and few values fell far from it. Respondents perceived Eurikon to be less violent and more irritable (whatever that may mean) than ITV; less worthwhile than BBC1 and BBC2; and more international than all four of the UK terrestrial television channels. The IBA's findings were echoed by RAI and NOS (RAI 1983: 26 and 29; NOS 1983: 20).

British, Dutch and Italian respondents seldom identified striking differences between Eurikon and the television of their own country (using the bi-polar scales). However, when evaluating Eurikon, the viewers in the UK, in Italy and in the Netherlands expressed emphatic, often negative, judgements. UK research on the second, RAI, week of programmes found that 'six out of ten

*Table 10.1* Tabulation of viewers' responses to comparative evaluation of Eurikon with British TV channels

| | Eurikon compared with | | | | |
|---|---|---|---|---|---|
| | BBC1 | BBC2 | ITV | C4 | |
| Interesting 5 | 2.2 | 2.0 | 2.1 | 2.2 | Boring 1 |
| Serious 1 | 2.5 | 2.1 | 2.6 | 2.6 | Light-hearted 5 |
| Unusual 5 | 2.6 | 2.3 | 2.4 | 2.6 | Commonplace 1 |
| Cheerful 5 | 2.5 | 2.5 | 2.3 | 2.2 | Sad 1 |
| Violent 5 | 2.1 | 2.4 | 1.8 | 2.1 | Non-Violent 1 |
| Relaxing 1 | 2.4 | 2.2 | 2.7 | 2.3 | Arousing 5 |
| Difficult to follow 5 | 3.4 | 2.5 | 2.6 | 2.8 | Easy to follow 1 |
| Humorous 5 | 2.1 | 2.0 | 1.9 | 2.4 | Irritable 1 |
| Unenjoyable 1 | 2.9 | 2.6 | 2.6 | 2.5 | Enjoyable 5 |
| Important 5 | 2.1 | 2.1 | 2.2 | 2.5 | Trivial 1 |
| Dull 1 | 2.9 | 2.5 | 2.4 | 2.9 | Exciting 5 |
| Noisy 5 | 2.5 | 2.4 | 2.1 | 2.2 | Quiet 1 |
| Worthwhile 5 | 1.9 | 1.8 | 2.2 | 2.4 | Worthless 1 |
| Pleasant 5 | 2.2 | 2.2 | 2.1 | 2.6 | Unpleasant 1 |
| National 5 | 1.1 | 1.4 | 1.3 | 1.7 | International 1 |
| Slow 1 | 2.7 | 2.1 | 2.8 | 2.4 | Fast 5 |
| Something for everybody 5 | 2.1 | 2.2 | 2.2 | 2.7 | Only cater for special groups |
| Good variety of programmes 5 | 2.1 | 2.1 | 2.1 | 2.3 | Poor variety of programmes 1 |

*Note*: Respondents were asked to use a five point scale when articulating their responses to the questions. The mid point in the scale (scoring three) was identified as 'virtually no difference', adjacent points (scoring two and four) were identified as 'a bit more' and the boundary points (scoring one and five) were identified as 'much more'.

viewers on the panel felt that the selection of programmes available on Eurikon was boring compared with those usually found on British television' (Gunter 1982: 5, 1982b: 3). Research on the first, IBA, week of the Eurikon service had shown 'that the majority of panel members judged Eurikon's choice of programmes to be worse than that on each British TV network' and that 'nearly 80 per cent of the panel said that they would watch Eurikon less than once a week if at all' (Gunter 1982a: 3, 1982: 11 and 12).

Drawing on UK subjects' responses to the IBA and RAI weeks Gunter gave a melancholy answer to the question '[A]re there any indications that a new European TV service such as Eurikon is welcomed and would be viewed by people in Britain?'

> The findings of the current experiments do not unfortunately offer much encouragement. Many more people from both panels who took part in these studies considered *Eurikon* in unfavourable terms than who looked upon it favourably. . . . It also needs to be borne in mind that . . . the samples were not representative. Instead both panels were heavily weighted towards better educated ABC1 people. Given that it is this section of the population at which Eurikon is primarily targeted, the fact that so few said they would be likely to watch, or said that they liked what they saw offers even less encouragement.
>
> (Gunter 1982: 15)

Moreover, Gunter's report closed with a poor prognosis for pan-European services:

> Intentions to watch before a new service comes into operation do not always match up with actual viewing behaviour . . . a survey . . . carried out by the IBA's Research Department indicated that optimistic state- ments about Channel Four were agreed with. . . . Despite this apparent optimism, however, the early viewing figures for Channel Four show that very many of its programmes are attracting very small audiences. If the same pattern follows for Eurikon, for which the numbers of expected viewers are already small, *actual* viewing figures for the service in its current form could be very low indeed.
>
> (Gunter 1982: 16)

UK researchers' melancholy findings were echoed by their Italian colleagues.

### *Italian research*

RAI undertook two research projects. One closely followed the common research plan (in which fifty respondents viewed a compilation of Eurikon programmes) (RAI 1983), but the second, more extensive, enquiry used a sample of 210 respondents who considered all the Eurikon output; this study was the most extensive research undertaken on Eurikon (1983a).

The first study showed that Italian viewers' response to Eurikon was 'decidedly unfavourable'. Respondents identified the 'following defects' in Eurikon programmes: they were, uninteresting, boring, worthless, trivial, incomprehensible, incomplete and inferior to RAI programmes (RAI 1983: 20). However RAI found (in contrast to the IBA) that respondents of different social classes responded differently to the different forms of re-languaging (subtitling, dubbing etc.). Here, 'positive judgements were expressed almost exclusively by those respondents belonging to the upper-middle and upper classes' (1983: 32). However even these, upper and upper-middle class viewers' judgements were mostly negative.

Broadly, RAI's research showed that Italians shared British dissatisfaction with Eurikon's programming. 'On the whole two thirds of the people interviewed in all four weeks declared that the Italian audience would have been unsatisfied [sic] with the evening proposed by the European channel' and 'even the Italian week met with a substantially negative judgement' (RAI 1983a: 20). RAI found that 'the degree of dissatisfaction resulted to be substantially the same in all the demographic and behavioral segments that were subjected to the parametric analysis, even though the interviewed people belonging to an upper socio-economic class resulted to be more dissatisfied than the rest' (1983a: 20).

Yet, in spite of respondents' generally adverse judgements, Italian researchers found a marked enthusiasm for a European channel in Italy. The researchers commented 'it is an idea that "fascinates" the Italian audience, especially on account of the role it may play within the framework of a progressive strengthening of the European Community relations' (RAI 1983a: 32). Possibly Italian respondents' enthusiasm was more closely linked to Italians' generally favourable perception of the European Community and European unification than to the Eurikon channel.[7] RAI supported Gunter's conclusion that there was a need to 're-think . . . programming policies' (Gunter 1983: 14). RAI urged change: 'The prevailing opinions in respect of the various scheduled broadcasts uniformly point to the excessive presence of cultural and information programs and the scarce attention paid to actual entertainment' (RAI 1983a: 22).

### Dutch research

Dutch viewers found Eurikon more attractive than did UK and Italian viewers.[8] They liked Eurikon for:

- its international and informative character
- its greater depth and variety
- greater length of transmission time
- special items and 'On the Road in Europe'[9] in particular.

194

They disliked Eurikon for:

- its absence of anything new
- its voice-over translations
- an uninteresting and dull programme mix
- its international and informative character
- its disorderly and superficial coverage.

(Derived from NOS 1983: 5)

Dutch viewers therefore *both welcomed and disliked* the international and informative character of Eurikon programmes. Their judgement is only superficially paradoxical. Programmes which elicit high indices of appreciation from some viewers may be strongly disliked by others. Indeed, programmes (and channels) with marked characteristics tend to provoke emphatic responses from viewers, whether negative or positive. However, Dutch respondents, like their UK and Italian equivalents, found Eurikon less attractive than the terrestrial channels with which they were familiar (and with which any pan-European service had to compete). NOS found that 'they will spend less time viewing Eurikon than they spend viewing other channels' (derived from NOS 1983: 7).

Viewers responded strongly to Eurikon's different types of re-languaging. But, here too, there were significant national differences. Italian viewers favoured dubbing – 'this translation system met with the favour of test viewers because it was more natural and familiar to them than subtitling' (RAI 1983: 31). Whereas Dutch viewers disliked dubbing – 'they think it confusing, annoying, irritating, dull, unnatural etc.' (NOS 1983: 27). UK viewers' responses to dubbing were close, but not the same as, Dutch viewers'. UK research found that '[T]wo-thirds . . . [of respondents] . . . felt . . . that this technique of translation would not be acceptable for regular TV viewing' (Gunter 1983: 9). The different responses of the national viewer groups seem best explained as an expression of each group's preference for the re-languaging system with which it was familiar. Italian viewers are used to dubbing, Dutch viewers are used to subtitling, UK audiences are used to television made in English and are unready to accept any form of re-languaging.

### Austrian, Swiss and Portuguese research

Research on Eurikon was also undertaken in Austria, Switzerland and Portugal. None of this research conformed to the standard research design, but it contained (as the Operations Group report put it), 'elements relevant for purpose [*sic*] of the cross national project' (EBU/OTS 1983: 22). RTP undertook extensive research on Portuguese viewers' responses to Eurikon and screened the whole week of ARD programming (except the programmes transmitted on the evening of Thursday 25 November 1982), to eighty-two subjects. Viewers watched complete evenings of Eurikon transmissions (with a

195

thirty-minute dinner break). However, in spite of the different research methodology findings were similar to those elicited elsewhere. Portuguese viewers were ill disposed towards Eurikon's output:

> 44 pour cent des participants ont signalé que la session à laquelle ils venaient d'assister ne leur avait fait aucune impression – ni favorable ni défavorable. Les autres résultats obtenus ont été plutôt négatifs: pour 32 pour cent des spectateurs l'émission ne leur avait pas beaucoup plu ou même pas du tout, tandis que 24 per cent déclaraient qu'elle leur avait beaucoup plu ou vivement plu. [44 per cent of participants indicated that the session in which they had participated had made no impression on them – favourable or unfavourable. The remaining responses were somewhat negative: 32 per cent of viewers had either not responded favourably to the transmission at all or had not found it particularly pleasing, whilst 24 per cent stated that they had responded favourably or very favourably.]
>
> (RTP 1983: 3)

Indeed, most Portuguese viewers did not fully understand Eurikon transmissions (RTP 1983: 3) largely due to the imperfections in the ARD voice-over translations. Sixty-three per cent of Portuguese respondents favoured subtitling (1983: 11) and 78 per cent rejected the ARD's 'vertical schedule' (1983: 12).[10]

Only about a quarter of the Portuguese sample liked Eurikon and their enthusiasm was balanced by the dislike expressed by about a third of viewers. The largest single group of Portuguese viewers expressed neither positive or negative responses. Given that the Portuguese were almost alone in Europe in having access to only a single national television channel their temperate response to the alternative presented by Eurikon did not bode well for the success of a similar operational service.

## Conclusions

De Bock summarised the findings from research on viewers' perception of Eurikon, he emphasised the positive elements of subjects' responses:

> Depending on the extent to which national television carries foreign programs, Eurikon is considered moderately to quite different from the national channels both in content and in form. Viewers see Eurikon as more international, more informative, more cultural and more serious.

and that

Eurikon's international character is considered its most distinguishing element. Viewers spontaneously recognize its possibilities to support the development of the European community and to break through barriers of nationalistic feelings.

However

Eurikon's voice-over translation techniques as tested in 1982 are heavily criticized because of professional and technical imperfections; voice-over translation is not acceptable for regular viewing unless its quality equals national dubbing standards. If not, subtitling of high quality is the better choice for translation.

(de Bock 1983: 2)

In spite of de Bock's delicate drafting, research findings did not auger well for future services. De Bock concluded: first, 'solving the language accessibility problem is essential for Eurikon's future . . . continuing the 1982 developments in voice-over and subtitling translation techniques should be high on the priority list'; second, 'Eurikon news has the potential of becoming one of its more important programs . . . the Eurikon news formula should include: efforts to increase the viewers' familiarity with the European institutions, attempts to *explain* the European interdependence, items which clarify national conse- quences of European policy making, stressing once more Europe's very personal relevance to the individual viewer', and; third, 'Eurikon's popularity will increase by including into the program schedule a larger share of light information and entertainment fare' (de Bock 1983: 3).

De Bock's conclusions (on the importance of solving the language problem, the attractiveness of news and the importance of entertainment programming) were incorporated into the Operations Group's report. The Operations Group drew a fourth conclusion from the audience research, it concerned 'national sensitivity'. The Operations Group asserted that 'Eurikon should regularly contain programmes on all countries it considers its direct market. So, viewers in these countries will come to see Eurikon as "also our channel" and not "just another foreign channel"' (EBU/OTS Operations Group 1983: 34).

In spite of viewers' very qualified enthusiasm for Eurikon the Operations Group claimed that audience research had shown that viewers would welcome a pan-European service. Clarke reported to the EBU's Working Party on Television News that Eurikon had

in general, been considered a success. Of a total of 200 hours of programmes during five non-consecutive weeks, originated by five different organisations (UKIB, RAI, ORF, NOS, and ARD), 40 per cent had been devoted to information. Ninety-nine per cent of the information material had been compiled from material supplied by

EBU members or news agencies, the remaining 1 per cent being provided by the European Parliament and the Council of Europe. Research conducted in seven of the 15 countries participating in the 1982 experiments had shown that viewers recognized the Eurikon service as distinct from their national services, as distinctively European and as an additional option which they would welcome.

(Com.TV/GT TV News (r) SPG 2136/Feb.83: 20)

Moreover, Clarke continued, 'the 1982 Eurikon experiments had shown that a pan-European television service was, despite some outstanding problems, feasible and that it would be welcomed by viewers as a complementary but not competitive national service' (Com.TV/GT TV News (r) SPG 2136/Feb.83: 21).[11]

Clarke's account of audience research findings painted Eurikon in rosier colours than research findings actually warranted. Researchers found less enthusiasm for the Eurikon service, and less hope for pan-European satellite television, than the elites which supported and orchestrated the pan-European services wished. In consequence research findings which cast doubt on the strategy of establishing pan-European satellite television services did not receive the attention which they deserved. The EBU's Television Programme Committee's judgement that the Eurikon experiments had yielded 'extremely positive' results (Com TV. SPG 2081 19.10.82) cannot be reconciled with the judgement of the UK researcher, who conducted the IBA research on audience responses to the Eurikon service, that '[T]he findings of the current experiments do not unfortunately offer much encouragement' (Gunter 1982: 15).

Three main findings emerged from audience research on pan-European television. It revealed marked *differences* in the attitudes, preferences and behaviour of television viewers in different European countries; weaker linkages between television viewing and attitudes towards Europe and European union than had been supposed; and less enthusiasm for pan-European satellite television among viewers than the proponents of the new services had been wont to suggest. In the light of this evidence the pan-European EBU satellite television channels of the 1980s may appear perverse enterprises, inspired by entrenched public service broadcasters' obdurate commitment to time honoured practices and by a blinkered ideological enthusiasm of European unionists rather than by intelligent concern for the needs and interests of European television viewers. But such a view is tenable only with hindsight. Much of what we now know derives from studies undertaken during or after the pan-European experiments which form the principal focus of this study.

The findings from these studies which, almost without exception, were unfriendly to pan-European initiatives and which showed how *different* were European television viewers were not available to those who initiated the EBU's stream of successive satellite television initiatives with Eurikon. However, evidence from Eurikon *was* available to those who launched Europa, Eurosport and Euronews. That pan-European public service satellite television has continued after the findings of the Eurikon experiment and the Europa debacle testifies to the strength of political and institutional considerations. These were the imperatives which drove European broadcasters and proponents of European union to persist with pan-European television when research findings had shown that such ventures were unlikely to succeed.

## Differences in European television audiences

The first transnational comparative survey of European television audiences (conducted in 1987 by PETAR – Pan European Television Audience Research – a consortium supported by several, mostly commercial, European satellite television enterprises) found marked differences in the viewing behaviour of satellite television viewers in different countries. PETAR examined the responses of viewers in various European countries to the UK based commercial satellite channel Super Channel. It found striking differences in viewers' response to a common television programme schedule, as seen in Table 10.2.

Not only did the most popular Super Channel programmes achieve strikingly low audience shares in each of the national markets shown, but audiences in different countries appear to have valued different Super Channel programmes most highly. The PETAR findings suggest that a change to the schedule of a transnational channel designed to appeal to the preferences of viewers in one market (and therefore build audience share for the channel), was unlikely to build, and might even lose, the channel's share in other markets. To screen more programmes of the *European Top 40* type *might* reinforce viewing in Switzerland but a quite different strategy (perhaps screening more programmes of the *Benny Hill* type), seemed likely to be required if audience share in the Netherlands were to be increased.

## Souchon's findings

Other studies also identified profound differences in the behaviour and preferences of European television viewers. Souchon, in a study for the Assises européennes de l'audiovisuel (1989: 77–92) found significant differences in the behaviour of television viewers in Francophone Belgium, France, Hungary, Netherlands, Poland, Spain, Sweden and the UK (BBC only) in 1987. Souchon classified broadcasters' programme offer and viewing behaviour for four types of programmes; education and culture, information, fiction and other entertainment.

In all West European countries Souchon found that fiction and entertainment were the most watched categories of programming. However, how much these two categories of programmes were viewed varied from country to country (precise percentages are impossible to identify from Souchon's bar charts – but these categories of programmes accounted for between 55 per cent

*Table 10.2*  The marked differences in the viewing behaviour of satellite television viewers in different countries

| | Average shares | | |
|---|---|---|---|
| Men aged 16+ | (%) | Women aged 16 + | (%) |
| Netherlands | | | |
| *Benny Hill* | 2.9 | *Benny Hill* | 1.8 |
| *Kenny Everett* | 1.8 | *Mistrals Daughter* (US mini series) | 1.3 |
| *Survival* | 1.6 | *Kenny Everett* | 1.3 |
| *Super Sport* | 1.4 | *Armchair Adventure* | 1.2 |
| West Germany | | | |
| *Spitting Image* | 2.1 | *Life on Earth* | 0.8 |
| *News* | 0.9 | *Wild World* | 0.8 |
| *News* | 0.7 | *Shirley Bassey* | 0.7 |
| *News* | 0.7 | *Great Railway Journeys* | 0.7 |
| Scandinavia | | | |
| *Benny Hill* | 6.6 | *Benny Hill* | 5.6 |
| *Benny Hill* | 5.3 | *Princess Daisy* | 5.4 |
| *Kenny Everett* | 4.7 | *Mistral's Daughter* | 5.2 |
| *Princess Daisy* | 4.1 | *Limestreet* | 3.7 |
| Belgium | | | |
| *Super Sport* | 1.8 | *News* | 1.0 |
| *Super Sport* | 1.8 | *Princess Daisy* | 1.0 |
| *Super Sport* | 1.8 | | |
| *Princess Daisy* | 0.9 | | |
| Switzerland | | | |
| *European Top 40* | 1.8 | *European Top 40* | 0.9 |
| *Countdown* | 0.9 | | |
| *Living Body* | 1.1 | | |
| *Busman's Holiday* | 0.9 | | |

*Source*: PETAR survey March – April 1987

and 65 per cent of viewing). But although viewers everywhere principally used television for entertainment, Souchon found striking differences between viewers in different countries who neither shared tastes in programmes nor ranked the same types of programmes highest in their orders of preference.

In France, films shown at 20:30 have the highest ratings. In the FRG and Great Britain, television series get high scores. Sports and varieties are highly rated in Italy; they come in second in the FRG and have a slightly lesser rating in Great Britain. The FRG gives high ratings to game shows.

(Assises européennes de l'audiovisuel 1989: 90)[12]

Souchon found that markedly less information programming was watched in the Netherlands, Spain and the UK than in Belgium, France and Sweden (c.8, 8, 10 and 18, 18 and 20 per cent respectively (Assises européennes de l'audiovisuel 1989: 88)). And so on. Further research by the Commission of the European Communities also revealed striking differences in Community citizens' use of television. Markedly higher percentages of viewers watched television news daily in Germany (77 per cent), the Netherlands (77 per cent), Ireland (76 per cent), Italy (76 per cent), Luxembourg (75 per cent) and the UK (75 per cent) than did in Portugal (53 per cent), France (58 per cent), Belgium (60 per cent), Denmark (60 per cent), Greece (63 per cent) and Spain (64 per cent) (Commission of the European Communities 1991: A41).

Not only do European viewers watch different programmes but they watch them at different times. Souchon found that in the UK and Spain (and to a lesser extent in France) daytime viewing is high. Whereas in other European countries, where viewing 'is concentrated during specific time periods', it was not. Prime-time varies from country to country but, in most countries, falls between 19:30 and 22:00. But in Spain prime-time peaks between 22:30 and 23:00 (Assises européennes de l'audiovisuel 1989: 83).[13] Ten years after Eurikon, Henri Perez (Director of the EBU Television Programme Department), identified differences in prime-time in different European countries as a major obstacle to the successful establishment of transnational European television services. He stated:

> Viewing habits vary enormously from country to country, beginning with the timing of the prime time period. The further south one goes, the later it is: 19:30 in the UK, 20:30 in France, and around 22:00 hours in Spain.
>
> (Perez in *Espace* No. 12 [1992]: 4)

## Cultural screens and their challenge to broadcasters

The difficulties for a pan-European television service presented by the differences in European viewers' programme tastes, habits of consumption and time budgets need no emphasising. Indeed, the Eurikon Operations Group had been forced to recognise that differences in prime-time and viewing habits from region to region and country to country across Europe made it impossible to co-ordinate a pan-European channel with national channels. Eurikon's (and future services') schedules could not be made to complement, rather than compete with, EBU member broadcasters' established terrestrial services because these services were tailored to the idiosyncratic viewing habits of different countries.

Clearly, if viewers have available, as they have, services which are tailored to their programming and scheduling preferences they are likely to adopt such services in preference to rival services which address a common denominator in European television consumption. Desgraupes, in a study of the possibility of establishing a European satellite television channel devoted to culture (Desgraupes 1985) cited telephone interview research in Belgium, France, Germany, Italy, Netherlands, Spain, Switzerland and the UK in 1985 which showed that 'les téléspectateurs européens ont plutôt une bonne opinion de leurs chaînes de télévision. Les qualitatifs négatifs sont largement compenses par des qualificatifs positifs' [European television viewers have quite a good opinion of their television services. Their negative judgements are outweighed by their positive evaluations] (Desgraupes 1985: 45). The same research showed that few viewers expressed an interest in pan-European programming.

## The pull of national services

During the 1980s, both public service and commercial broadcasters learned how strong was European viewers' commitment to national television services. UK based broadcasters such as Sky Channel and Super Channel, who had blithely believed that, because English was the lingua franca of Europe, they could establish profitable pan-European niche markets, were forced to withdrew from the European market. Satellite television in Europe changed from a pan-European to a national phenomenon. New channels were launched to establish, or intensify, competition in national (or more precisely linguistic) markets rather than to serve chimerical pan-European markets and services (see Collins 1992). Gunter's finding that 'there is no emerging, overwhelming commonality of viewing behaviour' (Gunter 1991: 20) was supported by both research findings and broadcasters' bitter experience.[14]

## Why pan-European television?

But in spite of the weight of research findings, several pan-European satellite television services continued to be launched. Why? Two possible explanations seem valid. First, much of the research cited post dated the launch of the first services. It took the experiments to happen for the findings to be available. But this explanation is not wholly satisfactory. Several services – not least Europa – post dated these findings. A second explanation is therefore required. Here Desgraupes' interpretation of research he commissioned prior to the possible launch of a French pan-European service provides a clue. Degraupes interpreted the finding that 'un tiers du public potentiel du satellite refuse de se laisser enfermer dans le microcosme socio-politique de son propre pays et se déclarer très intéressé par des journaux télévisés en provenance de pays voisins' [a third of the potential public for satellite television refuses to remain shut up inside the boundaries of its own country and expresses a strong interest in television news from neighbouring countries] (Desgraupes 1985: 49), as evidence of European viewers' demand for pan-European television.

However these findings, which Desgraupes cited as evidence of demand for a pan-European cultural satellite television channel, could more plausibly be interpreted negatively. They show that the majority of the European television audience indeed preferred 'de se laisser enfermer dans le microcosme socio-politique de son propre pays' [remain shut up inside the boundaries of its own country]. What the findings show may be interpreted as a glass one-third full, as Desgraupes did, or as a glass two-thirds empty. Clearly, those whose careers depended on development of new ventures, rather than on finding reasons not to do so, might have been predisposed to find glasses one-third full rather than two-thirds empty.

But if, as Desgraupes chose not to think, European television audiences were generally satisfied with their domestic television services then the chances of successfully establishing a competing pan-European service were not encouraging. If, as Souchon found, European viewers principally use television for fiction and entertainment then a channel dedicated to a programme mix emphasising non-fiction and non-entertainment programming invited failure. And if, as Souchon, PETAR and the Commission of the European Communities had found, European viewers do watch television at different times then a common European programme schedule was unlikely to compete successfully against channels tailored to the preferences of viewers in specific national markets. In short, what was (and is) known about European television audiences offered scant encouragement to those who sought to establish pan-European satellite television channels – particularly those (like Eurikon and Europa) with a high proportion of cultural programming. The cherished collective European consciousness and collective identity central to the project of European unionists seemed more evident in unionists' dreams than in the practices of European television viewers.

Research conducted by the Commission of the European Communities suggested that citizens of the European Community display strikingly different attitudes towards the Community. Asked how often they thought of themselves as European, 69 per cent of respondents in the UK answered 'never' whereas only 27 per cent of Luxembourg respondents answered 'never' (Commission of the European Communities 1991: A22).[15] Moreover, respondents in the UK viewed European Community membership less favourably than did respondents in other Community Member States.[16] Although more respondents in the UK than in Luxembourg and Denmark favoured the unification of Western Europe (but fewer in the UK than in the other nine Member States), more in the UK than in any other Community Member State said that they would be 'very relieved' if the European Community was scrapped (Commission of the European Communities 1991: A10 and A11).[17]

How far the differences in sentiment which this research detected are a consequence of the absence of a shared broadcasting service across the

Community (as proponents of European union and of broadcasting as a means to promote union might claim), cannot be known. However, differences in the basic attitudes of Community citizens and in their conceptions of their collective identities suggest both that there is no single, normative, European identity and that (because of European Community citizens' differences in self perception and in their relation to the Community and its institutions), a European broadcasting service that addresses the different experiences and self perceptions of Europeans will either be impossibly diffuse or impossibly normative. In either case such a broadcasting service is likely, at best, to attain only a marginal place in the Community's broadcasting markets.

## Research findings before pan-European television

UNESCO commissioned a seven country study,[18] titled 'Three Weeks of Television' (UNESCO 1982), in 1979 which was carried out using a sample of programmes screened in the winter of 1978–9. The authors found that programming and scheduling characteristic of public service broadcasting does not match viewer preferences well.

> Demand from country to country differs less than supply. Despite the diversity of programme structures and schedules the response is virtually identical. The viewers' 'demand' appears to approximate to the following figures: around 70 per cent entertainment, 21 per cent information and 5 per cent culture and education. Everywhere entertainment is 'over-consumed', the more so in that it is 'undersupplied'. Information, culture and education are everywhere 'under-consumed', the more so for being 'over-supplied'.
>
> (UNESCO 1982: 34)

This mismatch, evident in all the countries studied by the authors of the UNESCO study, served Eurikon and Europa ill (which were set up to extend public service broadcasting's philosophy and practices into the domain of satellite television). A later study by Bekkers (1987) confirmed the UNESCO findings and suggested that the programmes and schedules of the EBU channels were unlikely to appeal strongly to viewers. These findings may not have been available at the time Eurikon was launched but were available to those who supported and ran Europa, as were the findings arising from the Eurikon experiment itself which supported the discouraging findings of other research (e.g. Assises européennes de l'audiovisuel 1989; Desgraupes 1985; PETAR 1987; UNESCO 1982).

Cultural differences between distinct groups of European television viewers were marked and the mixed programme and rather highbrow television schedule characteristic of European public service broadcasters, and on which the Eurikon schedule was modelled, was not well adapted to the attraction and retention of viewers. These findings were reinforced by the direct experience of formidable practical and financial difficulties in re-languaging programmes (to reduce cultural and linguistic discount), during the Eurikon experiment. However, these melancholy findings were either not presented to, or were passed over by those who made the decision to launch an operational pan-European public service satellite television channel, Europa.

# CONCLUSION

European media policy . . . is a touchstone for judging whether the Member States, and public broadcasting corporations, are prepared to take European unification seriously and adopt a common policy on the media.

(European Parliament 1985: 35)

## New technology – new policy

Pan-European public service television was the child of technological innovation. Communication satellites in Clarke orbits made possible television services serving the whole of Europe. The new technology presented European public service broadcasters with both threats and opportunities: the threat of competition and the destruction of their time-honoured monopolies; the opportunity to strengthen European viewers' collective identity and thereby further advance towards 'the ever closer union' prescribed in the Treaty of Rome. It was the public service broadcasters' misfortune that the threat was more potent than the opportunity, and that their belated attempts to meet that threat were insufficient to counter the resurgent power of new commercial services.

Freeman (1994) has identified four stages in technological innovation: incremental; radical; the establishment of new technological systems; and a change in the dominant techno-economic paradigm. Incremental innovation occurs, he argues, within an established technological system. From this point of view, technological change in terrestrial television broadcasting from 1936 (when a regular high definition television transmission service began) to, say, 1992 could be characterised as incremental innovation. The succession of changes between 405 line monochrome and monoaural broadcasting to 625 line colour and stereo broadcasting constituted an incremental series of innovations within an established technological system. In contrast, radical innovation occurs when a new technology is operationalised and in some important sense breaks with related technological systems. Satellite television in Europe in 1982 exemplifies this kind of radical innovation in that it had fundamentally different technological characteristics to those of established terrestrial television services.

Satellite television has not yet realised the third type of innovation which Freeman identified – the establishment of a new technological system. Although one might argue that the striking success of BSkyB's satellite-delivered UK services contradict this assertion. However, the essence of BSkyB's success is not the innovatory transmission technology of satellite television it uses but its innovatory conditional access, payment and charging system; just like the terrestrial pay television services in other national markets. It might be further objected that transnational, indeed pan-European channels such as Eurosport *do* exemplify the successful establishment of a new technological system – cross-border satellite television. Perhaps they do. But if so it is also striking how insignificant they are relative to services addressed to distinct national markets – whether delivered by terrestrial or by other means.

The vision of successful establishment of a new technological paradigm in television continues to hover seductively just out of reach. Any or all of the 'new televisions' deriving from the convergence of hitherto distinct technological domains – telecommunications, television and computing – promise just such a change (although a dial-up video-on-demand service still seems some way away). But, once implemented, such a service will set public service broadcasters further challenges: should they too enter this new territory? Should licence payers money be so risked? Is such a new service an essential part of a public service mandate?

Finally, change in the dominant techno-economic paradigm, the last and most fundamental form of change arising from technological innovation, involves qualitative changes in the attitudes and intellectual paradigms of the humans who use new technologies. Satellite television has yet to engender change of this kind. As Barrand (1982), Daly (1982), Fleming (1982) and Reiler (1982), recognised pan-European television required a new type of person to work in it. A person endowed with a novel combination of journalist's and interpreter's skills and who *thought* differently to journalists and interpreters. But, if *producers* had to be different for pan-European television to work so, *a fortiori*, did viewers. Because this was not the case, pan-European satellite televsion failed.

Freeman's taxonomy illuminates the changes to European television which took place between 1982 and 1992. Satellite television was a *radical* innovation and broadcasters, notably the European public service broadcasters, accustomed, for the most part, to incremental innovation found it difficult to cope with radical innovation. In their satellite television ventures, and most notably with Eurikon and Europa, they attempted to establish pan-European broadcasting services using a radically innovatory technology in conjunction with practices and procedures developed during a regime of, at most, incremental innovation (and, for the majority of European public service broadcasters, a stasis in which they maintained their monopolies), a regime in which they controlled the pace of change.

The broadcasters who launched Eurikon and Europa developed neither the administrative and organisational forms nor the programming and scheduling mixes necessary for successful implementation of a radically new technology. Although their achievement in successfully establishing Eurikon at short notice and on a precarious financial foundation was very impressive (and eloquently testifies both to the personal skills and determination of Clarke and his colleagues and to the strength and flexibility of the EBU's working arrangements), neither with Eurikon nor – fatally – with Europa did public service broadcasters successfully devise the new working practices and new programming forms required to shift successfully to a new techno-economic paradigm. But with both Eurosport and Euronews public service broadcasters broke with their old ways and struck out towards a new paradigm. With Eurosport they established an unprecedented partnership with their arch commercial rival, Rupert Murdoch, and with Euronews they established close working relationships with European political authorities. Many public service broadcasters, attached to time-honoured ideals of broadcasters' independence of political and commercial interests, thought these initiatives incompatible with the very existence of public service broadcasting.

Commercial broadcasters were more successful in implementing the radically innovatory technology of satellite television. Perhaps (although this proposition requires to be tested with more research) because they had fewer old habits to unlearn. Europa and Eurikon failed because they did not match programme offer to audience demand. Euronews seems scarcely more likely to succeed. In contrast, the corporate background and centres of gravity of the commercial satellite broadcasters lay in the market driven sectors – notably newspaper and magazine publishing. This served them better in implementing a radical innovatory technology than did the inherited assumptions of public service broadcasters. Assumptions and habits formed in the comfortable matrix of monopoly and incremental innovation. For Sky and RTL+, ruthless control of costs and orientation to audience demand served them well in the race to implement satellite television. In comparison, the gentler habits and high cultural orientation of public service broadcasting were poorly adapted to the challenge.

Public service broadcasters were not alone in failing to implement successful pan-European television services. The sky barons (Clarke and Riddell 1992) were no more successful in establishing pan-European services. Their success in satellite television derived from their recognition that European television continues to be a series of national televisions. The experiences of public and commercial broadcasters suggest two conclusions. First, that the decisive factor in the success or failure of television is the degree to which programme offer is matched to demand: viewers watch programmes, they do not consume technologies. Effective implementation of a new broadcasting technology is a necessary, but not a sufficient, condition of success. Second, the screens of language and culture which separate Europeans are insufficiently permeable to television for it to play a major role in fostering a collective European consciousness and culture. The idealistic 'good Europeans' who slogged to make Europa a success were bound to a Quixotic enterprise.

Nonetheless, although neither public service nor commercial broadcasters successfully established pan-European services, it is striking how far the public service broadcasters fell, and how high the commercial broadcasters rose, between 1982 and 1992. Technological and regulatory change reduced the barriers to entry to broadcasting which formerly preserved television as the privileged domain of national public service monopolies. Pervasively, contemporary competition in television in Europe derives from the introduction of a new technology and the re-regulation of broadcasting on the basis of the values of 'negative liberty' (Berlin 1969) enshrined in the Treaty of Rome and the European Convention on Human Rights, and specifically embodied in broadcasting regulation through the *Television without Frontiers* Directive (Council of the European Communities 1989) and the *European Convention on Transfrontier Television* (Council of Europe 1989).

These changes have been anathematised both by proponents of public service broadcasting (see *inter alia*, Blumler 1992; Garnham 1990, 1992; Keane 1991) and of European union and culture, (see, *inter alia*, Barzanti 1990; Lang 1988). Increased competition was perceived to threaten European cultural values and European identity as well as the 'public sphere' deemed necessary for a democratic European polity. Some of this critique can be dismissed as special pleading for producer interests, as based on undemonstrated presumptions of the powerful effects of television, and that not-for-profit organisations necessarily better serve the interests of users than do organisations working for profit. But not all can be so lightly dismissed.

Two difficult clusters of theoretical and empirical questions lie at the heart of this debate. The first concerns the degree to which individuals' collective cultural identities are shaped by television, how far cultural identities are linked to political identities or citizenship, and how far political institutions (such as states or, as here, the European Community 'superstate') can be stable and legitimate only in so far as they are congruent with the collective identities of those who are citizens in them. The second concerns the extent to which markets or administered allocations are likely to best serve the public interest, the balance between the right and the good in the public interest, and how far individuals are the best judges of their own interest or require education or 'tutelage', to realise their interests. To take the second question first.

## Public service broadcasting. What next?

Berlin's distinction between positive and negative liberty offers a useful basis for analysing contemporary broadcasting policy issues and debates: debates characterised by an unproductive dualism of attack and/or defence of a particular principle of organisation rather than discussion of how best the ultimate goals of broadcasting policy may be achieved. Berlin's scheme is not without difficulties, but his notions of the complementarity of negative and positive liberties, of the necessity of both and the insufficiency of either concept alone, offer a productive basis for thinking beyond the sterile dualism in which the broadcasting policy debate has become mired. Neither positive nor negative liberty are sufficient and neither public service nor the market have delivered both kinds of freedom in broadcasting (see Collins 1992a and 1993).

However, critics of the 'marketisation' of European broadcasting see a categorical difference between market and public service broadcasting systems. Here Blumler's formulation is representative. One paradigm, he contends, is rooted in a 'standpoint of social ethics'; the other is animated solely by the 'capture of audience as market as the prime, normative and pragmatic goal of the broadcasting business' (Blumler 1992: 2). It is undoubtedly true that the 'capture of audience as market as the prime, normative and pragmatic goal of the broadcasting business' justly characterises some contemporary European broadcasters. But it does not accurately represent the outlook of all proponents of broadcasting markets. Nor does it acknowledge the force of arguments for markets as means for the realisation of consumers' and citizens' preferences. Indeed, much of the power of the market idea has been its ethical component (see, *inter alia*, Friedman and Friedman 1981; Hayek 1972). And many criticisms of public service broadcasters are grounded in the recognition that reconciling public service broadcasters' practices of intransigent defence of their historical monopolies, subordination to party political agendas, disdain for popular taste and their own commercial practices, can only with difficulty be reconciled with a 'standpoint of ethics'.

Blumler's antithesis between 'social ethics' and 'capture of audiences' is untenable. It is only through a Nelsonian eye that European broadcasting history can be so seen. More importantly, Blumler's antithesis misses the point: outcomes may be closer to optimal in circumstances of public service *and* the market rather than public service *or* the market. Indeed mixed, public service and the market, broadcasting systems are sufficiently widespread and sufficiently long established to demand recognition not as deviant sport of a fundamentally binary system (public service or the market), but as a distinctive formation with policy questions and organisational configurations of its own. As the EBU, prompted and coaxed by the BBC, recognised with Eurosport.

Public service broadcasters do not enjoy a monopoly of the characteristics which Blumler identified as distinctive properties of public service broadcasting. Properties such as 'independence of vested interests and governments' and 'catering for all interests and tastes' are neither the exclusive property of public service broadcasters nor invariably absent in commercial broadcasting. Moreover where such properties are evident in public service broadcasting they have often developed[1] through public broadcasters' interaction and competition with commercial broadcasters. They developed, in short, because of, rather than in spite of, competition, as leading public service broadcasters have testified. Massimo Fichera of RAI described the changes to RAI following the introduction of competition in Italy as leading to a 'fruitful balance between market forces and public service requirements' (Fichera 1989: 23). Alasdair Milne (when Director General of the BBC) also testified to the positive impact of competition on RAI. Milne stated (to the Administrative Council of the EBU) that: 'competition from newcomers need not be feared unduly. It could have stimulating effects: had not the RAI, for example, when threatened some years ago been stimulated by the competition and had it not been able to meet it in a remarkable way?' (CA 1704 SPG 2653 May 1984: 37).

Thus the antinomy which Blumler proposed misrepresents both the historical *interaction* between public service and market-based broadcasters and the growing (sometimes grudging) acceptance by public service broadcasters of the positive consequences of competition. Indeed, the Peacock Committee (whose report made a powerful and intellectually coherent case for the market as a means of organising broadcasting) vigorously refuted assertions that the market and public service were incompatible 'The fulfilment of this goal [ie transition to a broadcasting market] so far from being incompatible with public service activities positively requires them in a sense of public service' (1986: 125).

## The public sphere and the future of public service broadcasting

Just after ratification of the Maastricht Treaty on European Union the EBU testified to its, and public service broadcasting's, commitments: 'The broadcast media sector', it stated, 'lies at the heart of the democratic, social and cultural development of all the countries and regions of Europe. To abandon it completely to the laws of the market place would not only seriously impede the performance of its mission to the public, but would be contrary to the constitutional principles of a number of states' (*Espace* No. 21 November [1993]: 7). Laudable though the EBU's commitments to 'the democratic, social and cultural development of all the countries and regions of Europe' were, it was unable to reconcile these commitments with the laws of a changed broadcasting market.

The EBU's relationships with European political structures and authorities confirm and challenge neo-Habermasian propositions about public service broadcasting and the contemporary public sphere (see especially Garnham 1983, 1992; Keane 1991). In 1989 the EBU explicitly defined creation of a modern public sphere (public forum)[2] as part of public service broadcasters' contemporary role (see EBU 1989 and 1989a):

[the] essential task of public service broadcasters at the present time is
to widen the public platform they already offer nationally to the

dimensions of Europe, thus participating in the construction of a Europewide public forum.

(EBU 1989: 16)

The public forum, or public sphere, was largely to be realised through maintaining the EBU's established activities but included a return to pan-European broadcasting. The European public forum sought by the EBU was to include:

- news exchanges;
- production of common programmes in all fields of information, education and drama;
- partnership with the cinema and with national and international cultural industries and institutions;
- programming of European works in the original language;
- common technological research;
- development of transnational channels.

(EBU 1989: 16)

However, as I have shown, the EBU was unable to develop its 'transnational channels' – Eurosport and Euronews – except through dependent partnerships with commercial and political power centres which it, and the neo-Habermasians, regarded as at best alien, and at worst hostile, to the development of an authentic public sphere. The funding and practical organisation of positive liberty in pan-European broadcasting remains elusive. Not least because of the contradiction between, on the one hand, European public service broadcasters' time-honoured forms of organisation and of practice and, on the other hand, the competition provisions inscribed in the Treaty of Rome and its successor, the Maastricht Treaty. This contradiction has led both to the 'two scorpions in a bottle'[3] relationship of the EBU and DG IV and, latterly, to attempts to protect European public service broadcasters from the depradations of Treaty provisions formulated long before anyone might have conceived that competition law would be applied to public service broadcasting. Notable here have been the European Parliament's Resolution on the role of public service television in a multi-media society (of 19.9.96),[4] Carole Tongue MEP's report *The Future of Public Service Broadcasting in a Multi-Channel Digital Age* (Tongue n.d.) and the public service broadcasting protocol added to the European Union Treaty in the course of the Netherlands' Presidency of the European Union in early 1997.[5]

## The mixed system and the end of national monopoly

Clearly, a system which combines both positive and negative freedoms is required. For it is not only the economic market that remains imperfect, so too

212

does the 'political market' through which public service and public sector broadcasters are controlled. As Berlin stated: what is required is, 'logically untidy, flexible, and even ambiguous compromise' (1969: 39). Unfortunately, few advocates of public service broadcasting have faced this problem of access and accountability (but see Heller 1978). Changes in the organisation of broadcasting and the halting establishment of, still imperfect, markets have improved the responsiveness of the supply of broadcasting services to demand. Not, it is true, in the most important sense of access of viewers and listeners to control of the offer and the accountability of service providers to final consumers, but in terms of access to audiences (and vice versa) for independently produced programmes and the extension of more viewing choices to viewers.

The historical evidence suggests that a system combining positive and negative freedom exists neither in circumstances where public service broadcasting has a monopoly nor where for-profit commercial broadcasting (the market sector) is overwhelmingly dominant. A mixed system is required. This may seem an underwhelming conclusion, but it is not one which can be derived from the arguments of either neo-Habermasians such as Garnham or Keane or the market theorists. Moreover, a principal contribution of the market theorists to the broadcasting debate lies in their foregrounding of the importance of both the preferences of viewers and a satisfactory feedback system between consumers and providers of broadcasting services. The relationship between consumers and producers has often been ignored by public service broadcasters.

Satellite television has made national regulation and control of television more difficult than heretofore, has enabled for-profit broadcasters to offer a geographically universal service without thereby raising the cost of providing service, has increased negative freedom in broadcasting and, as Garnham argued, has given the broadcasting policy of European states an inescapably pan-European dimension. Formerly the Europeanisation of television was a matter which could be left to broadcasters as a matter of broadcaster to broadcaster relations. Public service broadcasters collaborated within the EBU and the Europeanisation of broadcasting, such as it was, existed in the provision of *producer*, (i.e. broadcaster-to-broadcaster), rather than consumer (i.e. broadcaster-to-viewer) services. But with the establishment of satellite television pan-European television became a consumer service rather than, as was and is Eurovision, a broadcaster-to-broadcaster, producer, service. Service providers, including public service broadcasters, had to take viewer preferences and behaviour patterns into account more than ever before. So too did they have to adapt to a changing regulatory environment in which pan-European political institutions became unprecedentedly important to broadcasters and broadcasting.

## European broadcasting and European identity

The first of the two difficult theoretical questions to which I alluded above concerns the relationship between collective identity, television and political institutions, specifically the European Community 'superstate'. European politicians and European public service broadcasters shared much in their approach to this question. Indeed the Hahn Resolution of 1982 stated that the European Parliament '[c]onsiders close co-operation with the European Broadcasting Union to be imperative' (1982a: 112). European Parliamentarians and the OTS/Group of Experts, which brought Eurikon into existence, argued that television could, and should, foster and inculcate[6] European consciousness. They did so from a cluster of assumptions which were and are classically nationalist. Nationalist, not in the sense of chauvinist partisanship for an exclusive normative status of a single one of the plurality of collective national identities extant in Europe, but in the sense of stipulating that a European political identity, derived from a shared cultural identity, should be congruent with European political institutions. In the words of the Hahn Report:

> European unification will only be achieved if Europeans want it.
> Europeans will only want it if there is such a thing as a European identity. A European identity will only develop if Europeans are adequately informed. At present, information vis à vis the mass media is controlled at national level.
>
> (European Parliament 1982: 9)

Here the Hahn Report explicitly links European political union to the sentiments of Europeans. And, although implying a singular, normative, identity for Europeans (a doctrine offensive to many of them) the political programme it foreshadows is profoundly democratic: political change follows European citizens' aspirations. Nonetheless, implicit in the model propounded by Hahn are notions of the subordination of information media to political objectives (see Commission of the European Communities 1993 for a contemporary instance of this doctrine) and of the necessary singularity of European identity if a European political union is to grow and survive. Hahn's doctrine is then an instance of nationalist doctrine. It exemplifies what Gellner rightly identified as the core nationalist presumption: 'the principle of homogeneous cultural units as the foundation of political life and of the obligatory cultural unity of rules [sic] and ruled' (Gellner 1983: 125). It is not surprising that the presumptions which Elie Kedourie (another notable European theorist of nationalism) described as having become 'thought to be self-evident' (Kedourie 1966: 9) have directed powerful currents in European broadcasting policy. But it is important to recognise that, whilst European cultural nationalism has been a very powerful element in the shaping of European television and is a major policy strain of the European Community in particular, such beliefs have neither been universally held nor are they universally deemed necessary to European union.

Functionalist political theory, for example, places considerably less emphasis than do nationalist theories on the necessity of the congruence of polity and culture for the construction of stable, popular and legitimate political arrangements. Indeed functionalists, who emphasise the establishment of practical mechanisms of co-operation and collaboration for the realisation of mutual interests as the primary motor of developing political unions, sometimes regard the harmonisation of culture (perceived by nationalists as a necessary condition of enduring political unions) as an obstacle to practical, enduring and union-building political arrangements. The 'father' of functionalism, David Mitrany,[7] developed his theory (or what he modestly described as an uncovering and clarification of 'the relation of things' [Mitrany 1975: 17]), in response to the blight of nationalism; a doctrine which he characterised as a 'ruthless political stress for uniformity' (Mitrany 1975: 143).

Functionalism supposes separation, rather than the congruence customarily stipulated in nationalism, between culture and political structures. A functionalist route to European union takes a different direction to the nationalist route which underpinned the political Europeanisation of television and influenced the trajectory of the EBU-sponsored satellite television channels. Indeed, Jean Monnet (1978) followed a very functionalist path to European union as his memoirs make clear.[8] Monnet, moreover (in spite of his celebrated statement to the effect that if he were to start again on the road to European union he would start with culture) was rather contemptuous of the pursuit of a chimera of European identity. As he stated: 'While fifty-five countries were meeting in Lomé or Brussels to seek their common interests, our diplomats were holding pointless debates about a "European identity"' (Monnet 1978: 499).

In fact a functionalist perspective may provide some comfort to European unionists faced with the disinclination of European television viewers to watch pan-European television so eloquently manifested in their responses to Eurikon and Europa; to the costs and intractable difficulties, which Eurikon and Europa forced into visibility, of re-languaging television programmes and services so that they were intelligible and attractive to viewers across Europe. Rather than obdurately persisting with a Quixotic project of making European polity and culture congruent, as a consistent application of nationalist doctrine requires European unionists to do, functionalism suggests that European unionists might enjoy more success through the pursuit of pragmatic measures, like those Monnet enjoined in the statement cited above, rather than by pursuing the (more frequently cited) programme he is thought to have urged elsewhere: 'If we were beginning the European Community all over again we should begin with culture' (cited in Commission of the European Communities 1984: 10). As the EBU's experience with Eurikon and Europa demonstrated, beginning with culture is more easily said than done.

Scholars, no more than television viewers, have a singular identity, and it is well to recognise that they are also citizens and that any disjuncture between their, more or less active, political identities and their scholarly pursuits is always imperfect. To evaluate whether or not a nationalist or functionalist approach to European broadcasting policy is more likely to succeed in advancing European union begs the question (which scholars may believe they can escape but which is an inescapable issue for all citizens of what now, post-Maastricht, we must learn to call the 'European Union'): is European union desirable?

UK commentators and politicians are notorious for their usual reply to that question. My critical account of pan-European television and my evident unease at the prospect of a developing symbiosis between the EBU and the Commission of the European Communities in a collaborative European news service may suggest that I am content to be read as a ventriloquist's dummy mouthing the 'defensive and adversarial vocabulary adopted consistently for the past 40 years by almost the entire political class in Britain towards the European Community' (*Financial Times* 12.12.91: 3). I am not. There can be no doubt that the European Community has increased the mobility of Community citizens who now enjoy novel rights of residence, establishment, and to employment (although these augmented rights for European 'insiders' are often traded off against reduced rights for 'outsiders'). The European free trade area established under Community auspices has offered European economies and enterprises potential economies of scale and scope and the interrelatedness of Western Europe's economies has, as Monnet dreamed it would, made intra-Community war unimaginable. All this is very much to the good: although the benefits I see accruing to European citizens from their membership of the European Community are, largely, increases in 'negative freedom'.

The comfortable reflexes which have led UK commentators to decry the European Union (or Community) and all its works have not served the UK well. Abstention from participation in the pan-European policy fora of the Community and Council has resulted only in the policy agenda, to which the UK perforce has to respond, being set by others. Not least in broadcasting and the audio-visual does the UK have no alternative to continued membership of the European Union. For, increasingly, the economic viability of the UK's audio-visual sector depends on the state of its trading relationships with European partners. In 1989 the European Community became more important a customer for UK television programmes than was North America, hitherto the most lucrative destination for UK television exports, and since 1989 the importance of the European Community as a customer has steadily grown. In respect of film exports the same story obtains, although it was not until 1990 that the European Community displaced North America as the most important customer for UK film exports (CSO 1993: 2, 4). The characteristic UK policy of abstention and obstruction (represented perfectly in the words of a UK official, interviewed 10.2.92, who characterised its policy towards the Council of Europe's initiatives on the media 'as entirely negative, to stop it doing things, it's [the Council of Europe] going far beyond what it's capable of achieving') ill serves fundamental UK interests.

But if I strongly favour closer UK involvement in the European project I see reasons to be uneasy about the growing closeness of European public service broadcasters and European political institutions. The contemporary mutuality of interests between the EBU and the Commission of the European Communities may compromise the political impartiality at the heart of public service broadcasting, particularly because of the European Community's existing 'democratic deficit' (Commission of the European Communities and European Parliament 1990: 6).

However, in spite of the growing resurgence in collaboration between European public servcice broadcasters and the European Union, not least in Euronews, there seem relatively few possibilities for the Community to play a positive role in extending 'positive freedoms' in the cultural and broadcasting domains. Not least because the cultures of the Community are so diverse. And when they are similar to each other they are also similar to the cultures of 'Les Enfants de l'Europe' overseas as Louis Hartz (1964) and others have shown.[9] If membership of the Community is to be widened and the benefits of member- ship extended to more people, European cultural diversity will become more pronounced. The really exacting challenges to the European Community, and indeed to Europe as a whole, in human rights, in culture, and in economic development, come not from Western Europe but from the south and east. How far are rights of abode and work enjoyed by Community citizens to be extended? To Turkey and to Russia? How far are prosperous Western states prepared to expend 'cohesion' funding to impoverished and brutal societies? How far are the Catholic and Protestant traditions of Western Europe able to embrace the Muslim and Orthodox south and east?

It seems inconceivable that the answers to such questions are to be found in a nationalism in which the political structures of a European superstate are to be founded in a common consciousness and culture. Empirically, as Eurikon and Europa showed, the European collective identity stipulated by nationalists for such a programme does not exist. How much more fanciful is it to imagine that such an identity could be found to cover the east and the south as well as the west. However it is only within the theoretical framework of nationalism that the lessons taught by the EBU's bold pan-European ventures appear so gloomy. From a functionalist point of view many other possibilities are open.

## The lessons of pan-European satellite television

In this respect the EBU's merger with the OIRT has shown the way: an impor- tant pan-European broadcasting initiative is taking place through unpretentious functional integration rather than under the banner of a spurious European cultural unity. Indeed, the troubled relationship which European public broad- casting enjoyed with proponents of European union between 1982 and 1992 suggests that the enduring values of European public service broadcasting – impartiality, universality and diversity – are best realised in changed contemporary circumstances not in the pursuit of a chimera of pan-European television programming, a consumer service, but rather, in strengthening of the EBU's repertoire of producer services. For example, through a reinforcement of programme exchanges along the lines of the well established Eurovision news exchanges. Programme exchanges increase welfare, they enable poor countries and viewers to have access to a diversity and quality of programmes which they would not otherwise enjoy and they realise the core value of public service broadcasting – universal service. Moreover, because final editorial control remains in local hands, the product made available to local consumers may be tailored to local tastes and requirements from the raw material made available to the local broadcaster through the EBU.

The EBU has recognised that diversity in broadcasting is no longer best realised through single monopoly organisations but instead through a plurality of different broadcasting organisations – commercial and non-commercial – delicate though the task is of managing the transition (and not helped by the Marino decision), from an EBU composed exclusively of public service broadcasters to a pluralistic organisation. The admission to membership of the French GRF (which includes commercial broadcasters in TF1 and Canal Plus) and the opening of the Eurovision Permanent circuits to commercial broadcasters' signals testifies to the impossibility of the EBU holding a consistent line between public and commercial broadcasting.

There are obvious dangers in generalising from so recent and short lived a phenomenon as satellite television in Western Europe; a phenomenon which has existed for only a decade. The lessons which can be drawn suggest overwhelmingly that the differences between European television viewers are more important than the similarities. Moreover, the history of the EBU-sponsored pan-European satellite television services suggests that the generally high level of satisfaction with national broadcasting services expressed by European television viewers has been more important than the interest, expressed by a third of them (Desgraupes 1985: 49) in pan-European services. The fall of pan-European public service television is best explained by viewers' resistance to its programme offer; its rise by the policy imperatives of the major pan-European institutions, notably the EBU and the European Community.

The response of European public service broadcasters, and their collective embodiment, the EBU, to technological change tested to destruction the time-honoured model of European public service broadcasting. Audience response to the new commercial services testified to their hunger for a more entertaining and demotic programme mix than had been provided by public service broadcasting monopolies, and the attempt to translate the old public service programme mix into a new pan-European idiom in Eurikon and Europa proved a resounding failure. All seemed to be captured (as Sue Summers smartly spotted in the title of her review 'Pass the drinks – this is Euro TV') by the infamous Roger Garaudy/Irene van Lippe discussion, 'On the lack of appreciation for the feminine'. Here, if ever one were to be needed, was an instance to confirm the justice of an application of Bauman's snarky jibe at Habermas – that he conceived society as a sociology seminar (Bauman 1992: 217) – to European public service broadcasting.

But the EBU-sponsored pan-European satellite services showed both sides of the Janus face of public service broadcasting. If the programme mix offered on Eurikon and Europa reflected the sclerotic habits of organisations which had succumbed comfortably to what White identified as the greatest danger of middle-age – 'the danger of being satisfied' (White 1980: 59) – the speed with which EBU members combined to launch Eurikon testified to the competencies of middle age, competencies conferred by experience, established working relationships and abundant know how which, combined with an ambition to do new things, testified to the vigorous presence of the 'creative fire' which White had found lacking in the EBU and its members.

Pan-European public service satellite television owed its rise to the institutional interests of the major pan-European institutions; notably the EBU and the European Community. What else can explain the EBU's persistence in launching channel after channel when positive response from viewers was so conspicuously lacking? Latterly these imperatives have led to public service broadcasters' dependency on commercial and political interests not readily compatible with public service broadcasting's traditional commitments. In order to maintain its access to sports programming, the EBU entered a 'creatively' funded partnership with News International – brokered by Europe's most successful public service broadcaster the BBC! To improve its lobbying power in Brussels (albeit to resist the lethal assaults of the Competition Directorate), the EBU launched Euronews as a frankly 'political file' because the 'EBU's image with the European institutions was at stake' (CA 2116 SPG 5254 18.2.91: 17). These strategies are difficult to reconcile with the independence 'of government and parliament, and of any other entity or force within the society' which Albert Scharf, President of the EBU, proudly defined as the essence of public service broadcasting.[10] Doubly ironic that the recurrent nemesis of the EBU, the Competition Directorate of the Commission of the European Communities DG IV, has again secured a ruling against the working practices central to the very existence of the EBU.[11]

European public service broadcasting and the EBU display little of the senescent complacency in the early 1990s which White (1980) detected in them a decade before. The EBU has successfully incorporated the OIRT and many public service broadcasters have reoriented their programming to successfully win back the audiences lost to commercial competition a decade earlier. A host of inventive production methods and organisational innovations have been implemented and the EBU and its members have increasingly built on the EBU's Eurovision news exchanges and collective acquisition of sports rights to strengthen their competitiveness. But the creation of a single European market in television – a 'Television without Frontiers' – has exposed the EBU to the potential lethal impact of the European Commission's Competition Directorate and has consequentially necessitated a courtship of other interests in the European Commission to countervail the power of DG IV. This strategy carries the attendant risks of compromising European public service broadcasting's political independence and of being subject to capture in the service of further pan-European integrationist projects via TV.

One lesson that the unhappy experience of Eurikon and Europa has taught unequivocally was that the EBU's established pan-European practices of programme and news exchanges were incomparably more effective than the creation of pan-European channels. The EBU's experiences suggest that pan-European television works at the level of producer services, not at the level of consumer services. Or, to put it another way: pan-European television works at a wholesale but not a retail level. It would be tragic if this hard won lesson had to be learned again. Ironic that it may have to be, for much of the EBU's, and European public service broadcasting's, successful reorientation, albeit still incomplete, can be attributed to the lessons learned from its bold pan-European ventures of the 1980s. It is unfortunate that so many of the lessons were, as Jean-Pierre Julien aptly stated, lessons about what not to do.

# APPENDIX I

## Why Eurikon and why not? Speculations on motives

If the EBU's sponsorship of Eurikon can readily be explained as the collective response of European public service broadcasters to the threat posed by the unprecedented entry of commercial services delivered via satellite into what had hitherto been national broadcasting monopolies, how can the participation of the individual broadcasters directly participating in the experiment be understood? Clearly some special factors were at work, for fewer EBU members participated in Eurikon than stayed on the sidelines. Although nine EBU members (ARD, BRT, NOS, ORF, RAI, RTE, RTP, SSR and UKIB) had expressed their willingness to participate actively in Eurikon, only five did so. Why did the ARD (West Germany), NOS (Netherlands), ORF (Austria), RAI (Italy), UKIB (UK) take part?[1] Explanation, as so often in the course of European affairs, has to encompass the differences between the course taken by the mainland European majority and that taken by the EU's 'awkward partner' (George 1990) – the UK.

### The majority view

The ARD's, RAI's, NOS' and ORF's interests in Eurikon can be readily identified. In general, all sought to maintain their institutional power and influence which was threatened by emerging commercial rivals. The large broadcasters, RAI and the ARD, had particular reasons for alarm. RAI was already strongly challenged by a troubling domestic rival, the Fininvest channels controlled by Silvio Berlusconi. RAI's domestic monopoly had been broken in 1974 by the Italian Constitutional Court's celebrated 'Tele Biella' judgement permitting cable redistribution of television. But it was the Constitutional Court's Decision 202 in 1976, permitting commercial over-the-air broadcasting, that made Fininvest's powerful challenge to RAI's hegemony possible. Accordingly, RAI had a strong incentive to pre-empt the entry of commercial satellite services to the Italian market. The ARD also feared entry of commercial services into West Germany – the most attractive European television market for commercial broadcasters. German public service broadcasters, the ARD and the ZDF, scheduled few entertainment programmes and provided advertisers (in

Europe's biggest economy) with insufficient television advertising opportunities. Accordingly, commercial services rapidly emerged in Germany in the early and mid-1980s, first using the new cable systems (for example, Sat Eins began on the Ludwigshafen cable system in 1985) and later satellites, sparking a significant decline in public broadcasters' audience share.

The NOS and ORF were also vulnerable to competing commercial services. Like RAI and the ARD, both supplied a less than optimal medium for television advertisers and were similarly vulnerable to a migration of audiences towards a more entertaining programme mix delivered by commercial broadcasters. Moreover they were (and are) less able than big country broadcasters (such as RAI and the ARD) to fund new competitive streams of programming in response to commercial rivals. But the IBA's motivation is not so easily explained. It was not threatened in the same way as were its Eurikon partners. Indeed the ITV network (with the prudent exception of its largest member, Thames Television) developed its own satellite television service, Superchannel, and its terrestrial service had little to fear from Sky Channel in the early eighties. Rather than the competition from commercial broadcasters which its Eurikon partners feared, the IBA was alarmed by competition from a public service broadcaster – the BBC.

Although institutional rationales for participation in Eurikon can be identified, to do so is to risk underestimating the importance of individual agency, which clearly played a major part in the genesis of Eurikon and its successors. The Operations Group were men who had experienced the aftermath of the Second World War and who were all described as 'idealistic and enthusiastic Europeans'. Their supra-national, European, sympathies, their lifetime commitment to public service broadcasting together with their obvious motives to build a career for themselves in, what they hoped would be, the vanguard of the new European broadcasting order, goes far to explain the persistent extraordinary dedication, often in the face of intimidating obstacles, of those who built the EBU-sponsored satellite channels. Indeed, at least one observer believed, the Eurikon Operations Group 'went much further with Eurikon than their parent organisations wished and expected'. Most remarkable, this source believed, was 'the success of Neville Clarke given the private, for profit, nature of ITV' (Council of Europe official interviewed 17.12.91).

## Participation (and non-participation) by the awkward partner

It was not ITV, but the IBA, which drove the UK's participation in Eurikon but, nonetheless, the UK's participation still needs to be explained. Formally, it was the IBA which held membership in the EBU as UKIBA in virtue of its responsibility under UK statute law as broadcaster to whom the ITV companies contracted for the supply of programmes. Formalities aside, the ITCA, the association of ITV franchisees, played a partnership role with the IBA in respect of

EBU membership. And the ITCA was always sceptical about the benefits which might accrue from Eurikon and became increasingly alarmed by the cost of UK participation for which it shared responsibility. Later, the majority of ITCA members participated in a UK-based commercial pan-European satellite television channel, Superchannel.

Moreover, Neville Clarke, in his capacity as the Senior Television Programme Officer of the IBA,[2] had to fight hard for the IBA to maintain its commitment to the 'close and active' involvement with the EBU initiatives which he had advocated (Clarke to the Director of Television [Colin Shaw] in an internal IBA memo dated 3.12.80). As late as November 1981 the IBA had made no definite commitment to Eurikon. Clarke was forced to acknowledge that 'it is difficult to assess the value to UKIB of the proposed L-Sat programme experiments, or to express a view on whether our interest would lie in European or national experiments' (memo from Clarke to Shaw titled 'Draft telex to Miro Vilcek' 13.11.82).

The crucial decision which sealed the IBA's participation in Eurikon was taken between December 1981 and January 1982. This was a busy time for the IBA, since new franchises for the terrestrial commercial television companies which made up the ITV network came into effect in January 1982. This was also the year when Channel 4, a wholly owned subsidiary of the IBA, began its transmissions. The satellite initiative for which Clarke sought support was seen as a further, and unwelcome, complication. But senior IBA staff's preoccupation with their new terrestrial responsibilities also enabled Clarke to advance his initiative with more success than might have been possible when his colleagues were less preoccupied than they were in early 1982. Moreover, Clarke was fortunate to enjoy the support of a new, very pro-Europe, Chair of the IBA.

George Thomson became Chairman of the IBA early in 1981. He had formerly been a Member of the House of Commons (he had held office as Chancellor of the Duchy of Lancaster and as Deputy Foreign Secretary with special responsibility for European Affairs and Common Market Negotiations). Thomson subsequently became a Commissioner of the European Communities and a Member of the House of Lords. He was a committed pro-European who claimed to 'yield to no one in my enthusiasm for progress in the search for European unity' and, as a newly appointed IBA Chairman, he was keen to make his mark. His support, together with the IBA's concern to ensure it was not outpaced in satellite television by the BBC, ensured that Clarke enjoyed sufficient support in the IBA to advance his pan-European ventures.

On 21.12.81 Clarke sent a memo to the Deputy Director of Television at the IBA stating that a decision on participation in the OTS experiment was required and that 'If Independent Broadcasting in the United Kingdom passes this opportunity by it will not be offered again'. He prudently stated: 'There is no question at this stage of financial commitment'. The following day the memo was initialled by the Deputy Director of Television who annotated it in manuscript, authorising IBA participation on the basis Clarke had suggested. By

January 21st 1982 the IBA had become one of the five active participants in the experiments and the IBA hosted the OTS Operations Group meeting in London the following month.

## Deadly dualism: BBC versus ITA

George (1990) suggests that much of the curious history of the UK's relations with and within the European Community can only be understood as the expression on a European stage of internal, UK, political dynamics. George's model explains the IBA's participation in Eurikon very well. The IBA participated in the EBU satellite television venture as a gambit in its rivalry with the BBC. Clarke had shrewdly mentioned (in his memo of 21.12.81) the news that the BBC Kingswood Warren engineering establishment had offered to participate in the OTS experiments.[3] Clarke's drafting doubtless sharpened apprehensions among senior IBA officials that, if the IBA did not participate, it might be pre-empted by the BBC and excluded from satellite television. It had some grounds for this fear.

In March 1982 William Whitelaw, then the UK Home Secretary and thus the UK Minister responsible for broadcasting, gave the BBC responsibility for the UK's DBS services (which were planned to begin in 1986). The BBC was given what it came to regard as a poisoned chalice: government believed that quick action was necessary and that the BBC could develop a satellite service quicker than the IBA. This was not least because the BBC's Charter permitted the BBC to do all it is not specifically prohibited from doing, whereas new primary legislation would have been required for the IBA to have launched a satellite service.

In charging the BBC with responsibility for DBS the UK Government thus moved to implement the 'Option C' canvassed in its report on satellite broadcasting (Home Office 1981). The DBS service the BBC was charged to deliver was to be transmitted from a 'gold plated' UK manufactured DBS – Unisat – to be built by a consortium headed by British Aerospace. The BBC proposed to programme the new service with a subscription film channel and a 'Window on the World', drawing on 'the best television from round the world' (*Ariel* 10.3.82). The IBA fiercely resented its exclusion from what it judged would become an important television market and by the changed balance between its and the BBC's responsibilities. From being responsible (as the ITA) only for a single commercial television channel the ITA had successfully added radio (and accordingly had been redesignated the IBA) and a second television channel (Channel 4) to its responsibilities. Only with Channel 4 in 1982 had the IBA regained the 'parity' with the BBC it had lost in 1964 when BBC2 had been established. The IBA's hard won equality with the BBC seemed to disappear with the Home Secretary's announcement that the BBC would be responsible for Direct to Home Satellite Broadcasting (for a useful discussion of the BBC's, brief, responsibility for DBS see Negrine 1988).

Neville Clarke's public comment gave a flavour of the IBA's response:

> The Europeans were totally amazed by the Government decision. The IBA have been the only ones working in Europe on satellite broadcasts. We were the ones who took the initiative. What a shock when after years we finally got Channel 4 which would establish some sort of parity with the BBC but with one stroke of the pen, the Government re-established the BBC monopoly.
>
> (interviewed in *Broadcast* 5.4.82: 55)

Concern over the IBA's exclusion from satellite television was pervasive in Brompton Road. Colin Shaw's deputy (the Deputy Director of Television or DDT as he identified himself in internal IBA communications) annotated a memo concerning Eurikon on 15.3.82 in manuscript:

> I am sure you would agree that we can't afford to get egg all over our face on this, *particularly* [original emphasis] as we are now trying to rebuild our credibility in the space segment following recent Gov. decision which to the uninformed appears to dismiss us as having nothing to offer by way of ideas, skills or experience.
>
> (Waddington to Clarke, dated 23.3.82)

The IBA sought to steal a march on the BBC and establish its credibility in satellite television through participation in Eurikon. Brompton Road doubtless drew considerable satisfaction from *Broadcast*'s headline: 'IBA first in satellite TV' (*Broadcast* 5.4.82: 55) and the nightmare which unfolded for the BBC in consequence of its becoming mired in the Unisat project from which it eventually disentangled itself in 1985.[4]

A memo from Colin Shaw (when IBA Director of Television) to the Director General of the IBA dated 4.8.82 reported that John Whitney[5] had information identifying 'financial difficulties on the part of the BBC in meeting the costs of its proposed satellite services, initially because of the high costs being quoted by the British consortium manufacturing and launching the satellite'. The BBC's difficulties, Shaw argued, offered 'the opportunity of getting an IB [Independent Broadcasting] service of some kind into operation as early as 1986'.[6]

In December 1982 the newly appointed Director General of the IBA, John Whitney, lent his support to the IBA officials who advocated an IBA/ITV commitment to satellite television.[7] Whitney told the IBA's Standing Consultative Committee (the forum for meetings between the Authority and the commercial television companies) that:

I believe it is in the interests of Independent Broadcasting, and not only in order to maintain our competitive position in relation to the BBC, to seek to launch a DBS service at the earliest opportunity.

(IBA SCC Paper 31 [82])

## Commercial caution

However strong the IBA's enthusiasm for satellite television, it experienced real difficulties in securing support from the ITCA. Whilst IBA proponents of Eurikon were able to secure involvement in Eurikon, thanks to the enthusiasm of the new Chairman and Director General,[8] institutional rivalry with the BBC and staff preoccupation with the launch of Channel 4 and the performance of the newly franchised ITV companies, plus the continued absence of ITCA support made IBA involvement in the EBU's satellite ventures after Eurikon almost impossible. Members of the ITCA preferred to develop their partnership with Virgin in the Superchannel satellite television service rather than embroil themselves in a European joint venture offering uncertain benefits and entailing unidentified costs.

## Turning to home

The IBA's priorities also remained in the UK. It declined to follow its participation in Eurikon and join its erstwhile partners in Europa. The flavour of ITV attitudes in 1983, when Europa was getting underway, is caught in the public explanation (attributed to an unnamed senior ITV source) of its non-participation in Europa: 'That's just gilt on the gingerbread. DBS is much more fundamental to us' (*Stage and Television Today* 3.11.83: 20). By 1983 its experience of satellite television, acquired through Eurikon, coupled with the appointment in 1983 of a new UK Home Secretary, Leon Brittan,[9] who was more sympathetic than his predecessor to commercial broadcasting, meant that (in spite of the BBC's leading role in funding the UK DBS),[10] the IBA and BBC enjoyed equality of representation on what Lord Thomson, the Chairman of the IBA, referred to as the 'shadow' Satellite Broadcasting Board.[11] The IBA's costly and controversial involvement in Eurikon seemed to have borne fruit.

The Board was established in January 1984 with six members: three Governors of the BBC and three Members of the IBA (Thomson 1985: 10). Chairmanship of the Board alternated between the BBC and the IBA. In September 1984 the UK government announced that the IBA would be permitted to allocate at least one of the licences associated with the planned UK DBS. Moreover the IBA's MAC (Mulitplexed Analogue Component) transmission standard was chosen as the European standard in preference to the BBC's choice of an enhanced PAL (Phase Alternation Line) standard. By late 1983 the IBA had therefore won back its cherished position of parity with the BBC and domestic UK considerations no longer impelled it to participate in pan-European satellite television ventures.

Institutional rivalry between the BBC and IBA continued even after the cessation of the Eurikon experiments and the BBC's withdrawal from the UK's first DBS project. The BBC sought to maintain its expertise and ensure it maintained effective working relationships with other broadcasters so that, if necessary, it would be able to mobilise an international joint venture in satellite television. On 30 March 1983 (at a time when the news led Europa was under active development), the BBC convened a meeting in London (chaired by Nobel Wilson) of 'a small group of experts' to 'explore informally what was presently being done in the area of documentary and current affairs coverage of Europe – considered in the widest continental as well as political (EEC, etc.) sense – and to consider what more might be done to stimulate co-operation in this field'. The group's members came from Antenne 2, ZDF, and NOS as well as from the BBC. With the exception of NOS, none of the organisations invited by the BBC had participated in Eurikon or in Europa. Rather, the constellation put together by the BBC became the key players in the establishment of Eurosport – the EBU's next satellite television channel following the ignominious failure of Europa.

In 1986 the IBA, now given regulatory authority over UK DBS, licensed what it envisaged would be the UK's monopoly DBS service, BSB, with a fifteen-year franchise. However the IBA's success in winning back the satellite initiative from the BBC proved hollow. As is well known, BSB's services were pre-empted by Sky Television, which began transmitting its satellite television services to the UK from the Luxembourg satellite Astra in early 1989. BSB launched its service the following year and in November 1990 merged, on unequal terms, with Sky Television to form BSkyB. The BSkyB merger took place without either the IBA's permission or prior knowledge. The merger meant cessation of services from the BSB satellite and an absence of UK licenced services in what was the largest DBS television market in the world. The success of Eurikon (albeit a success very expensively bought) in reinstating the IBA in the UK satellite television field left the Authority implicated in a major debacle – the collapse of BSB and the successful 'endrunning' of UK regulation by Rupert Murdoch's News International. In contrast, the BBC participated in Eurosport's success.

# APPENDIX II

## Pan-European institutions[1]

The principal post-war pan-European Western political institutions, the Council of Europe and the European Communities, grew from similar roots. Although utopian proposals for European union may be found as far back as the seventeenth century (and perhaps earlier), for example, in the works of Penn and Sully, and during the inter-war period in the writings of Coudenhove-Kalergi (1926, 1943, 1948) it was the disaster of the Second World War which stimulated many Europeans to take practical steps to realise what had hitherto been only a fantasy. Just as the mass slaughter of the First World War stimulated a reconstruction of Europe on the nationalist lines prescribed by the Sèvres and Versailles Treaties, so the mass slaughter of the Second World War, perceived to have grown from the poisoned soil of the nationalist vision of Versailles stimulated European reconstruction: this time on transnational, pan-European lines. Both east and west of the Elbe integrated, post-national, Europes developed. East of the Elbe a sphere of notionally proletarian internationalism and interdependence sponsored by the USSR and CPSU. West of the Elbe two main pan-European institutions blossomed – the Council of Europe (based on intergovernmental agreements) and the European Communities which embodied the more radical, integrationist, vision of Jean Monnet and the other founding fathers of the European Communities such as Walter Hallstein and Altiero Spinelli. Sponsors of both Council and Communities stressed the inadequate size of national markets in Europe and the need to create political and economic relationships in order to inhibit further European wars.

## The European Union

The European Union consists (in 1997) of fifteen Member States which have joined to share some aspects of sovereignty, notably economic sovereignty, to establish a single market and progress towards the 'ever closer union' prescribed in the European Union Treaty – the Maastrict Treaty of 1991 – and the earlier Treaty of Rome. The Union was formerly known as the European Community, more properly referred to as the European Communities, which embraced the European Coal and Steel Community (founded under the Schuman Plan and established by the Treaty of Paris in 1951), and the European Atomic Energy Community and the European Economic Community (both established under the Treaty of Rome of 1957). These three communities constituted the European Community which was renamed the European Union in 1991. The Treaties of Rome, the Single European Act of 1985 and the Maastricht Treaty on European Union of 1991 constitute the European Community's 'constitution'.

Belgium, France, Germany, Luxembourg, Italy and the Netherlands were the six founding members of the European Community. In 1972 Denmark, Ireland and the UK joined the six; in 1981 Greece; in 1986 Spain and Portugal; and in 1995 Austria, Finland and Sweden. Citizens of Norway and Switzerland have voted against membership but further accessions to the European Union can be anticipated by Cyprus and Malta possibly followed by Turkey and the 'Visegrad' states of the Czech Republic, Hungary, Poland and perhaps Slovakia. Because it was the European Community, rather than the European Union, which existed between 1982 and 1992 (the dates which bound this study), I refer to the European Community. Where I refer to the European Union, the term signifies arrangements after ratification of the Maastricht Treaty on European Union.

The European Community is but one of a number of pan-European institutions which have shaped, and continue to shape, the broadcasting and audio-visual landscape of Europe. But, important though others have been, the European Community is by far the most important. Its importance for its members is obvious. But its rule making and pro-active initiatives in the broadcasting and audio-visual sphere have also had a striking impact on broadcasting in European states outside the Community, not least because of the impact of Community competition policy on long-established practices of the EBU to which the public service broadcasters of all European states belong.

## The political structure of the European Community

The European Community's political structure includes a parliament (the European Parliament), a supreme court (the Court of Justice) and an executive (the Commission of the European Communities). It thus appears to follow a well-established Western tradition of a division of powers between legislature, judiciary and executive. However, not only does the European Community include several, sometimes unfamiliar, institutions (such as the Economic and Social Committee, the Council of Ministers, the Court of Justice and the Court of Auditors[2]) but, most important, the balance of power between the European Community's institutions of government is different to the customary arrangements of Western democracies.

In the European Community the executive – the Commission of the European Communities – has very considerable powers and the Parliament is relatively weak. The Parliament's power is vested in its right to dismiss the

Commission. However it may exercise this power only through an affirmative vote of two-thirds of its members and may not selectively dismiss a single Commissioner, or Vice President or, indeed, the President of the Commission, but only the Commission in toto. Moreover the Community has an additional powerful body, a Council of Ministers[3] composed of a representative of each of the governments of the Community's member states. The most important loci of power in the European Community are the Commission and the Council.

Community policy is customarily initiated by the Commission of the European Communities, (indeed it is only the Commission which formally disposes of the power to initiate), that is by the permanent officials of the Community. Proposals from the Commission, when they are of general applicability or of particular importance, do require to be ratified by the Council of Ministers. However, although the Council is described by the Community as its 'decision maker' (Commission of the European Communities 1992: 37), if proposals are not initiated by the Commission then the Council 'is paralysed' (Noel 1988: 23). Moreover the Council is empowered to amend a Commission proposal only if it achieves unanimity. A Commission proposal may be accepted, but only in toto, by a majority vote in the Council. As Noel (1988: 24) states, 'the Commission is always in a position to sway the outcome'.[4]

The powers of the Commission can be vividly exemplified by an example taken from the Community's broadcasting policy. The most important of the Community's acts in respect of broadcasting,[5] – the establishment of a single market through the *Television without Frontiers* Green Paper and Directive (Commission of the European Communities 1984a; Council of the European Communities 1989) – was initiated by Commission officials in DG III. The integration of European broadcasting markets into a single market was not proposed by the Parliament, the European Council or the Council of Ministers but by Commission officials.

## The politics of audiovisual policy

European Community audio-visual and broadcasting policy has evolved within the framework established by the major European treaties and declarations, notably the Treaty of Rome and the European Convention on Human Rights (which although promulgated under the aegis of the Council of Europe has been signed by all member states of the European Community). However the legal foundations on which Community policy has been built were insufficient to support comprehensive initiatives in the cultural – including audiovisual – field. In consequence Community institutions, notably the Commission supported by the Parliament (and in particular by its Committee on Youth, Culture, Education, the Media and Sport) and some Member States sought specific cultural powers either by revision of the Treaty of Rome or by successfully including a culture article – Article 128 (albeit with limited powers) – in the Maastricht Treaty on European political union.

The Maastricht Treaty has provided grounds for the Commission to exercise jurisdiction in the cultural domain for the first time. It has been welcomed by prominent members of the dirigiste camp and one of these, Roberto Barzanti formerly the Chair of the European Parliament's Committee on Youth, Culture, Education, the Media and Sport, made it clear that the inclusion of culture within a revised Treaty (i.e. the Maastricht Treaty) was necessary to ensure that Community initiatives in the audio-visual sector were effective. He stated: 'Il faut qu'initiatives comme le programme MEDIA, constamment menacé par les atteintes pendantes portées à la faiblesse de ses bases juridiques, deviennent l'ésprit même de l'action communautaires dans le secteur' [It's imperative that initiatives like the MEDIA programme, which are always under threat because of their insecure legal foundation, become the animating spirit of the Community's actions in the audio-visual sector.] (Barzanti 1990a: 36).

Not surprisingly Article 128 has been firmly opposed by the UK. The minutes of a meeting of UK officials in September 1991[6] (in preparation for negotiations on the Maastricht Treaty), recorded that the UK government 'was not convinced of the need for a new Treaty article . . . effective cultural co-operation already existed and the addition of a cultural article extending Community competence would mean increased Community expenditure. Any increased UK contribution would be at the expense of OAL's domestic spend. . . . we were concerned about the scope of "artistic and literary creation"; about the inclusion of audiovisual; and heritage' (note of meeting to discuss European Cultural Co-operation at the Office of Arts and Libraries 17.9.91).

The UK did not succeed in excluding the Culture Article from the Treaty but did succeed in limiting its scope. The text of Article 128 confines the Community's competence in the audio-visual to 'artistic and literary creation, including *in* (my emphasis) the audio-visual area'[7] rather than opening the whole of the audio-visual sector to Community intervention. Moreover Article 128 provides that Council decisions in cultural matters should be taken unanimously, rather than by qualified majority voting. Thus, although the Maastricht Treaty will permit more powerful interventionist initiatives by the Commission in the broadcasting and audio-visual sectors, the UK (the 'ultra liberal' Member State par excellence) achieved a significant success by maintaining a single state veto over Community cultural initiatives.

Article 128 of the Treaty on European Union reads:

1 The Community shall contribute to the flowering of the culture of the Member States, while respecting their national and regional diversity and at the same time bringing the common cultural heritage to the fore.
2 Action by the Community shall be aimed at encouraging co-operation between Member States and, if necessary, supporting and supplementing their action in the following areas:

- improvement of the knowledge and dissemination of the culture and history of the European peoples;
- conservation and safeguarding of cultural heritage of European significance;
- non-commercial cultural exchange;
- artistic and literary creation, including in the audio-visual sector.

3 The Community and the Member States shall foster co-operation with third countries and the competent international organizations in the sphere of culture, in particular the Council of Europe.
4 The Community shall take cultural aspects into account in its action under other provisions of this Treaty.
5 In order to contribute to the achievement of the objectives referred to in this Article, the Council:

- acting in accordance with the procedure referred to in Article 189b and after consulting the Committee of the Regions, shall adopt incentive measures, excluding any harmonization of the laws and regulations of the Member States. The Council shall act unanimously throughout the procedures referred to in Article 189b;
- acting unanimously on a proposal from the Commission shall adopt recommendations.

(Treaty on European Union. Article 128)

Although the UK had sought to forestall inclusion of a Culture Article in the Treaty both Conservative and Labour UK MEPs on the European Parliament's Committee on Youth, Culture, Education, the Media and Sport (interviewed in November 1991) joined their colleagues on the Committee in supporting the inclusion of Article 128. Indeed, a Conservative MEP, Miss Patricia Rawlings, wrote the Committee on Youth, Culture, Education, the Media and Sport's official Opinion (sent to the Parliament's Committee on Institutional Affairs) on the matter. Rawlings' Opinion stated the Committee's support for 'a paragraph on cultural affairs [being] included in the revised Treaty of Rome' (European Parliament 1991: 3). The Opinion began with Matthew Arnold's celebrated definition of culture in *Culture and Anarchy* (1963 [1869]) as 'the best that has been known and said in the world'. It identified two distinct meanings of culture. 'Firstly . . . an artistic concept, which includes all the arts. . . . Secondly as a social concept. This is the broader definition incorporating the socio-culture of individual countries, their food, language, attitudes, philosophy and behaviour'. Culture is, the Opinion states, 'at the very foundation of Europe. It reflects each country's individuality, as well as being a means of communication and integration between Member States' (European Parliament 1991: 3).

The Community's audio-visual policy is therefore not the product of a single and unified Community vision of the audio-visual sector. Rather it is a result of the interaction of differing priorities and perspectives of several distinct power centres. These power centres include the Member States of the Community, the European Parliament and, not least, rival power centres within the Commission of the European Communities. As Community officials in the Directorate concerned with Competition Policy, DG IV, confirmed (interview with author 11.11.91) 'the views and interests of DGs are different'.

## The role of the European Parliament

The European Parliament[8] has little power relative to the Commission. Indeed, the Parliament's weakness has led to the perception that the European Community has a 'democratic deficit' (Commission of the European Communities and European Parliament 1990: 6). The most significant of the Parliament's powers are those it exercises over the Commission's discretionary expenditure.[9] The Parliament can also call Commission officials to account for their work and policies (before its committees and through Parliamentary questions). Moreover the Parliament may, on a two-thirds majority in a vote of censure, dismiss the Commission. But, as a Conservative UK MEP ruefully stated 'The Commission tries to do as much as it can without involvement of the Parliament' (interview 6.11.91).

Not only is the Parliament weak in comparison to the Communities' major power centres, the Commission of the European Communities and the Council of Ministers, but its Committee responsible for the media (including television) is perceived to have low status and little influence. UK MEPs from both Conservative and Labour parties (interview November 1991) commented that the Committee on Youth, Culture, Education, the Media and Sport enjoyed the lowest status of any of the European Parliament's Committees. One Labour MEP observed that Denmark described it as 'the illegal Committee'![10] The other said 'its work means sod all. It's the bottom of the pile in terms of importance, at the end of the day the Council of Ministers will decide, end of bloody story'.

A Conservative MEP characterised the work of the Committee on Youth, Culture, Education, the Media and Sport as 80 per cent examination of proposed legislation (ie responding to Commission initiatives) and 20 per cent 'own initiative' work. Characteristically, the Committee responded to the Commission's agenda for the Community rather than setting the agenda itself. Mary Banotti MEP, the Irish Vice Chairman [*sic*] of the Committee on Youth, Culture, Education, the Media and Sport confirmed that the Parliament's role was essentially reactive. She stated that the Committee 'plays a significant part in amending Community legislation' (Banotti 1992: 6). Few MEPs have a specialised knowledge or interest in the media and, in consequence, the Parliament's views on media tend to be set by a few expert members. As Banotti testified 'each Committee contains a very mixed group of people in terms of experience and specialised knowledge. One or two people tend to deal with a piece of legislation and the others concur with their conclusions' (Banotti 1992: 6). None of the UK MEPs interviewed in 1991 regarded the media as one of their primary interests or areas of expertise. Indeed only the Chairman of the Committee[11] and two of its substitute members[12] were thought to have the media as a particular area of interest and expertise.

Nonetheless, as the Dutch MEP, Gijs de Vries,[13] put it: 'limited powers do not necessarily imply limited influence' (European Parliament 1987b: ii). In spite of the Community's overall 'democratic deficit' and the 'illegal committee's' relative weakness, de Vries has made strong claims for the importance of the Parliament's influence in Community broadcasting policy. Indeed, he claimed that the Parliament, rather than the Commission or the Council, initiated key elements of the Community's broadcasting and audiovisual policies. The Parliament, he claimed, 'prompted the Commission into publishing, first the Interim Report, and in 1984, the Green Paper on the Internal Market in broadcasting. . . . Parliament has thus *de facto* initiated legislation' (1987: ii). Roberto Barzanti, formerly Chairman of the Parliament's Committee on Youth, Culture, Education, the Media and Sport, echoed de Vries' claims. Barzanti described the Parliament's Hahn Resolution (European Parliament 1982) as the 'premier pierre' of Community audio-visual and broadcasting policy (interview with author 8.11.91). Elsewhere, Barzanti made strong claims for the Parliament's importance, stating:

> Le parlement européen est depuis toujours chef de file parmi les institutions européennes pour affirmer le role de la communauté dans les débats et les initiatives qui se produisent en Europe autour du secteur audiovisuel. Il s'agit, bien évidement, d'un secteur de l'industrie: mais il s'agit aussi, et dans aussi une mesure du moins aussi importante que l'autre, d'une activité culturelle. [The European Parliament has always been in the front line among European institutions in advocating a Community role in the European debates and policy initiatives concerning the audiovisual sector. The issue, obviously, concerns an industrial sector but it also concerns a cultural activity which is no less important.]
>
> (Barzanti 1990a: 35)

## The Council of Europe

The Council of Europe was established in 1949 with ten members, by 1992 its membership had grown to twenty-five states and promises to grow further.[14] It was born in the late 1940s from the International Committee of the Movement for European Unity (later the European Movement) founded in 1947 following Winston Churchill's celebrated Zurich speech of 1946. The founders of the Council of Europe placed considerable importance on a supernational

European authority to guarantee human rights. Hence the formulation of the European Convention on Human Rights and the early establishment of the European Court of Human Rights under the aegis of the Council of Europe and its Parliamentary Assembly.[15] Council decisions are made by the Committee of Ministers, that is by the Ministers of Foreign Affairs of member states. The 192 member Parliamentary Assembly (between 2 and 18 members are appointed from each member country by the parliament of each member state) has a consultative status.

The chief significance of the Council of Europe for broadcasting policy lies in the guarantees of freedom of access to information (and consequential limits on the powers of governments) which the European Convention on Human Rights affords. The Convention's safeguards were further affirmed by the Council's Convention on Transfrontier Television, Article 4 of which provides for 'freedom of expression and information . . . freedom of reception and . . . retransmission . . . of programme services' (Council of Europe 1989) which came into effect on 1.5.93. However the Council has also provided an important agency for positive initiatives in respect of broadcasting and the audio-visual: notably through the use of European 'variable geometry' to establish the Eurimages programme.

Council initiatives, such as Eurimages and the Convention on Transfrontier Television, are notable examples of the way in which the Council has enabled Members to achieve objectives impossible to achieve in the context of the European Community because of opposition to such measures by other Community Member States and/or because of the absence of EC jurisdiction in the area in question. Moreover, the Council has enabled Members to create rules and agreements in a less binding form than the EC permits (eg the Convention on Transfrontier Television). As one Council official stated (interview 17.12.91), the Council 'gives options for partial agreements'. Thus the Council has enabled members, (notably France and its allies) to develop European film support policies which they had been unable to develop within the EC, and has enabled members (such as the UK and its allies) to establish agreements on transfrontier broadcasting, extending 'negative freedom'[16] of a character different to that possible within the European Community. Indeed, the Council has been regarded by several Member States of the European Community (Gavin 1991: 20, mentions Belgium, Denmark and Germany) as a more appropriate body for media regulation than the Community itself.

Council resolutions have been passed on a variety of media and cultural matters, including the educational and cultural use of radio and television (Resolution (70) 19). Council Resolutions may, or may not, lead to action, (Eurimages, for example, was established in consequence of a Resolution (88) 15), but Resolutions are chiefly important in that they pave the way for intergovernmental agreements known as Conventions. Several Conventions relevant to the mass media have derived from Council Resolutions. For example, those on television programme exchanges (Nr 27 in 1958) and on protection of copyright in television broadcasts (Nr 34 1960).

The most important convention in respect of the mass media to derive from Council activity is the European Convention on Human Rights (which has been ratified by all the Member States of the European Community). The Convention guarantees every person freedom to receive and impart information and ideas without interference by public authority regardless of frontiers. The Convention was signed on 4 November 1950 and entered into force on 3 September 1953.[17] In 1982 (29 April) the Committee of Ministers of the Council of Europe adopted a Declaration on the Freedom of Expression and Information which further affirmed the general principles enunciated in the Convention. Latterly the Convention on Transfrontier Television has been promulgated and has received ratification by seven Member States of the Council of Europe, permitting its coming into force on 1.5.93.

The Council's Human Rights Directorate, through its Steering Committee on the Mass Media (CDMM[18]) and its sub-committees and working parties, was given formal responsibility for media policy within the Council because

> The proper functioning of free and autonomous media and the availability of a plurality of information sources and of communication links are essential for democracy and international understanding. Freedom of information is not only a fundamental right *per se* but also facilitates the exercise of other fundamental rights.
>
> (Council of Europe 1991b: 6)

This formulation expresses the Council's overriding commitment to negative freedom in communications and the status and influence of the CDMM (particularly relative to the CDCC or Council for Cultural Co-operation) testifies to the strength of the Council's commitments in this respect. The 1980s, the period in which the Council formally took up media issues, were characterised by a Council official (interviewed 18.12.91) as a time of 'tremendous technical change' when members of the Council had become alarmed by the development of doctrines which they believed threatened freedom of expression and communication; notably the doctrines of 'prior consent' for reception of satellite television signals and licensing of journalists espoused by UNESCO. Publication of the UNESCO-sponsored MacBride report *Many Voices One World* in 1980 (UNESCO 1980) focused these concerns. In 1981 the Parliamentary Assembly of the Council of Europe adopted a recommendation (n 926) on 'Questions raised by cable television and by direct satellite broadcasts'. The recommendation welcomed satellite television and affirmed that the development of policy for these new media must be based on recognition of 'freedom of the press and television, as a fundamental component of freedom of expression' (Council of Europe 1991c: 34) and urged 'concrete legal co-operation, possibly in the form of a convention' (1991c: 37).

In 1982, the Committee of Ministers of the Council of Europe adopted a

Declaration on the Freedom of Expression and Information (Council of Europe 1991a: 63) which was grounded in Article 19 of the Universal Declaration of Human Rights and Article 10 of the European Convention on Human Rights. The 1982 Declaration (sometimes known as the European Media Charter) was notable for its explicit commitment to free flows of information across borders and to its commitment to the 'protection of the right of everyone, regardless of frontiers, to express himself, to seek and receive information and ideas, whatever their source'. The Declaration also specifically rejected 'arbitrary controls or constraints on participants in the information process'. The '21' (as it then was) members of the Council of Europe therefore explicitly and unequivocally rejected the central propositions advanced by the MacBride Report. It was in this context that the CDMM was established within the Council's Directorate of Human Rights.

# NOTES

## INTRODUCTION

1 The author had access to extensive primary documentation (notably the IBA files concerning Eurikon and recordings of the channel's five weeks of transmissions), on which this case study is based.

2 Audio-visual trade statistics are notoriously unreliable but there is little doubt that European imports of American works has experienced striking increases. Dibie (1993: 10) states that 'European turnover of American distributors of audio-visual programmes went from $700 million in 1988 to $2.5 billion in 1990'; Maggiore (1990: 45) states that between 1985 and 1986 the Western European audiovisual trade deficit with the USA worsened and fell from $911 million to $1260 million. The US Bureau of Economic Analysis stated that the positive US worldwide trade balance for film and television programmes improved from $1090 million in 1987 to $2122 million in 1991 (NTIA 1993: 20).

Stephane has identified the European audio-visual market as 'rapidly becoming enslaved to American production'. He cites the following statistics to show Europe's enslavement to the USA (Stephane 1988: 15).

Proportion of American films shown by European television in 1985 by channel:

ZDF 36.1 per cent
RTBF 43.7 per cent
TF1 37 per cent
A2 35.3 per cent
FR3 28.1 per cent
RAI 57.4 per cent
RTL 50 per cent
NOS 51 per cent
BBC 55 per cent
ITV 38 per cent

See also UNESCO (1989: 145–8) and Sepstrup (1990).

3 The official title of the European Community changed to the European Union in 1993, after ratification of the Maastricht Treaty on European Union, and likewise the title Commission of the European Communities changed to European Commission. However I have used the pre-Maastricht titles for these institutions because these

238

were the titles extant at the time of the events considered in this study (except where I refer to later instances).

4 See, *inter alia*, the German Federal Constitutional Court's judgement of 16.6.81 which states 'Article 5 (1), second sentence, Basic Law, prescribes legislation which ensures freedom of broadcasting. This is also necessary where the scarcity of transmission frequencies and the high cost of production are offset by modern technology' (Internationes 1989: 20).

5 Reprinted in Clarke, A. (1992) pp 272–9.

6 See Collins 1992a and 1993.

7 From 4,168 hours in 1973 to 5,409 hours in 1986 (Bekkers 1987: 32).

8 The contemporary importance attributed to such matters cannot be doubted: the first named of the three qualifications, (defined by the Commission of the European Communities), for a state's accession to membership of the European Communities is 'European identity', the other two being 'democratic status' and 'respect of [*sic*] human rights' (Commission of the European Communities 1993a: 1).

9 Bourges was replaced by Jean-Pierre Elkabbach, a nominee of the new Conservative administration, in December 1993. He subsequently became président du Conseil supérieur de l'audiovisuel (CSA).

10 Many European public service broadcasters suffered dramatic declines in their share of television viewing between 1982–1992. Hervé Bourges, who was Chairman of France Television until December 1993, (and formerly of Antenne 2 and FR 3), stated 'Like their counterparts elsewhere in Europe, like the RAI, the ARD, the ZDF and TVE, the French public service channels' audience share dropped from 100 per cent to 50 per cent, or even less, when the commercial broadcasters started up' (Bourges 1993: 2–3). The analysis of public service broadcasting and its problems advanced by Bourges, (published in summary form in Bourges 1993), was described by Silj as 'undoubtedly the most lucid and concrete analysis of the problems currently facing public broadcasting' (Silj 1992: 42).

11 See, *inter alia*, *Independent* 25.8.93: 3.

## 1 EUROPEAN CULTURE AND IDENTITY

1 Jacques Boutet was President of the Conseil Supérieur de l'Audiovisuel.

2 When President of the British Film and Television Producers Association.

3 On 'Connexions', the promotional programme made to publicise the EBU's Eurikon experiment and to proselytise for the establishment of a pan-European public service satellite television channel which was screened at the Palais de l'Europe in Strasbourg on 13.10.82.

4 The genesis of the Council of Europe and the European Union are sometimes traced to utopian projects of European Government, notably to the Duc de Sully's "Grand Design for a Union of European Christendom" (see Sully's "Mémoires" notionally published at Amsterdam in 1638) and William Penn's "Essay towards the Present and Future Peace of Europe by the Establishment of a European Diet; Parliament or Estate" of 1693, but are usually dated from the foundation of the International Committee of the Movement for European Unity in 1947 (which was inspired by Winston Churchill's speech in Zurich a year before).

5 The role of the Western Occupying Powers in Germany was, of course, to do just that.

6 The CDMM (Comité directeur des moyens de communication de masse) comprises experts from each of the member states of the Council from the Commission of the European Communities and from the Parliamentary Assembly. Other organisations including the Audiovisual Eureka, the EBU and ACT have observer status on

CDMM. The membership of CDMM (and the sub-committees MM-JU, Committee of Legal Experts in the Media Field, and MM-R-PD, Select Committee of Experts on the Production, Distribution and Marketing of European audio-visual works) is specified in Council of Europe (1991b: 130–1).

7 And on the degree to which the choices are realisable, how important they are relative to each other and what social constraints obtain in determining which choices are made.

8 Indeed the Commission of the European Communities has defined the four fundamental freedoms of the European Community as negative freedoms: 'the free movement of goods, services, people and capital' (Commission of the European Communities 1992: 2).

9 Hahn was a German Christian Democrat refugee from East Prussia.

10 The resolution was also referred to the Committees on Budgets, Political Affairs and Legal Affairs. The Committee on Budgets did not submit a view on the resolution. The reports of the committees are in European Parliament (1982).

11 In *Realities and Tendencies* (Commission of the European Communities 1983: 6), the Commission specifically nominated the EBU's Eurikon experiment as foreshadowing 'the common European programme'. It named Eurikon's main aims as:

> to develop a truly pan-European service to reach out beyond the traditional barriers of nationality and language to a new audience more than 300 million strong;
>
> to establish the nucleus of a European editorial structure, ie a team of highly qualified broadcasters who, with the support of the organizations they come from, are convinced of the value of their work and believe in its future;
>
> to identify the proposed project's inherent technical, legal, cultural, linguistic and economic problems.
>
> (Commission of the European Communities 1983: 26–7)

Clearly the Commission supported these aims and, although its support for Eurikon was principally rhetorical, granted Eurikon's successor, Europa, 1 million ECU in subventions.

12 A source in the Council of Europe (interviewed 17.12.91) stated that there was 'no doubt that the European Parliament wanted increased coverage of the Parliamentary proceedings' and that the Council had provided free facilities to Eurikon to raise the profile of the Council and the Parliamentary Assembly with European viewers. The Council remains 'very interested in news' the source said.

13 The broadcasting trade journal *Television Business International* (October 1989: 127–34) listed 442 international co-productions in progress, or recently completed, at October 1989. However, although co-production is becoming increasingly important, it should not be forgotten that co-productions 'represent but a low proportion of first-run broadcasts in Europe: 3 per cent to 5 per cent on average' (*Espace* No. 10 [1992]: 4).

14 Hoskins and McFadyen, in their study of international joint ventures in television programme co-production, identify eight potential benefits for partners as follows: benefits of pooling financial resources, access to foreign governments' incentives and subsidies, access to partner's market, access to third country markets, learning from partner, risk reduction, cheaper inputs in partner's country, and access to desired foreign locations. But international joint ventures are not necessarily wholly beneficial. They can entail additional transaction costs, loss of control over the product and

its cultural specificity, exploitation by a foreign partner and creation of a more formidable competitor.

15 Chenevière was Director of the Programme Committee of the European Co-production Association and the Programme Director of Télévision Suisse Romande. He later became Director General of Télévision Suisse Romande.

16 Jurgens' proposals came to fruition (in respect of cinema films) through establishment of Eurimages and (in respect of television programmes) the European Co-production Association. Collaboration between small and medium-sized European broadcasters, which he sought, developed through an association of the public broadcasters of eleven European states which established a group for the Development of an Audio-Visual IDentity for Europe – DAVID.

Broadcasters from Austria, Belgium, Denmark, Finland, Greece, Ireland, Netherlands, Norway, Portugal, Sweden and Switzerland established DAVID in 1988 following concern that the consequences of the Television Without Frontiers Directive would be disadvantageous to small country broadcasters. (See *EBU Review. Programmes, Administration, Law.* Vol. XXXIX, No. 5. September 1988: 46). DAVID is therefore a response to the intensified division of labour within the Community (and between the Community and other European states) that the *Television without Frontiers* initiative anticipated. In 1991 the Commission of the European Communities established an analogous programme SCALE (Small Countries improve their Audio-visual Level in Europe) under the MEDIA 95 umbrella.

## 2 THE EUROPEAN BROADCASTING UNION

1 Also known as the UER after the initial letters of the words Union Européenne de Radiodiffusion.

2 The founding Statutes of the Union Internationale de Radiophonie (IBU) are reproduced in Briggs (1961: 413–15). The statutes admit to membership 'all societies or associations exploiting public broadcasting enterprises'. The genesis of the IBU is described by Briggs (1961: 308–22).

3 Czechoslovakia, Hungary and Poland joined the EBU in 1990 whilst remaining members of OIRT. They were joined by broadcasters from Belarus, Bulgaria, Estonia, Latvia, Lithuania, Moldova, Romania, the Russian Federation and the Ukraine in 1993.

4 Head of EBU Data and Reference Centre.

5 Membership of the Council was expanded to 19 following union of the EBU and OIRT.

6 SSR is a permanent member of the Council. An EBU official stated (24.2.92) that it was 'unthinkable' for the UK, Germany, Italy and Spain not to be represented on the Administrative Council and that it would be highly unusual to have France unrepresented. Other Administrative Council positions are divided on 'a gentleman's agreement' between a number of regional groupings: the Nordic grouping (in which Denmark, Finland, Norway and Sweden share representation), a Benelux grouping (in which the Netherlands and Belgium alternate as members of the Council), a North African grouping, (in which both Libya and Israel are located, although neither of these states have been represented on the Administrative Council), and a residual category where Council membership has rotated between broadcasters from Turkey, Austria, Yugoslavia (when that state existed) and Ireland.

7 The EBU paid no fee for the rights to the soccer World Cup final but guaranteed the Swiss Football Association up to 10,000 Sfr if its gate receipts were in deficit.

8 In 1989 the BBC originated 124 hours 54 minutes and received 212 hours of Eurovision programmes, a ratio of c.1 : 1.7. Danmarks Radio originated 17 hours 45 minutes and received 451 hours 02 minutes, a ratio of c.1 : 25.4. In the same year the ARD originated 364 hours 29 minutes and received 557 hours 33 minutes, a ratio of c.1 : 1.52, whereas Radio Monte Carlo originated 12 hours 09 minutes and received 1,147 hours 16 minutes, a ratio of c.1 : 95.6 (*EBU Review. Programmes, Administration, Law* Vol. XLI No. 3 May 1990: 24).

9 In 1989 actuality programmes accounted for 7.7 per cent of Eurovision programmes, folklore 0.2 per cent, religion 1.5 per cent, sport 87.4 per cent, light entertainment 2.2 per cent and music and jazz 1 per cent.

10 Since this study was completed Cohen, Levy, Roeh and Gurevitch (1996) have published a study of the Eurovision news exchange.

11 The news exchanges are EVN-E/EVN-M at 04.30 CET, AVN at 08.30 CET, EVN-Y at 09.30 CET, EVN-0 at 11.00 CET, YNE at 13.00 CET, EVN-W at 14.15 CET. (This exchange was also known as IVN and was the principal occasion for the exchange of news with the OIRT Intervision network), ERN-E at 14.45 CET, EVN-1 at 16.00 CET and EVN-2 at 17.40 CET (*Espace* No. 21 November [1993]: 2). There are also *ad hoc* 'flash' news exchanges.

12 On 9 September 1993 Sky Television announced the establishment of a satellite television news exchange between Sky News, VTM (Belgium), CBS (USA) and TBS (Japan) (Sky Television press release). CNN has mimicked Eurovision in its organisation:

> The contributing news organisations pay all costs of production and delivery of their reports to CNN each week, either by satellite or air freight. CNN assumes all costs of assembling the newscast and transmitting it via satellite to earth stations in contributing countries. Contributors are invited to down-link and rebroadcast the programme locally in its entirety, or tape the programme for later use in any way they like.
>
> (Flournoy 1992: 10)

Curiously Flournoy does not acknowledge the precedent of Eurovision in his discussion of television news exchanges.

A BBC source interviewed on 9.12.91 stated that the EBU Eurovision news service was superior to that offered by television news agencies.

See also Cohen *et al.* (1996).

13 The satellite television channel Super Channel, for example, purchased access to Eurovision news exchanges in 1987 for Sfr 880,000 per annum (CA 1915 SPG 3848 26.2.88: 23).

14 'The basic units are based on the potential television audience . . . or, in the absence of more precise data, on the estimated number of sets in use' (SG/AF/9857 17.12.91: 1). Transnational entities adhering to the EBU, (but not formally members), also pay subscriptions calculated in basic units: in 1992 3Sat was liable for 7 basic units, TV5 for 11 basic units and Eurosport 10 basic units (CA 2173 SPG 5732 23.1.92: 25).

15 Eugster gave the complicated bases for price calculation as follows:

> basic units (BU) = square root of *licences*/10,000

This formula remains the basis on which members' liability to pay basic units is calculated. Modifications applied to the basic units formula (the Wallquist system) to yield 'rectified basic units' result in a modest rise in liabilities for large and/or rich countries and a consequential decline in liabilities for small/poor countries.

Thus (for 1992), the liability of the ARD (the largest single contributor to the EBU's finances) under the Wallquist system rose from 35 to 37 basic units (and the BBC's from 22.5 to 23.75) whereas Turkey's declined from 25 to 23.5. The only instances of decline in a rich country's liability to pay were the cases of Norway (from 13 to 12.5 basic units) and Luxembourg (from 7 to 6.5 basic units).

Transnational member broadcasters (such as TV5, Eurosport and Radio Monte Carlo) pay on a basis decided case by case. The annexe to SG/AF/9857 of 17.12.91 states 'For transnational activities, the basic units calculated according to a special rule approved by the Administrative Council are not automatically applied'.

In theory vision units are distance related and calculated from a notional network centre point. Thus members distant from the network centre will tend to pay more in vision unit charges than members geographically closer to the network centre.

For 1992, however, the liability to pay vision units was identical to the liability to pay basic units except for one case; that of Libya. Libya's vision unit liability was inflated by 4.5 excess cost units.

Each member is also liable to pay circuit costs. These costs are mitigated by the credits members accumulate by originating unilateral contributions to the Eurovision system. Thus the net cost of vision circuits are calculated by subtracting the unilateral credit from the circuit cost.

In 1992 the notional value of 1 basic unit was set at 130,000 Gold Francs (Eugster 1983; SG/AF/9857).

Pelieu (interview 26.2.92) stated that the cost division for Eurovision events was increasingly negotiated on a case by case basis. Moreover, there were cases when there was insufficient financial commitment by members to the acquisition of specific rights and in consequence rights were acquired by an individual EBU member and then sub-licensed to members (and non-members).

16  The Technical Director of the EBU (interviewed 24.2.92) stated satellite transmission had led to 'an enormous increase in traffic' and that the annual growth in Eurovision traffic had risen to 25 per cent (from 10 per cent) with use of four Eutelsat transponders for Eurovision.

17  See Komiya (1990) for an interesting discussion of the case of Intelsat.

18  Eugster states, 'At Torquay [where the EBU held its founding conference in 1950] in 1950, West European broadcasters were worried that they would have to pay higher royalties to directors, artists, authors and musicians. . . The seriousness of the matter made necessary a formal examination of ways by which broadcasters can protect themselves from higher program rights costs'.

19  See Eugster 1983 for EBU Statutes prior to 1982.

20  In fact this projected public conference did not take place until 1989 when, during the European Film and Television Year, the EBU held a Symposium in Brussels (see EBU 1989a).

21  Boni was a member of the socialist faction in RAI and an active participant in the group who developed and implemented the EBU's Eurikon satellite television service.

22  Of the member organisations consulted the ARD [Germany], BBC [UK], DR [Denmark], NOS [Netherlands], NRK [Norway], SR [Sweden], UKIB [UK] and YLE [Finland] responded. It can be seen therefore that it was North European broadcasters, including British broadcasters, who were particularly active in contributing to the EBU's self-examination.

23  Enkelaar was a member of the Group of Experts which progressed Eurikon and was Managing Director of NOS Television Programmes and Vice Chairman of the EBU TV Programmes Committee. Kimmel became Head of the International Affairs at

ZDF and was described by a member of the EBU Permanent Services as 'one of public service broadcasting's deepest and most important thinkers' (interview 26.2.92). MacConghail became Controller of Programmes at RTE, (and subsequently became an independent producer), where he was tipped as a future Director General, albeit described as the 'stormy petrel of the RTE' (Cairnduff 1984: 118). Johnson was Chief Assistant to the Managing Director of BBC Television and later became (before his retirement in 1993) Head of International Television Liaison for the BBC.

24 A reference to the equal voting power given to EBU Member States independent of their size. Thus the BBC had and has less formal voting power in the EBU (because the UK vote has been shared between the BBC and UK commercial broadcasters and the IBA) than had and has Radio Monte Carlo.

25 In 1985, for example, Vittorio Boni, a member of the Wangermée Group (and also Head of RAI's International Relations Department, Chair of the EBU Television Programmes Committee and a member of the Eurikon Operations Group) urged that the EBU extend its collaboration in news and sport to drama, and that the EBU should establish new services and engage in extensive research on European audiences (Boni 1985).

26 Mariano Maggiore of DG X, the Commission's observer on the Eurikon Operations Group, served as Vice Chairman of BABEL.

27 The Marino Charter states:

> Meeting at Marino, Italy, on 6 April 1990, the directors general of Administrative Council member organizations stated their views on the Union's general policy.
>
> They considered that, within the framework of the turmoil of the European audiovisual scene, it was more than ever necessary to maintain and promote the richness of European cultural and linguistic diversity. To be best able to do this, the European Broadcasting Union had to tighten relations between its existing members and reinforce its role as the spokesman and the body for cooperation of public service broadcasters and of other broadcasters with a cultural mission, irrespective of their funding. It shall apply the statutory criteria for admission of new members accordingly.
>
> The European Broadcasting Union will cooperate with non-member broadcasters on a contractual basis and with reciprocity, directly or with associations which these organizations might set up or develop.
>
> To attain these objectives, the Union's members strongly reaffirmed the principles of solidarity which are the basis of their cooperation, in order to maintain high professional and technical standards as well as to offer to the whole public, including minorities, a diversified quality programme. They wished to redefine the EBU, to render it dynamic and make it the performing instrument of their common mission. They undertook to make available to the EBU the necessary financial and human resources to attain the following objectives in particular:
>
> 1　Intensify the EBU's action towards European institutions and participate actively in various projects launched under their auspices.
>
> 2　Integrate or coordinate the various activities of EBU members clearly attached to the objectives of the Union, but which have developed outside it, in order to create synergies and to add an extra public relations value to the efforts of the public service broadcasters.
>
> 3　Intensify cooperation between members through coproduction, especially in the cultural area and promote other forms of joint European initiatives.

4    Maintain collective negotiation for the purchase of sports rights by setting in motion more rapid and more flexible procedures, making available considerable financial resources required by increased competition and developing as needed other negotiating assets.

5    Confirm the principle of free reciprocity which promotes exchanges for small as well as for big organizations, on condition that members hold to it without exception.

6    Widen the use of the Eurovision network for the benefit of all broadcasters, members or non-members, and reinforce the EBU's role as network operator.

7    Develop and establish a strong and clear image of the Union as a community of broadcasters with an obligation to provide varied and balanced programming for all sections of the population.

8    Review the sharing of financial charges within the Union, so that the increased burden resulting from this policy be better distributed on the basis of members' capacity, the use they make of services and the value of rights according to the various markets.

9    Strengthen the ties with OIRT and its European members with the aim of extending collaboration between broadcasters from the Atlantic to the Urals, such as already covers the entire Mediterranean basin.

These objectives have consequences for the Permanent Services and for members.

The Permanent Services will re-examine their activity in order to make available the means necessary for new directions, through a revision of priorities and working methods. They will review the financial system to make it the tool of a management by objectives and increase the transparency of costs according to activities (as a first step, a separate radio budget should be established). They will develop qualitative and quantitative personnel management. They will, finally, take the necessary organizational measures for an increased dynamism and an interdisciplinary approach to all questions.

Members will see to it that all their staff concerned work with a view to the objectives fixed and act in such a way that decisions may be taken rapidly by competent people. They will in addition make available the required financial means.

28  La Cinq, M6, RTL-TVi, RTL+, Premiere, Telefünf, BSkyB, Super Channel, VTM, Teleclub, TV3, Telecino, Antenne 3 and Telepiu subsequently joined the ACT.

29  The ACT Charter asserts the creative role of commercial broadcasters in 'developing the European identity and cultural heritage'; in providing programmes which are 'varied and up to the quality expected by the public'; in reflecting 'existing diversity' and giving an impetus to 'constantly evolving aspirations and expectations of the people' (cited from Maggiore 1990: 201–2).

30  Channel 4 indirectly participated in the EBU: it was a wholly owned subsidiary of the UK's regulator of commercial television, the IBA, which was a member of the EBU through its own participation in the UKIB consortium made up of the IBA and the trade association of the UK's commercial television stations, the ITCA.

31  An EBU official (interviewed 26.2.92) stated that German and Italian members' resistance to the admission of commercial broadcasters was particularly strong. French and UK members were less opposed. However the BBC voted for the exclusion of commercial broadcasters at Marino. Although a BBC official (with a long history of active participation in the EBU) reported (interview 9.12.91) that the

Director General of the BBC to have said that the BBC's decision to vote for exclusion of commercial broadcasters from the EBU at Marino was very finely balanced.

32 In spite of the relationship with commercial broadcasters having been the focus of EBU policy debates in recent years an EBU official stated (24.2.92) 'Our main problem is not the private broadcasters but the PTTs – they are the last bastion of monopoly'. Indeed the EBU carries commercial broadcasters' signals on its Eurovision network and is developing satellite transmission and relay of signals between members (with earth stations on broadcasters' premises) in order to reduce its dependence on the PTTs for its 13,800 km of terrestrial links.

33 See Collins 1994 for discussion of the conflict between liberals and *dirigistes* in the European Community.

## 3 PUBLIC SERVICE BROADCASTING

1 Now usually known as the orbit/spectrum resource. The orbit resource is the finite number of locations at which a satellite can be located in geosynchronous orbit. A satellite in geosynchronous orbit (or geostationary orbit) maintains the same position relative to the earth's surface and can thus relay signals from the earth to a wide area of the earth's surface using radio frequencies which were hitherto (before the successful implementation of communication satellites) unusable for communication. Thus successful exploitation of the geosynchronous orbit resource has mitigated the scarcity of the radio frequency spectrum whilst the combined orbit/spectrum resource still remains a finite resource.

2 See Coase (1950) for an argument that the principal reason for the restriction of broadcasting in the UK to the BBC was not scarcity in transmission capacity but policy makers' choices. Coase examines policy elites' attempts to suppress cable radio and advertising-financed radio in English from overseas. He cites the Crawford Committee Report of 1926 to illustrate the roots of monopoly: 'It is agreed that the US system of uncontrolled transmission and reception is unsuited to this country, and that Broadcasting must accordingly remain a monopoly – in other words that the whole organisation must be controlled by a single authority' (Crawford Committee Report para 4 , cited in Coase 1950: 59).

3 Not least the peculiar economic characteristics of broadcasting, which mean that the theoretical criteria of well-functioning markets can only be satisfied at the expense of significant welfare loss, and which therefore provide solid grounds for intervention in broadcasting markets. Cave (1985) and Garnham (1990: 120) have pointed out that spectrum scarcity is not the only rationale for the regulation of broadcasting. Garnham has argued that a range of social, political and cultural public policy goals legitimise intervention and that market arrangements will entrench information poverty and disempower the poor. Both contend that welfare is likely to be maximised through forms of public provision of services.

Cave, (following Coase), has argued that the public good, non-excludable, character of market failure in broadcasting provides powerful reasons for intervention which are independent of spectrum scarcity and that, moreover, establishment of excludable services will not satisfactorily rectify market failure.

Because one person's consumption of a broadcast signal deprives no other person of the opportunity to consume it broadcasting is considered to be a 'non-rival' good. Moreover, because viewers and listeners cannot be excluded from consuming broadcast signals broadcasting is, unlike most other goods and services, 'non-excludable'. The 'non rival' and 'non excludable' characteristics of broadcasting have meant that, (until recent developments in communication technologies, notably the development of robust and inexpensive systems for encrypting broadcast signals), broadcasting markets were 'failed markets' and that, therefore, political intervention is both necessary and legitimate.

Cave argued (Cave 1985: 26) that excludable services (such as subscription television) will tend to undersupply broadcasts and that even a broadcasting market offering a range of satellite supplied encrypted services will be a failed market in which intervention is required to maximise welfare.

4 Since all markets are to some degree failed markets, market theorists can argue that even a market which is acknowledged to be imperfect may be the 'least worst', even if not the 'first best', basis for the organisation of broadcasting services.

5 See case NN 141/95 – Portugal, and also commentary in Competition Directorate-General 1996: 48–9 and in European Commission 1997: 66–7.

6 The Peacock Report, properly known as the *Report of the Committee on Financing the BBC*, was commissioned by the UK government and published in 1986. It is known as the Peacock Report (and the committee which wrote it is known as the Peacock Committee) after Alan (now Sir Alan) Peacock, the committee chairman.

7 Other definitions may be found in McDonnell (1991: 78–83) and in Raboy (1996: 15). My thanks to Joseph McElligott for bringing these to my attention.

8 Austria, Belgium, France, Germany, Italy, the Netherlands, Portugal, Spain, Sweden, Switzerland, the UK.

9 One of the most interesting features of the proposal to establish a fifth terrestrial television service in the UK is that this service will *not* be universal. Large areas of the UK, including the southern littoral, will not be served. This decision represents an important shift in UK policy priorities: universal service has been subordinated to the goal of making the fullest possible use of the radio spectrum resource.

10 It is worth noting here that the BBC's comedy series *Fawlty Towers*, one of the most vaunted glories of public service broadcasting in the UK of recent years, was brought to German viewers by the commercial channel RTL+.

11 Blumler's attribution of a majoritarian ethos and vocation to commercial television and investiture of public service broadcasting with a necessarily minoritarian role overstates an important distinction. Public service broadcasting has often assumed the majoritarian role of nation building (the Australian Broadcasting Corporation is known not as a public service broadcaster but as a *national* broadcaster), and, *per contra*, commercial television has offered minoritarian (e.g. speciality) services. But Blumler was right to recognise (as BRU did not) the incompatibility of a minoritarian public service, and a majoritarian, nationalist, vocation for broadcasting. These two vocations can be reconciled only in circumstances of monopoly. One reason why European Public Service Broadcasters found the ending of their monopoly so difficult was that they were compelled to face this fundamental contradiction.

12 *Schwarzwaldklinik* is the best-known example of German broadcasters' attempts during the 1980s to develop popular programming on the lines of US high-budget drama series such as *Dallas* and *Dynasty*.

13 See Johnston (1979) for an excellent discussion of the influence of high culture values on German film making, and Collins and Porter (1981) for discussion of the relationship between German television and film-making, (and film-makers).

14 The 1987 Media Act provides that the Minister of Culture sets the levels of programming required of Dutch public broadcasters in each of four categories; education (5 per cent), culture (20 per cent), information (25 per cent) and entertainment (25 per cent).

15 Then of Antenne 2 and later an EBU official heading the Television Programmes Department. The members of the Perez Group were Henri Perez (Antenne 2), Carel Enkelaar (NOS), Michael Johnson (BBC), Hans Kimmel (ZDF) and Muiris MacConghail (RTE).

16 The Perez Group was one of four EBU groups to report to the Wangermée Group: the others were a radio group (chaired by Manfred Jenke), a legal group and a technical group.

17 See, for example, Murdock (1990), the deliberations of the Council of Europe Ministerial Conference on the Mass Media (see, *inter alia*, Council of Europe 1991e) and the European Parliament's successive Resolutions on media pluralism (see, *inter alia*, European Parliament 1982a and 1984a) and the Green Paper on *Pluralism and Media Concentration in the Internal Market* (Commission of the European Communities 1992a) produced by the Commission of the European Communities' internal market directorate.

18 The ACT was established in 1989 by CLT-RTL, Fininvest, ITV, Sat-1 and TF1.

19 The extent of the freedom of private broadcasters in Germany is dependent on the performance of public broadcasters. The Federal Constitutional Court Decision of 4.11.86 in respect of the Lower Saxony Broadcasting Law provides that 'As long as the fulfilment of this responsibility [i.e. to meet the 'basic needs' of viewers and listeners in respect of broadcasting services RC] by the public corporations is effectively guaranteed it would appear justifiable not to require private broadcasters to meet the same requirements with regard to range of programmes and degree of diversity. However, the appropriate legislation must make it possible for private contractors to achieve as much diversity of opinion as possible (Internationes 1989: 21).

20 See, for example, the Green Paper *The Future of the BBC* (Department of National Heritage 1992), which for the first time in an official UK Government publication defines a role for broadcasting in the construction of national identity.

21 Hearst had a long and distinguished career in the BBC and served as Controller of Radio 3, Controller of the BBC Future Policy Group and as Special Assistant to the Director General.

22 The Director of the Hans Bredow Institut attached to the University of Hamburg, Hans Bredow's place in German broadcasting history was rather like John Reith's in British broadcasting history.

23 Kimmel referred to the EBU as 'a successful and exclusive club of monopolist (or almost monopolist) PSB' (1982: 7): MacConghail asked 'what precisely is it we are to defend? It cannot be the status quo' (MacConghail telex to Vilcek 23.9.82).

24 The Pilkington Committee's arguments deserve to be read in full: 'the Governors' and Members' concern is to represent and secure the public interest in broadcasting. It is for them to judge what the public interest is, and it is for this that they are answerable. They must not do so by assessing the balance of opinion on this or that element of programme content, and then adopting the majority view as their own; for as we have already noted, this would be to mistake "what the public wants" in the misleading sense implied when the phrase is used as a slogan – for the public interest. Their task is, as we have said, to be thoroughly aware of public opinion in all its variety, to care about it and to take proper and full account of it. Having done so, they must then identify the public interest in broadcasting, and secure it through control of the executive arm (Pilkington 1962 para 408).

25 Habermas' ideas about the public sphere were first introduced to English language readers in 1974 when *New German Critique* published a translation of a brief essay (an encyclopedia article), by Habermas titled 'The public sphere'. Habermas' book *Strukturwandel der Öffentlichkeit* was published in German in 1962. An English translation was published in the UK in 1989. However for our purposes Habermas' impact on broadcasting studies dates from Garnham's essay of 1986 'The media and

the public sphere' which quotes from the seven-page essay first published by *New German Critique*.

26 Garnham has published two different essays under the title 'The media and the public sphere' (Garnham 1986 and 1992). Both have substantial sections in common but each essay contains much material which is absent from the other. However the intrinsic interest of the arguments posed in the later essay is such that those who do not read it, believing that it is simply a reprinted version of the first essay, will be denied valuable insights and much material for productive reflection.

27 The term also appeared in Garnham's editorial (1983a) to an issue of the journal *Media Culture and Society about Critical Theory*: 'After the Frankfurt School'. Here Garnham stated that 'Central to this whole debate is the concept of the public sphere, which takes the place within the tradition of ideology and hegemony' (1983a: 3).

28 An answer often given in the UK and other Western European countries is 'Via the licence fee'. However licence fees are simply a tax (and a particularly regressive form of taxation) under another name.

29 Habermas qualified his anathematisation of broadcasting by contrasting its development in Western Europe with the mode of development it assumed in the USA. However to state that 'In Great Britain, France, and Germany these new media were organized into public or semipublic corporations, because otherwise their publicist function could not have been sufficiently protected from the encroachment of their capitalistic ones' (1989: 188) hardly constitutes a rousing defence of public service broadcasting. Habermas' own work offers a meagre foundation for the neo-Habermasians' use of Habermas in their advocacy of public service broadcasting.

30 Jay's history of the Frankfurt school (Jay 1973) and exposition of its Critical Theory is deservedly well known.

31 However, Habermas does state explicitly that 'Today newspapers and magazines, radio and television are the media of the public sphere' (1974: 49).

32 As Habermas himself stated, his work 'leaves aside the plebian public sphere' (1989: xviii).

33 Reith's reflections on broadcasting and democracy read: 'Democracy had for years past been a ruling formula in this country and elsewhere. A philosopher's word, its actual as distinct from its theoretical content varied greatly. Further analysis of the theory was not of much avail; what was required was some mode of linking it to real life around; to the world as known to men and women as they were. Now broadcasting had emerged; was it the tempering factor that would give democracy for the first time under modern conditions a real chance of operating as a living force throughout the extended community as long ago it operated in the city state? It must cover more and more of the field of social and cultural life; become more and more valuable as an index to the community's outlook and personality which the statesman was supposed to read. The microphone could achieve where print and the philosophic formulation of doctrine had failed; could familiarise the public with the central organisation that conducted its business and regulated its inner and outer relations. Not the printable scheme of government but its living and doing, the bringing of the personalities of the leading figures to the fireside, which could unite governments and governed in democracy as in dictatorship' (Reith 1949: 135).

34 It would misrepresent Reith if the pawky self-deprecation with which he closed his statement were excised, he ended his statement 'Marvellous. That was the way one had to talk in those days' (Reith 1949: 103).

35 Fichera was a Vice President of RAI, one of 'Les Sages' appointed to review the pilot stage of the European Community's MEDIA Programme. He has served latterly as President and Chief Executive of Euronews.

36 Fichera stated that in 1985 RAI's share of the Italian primetime television audience had fallen to 37.44 per cent whereas that share achieved by Fininvest (Berlusconi) channels was 50 per cent. In 1989 RAI's primetime share had risen to 49.08 per cent and Fininvest's had fallen to 31.08 per cent. Fichera attributed RAI's success to scheduling a high proportion of its own productions, to coordinating the scheduling of its channels, to its reliance on mixed funding, (ie advertising and public funding), and to innovations in programming and technology (Fichera 1989: 22–23). In 1992 RAI lost some of the ground it had won back from Fininvest when its primetime share declined to 47.14 per cent and Fininvest's grew to 43.45 per cent (*Espace* No.18 February [1993]: 6).

## 4 EURIKON: THE DEVELOPMENT OF PAN-EUROPEAN TELEVISION

1 In the publication of one of the principle Dutch broadcasting societies associated with NOS and thus with the EBU-sponsored satellite television services.

2 The ESA was established in 1975 as the successor to ESRO (European Space Research Organisation) and ELDO (European Launcher Development Organisation) by eleven European partner states. In 1980 11 per cent of the ESA's budget came from the UK and 30 per cent from France. The Ariane launcher rocket is the best known of the ESA's initiatives but ESA also launched a series of communication satellites. The OTS-2 satellite was launched in 1978 after OTS-1 had been lost in a launch failure. The EBU had collaborated in the mid-1960s with ESRO in a study of the possible establishment of a television satellite network for the distribution of Eurovision (see Whyte 1989: 11).

3 Autin maintained his scepticism: whilst vigorously supporting the idea of a *European programme* stream he continued to express reservations about the L-Sat/Olympus delivery system which he referred to as 'a poor project' (CA 1704 SPG 2653 May 1984: 73).

4 See minutes of the 67th and 68th meetings of the Administrative Council (CA 1588 SPG 1773 1981; CA 1610 SPG 1923 1982). In 1982 a representative of RAI said 'if the EBU did not decide to use the L-Sat satellite the latter would be offered to other users which would be contrary to EBU's interests' (CA 1610 SPG 1923 20.10.82: 84). Muiris MacConghail of RTE, an active – if sometimes sceptical – participant in the EBU satellite initiatives confirmed that the threat of commercial competition motivated Eurikon participants: 'RAI, ARD and the IBA in particular were anxious to move ahead in relation to planning and to bring an experimental programme service into being as a demonstration of what might be done in pan-European programming and as a preemptive strike' (MacConghail 1983: 61).

5 The telex also asked members 'to decline any offers from this enterprise'.

6 In July 1996 the European Court ruled against public service broadcasters combining to acquire sports rights. Its decision destroyed one of the chief rationales for the very existence of the EBU which, throughout its history, had acquired programme rights on behalf of its members.

7 The meeting was opened by the newly appointed IBA Chairman, Lord Thomson.

8 RTL, the commercial broadcaster based in Luxembourg, was – thanks to perverse historical anomalies – an EBU member.

9 A telex (from J.-P. Julien to contacts in MBA, RTA, RTBF, RTT, TVE) dated 26 January 1982 refers to this meeting as having taken place on 20 February 1982. This eccentric dating follows that in a file draft telex by Clarke for Julien (dated 25 January 1982 in OTS Audience Research file). I have therefore assumed that the date of the meeting was in fact 20 January and that Julien's telex simply reproduces the

error originated in Clarke's draft. However the EBU/OTS Operations Group (1983: 22) account of the Eurikon experiments states that the Operations Group meeting took place in February – possibly following the original error. The group subsequently met in Geneva in March, in London in April, Hilversum in May, Rome in July, Vienna in August, Strasbourg in October and Baden-Baden in November 1982.

10 Giorgio Cingoli was an alternate member to Boni.

11 On occasion, (eg at the Rome, Vienna and Strasbourg meeting of the Operations Group), representatives of the major European institutions (such as the European Parliament, Commission of the European Communities, Council of Europe, European Space Agency, Eutelsat) attended the Operations Group's meetings.

12 In early 1982 Clarke attempted to draw in further EBU members into Eurikon. On 8 February he wrote to CBC, the Canadian Broadcasting Corporation, probably the most important EBU member outside the European broadcasting area, inviting its participation in Eurikon, (Canada was a member of the ESA whose satellite Eurikon used). However, Clarke's approach to the CBC was no more fruitful than were his courtship of EBU member broadcasters in the European broadcasting area who had not already made a commitment to Eurikon.

13 RAI consistently played a leading role in the EBU's satellite ventures: the Head of its International Department, Vittorio Boni, was a prime mover in Eurikon and his colleague, Ernesto Braun, became Chief Executive of Europa and later Chief Executive of Euronews (where he was succeeded by Massimo Fichera, formerly a Vice President of RAI).

14 The minutes record that 'The representatives of the European Parliament, the Commission and the Council of Europe all expressed satisfaction with the programme content and felt that the experiments had shown that there were enough programmes to make Pan-European broadcasting possible and viewable' (Minutes of The EBU/OTS Operations Group Meeting Rome 26.7.82: 1).

15 Even RTE, which committed only £10,000 to the operating budget of Eurikon and played no active part in the organisation and provision of the service, found it necessary to allocate a further £9,000 ('for freight, travel and associated administration and operational costs' [MacConghail 1983: 62]) to support its participation in Eurikon.

## 5 EURIKON PROGRAMMING

1 My accounts of Eurikon programming are based on the viewing of video recordings of transmissions, supplemented by reference to the IBA record of transmissions. Comprehensive description of the programming inordinately lengthy. I have chosen therefore to combine statistical accounts of categories of programme content with accounts of programming to give a 'flavour' of the channel's character.

Comparing recordings of the programmes actually transmitted with written records demonstrated the unreliability of the written sources. The IBA's record of Eurikon transmissions differs from the programmes actually transmitted. For example, it recorded two news reports, originated by NOS, of Cardinal Glemp's visit to Rome as the visit of 'the Polish Archbishop' and 'the Polish Ambassador' to Rome. Further examples abound.

2 Because programmes in the category 'adult education' accounted for less than 1 per cent of programmes screened, this programme category has been deleted from the table and is not shown in the minutage of programmes screened.

3 Undated and unattributed typescript notes in Eurikon programming file.

4 The team that made the news for the IBA week were led by Charles Barrand of UPITN supported by nine other staff of whom one came from NOS and the others

from UK ITV companies (Central and LWT) and from UPITN, assisted by two free-lancers (Barrand 1982: 2).

5 Records of news programme content during the IBA week are more comprehensive than for the RAI, ORF, NOS and ARD weeks. Viewing of one IBA news programme (transmitted Saturday 29 May 1982, the penultimate day of the IBA week) revealed that an item not listed in the IBA records was screened. The written record (used as the basis from which Eurikon news values were described) was therefore shown to be not wholly accurate.

6 Nineteen from UPITN, eleven from Visnews, eight from ITN, seven from the BBC, four from ITV companies (London Weekend, Thames, Tyne Tees, TVS) and one a pooled item from BBC/UPITN. In addition, five items were illustrated with graphics and did not include location visual material. Graphics were used only on the last two days of IBA transmissions.

7 Of the other news items screened by the IBA, six came from RAI, five from TDF and five from the ARD, four from CBS and from ORF, three from RTE, two from IRIB, two from TSS and one from each of RTP, RTBF, YLE, JRT, NOS, CNN, TVE, SRG, DR, Cuba and from the European Community.

8 There was no news on the first day of the IBA week (for technical reasons).

A common system of classifying news content was adopted for each of the five weeks of Eurikon programming. A single location was identified for each news item, using the IBA record of the running order and news schedule for all weeks of the Eurikon experiment. These locations were checked against the news transmissions for each day of Eurikon broadcasts that were viewed (at least one day in each week of transmissions). Some discrepancies were observed between the IBA record and the programmes actually transmitted but the correspondence between the written record and the transmission was sufficiently close to confirm that the written record was a reliable indicator of actual transmitted programme content.

Some news items showed more than one location; these were recorded only under one category. In the majority of cases the geopolitical location of the news item was a good proxy for the content of the item: a European location generally signified a European news subject. However the presence of a European dignitary in, for example, Hong Kong was classified as 'Hong Kong'. And the locations 'South Atlantic' and 'Ascension Island' during the IBA week, though suggesting an extra-European focus to the news, in fact appeared in consequence of the contemporary conflict between the UK and Argentina over the sovereignty of the Falkland/Malvinas Islands. Thus European content was somewhat under-represented under the classification system used. However the majority of news items screened which depicted non-European locations concerned non-European issues (albeit ones relevant to Europe and to European viewers).

Geopolitical unit shown in Eurikon news items during the IBA week 24–30.5.82, by number of occurrences.

UK 15
France 10
USA 6
Italy 6
Lebanon 5
South Atlantic 5
Austria 4
Argentina 4
Ireland 3

Germany 2
Spain 2
Yugoslavia 2
United Nations 2
USSR 2
Ascension Island 2
Netherlands 2
Iran 2
Poland 2
Vatican 2
Australia 1
Brazil 1
Denmark 1
European Community 1
Finland 1
Israel 1
Japan 1
Nicaragua 1
Norway 1
Portugal 1
Senegal 1
Sweden 1
Switzerland 1
Turkey 1

Total 92

*Note*: South Atlantic = Falklands and adjacent waters
*Source*: Eurikon news listing.

9 Attribution of national origin to audio-visual works is more difficult than it may seem. I have used the data recorded in the Operations Group's report on Eurikon (EBU/OTS Operations Group 1983) in my calculations. However this data is almost certainly based on an attribution of national origin to complete programmes and therefore overstates both the proportions of European content and of programme content originating from Austria, Germany, Italy, the Netherlands and the UK in the Eurikon schedules.
10 The first item in the RAI news (on a meeting of the Commission of the European Communities) had no voice-over interpretation.
11 The IBA record states that the film screened was 'Bolero', an alternative title for 'Les uns et les autres'. However the theme of Lelouch's film, a family spanning the world, was obviously appropriate for Eurikon.
12 The sexist character of the biscuit making demonstration contrasted sharply with the tediously insistent feminism of 'On the Lack of Appreciation for the Feminine' and exemplified, if not the differences in the values of European television viewers, the differences in values of European broadcasters.
13 The IBA commented that this 'seemed to make very little sense – there was no explanation of the item and the interpreters found it heavy going'. However RAI evidently believed that viewers' interest in physiognomy was sufficient for the item to appear regularly in its Eurikon schedule.
14 Geopolitical unit shown in Eurikon news items during the RAI week 19–25.7.82, by number of occurrences.

UK 20
Italy 19
France 18
EC 16
Lebanon 16
USA 10
Germany 6
Vatican 6
Japan 5
Poland 5
Iraq 4
Syria 4
Netherlands 3
Greece 3
China 2
Falklands 2
Iran 2
Saudi Arabia 2
Spain 2
Argentina 1
French Guyana 1
Gibraltar 1
San Marino 1
Somalia 1
Tunisia 1

Total 151

*Source*: Eurikon news listing.

15 For example, a blank screen and unsynchronised sound and vision in the fade up to the documentary on Hungarian cinema.
16 *Der Verschwender*, when first shown in Austria, achieved a 19 per cent audience share and a 94 per cent satisfaction rating.
17 ORF proposed (to the EBU Television Programme Committee) that its innovation, pioneered in Eurikon, be adopted by the EBU in parallel to its established Eurovision song contest. However, the EBU did not take up ORF's suggestion; the low priority which the EBU traditionally gave entertainment is suggested by the lateness of the date – 1992 – of its establishment of a formal working party on light entertainment.
18 Geopolitical unit shown in Eurikon news items during the ORF week 27.9.82–3.10.82, by number of occurrences. (On Friday 1 October the ORF abandoned its 'top ten' news format in favour of covering the investiture of the new Chancellor of West Germany.)

Germany 31
USA 20
UK 17
Lebanon 13
Italy 12
Switzerland 10
France 9
Austria 8

Luxembourg 5
Netherlands 5
Spain 5
Iran 4
China 3
Israel 3
Bulgaria 2
Denmark 2
Hong Kong 2
Sweden 2
USSR 2
Vatican 2
Australia 1
Belgium 1
Canada 1
Czechoslovakia 1
EC 1
India 1
Iraq 1
Mexico 1
Poland 1
Saudi Arabia 1
South Africa 1

Total 168

*Source*: Eurikon news listing.

19 'Start in Finland, Finish in Friesland' achieved a 12.8 per cent share and a 69 per cent appreciation rating when first screened in the Netherlands.
20 Overall RTE contributed 390-minutes of programming to Eurikon (MacConghail 1983: 63).
21 This was not the case in respect of the IBA week. The IBA evening sampled included programmes – *Coronation Street*, 'On the Lack of Appreciation for the Feminine', 'Pop Around Europe' and *World in Action* – which portrayed significant numbers of women as well as some persons of colour. NOS also included copious representations of women and people of colour in its week and the ARD screened programmes specifically about and directed to minorities.
22 The display monitor would not lock onto the video signal for the first hour of the recording of the evening's programming. This was due to a fault in the scrambling system used for transmission of the video signal, an on-screen prompt appeared towards the end of the first hour of transmissions which stated that transmissions would be unscrambled from 19:15 due to technical problems. No difficulties were experienced in viewing recordings of the NOS signal transmitted after 19:15.
23 This bulletin used female presenters and location shooting. Its three items concerned the establishment of a nuclear free zone, surgery on the Netherlands' biggest tree and a street meeting of a safety for children campaign.
24 This, first, NOS bulletin had six items: the arrest of three alleged members of the Mafia in Italy; the meeting of the Pope and the Polish Cardinal; Lech Walesa's wife stripped by Polish prison guards; Israel's defence minister ordering Lebanese militia into refugee camps in Beirut; two murders in Northern Ireland; and Qaddafi's visit to China.

25 TROS is a major Dutch broadcasting society, i.e. one of the organisations licensed to programme television in the Netherlands.

26 Altersheim was distinguished by the active working lives led by its venerable inhabitants.

27 The news items were, the OTS (Eurikon) experiment, Ariel Sharon's testimony to the Israeli Commission of Enquiry into the massacres in the Beirut refugee camps, arrests of Italian bomb suspects, sectarian murders in Northern Ireland, Qaddafi in Beijing, Danuta Walesa visiting her husband, Cardinal Glemp visiting the Pope, President Karstens of West Germany in Italy, European Community Fisheries policy meeting, Strasbourg's aspiration to become the capital of Europe, the New York marathon. The news was followed by teletext coverage of the Wall Street crash and the arrest of American gamblers in Monte Carlo by French police.

Geopolitical unit shown in Eurikon news items during the NOS week 25–31.10.82, by number of occurrences.

Germany 18
UK 18
USA 13
Spain 10
Italy 7
Poland 7
Netherlands 6
European Community 5
Israel 5
China 4
France 4
Lebanon 3
Austria 2
Norway 2
Belgium 1
Guatemala 1
South Korea 1
Switzerland 1
Turkey 1

Total 110

*Source*: Eurikon news schedule.

28 The presence of ASBU visitors to SWF led to the screening of a thirty-minute UK production of 'Qatar – A quest for excellence' in the Eurikon schedule on Friday 26 November. The IBA noted that this was a 'specially procured propaganda film acquired for the sake of the members of ASBU, who were viewing that day in Baden-Baden. Went down well'.

29 In March 1983 a global news exchange, within UNESCO's 'Global Satellite System Project', was implemented, involving the EBU's partner organisations for Asia, the Arab world and Africa.

30 The twenty-minute bulletin covered the meeting of European Community Foreign Ministers in Brussels, delays in clearing imported video cassette recorders by French customs in Poitiers, budget cuts in the Netherlands, the meeting of the Central Committee of the Communist Party of the Soviet Union, the hijacking of a Polish aircraft, the new Hamburg–Berlin autobahn, Lebanon's celebration of its Independence Day, the Iran–Iraq war, formation of a new Christian Democrat

Government in Italy, meeting of union representatives from Ford UK's factories, Princess Diana's visit to a kindergarten, a Matisse exhibition in Zurich and European weather (including location coverage of actual weather in Vienna).

31 Geopolitical unit shown in Eurikon news items during the ARD week 22–28.11.82, by number of occurrences.

Germany 25
USA 17
France 14
European Community 13
Italy 13
Spain 10
Ireland 8
USSR 8
Vatican 8
Japan 7
UK 7
China 6
Egypt 6
Poland 6
Netherlands 5
GATT (Switzerland) 5
Israel 4
Lebanon 4
Libya 4
Belgium 3
Austria 2
Hungary 2
Luxembourg 2
Switzerland 2
Afghanistan 1
Algeria 1
El Salvador 1
India 1
Iran 1
Mexico 1
Norway 1
Romania 1

Total 189

*Source*: Eurikon news schedule.

32 Beer purity laws.
33 See Appendix 1.
34 'It became very clear early on that the co-ordinating organisations tended to fill the schedules with their material to the exclusion of others . . . we also found ourselves in competition with the IBA as to the English segment of the various schedules' (MacConghail 1983: 63).
35 'Given that the broadcasting context in each of the member countries of the EBU is quite dissimilar one from the other, it is very difficult to construct an overall schedule which takes into account the varying needs of choice and complementarity which are

required. In any event it is very difficult, as we all know, to have a schedule drawn up by committee' (MacConghail 1983: 64).

## 6 FROM EURIKON TO EUROPA

1 Maggiore consistently refers to the dates of Europa as 1986 to 1987. In fact they were from 1985 to 1986.

2 The name Eurikon used for the first phase of the EBU/ESA satellite television partnership was discarded for several reasons, not least the obscene significance of the final syllable in some Romance languages.

3 Hahn instanced the Common Agricultural Policy of the European Community as an example of agreement on economic matters.

4 The terms 'horizontal' and 'vertical' are used metaphorically by broadcasters to describe different kinds of mixed programme schedules. A 'vertical' schedule has a distinctive and different character for each day of the week, a 'horizontal' schedule establishes programming continuities at particular times of the day (thus every day of a horizontally scheduled week might have a sports programme at 20:00, a game show at 21:00 and so on).

5 Eurikon had devoted 25.9 per cent of its schedule to news, information and current affairs, 13.7 per cent to the arts, and 7.6 per cent to drama.

6 Richard Dill (ARD), Adolf Aigner (ORF), Vittorio Boni (RAI), Carel Enkelaar and Klaas-Jan Hindriks (NOS), Jean-Pierre Julien (EBU) and Neville Clarke (IBA) – all of whom had been central and very active figures in Eurikon – participated in the meeting to discuss the L-Sat service. Colin Shaw of the IBA, Nobel Wilson of the BBC and representatives from nine other EBU member broadcasters were also present.

7 Later the ARD joined its erstwhile Eurikon partners, NOS and RAI, in Europa and one of its representatives, Dietrich Schwarzkopf (BR) chaired the governing board of the Europa Consortium.

8 The vertical schedule has been advocated consistently by German participants in pan-European services, in Eurikon, Europa, and latterly ARTE where German participants advocated a vertical 'theme day' organisation of the schedule.

9 RAI screened programmes which originated from Italy and the UK, on its cinema day (19.7.82), but which contained significant elements of American programming. Granada Television's repackaging of Warner animations and RAI's news feature accounts of cinematic stunting history and contemporary art thefts both included numerous American items and similar examples of a European wrapping of American content can be found elsewhere in Eurikon programming.

10 Barrand's judgement was reproduced verbatim in the Operations Group's report on the Eurikon experiment at EBU/OTS Operations Group 1983: 12.

11 TV-AM made regular use of this news resource and, had it not lost its UK franchise, proposed to join the EBU's Euronews consortium.

12 George Waters attested (personal interview 24.2.92) that Europa was driven by NOS.

13 They mentioned HTV's 'interest' in selling the pan-European service to UK cable companies, 'considerable interest' from Thames Television, that TV South was 'considering' financial involvement in the pan-European initiative and that Channel 4 and S4C 'have both shown keen interest' (Clarke and Hindriks 1984: 4 and 5). However Clarke and Hindriks were unable to specify firm commitments from either ITV companies or from the ITCA.

14 A revised version of the report was prepared in December 1983. Funding for the feasibility study (for the period 1.7.83–21.10.83), of 100,000 Sfr was provided by

ARD, ERT, NOS, RTE, RTVE, SSR, SVT and YLE (memo from Clarke to Small and Enkelaar 1.11.83). Clarke was seconded from the IBA to act as project coordinator (in spite of the IBA declining to participate financially in further European public service satellite ventures).

15  Finn subsequently became Director General of RTE.

16  The Europa Board (meeting in September 1986), received Airtime International's report (a subsidiary of Scottish Television which had been appointed in May 1986 to sell advertising space on Europa), which reported that the channel's advertising revenue for the previous three months had been only £140,000, far from the levels of revenue envisaged either by the EBU Finance Group or in the feasibility study. Far from pan-European satellite television making inroads into the main European television advertising markets Airtime regarded Portugal as the most promising market for development because it was there that Europa was distributed via terrestrial transmissions.

17  The arguments advanced by NOS in the early 1980s were to be echoed later. Establishment of the EBU's Euronews channel was strongly encouraged by the European Community on the grounds that Europe needed a source of indigenous television news to counterbalance the influence of the US' channel CNN. A UK broadcaster (personal interview 9.7.92), who had worked on Europa stated that the majority of European public service broadcasters were anti-American, however (this source believed) broadcasters' anti-Americanism led to contradictory and self-defeating policies in that the desire to countervail American values led to European broadcasters eschewing American programming values and rhetoric, which have proven attractive to European viewers, and to a reluctance to use English, the European language most widely understood across Europe, because it is the language of the USA.

Broadcasters' reluctance to use English meant that services were confined to one language community (or a plurality of expensive linguistic re-presentations were required); the decision to eschew American programme rhetoric meant that a rhetoric well suited to pan-European services was rejected. American television, this UK broadcaster argued, is rooted in Hollywood and Hollywood is rooted in the silent movies. The silent cinema was driven by action and simple narratives in order that it be intelligible to a polyglot, multicultural immigrant public, 'it was driven by action not by words'. However, European broadcasting (including British) is too wordy to be successful across language barriers. Certainly the programming and scheduling of Europa was insufficiently attractive to viewers to render the service economically viable.

18  The ARD had encountered competition from commercial services established *within* Germany for the first time in 1984 with the opening of the 'pilot' cable television project at Ludwigshafen. The pilot cable projects were the 'Trojan Horse' of commercial television in Germany, thus the ARD had a particularly acute – and well founded – fear of commercial television at the time of its participation in Eurikon and Europa.

## 7  EUROPA: THE CASTLE IN THE AIR

1  The Olympus (formerly the L-Sat) satellite was planned to enter service in 1987 but did not enter operational service until 1989. The satellite has had a troubled history, it has been underused and in May 1991 Olympus began to drift in space; control was regained in July 1991. Human error (reputedly involving an absence of response to more than fifty warning signals transmitted from the satellite to ground station operators at the Italian control centre at Fucino) whilst re-orienting the satellite in order

to move its footprint further north resulted in loss of the satellite. Control was later regained.

2 Eutelsat was established under an agreement between twenty-six European PTTs in 1977 as a satellite telecommunications carrier. Its first satellite, Eutelsat I, was commissioned in 1983 and its second generation of higher powered (60 as opposed to 20 watt) satellites, Eutelsat II, came into service in 1990.

3 The Netherlands, Europa's principal market, has about 5.7 million television households, of which 4.8 million were cabled.

4 64 million Sfr (before programme costs) over four years.

5 The children's programmes on the first day of Europa, a Saturday, were *Tic-Tac*, *Bolke the Bear*, and *Herman and the Six*. They were followed by sports reports, commercials, a weather report, more commercials, a music show *La chauve souris*, more commercials and a programme preview for the following day.

6 On the first day of this week, a Saturday, *Emilie*, *Rexie Dog* and *Thunderbirds* (all children's programmes) were screened, followed by sports reports, weather, Irish folk songs, a documentary on the Dutch painter Jan Steen, *The Persuaders* series and a feature film *Twinky*.

7 *Countdown* was based on the Eurohitparade format developed by ORF for Eurikon. De Mol produced the DJ Kat show, one of the most successful programmes in the schedules of Sky Channel during the 1980s.

8 Indeed Taylor argued that a pop music channel, rather than the sports or news channel formats adopted by the EBU in Euronews and Eurosport, offered the best possibilities for the successful establishment of a pan-European television channel.

9 Europa was carried on some, but not all, Dutch cable networks, and was distributed via cable and MATV (Master Antenna Television – small scale cable networks) in Austria, Denmark, Finland, Germany, Luxembourg, Norway, Sweden and Ireland. In May 1986 rebroadcasting of three and a half hours daily of Europa programming had begun on RTP's terrestrial network.

10 Europa was consistently supported by both the European Parliament and the Commission of the European Communities; the Commission allocated 1 million ECU subsidy in 1986 and the Parliament's attempt to allocate a further 5 million ECU in the Community budget for 1987 was defeated by only two votes.

The Commission, in its first major review of television policy, specifically nominated 'creation of a common television programme' as a Community policy goal (Commission of the European Communities 1983: 5). In consequence the Commission specifically mentioned Europa in its action programme for European audio-visual production as the 'first concrete step' taken in the direction of multilingualism in European television (Commission of the European Communities 1986: 10).

The EBU had noted European institutions' desire for a pan-European television service. The EBU's Study Group on the Future of Public Service Broadcasting (the Wangermée Group) stated, 'Several Members of the Union desire that under EBU auspices there should be active preparation of projects for European programmes which would use the L-Sat satellite. The idea of a European programme, which fifteen Union members experimented with for the first time using OTS in 1982 (Eurikon) is of great interest to European institutions (Council of Europe, European Parliament) which have communicated to the EBU recent resolutions adopted on this subject' (AG 551 SPG 2641 June 1984: 16).

11 Ernesto Braun and Ripa di Meana, the Commissioner responsible for the European Community's audio-visual policies were personal friends.

12 Johnson's concern was recognised by those who developed Europa. Carel Enkelaar specifically referred to the need to protect Europa's editorial staff 'against one-sided influences from the hinterlands of broadcasting organisations, as well as against

supranational organs, including the European Parliament and the European Commission' (interviewed in *Broadcasting News from the Netherlands* 1984, 2: 2). Bouke Beumer, the Dutch PPE MEP who chaired the European Parliament's Committee on Youth Culture Education Information and Sport, also recognised the importance of journalistic independence: 'the European programme must be independent from commercial influences . . . .We are not against advertising, but it should not determine the contents of the European Programme . . . the Programme must [also] be independent from the European Community, and have an independent team of journalists' (interviewed in *Broadcasting News from the Netherlands* 1984, 2: 3).

13 He spoke before the accession of Portugal and Spain to the European Community.

14 It cannot be taken for granted that Europa was run as economically as possible. *Variety* (3.12.86) reported 'heavy wastage and overspending on facilities' at Europa. A UK source, formerly employed by Europa, commented on the 'vast numbers of people and enormous resources' devoted to Europa by NOS (personal interview 9.7.92). This source also characterised NOS as 'the biggest broadcaster you have ever seen'. Further evidence of NOS' and Europa's profligacy (at least as perceived by anglophones), is given in a letter to Neville Clarke from Ron Wordley (then the Managing Director of HTV) on 26 October 1983. Wordley wrote:

> I was particularly pleased that you had arranged for us to look over NOS. I obtained the impression of a large and happy staff in a wonderful working environment working with superb equipment and resources, but mostly devoted to mainly mundane programmes in UK broadcasting terms. I was particularly amused to hear that Outside Broadcast units are used for sport and not for location work on other programmes and that filmed inserts were restricted to news items only. With all respect to our kind and charming friends at NOS this is an attitude which UK television discarded about 15 years ago.

15 RTE disputed its liability to defray a share of Europa's debts on the grounds (which it adamantly maintained in many letters and statements to Europa and EBU meetings) that RTE's contribution to Europa was always to have been in kind rather than in cash.

16 Vilcek also noted that cessation of Europa transmissions left the Union with a difficult problem *vis à vis* the European Space Agency. Not only had the Union contracted with the Space Agency 'to transmit a comprehensive and unified programme, designed to arouse European audiences' interest in direct broadcasting', but, Vilchek stated, any inability of the EBU to honour its contract with the ESA left it vulnerable to the ESA replacing the EBU 'by some other outside body with objectives running counter to those of Union members' (EBU 1987: 18).

17 Indeed the mission statement drafted by FR 3 for the French satellite channel Canal 1 (later La Sept), included competition with Europa as one of the four chief elements of the new channel's mission (Emanuel 1991: 101).

18 Further questions relating to Europa were put by other members of the Parliament (OJ C 226 24.8.87: 46; OJ C 240 7.9.87: 25) to which the Commission replied that it reserved its right to sue for the return of its subsidy, that it regretted the demise of Europa, and that it awaited the unfolding of events (European Parliament 1982a; 1984a; and OJ C 226. 24.8.87). Di Meana was reported to have deplored Europa's refusal to accept partnership with commercial interests and to have blamed the 'myopie politique et l'absence de courage des télévisions publiques' (in *24 Heures* Brussels 29.11.86) for the channel's failure.

19 Following Europa's demise the Commission of the European Communities used the UK based satellite television channel, Super Channel, to disseminate European programming and information about Europe to viewers and assisted Super Channel by giving the channel access to its technical facilities (OJ C 261 30.9.87: 54).

20 Heinsmann was interviewed by Elizabeth Jacka to whom I express my thanks for this information.

21 Strictly speaking the EBU has participated in none of the satellite television initiatives considered here: it is EBU *members* which have (or have not) participated. The EBU has simply provided a forum in which collaboration has developed.


## 8 EUROSPORT AND EURONEWS

1 The title of both Eurikon and Europa sports programmes was Eurosport.

2 A total calculated on the basis of the incremental costs which attached to the pilot, and not the fully attributed cost of use of Europa, the Eurovision system or the costs of rights and Eurovision circuits

3 The note of a meeting between Europa (represented by Richard Dill, Klaas-Jan Hindriks and A. de Souza), and the sponsors of the Sport Channel from the EBU's Permanent Services (Richard Bunn and Willem van den Berg), records that the cost of the sports channel was estimated to be 3.5 million Sfr per annum 'not taking account of the fact that Europa TV would offer its existing infrastructure and related personnel, as well as the satellite transponder, advertising agent and the possibility to use its schedule without costs' (SG/S/457 26.6.86: 3–4).

4 Noble Wilson, formerly Controller of International Relations at the BBC and Vice Chairman of the EBU Television Programme Committee stated that 'the members of Eurovision transmit between 15 and 20 per cent of all the sports events for which they have the rights' (Wilson 1988).

5 Boni sponsored the preparation of a Business Plan for the Sports Channel by the UK company Parallel Media (in which Mike Luckwell – formerly the Managing Director of Carlton Communications – played a leading role). In 1986, during Europa's terminal crisis, Parallel Media had offered to acquire a share in and to undertake the management of Europa. RAI (and RTP and RTE) supported this proposal and advocated a partnership with Parallel Media after Europa was wound up on the basis of Parallel Media's business plan which proposed co-operation with Sky Television, hitherto the EBU's arch antagonist.

6 Named after its Chairman, Alan Hart of the BBC. Hart had been Controller of BBC1 and, in 1984, became Special Assistant to the Director General with special responsibility for relations with the EBU. Hart subsequently became Controller of International Relations for the BBC.

7 The BBC collaborated with Sky Channel in joint acquisition of UK sporting rights in order to strengthen their respective competitive positions *vis à vis* their shared rival ITV.

8 Eric Jurgens wrote to de Kalbermatten stating 'it is wiser, when reflecting on possible changes, to take notice of the maxims of BBC's founding father Reith than of the press bulletins of Mr Rupert Murdoch' (Jurgens' letter to de Kalbermatten 3.4.84: 4).

9 A brief, official, statement by the BBC describing Eurosport is to be found in House of Commons 1988 V II: 289–90.

10 ORF, BRT, RTBF, DR, YLE, TF1, A2, ERT, RUV, RTE, RAI, NRK, RTVE, SVT, BBC, SRG. Subsequently TF1, A2, left and JRT, TRT, CYBC, and IBA joined the Consortium. Although the initial conception of Eurosport, ZDF's programme concept 'Project B', originated in Germany neither the ARD nor ZDF joined Eurosport. The legal basis for German public broadcasting did not permit German

EBU members to participate in a commercial venture such as Eurosport. Other members subsequently joined the Consortium and the German Länder modified the rules which had hitherto inhibited the participation of public broadcasters in commercial transnational television services. However the new arrangements (New Media Markets 18.7.91: 66) required the unanimous approval of the sixteen Länder broadcasting authorities for ZDF or the ARD to participate (up to 49.9 per cent in any enterprise which did not carry advertising directed exclusively to German viewers) in transnational ventures.

11 A full account of the corporate structure of Eurosport (when run under the agreement between the Consortium and Sky Channel) is given in OJ L 63/32–44 9.3.91).

12 Screensport (sometimes Screen Sport or ScreenSport) was 75 per cent owned by W.H. Smith Television and 25 per cent by ESPN (the US satellite cable company owned by ABC/Capital Cities). In 1991 W.H. Smith Television was divested by its parent company and became ETN (European Television Networks) with ABC/Capital Cities holding 50 per cent of the new company.

13 Before joining the Commission of the European Communities Brittan was Home Secretary, the Minister responsible for broadcasting, during much of the Thatcher era. He appointed the Peacock Enquiry (Peacock 1986) on Financing of the BBC which recommended increasing competition in UK broadcasting and challenged what it saw as a comfortable BBC/ITV duopoly.

14 La Cinq was permitted to sub-license access to Eurovision material from 1 October 1988 (CA 1988 SPG 4245 9.3.89: 40).

15 The Commission argued that the commercial broadcasters inside the EBU (such as Canal Plus and TF1), discharged 'public interest obligations' (OJ L 179 22.7.93) and thereby merited treatment different to commercial broadcasters who were not EBU members.

16 But it should also be recognised that sports rights acquired by the EBU on behalf of its members were often unused. Thus the effect of the EBU's collective acquisition of rights was to deny competing broadcasters (and thus their potential viewers), access to sports programming which EBU members would not screen. Some estimates suggest that as much as 85 per cent of the sports programme material acquired by the EBU was never screened.

17 Paasilinna is, at the time of writing in 1997, an MEP.

18 Following Sky's withdrawal Eurosport ceased transmission between 6–22 May 1991. The Eurosport Consortium subsequently re-established the Eurosport service in partnership with the French commercial broadcaster (and EBU member) TF1.

19 The European Parliament called on the Commission to support Euronews in 1992 (OJ C 284 2.11.92).

20 Ripa di Meana was not the only senior Community figure who had sought to establish a European television news channel. Roberto Barzanti, when Chairman of the European Parliament's Committee on Youth, Culture, Education, the Media and Sport, initiated a report on the audio-visual industry (the Barzanti Report), which specifically sought to foster Euronews and to recruit Community support for it. Barzanti wrote:

> The MEDIA programme is intended to encourage the launching of a European television information service which will be multilingual and managed jointly by State television companies after the pattern of the Euronews project drawn up in the context of the European Broadcasting Union.
>
> (European Parliament 1990: 32)

21 Hjarvard, in his excellent account of the EBU's development of a European news service, also stresses the strength of EBU members' commitments to a Europe wider than the membership of the European Communities and to journalistic independence (Hjarvard 1991: 18–20). An independence, and a conception of Europe (looser, wider and more pluralistic than that of the Community's integrationists) which public service broadcasters of Vandersichel's stripe feared would be compromised by funding from the Commission of the European Communities.

22 The President, Albert Scharf, said to the Administrative Council's discussion of Euronews in December 1990 that 'the EBU had to prove its capacity to conclude an operation for which it had taken the initiative and where it would be a partner of European institutions with which it wished to strengthen its ties' (CA 2116 SPG 5254 18.2.91: 19).

23 In 1992 the Commission granted Euronews 3 million ECU (and a modest subsidy to provide an Arabic language news service) and in 1993 the Commission authorised a subsidy of 2.2 million ECU. The Commission's contribution in 1993 was to redress an anticipated shortfall in advertising revenue.

24 'United Kingdom organisations ... participation was necessary due to their high professional level' (CA 2116 SPG 5254 18.2.91: 17).

25 TV-AM was to have joined Euronews had it been successful in its application for the UK Channel 3 commercial breakfast news franchise in 1991. Two former EBU employees, Neville Clarke and Harry Dennis, were employed by TV-AM as consultants on the franchise bid.

26 The EBU Secretary General, Jean-Bernard Münch, observed that if the EBU had access to venture capital finance to establish Euronews 'the risk we should have to underwrite is estimated at somewhere between ECU 45m ... and ECU 25m'. Whereas without access to venture capital, the customary condition of public service broadcasters and the basis on which Euronews was established, 'the cumulative funding requirements form the end of 1990 up to and including 1998 would be ECU 229 million, which would represent the maximum risk we should have to underwrite if Euronews were financed solely by public service funding' (SG/2975 8.6.90: 1).

27 The withdrawal of Havas, the designated advertising agency for Euronews, in 1992 was not an encouraging signal.

28 The Commission of the European Communities included a budget line for Euronews in the 1992 Draft Budget. However, because the Commission is able to authorise subventions (subject to the concurrence of the European Parliament), to Euronews from its own resources only if the budget line amounted to less than about 6m ECU the Commission's support is unlikely to amount to more than about half the sums that Euronews envisaged receiving from public funds. DG X offered to support Euronews but only in a sum of less than 100,000 ECU (below the threshold for reference to the MEDIA Consultative Committee. Reference to the Committee would, the Euronews Assembly thought, entail 'dangers of opposition' ED 022 16.7.91: 3). However the EBU's lobby of members of the European Parliament's Committee on Youth, Culture, Education, the Media and Sport was successful and the Parliament voted a subsidy of 3 million ECU to Euronews in 1991 a level of support which it maintained to 1994.

Euronews received a further subvention on 8 February 1992 from the Audiovisual Eureka which committed 3 million ECU to Euronews for the year 1992. The Audiovisual Eureka used funds made available by the governments of Belgium (French Community), France, Italy and Spain (Audiovisual Eureka press release 8.2.92). In February 1992 Lyons was chosen as Euronews' base of operations after pledges of support by the city of Lyons. In June 1992 *Broadcast* reported that

France had undertaken to 'fill any gaps in the projected £35 million yearly budget' (*Broadcast* 12.6.92: 3). However the necessity of relying on subventions from France threatened to compromise Euronews' editorial independence. Indeed the Secretary General of the EBU had specifically recognised a danger in Euronews' dependence on subventions from national governments. He stated that the EBU preferred subsidies to Euronews from the Commission of the European Communities because the alternative – government subsidies via the Audiovisual Eureka – might compromise the editorial independence of Euronews. The Secretary General noted that support for Euronews, via the Audiovisual Eureka, from Spain, Finland, France and Italy was likely to be available (SPG 5424 5.4.91: 2).

## 9 THE LANGUAGE FACTOR

1 Danish, Dutch/Flemish, English, French, German, Greek, Italian, Portuguese and Spanish.
2 Luyken (1991: 7) estimates that there are thirty European language communities each of which has at least one million native speakers.
3 Luyken *et al.* (1991) prefer the term 'language transfer'.
4 MacConghail, perhaps relying on Clarke's estimate, cited the same figure (MacConghail 1983: 62).
5 In 1987 European Commission staff numbered 11,234 of whom 1,544 were translators and interpreters. (Noel 1988: 41). The outturn for 1990 from the Community's budget line for 'Promotion and Development of Multi Lingual Activities' (B5–5 0 1) – including automated translation – was 644,076,917 ECU (OJ L 26 3.2.92: 318).
6 Kilborn (1991: 18) reported that (within a context of exceptional resistance to foreign language television), UK viewers preferred dubbing rather than subtitling (see also Luyken 1991). However Kilborn noted 'these are average percentage figures which conceal the fact that within the national television audience there are significant differences in the pattern of preference according to the type of programme being watched and also to age and social class categories' (Kilborn 1991: 19).
7 In a letter to Neville Clarke's assistant Marc Wright. Dromgoole responded to Wright's letter of 2 August which requested HTV programmes with existing foreign language scripts for transmission on Eurikon.
8 Gentikow (1993) in an interesting comparison of the re-presentation of an episode of the UK television comedy *Fawlty Towers* in German, Norwegian and Swedish, not only shows the difficulties (and costs) of linguistic re-presentation but also the wholesale rewriting that is sometimes required if one country's television is to be presented successfully to viewers in another. Gentikow chose the – to English eyes and ears – hilarious *Fawlty Towers* episode 'The Germans' to show how the episode's most important running joke, the English characters' obsessive return to the subject of the Second World War, is simply extirpated from the German (but not Norwegian or Swedish) version. Clearly not everything is equally acceptable to those who putatively share a European collective identity.
9 Indeed the importance of the newscaster in UK television news was an important factor which contributed to the BBC's decision not to participate in the EBU's presenter-less European news channel Euronews. A BBC official stated that 'We don't think a service without a presenter will work' (personal interview 9.12.91).
10 'Il suffit, par exemple, de comparer les journaux télévisés britanniques, allemands et français pour sentir à quel point la nation demeure le cadre non seulement physique mais aussi mental de la programmation audiovisuelle' [it's only necessary, for example, to compare British, French and German television news to be aware of how

much each nation stays inside the framework, and not just the physical framework but also the mental framework, of its own audio-visual repertoire] (Desgraupes 1985: 14). However Desgraupes (1985: 15) also argued that, despite the differences between European television services and European publics, Europe *did* enjoy a common 'patrimoine culturel' [cultural inheritance].

11 A BBC source stated that the BBC's belief that presenter-less news would not attract viewers was an important factor in the BBC's decision not to participate in Euronews (personal interview 9.12.91).

12 Teletext was first broadcast publicly in the UK during a period of experimentation between 1974–6. Experiments were deemed to be successful and a regular BBC teletext service, known as Ceefax, continued after the end of the experimental period. Commercial television in the UK, ITV, began its broadcast teletext services in 1977 and its service, 'Oracle', was financed by advertising from 1981. For a history of broadcast teletext in the UK see Schlesinger 1985 and for a discussion of teletext's implantation into different European broadcasting systems see EBU 1985.

By 1982, and the inception of Eurikon, there were a million teletext receivers in UK television households: a penetration rate of c.5 per cent which was more or less equalled by the Netherlands (Bekkers 1987: 33) where teletext had begun in 1980. Broadcast teletext therefore seemed to offer a cheap and accessible means (a respectable sized and growing receiver population and producer personnel familiar with the technology and the problems of writing for and displaying information via teletext), of distributing written text together with a video and audio signal.

13 Clarke concurred; he wrote to Fleming on 6 December 1982 stating: 'I have just re-read the copy of your report on Week One to Mme. van Hoof. The points you made have been extremely valuable and we managed to incorporate some of your suggestions with success in later weeks' (Clarke to Fleming in OTS EEC/European Parliament/Council of Europe file). The Operations Group concluded that the similar methods used in the RAI week was similarly unsatisfactory (EBU/OTS Operations Group 1983: 18).

14 Although NOS was able only to transmit one set of titles at a time for technical reasons, it changed the language of titling from time to time.

15 Europa, based at the headquarters of the Dutch broadcaster NOS, used the translation based re-languaging system pioneered by NOS in its Eurikon week. The former Head of Press and Publicity for Europa, Jeremy Taylor, described the group of Portacabins behind the old NOS Headquarters in Emmastraat where Europa was located (personal interview 9.7.92). Here NOS translators re-voiced Europa programming in four languages. Taylor said that they would reinterpret and represent programmes 'rather like a BBC radio drama, with the translator playing different parts and using different voices'. However the results were, he claimed, 'pretty awful – even with all those resources it didn't work'.

Taylor explained that there were too few European viewers in Europa's target markets with teletext decoders to make teletext a viable form of re-languaging for the pan-European service. Furthermore, some European countries with teletext used different technical standards (the two main standards were the French Antiope and the UK Ceefax/Oracle standards).

ARTE, the Franco-German cultural channel, uses teletext titles in some of its programmes in French and German but has experienced technical difficulties in reconciling the German and French teletext technical standards. ARTE uses a variety of other methods of re-languaging – many reminiscent of those pioneered by Eurikon – including simultaneous translation, two presenters speaking different languages, dubbing and subtitling.

16 Golding was a Central Television journalist who worked on the UK news team.

17 Reiler states that translation was done by 'Konferenzdolmetschern' (conference translators).

18 In honour of members of the Arab Broadcasting Union's visit to the Eurikon experiment.

19 UPITN, in its bid for the Europa news contract (UPITN 1983), proposed teletext and titling on similar lines 'On the subject of sound, UPITN has proposals for treating the original 'sound bite'. We feel that this sound need not simply be 'wiped' and voiced over in the various languages but that it can be retained in its original form on all the audio channels and supplemented by multiple translation captions. In other words the text in the five remaining languages would be superimposed and preceded by a graphic symbol to catch the eye' (UPITN 1983 paras 15.2 and 15.3).

## 10 THE AUDIENCE FOR PAN-EUROPEAN TELEVISION

1 Made when Gunter was Head of Research at the IBA.

2 That is in Italy, where RAI was experiencing the first intense wave of competition from the commercial Fininvest channels (and where citizens' support for the European Community was notably high); in the Netherlands where viewers in one of Europe's most fully cabled markets had access to several channels of neighbour country television (and where, if somewhat less than in its fellow founder member of the European Community – Italy – there was general support for the European Community); in Portugal where the public service channel RTP still enjoyed a monopoly (in a country about to join the European Community); and in the UK where advertising financed commercial television had been established longer than in any other European broadcasting market (and where support for the European Community was lower than in most other Member States).

3 Although much research on the reception of Eurikon programmes was described as audience research the term 'audience' was one which Clarke sought to discourage. He believed the term would send the wrong signals to collection agencies and talent unions and would prompt them to seek payment in respect of performance rights.

4 ORF and RTP conducted research but did not use the standardised model of the IBA, NOS, RAI and RTE. SSR undertook no audience research but did analyse the content of Eurikon programming. The ARD did not undertake research because of lack of funds.

5 De Bock's text was reproduced verbatim in the Operations Group report on Eurikon which added further information including details of the actual number of test persons used by each broadcaster in audience research on Eurikon. That is: IBA: 95, NOS: 46, RAI: 54, RTE: 54, ORF: 15 and RTP: 82. (EBU/OTS Operations Group 1983: 24).

6 The early evening schedules for Tuesday 25 May 1982 and for Saturday 29 May 1982 were used for ascertaining responses to the IBA week. A ninety-minute selection from the following programmes was screened, using the first six–eight minutes of each programme.

   25 May. Eurikon News and Information (17:00–17:45), *Kanal Alligator* – an ARD cartoon detective story for children set in New York (17:45–18:05), *Avanti, Avanti* – the evening's language session in Italian from RAI (18:05–18:35), *Historia Senza Parole* – RAI film drama made without speech [erroneously described as a 'documentary about region in Italy' in Gunter 1982: 43] (18:35–19:35), Alberto Moravia in Africa – RAI film of Moravia on location in Africa giving his impressions of Africa (19:35–20:35), Folk Festival – Grampian Television compilation programme of Celtic music [erroneously described in Gunter (1982: 430) as an RTE programme] (20:35–21:01).

29 May. Eurikon News and Information (17:00–17:40), International Folklore Competition – an ARD entertainment showing folklore from around the world (17:40–18:40), Dizzy Feet – the Central Television Golden Rose of Montreux winning Wayne Sleep dance show [erroneously timed in Gunter (1982: 44) as 18:40–19:40] (18:40–19:18), Is there one who understands me? – RTE documentary on James Joyce (19:40–20:40), Concerto Europeo – RAI images of Europe accompanied by Beethoven's *Ninth Symphony* (20:40–21:05), Sports Review (21:05–21:59).

To ascertain responses to the Italian week viewers were shown a seventy-minute compilation of the first six–eight minutes of each Eurikon programme screened on Wednesday 21 July. These ten programmes were; News flash (17:00–17:05), a RAI children's cartoon of *The Magic Flute* (17:05–17:30), Buona Sera – RAI's introduction to the evening's programme theme of serious music (17:30–18:00), News and information (18:00–18:15), Eurikon News bulletin (18:15–18:30), Buona Sera part two – piano concert by Ivo Pogoleric (18:30–19:00), Act One of Verdi's *Otello* from La Scala (19:00–19:40), Verdi's Life – extracts from a biopic (19:40–20:15), RAI magazine programme including item on photo-magazine stories (20:15–20:50), RTVE ballet *Bodes de Sangre* by Gades from Lorca (20:50–21:50).

7  Commission of the European Communities research on public opinion in Community Member States has found that 'Italians are most likely to support Western European integration (89 per cent) and most likely to be sorry if the Community was scrapped (60 per cent)' (Commission of the European Communities 1991a: 7).

8  Dutch researchers screened a one hour compilation of Eurikon programming from the NOS week (similar to that used by IBA researchers), to forty-six Dutch respondents. Dutch respondents also saw a ten-minute compilation of Eurikon programming in order to test their responses to the different forms of re-languaging used by Eurikon.

9  A documentary compilation programme which showed curious and picturesque aspects of European life and was screened each weekday of the NOS Eurikon week.

10  A schedule structure consistently advocated by the ARD in the pan-European channels, Eurikon, Europa and latterly ARTE to which they contributed.

11  Earlier Clarke had reported that '[F]ive to 10 per cent said they would watch such a service regularly (4 to 6 days a week) and up to 50 per cent would watch occasionally over a period of a week' (Com.TV/GT TV News (r) SPG 2136/Feb.83: 20).

12  Federal Republic of Germany.

13  Local time varies in different European states.

14  Some caution should be exercised in drawing conclusions from the research findings cited here. Not only is data imperfectly commensurable but, since viewing behaviour clearly depends on programme offer, which differs from country to country, what viewers watch is not necessarily a guide to what they would watch in different circumstances (a point made strongly in UNESCO 1982).

15  Citizens of other Member States of the European Community answered as follows: 31 per cent Portugal, 31 per cent Spain, 32 per cent France, 35 per cent Belgium, 37 per cent Italy, 39 per cent Greece, 46 per cent Denmark, 50 per cent Germany, 53 per cent Netherlands, 59 per cent Ireland (Commission of the European Communities 1991: A22).

16  The percentage of those who stated that they thought European Community membership was 'a good thing' was 57 per cent in the UK, 62 per cent in Denmark, 70 per cent in France, 71 per cent in Germany, 75 per cent in Belgium, 76 per cent in Greece, 78 per cent in Ireland and Spain, 79 per cent in Italy and Portugal, 83 per

cent in Luxembourg and 89 per cent in the Netherlands (Commission of the European Communities 1991: A10).

17 Only Denmark came close to UK levels of discontent with the European Community. Seventeen per cent of UK respondents and 16 per cent of Danish respondents stated that they would be very relieved if the European Community was scrapped. (Commission of the European Communities 1991: A11).

18 Belgium, Bulgaria, Canada, France, Hungary, Italy, Japan.

## CONCLUSION

1 Here I collapse complex (and often still disputed) historical processes unduly. Of course public service broadcasting did not develop in the same way (or at the same time) in all countries.

2 The academic community has come to use 'public sphere' as the accepted translation of the term '*Öffentlichkeit*' used by Habermas even though the EBU's locution, 'public forum', is a preferable English version of Habermas' term.

3 The metaphor René Levesque coined to characterise the relationship between Canada and Québec.

4 The text is conveniently reproduced in Tongue n.d.

5 The Protocol reads: 'The provisions of the Treaty shall be without prejudice to the competence of Member States to provide for the funding of public service broadcasting in so far as such funding is granted to broadcasting organizations for the fulfilment of the public service remit as conferred, defined and organized by each Member State, and that such funding does not affect trading conditions and competition in the Community to an extent which would be contrary to the common interest, while the realization of the remit of that public service shall be taken into account.

6 A word not chosen lightly. A blatant contemporary instance occurs in the report of the Group of Experts charged with 'Reflection on Information and Communication Policy of the European Community', which referred to the problem that 'European identity has not yet been engrained in peoples' minds' (Commission of the European Communities 1993: 2).

7 Equally clearly, Mitrany's functionalism displays an affinity with the philosophical doctrine of functionalism; 'that things ought to be explained solely in terms of their social function' (Jarvie 1966). But to be a functionalist in Mitrany's sense does not necessitate adoption of the general doctrine of functionalism, as Jarvie (1965) points out.

8 And as Mitrany gleefully recognised in his citation of Altiero Spinelli's coupling of his and Monnet's names: 'Mitrany who became the theoretician of functionalism. Jean Monnet during the war years had elaborated the idea of applying the functional approach to that of the coal and steel industries and it was from this that there emerged the European Coal and Steel Community, the first . . . example of a functional supranational authority' (cited in Mitrany 1975: 75).

9 'Les Enfants de l'Europe' is the wonderfully chosen title of the French translation of Hartz's (1964) *The Founding of New Societies*.

10 Scharf's statement was made in response to the claim of the new President of Italy, Silvio Berlusconi, that 'there is not a single democratic state in which public service television raises its voice against the majority which sustains the government'. He rebutted Berlusconi's assertion and defined public service broadcasting as 'independent of government and parliament, and of any other entity or force within the society. Its very role is to serve the public by, *inter alia*, providing comprehensive, unbiased and correct information, and by contributing actively to the process

whereby the public can form its opinions freely and on the basis of the facts' (Open letter of Scharf to Berlusconi dated 9.6.94. EBU Press Release PR 11/94).

11 In July 1996 the European Court of the First Instance ruled that public service broadcasters' combination, in the EBU, to collectively acquire exclusive sports rights constituted an abuse of a dominant position.

## APPENDIX I

1 Other EBU members played minor roles. RTE, RTVE, RTP, SSR, TDF and YLE contributed programmes (MacConghail 1983: 61). French broadcasters, notably TDF, assisted by vacating the transponder they had been allocated on the OTS in favour of Eurikon, and TDF also supplied scrambling and descrambling equipment.

2 Clarke took part in Eurikon wearing what he described as his 'EBU hat' (memo from Clarke to Deputy Director Television 21.12.81).

3 The BBC had declined the EBU's invitation to participate in Eurikon for reasons noted as 'Uncertainty regarding costs and practical organisation of a European programme' (Telex from Miro Vilcek, Director EBU TV Programme Dept, to EBU Member Broadcasters TV Programme Executives 16.12.81). However Vilcek recorded the BBC's offer 'to help with Kingswood Warren Station' (Kingswood Warren was the BBC engineering research and development establishment).

4 The BBC made Chris Irwin, later responsible for its World Service Television initiative, responsible for the DBS project.

5 Whitney subsequently became Director General of the IBA but was then Managing Director of Capital Radio.

6 Leapman describes Shaw as an opponent of IBA participation in satellite television ventures who was successful in persuading 'his colleagues at the IBA to stay well out of the UK Unisat DBS initiative' (1987: 205). Additional evidence lends support to Leapman's account of Shaw's position: Shaw had earlier described satellite television as a 'glamorous diversion' (at the Economist/International Institute of Communication satellite conference held in Vienna in 1981).

7 Whitney proposed an independent broadcasting DBS channel of an ITN/TV-am twenty-four-hour satellite news channel financed by subscription and advertising.

8 Clarke observed the Chairman, Lord Thomson, had two priorities: 'to deal with the ITV franchises next time round in the growing climate of deregulation [and] ... to help equip commercial television for the new age of cross-border television' (Clarke and Riddell 1992: 162).

9 Brittan later appointed the Peacock Committee (The Committee on Financing the BBC), among the members of which was his brother Samuel. Brittan subsequently became a Vice President of the Commission of the European Communities responsible for competition policy and later the chief negotiator for the European Community in the closing stages of the GATT Uruguay round.

10 The UK DBS were to be provided by a consortium known as the '21 Club', in which the BBC had the largest share (50 per cent) followed by the ITV companies (30 per cent) and the UK electronics and entertainment industry (notably Thorn EMI) the remaining 20 per cent (Leapman 1987: 208).

11 See Great Britain. Parliament. House of Lords. Evidence. 1985: 45.

## APPENDIX II

1 For a fuller account of the Council of Europe and the European Communities, and of their broadcasting and audiovisual policies in particular, see Collins (1994).

2 The Court of Auditors monitors the Community's budget and expenditure; the Economic and Social Committee is a consultative body made up of representatives of various areas of economic and social life, and the Court of Justice ensures that Community law is followed.

3 The Council of Ministers is not to be confused with the European Council (which was established in 1974). The European Council meets biannually (or more often) and comprises the Heads of State or Government of Community Member States. The Council of Ministers is made up of Ministers from each of the Community's Member States. Thus, if foreign affairs is the business before the Council, foreign ministers attend, if agriculture ministers of agriculture. Presidency of the Council of Ministers rotates between Member States at six-monthly intervals.

4 Voting in the Council of Ministers is weighted. Luxembourg has two votes, Denmark and Ireland each have three votes, Belgium, Greece, the Netherlands and Portugal each have five votes, Spain has eight votes and Germany, France, Italy and the UK each have ten votes. The total number of votes is thus seventy six and a qualified majority is fifty-four votes.

5 There are significant differences and regularities in Community usage of the terms 'broadcasting' and 'audiovisual'. A useful, but not infallible, presumption is that use of the term 'broadcasting' implies a liberal, market-oriented, policy whereas the term 'audio-visual' suggests a more pro-active and dirigist emphasis. Indeed the Commissioner then responsible for DG X, Jean Dondlinger, stated explicitly that the economic imperatives which governed the Community's efforts to establish a single broadcasting market are inappropriate to the audio-visual sector.

> The European film and television industry is among the sectors most seriously endangered by competition from other markets more accustomed to a free and easy diffusion of broadcasts over large areas. The role of the Commission is, of course, that of providing consistent means for policy and coordination at Community level. It is also that of actively supporting a sector little-adapted to purely economic competition.
>
> (Dondlinger 1989: 3)

6 Representatives were from the Foreign and Commonwealth Office, the Office of Arts and Libraries and various UK cultural quangos.

7 Thus limiting Commission powers to the audio-visual sector only in so far as it is a vehicle for 'artistic and literary creation' rather than establishing the audio-visual sector itself as an authentic locus of artistic and literary creation.

8 Plenary sessions of the Parliament are held in Strasbourg. However its Secretariat is in Luxembourg and its committees meet in Brussels. The European Community's Court of Justice and Court of Auditors are located in Luxembourg whereas the Commission of the European Communities is permanently located in Brussels. The Community's Economic and Social Committee (an advisory body made up of representatives of interest groups such as trades unions, employers' associations and consumer groups) is also located in Brussels. The European Parliament has been directly elected by citizens of the European Communities in quinquennial elections since 1979.

9 The Single European Act (signed in 1986) came into force in 1987. It established a 'co-operation procedure' between Commission and Parliament which strengthened the Parliament's powers *vis à vis* the Commission. The Commission has now to secure the Parliament's assent to its expenditure on 'non-obligatory items' and the Council of Minister's assent in respect of 'obligatory' expenditure. For a useful summary of the contemporary constitutional issues in the Community see *Financial Times* 13.8.91: 2.

10 A reference to Denmark's recurrent argument that because culture is neither part of the Rome Treaty nor of the Single European Act, the Community has no jurisdiction in the cultural domain.

11 Then the Italian Member of the Party of the Democratic Left, formerly the PCI, Roberto Barzanti.

12 Dieter Schinzel, a German member of the SPD, and Karsten Hoppenstedt, a German member of the CDU.

13 A senior Dutch Liberal Democrat who was President of the European Parliament Intergroup Television,

14 The founder members of the Council were the UK, France, Belgium, Netherlands, Luxembourg, Sweden, Norway, Denmark, Italy and Ireland. They were followed by Greece and Turkey and then Iceland, Germany, Austria, Cyprus, Switzerland, Malta, Portugal, Spain, Liechtenstein, San Marino, Finland, Hungary and Czechoslovakia. Bulgaria, Poland and Yugoslavia had applications for membership under consideration in 1991.

15 The membership of the Parliamentary Assembly is drawn from members of the parliaments of the Council's Member States. The Court of Human Rights has one judge from each Member State, each of whom is elected by the Parliamentary Assembly to serve the Court for nine years.

16 Though the Convention provides for more stringent measures against pornographic television than does European Community regulation.

17 Article 10 of the European Convention on Human Rights states:

1 Everyone has the right to freedom of expression. This right shall include freedom to hold opinions and to receive and impart information and ideas without interference by public authority and regardless of frontiers. This Article shall not prevent states from requiring the licensing of broadcasting, television or cinema enterprises.

2 The exercise of these freedoms, since it carries with it duties and responsibilities, may be subject to such formalities, conditions, restrictions or penalties as are prescribed by law and are necessary in a democratic society, in the interests of national security, territorial integrity or public safety, for the prevention of disorder or crime, for the protection of health or morals, for the protection of the reputation or rights of others, for preventing the disclosure of information received in confidence, or for maintaining the authority and impartiartiality of the judiciary.

18 The CDMM (Comité directeur des moyens de communication de masse) comprises experts from each of the member states of the Council, from the Commission of the European Communities and from the Parliamentary Assembly. Other organisations including the Audiovisual Eureka, the EBU and ACT have observer status on CDMM. The membership of CDMM (and the sub-committees MM-JU – Committee of Legal Experts in the Media Field – and MM-R-PD – Select Committee of Experts on the Production, Distribution and Marketing of European audio-visual works) – is specified in Council of Europe (1991b: 130–1).

# BIBLIOGRAPHY

European Community and European Broadcasting Union documents, where not published, are cited using the internal reference numbers of those organisations.

Ang, I. (1996) *Living Room Wars: Rethinking Media Audiences for a Postmodern World*. London. Routledge.

Anonymous (1987) 'Dubbers and subtitlers have a prime role in the international distribution of television programmes'. *EBU Review. Programmes, Administration, Law*. Vol. XXXVIII, No. 6. November: 8–13.

*Ariel*. BBC Staff Newsletter. Weekly. London. BBC.

Arnold, M. (1963 [1869]) *Culture and Anarchy*. Cambridge. Cambridge University Press.

Ministère des affaires étrangères, Republique Française (1989) *Assises européennes de l'audiovisuel*. Projet Eureka audiovisuel Ministère des affaires étrangères, Republique Française and Commission of the European Communities. Paris.

AVRO (1982) 'Eurikon. Pan european experiment'. *Televizier AVRObode*. 25–31 October. Hilversum.

Bangemann, M. *et al.* (1994) *Europe and the Global Information Society. Recommendations to the European Council*. The Bangemann Report. Brussels. No Publisher.

Banotti, M. (1992) Interview in *Media Policy Review*. No. 4: 6–7.

Barnett, S. (1990) *Games and Sets. The Changing Face of Sport on Television*. London. British Film Institute.

Barrand, C. (1982) IBA/EBU Pan European Experiment. 24–30 May 1982. Unpublished mimeo report.

—— (1983) *Good Morning Europa. Proposals for a 4.5 hour Pan-European Television Breakfast Programme*. Unpublished typescript dated 12.3.83.

—— (1983a) Unpublished letter to Clarke dated 22.1.83.

—— (1986) 'Europa Television – the transponder's eye view'. In *European Broadcasting Union Review. Programmes, Administration, Law*. Vol. XXXVII, No. 2. March: 10–13.

Barzanti, R. (1990) 'La culture, parametre vital de la "société européenne"'. In *Coherence in Diversity: The Challenge for European Television*. Manchester. European Institute for the Media.

—— (1990a) 'Audiovisual opportunities in the Single Market'. In *MEDIA 92*. Newsletter of the MEDIA 92 Programme, 09/1990: 1. Brussels.

Bauman, Z. (1992) *Intimations of Postmodernity*. London. Routledge.

BBC (1992) *Extending Choice. The BBC's Role in the New Broadcasting Age*. London. BBC.

Becker, L. (1995) *Conflicting Goals, Confused Elites, Active Audiences: Some Thoughts on Canadian Media Policy*. Paper at the conference 'Media policy, national identity and citizenry in changing democratic societies'. Duke University. Oct 6–7 1995.

Becker, L. and G. Kosicki (1995) 'Understanding – and misunderstanding – the message-producer/message-receiver transaction'. In P. Wasburn (ed.) *Research in Political Sociology*. Vol. 7. Greenwich. JAI Press: 33–62.

Bekkers, W. (1987) 'The Dutch public broadcasting services in a multi-channel landscape'. In *EBU Review. Programmes, Administration, Law*. Vol. XXXVIII, No. 6. November: 32–35.

Berlin, I. (1969) 'Two concepts of liberty'. In *Four Essays on Liberty*. Oxford. Oxford University Press.

Blumler, J. (1992) *Television and the Public Interest. Vulnerable Values in West European Broadcasting*. London. Sage.

Boni, V. (1985) 'The implications of the new realities in European broadcasting'. In *European Broadcasting Union Review. Programmes, Administration, Law*. Vol. XXXVI, No. 6. November: 49–51.

Bourges, H. (1993) The public service channels in France: independence and responsibility. In *Diffusion*. Summer: 2–6.

Boyle, A. (1972) *Only the Wind will Listen*. London. Hutchinson.

Brecht, B. (1979) *Poems 1913–1956*. Ed. J. Willett and R. Manheim. London. Eyre Methuen.

Briggs, A. (1961, 1965, 1970, 1979) *The History of Broadcasting in the United Kingdom*. Oxford. Oxford University Press.

Brittan, S. (1987) 'The fight for freedom in broadcasting'. In *Political Quarterly*. Vol. 58, No. 1. January/March: 3–23.

British Screen Advisory Council (1992) *The Challenge of Language in European Film*. London. British Screen Advisory Council.

*Broadcast*. Weekly. London.

*Broadcasting Act 1990*. London. HMSO.

*Broadcasting News from the Netherlands Hilversummary*. Irregular. Hilversum. NOS.

Burgess, A. (1990) 'European culture: does it exist?' In *European Broadcasting Union Review. Programmes Administration Law*. Vol. XLI, No. 2. March: 17–21.

Burnett, C. (1989) 'Speaking in tongues'. In *Cable and Satellite Europe*. January: 38.

*Cable and Satellite Express*. Monthly. London.

*Cable and Satellite Europe*. Monthly. London.

Cairnduff, M. (ed.) (1984) *Who's Who in Ireland*. Dun Laoghaire. Vesey.

Cave, M. (1985) 'Financing British broadcasting'. In *Lloyds Bank Review*. No. 157. July: 25–35.

Central Statistical Office (CSO) (1993) *Overseas Transactions of the Film and TV Industry (1992)*. Newport: CSO.

Chenevière, G. (1990) 'The Europe co-production association is five years old. Towards a European TV drama industry'. In *European Broadcasting Union Review. Programmes Administration Law*. Vol. XLI, No. 6. November: 17–20.

—— (1992) 'European coproduction: a long road to haul'. In *Espace*. No. 10. April: 4–5.

Clarke, A. (1992) *How the World was One. The Turbulent History of Global Communications*. London. Gollancz.

Clarke, N. (1981) *Interim Report to the New Developments Group of the EBU Television Programme Committee by its Group of Experts Considering a European TV Programme Experiment*. (Unpublished.)

—— (1982) 'Pan-European TV?' In *Irish Broadcasting Review*. No. 14. Summer: 42–7.

Clarke, N. and K.-J. Hindriks (1984) *Pan-European Television Service*. Unpublished memo to Carel Enkelaar dated 16.1.84.

Clarke, N. and E. Riddell (1992) *The Sky Barons*. London. Methuen.

Clarke, N. *et al.* (1983) *Pan-European Television Service via ECS. A Feasibility Study*. Mimeo.

Coase, R. (1950) *British Broadcasting. A Study in Monopoly*. London. Longmans Green.

Cohen, A., M. Levy, I. Roeh and M. Gurevitch (1996) *Global Newsrooms, Local Audiences. A Study of the Eurovision News Exchange*. London. John Libbey.

Collins, R. (1990) *Satellite Television in Western Europe*. London. John Libbey.

—— (1992) *Satellite Television in Western Europe*. Revised edition. London. John Libbey.

—— (1992a) 'Public service broadcasting and freedom'. In *Media Information Australia*. No. 66: 3–15.

—— (1993) 'Public service versus the market ten years on. Reflections on critical theory and the debate on broadcasting policy in the UK'. In *Screen*. Vol. 34, No. 3: 243–59.

—— (1994) *Broadcasting and Audio-visual Policy in the European Single Market*. London. John Libbey.

Collins, R. and V. Porter (1981) *WDR and the Arbeiterfilm. Fassbinder, Ziewer and Others*. London. British Film Institute.

Commission of the European Communities (1983) *Interim Report. Realities and Tendencies in European Television: Perspectives and Options*. COM(83) 229 final, 25.5.83. Brussels.

—— (1984) *Towards a European Television Policy*. European File 19/84. Brussels. Commission of the European Communities.

—— (1984a) *Television Without Frontiers*. Green Paper on the establishment of the Common Market for broadcasting especially by satellite and cable. COM(84) 300 final. Luxembourg. Office for Official Publications of the European Communities.

—— (1986) *Television and the Audio-visual Sector: Towards a European Policy*. European File 14/86. Luxembourg. Office for Official Publications of the European Communities.

—— (1991) 'Public opinion in the European Community'. *Eurobarometer*. No. 35. June. Brussels.

—— (1991a) 'Public opinion in the European Community'. *Eurobarometer*. No. 36. December. Brussels.

—— (1991b) *Proposal for a Council Directive on Rental Right, Lending Right, and on Certain Rights Related to Copyright*. COM(90) 586 final – SYN 319. Luxembourg. Office for Official Publications of the European Communities.

—— (1992) *From Single Market to European Union*. Luxembourg. Office for Official Publications of the European Communities.

—— (1992a) *Pluralism and Media Concentration in the Internal Market.* COM(92) 480 final. Luxembourg. Office for Official Publications of the European Communities.

—— (1993) *Reflection on Information and Communication Policy of the European Community.* Report of the Group of Experts chaired by Mr Willy De Clerq Member of the European Parliament. RP 1051 93.

—— (1993a) *Background Report. The Enlargement of the Community.* ISEC/B15/93. London. Commission of the European Communities.

—— (1993b) *Growth, Competitiveness, Employment – The Challenges and Ways Forward into the 21st Century.* Luxembourg. Office for Official Publications of the European Communities.

Commission of the European Communities and the European Parliament (1990) *Europe, Our Future. The Institutions of the European Community.* Luxembourg. Office for Official Publications of the European Communities.

Competition Directorate-General of the European Commission (1996) *Competition Policy Newsletter.* Vol. 3, No. 2. Autumn. Luxembourg. Office for Official Publications of the European Communities.

Congdon, T. *et al.* (1992) *Paying for Broadcasting. The Handbook.* London. Routledge.

Coudenhove-Kalergi, R. (1926) *Pan-Europe.* New York. Knopf.

—— (1943) *Crusade for Pan-Europe.* New York. G.P. Putnam's Sons.

—— (1948) *Europe Seeks Unity.* New York. State University of New York. Institute of Public Affairs and Regional Studies.

Council of Europe (1982) *Council of Europe Activities in the Field of the Media.* Mimeo.

—— (1988) *Actes de la conférence ministerielle européenne sur la politique des communications de masse.* Strasbourg. Council of Europe.

—— (1989) *European Convention on Transfrontier Television.* 5.5.89. Strasbourg. Council of Europe.

—— (1990) *Explanatory report on the European Convention on Transfrontier Television.* Strasbourg. Council of Europe.

—— (1991) *Recommendations and Resolutions Adopted by the Parliamentary Assembly of the Council of Europe in the Media Field.* Strasbourg. Council of Europe Directorate of Human Rights.

—— (1991a) *Recommendations Adopted by the Committee of Ministers of the Council of Europe in the Media Field.* Strasbourg. Council of Europe Directorate of Human Rights.

—— (1991b) *Council of Europe Activities in the Media Field.* Strasbourg. Council of Europe Directorate of Human Rights.

—— (1991c) *Recommendations and Resolutions Adopted by the Parliamentary Assembly of the Council of Europe in the Media Field.* Strasbourg. Council of Europe Directorate of Human Rights.

—— (1991d) *Which Way Forward for Europe's Media in the 1990s? Media Economics and Political and Cultural Pluralism.* Report presented by the Steering Committee on the Mass Media. (CDMM). Strasbourg. Third European Ministerial Conference on Mass Media Policy. Council of Europe.

—— (1991e) *Which Way Forward for Europe's Media in the 1990s? Media Economics and Political and Cultural Pluralism.* Synthesis report on media concentration in Europe presented by the Enlarged Working Party on Media Concentrations on behalf of the

CDMM. Third European Ministerial Conference on Mass Media Policy. Strasbourg. Council of Europe.

Council of the European Communities (1986) *Council Directive on the Adoption of Common Technical Specifications of the MAC-packet Family of Standards for Direct Satellite Television Broadcasting: 86/529/EEC.* OJ L 311 6.11.86.

—— (1989) *Directive on the Coordination of Certain Provisions Laid Down by Law, Regulation or Administrative Action in Member States Concerning the Pursuit of Television Broadcasting Activities. 89/552/EEC.* OJ L 298 17.10.89: 23–30.

Curran, C. (1971) 'Broadcasting and society'. Speech at the Edinburgh Broadcasting Conference. In A. Smith (ed.) (1974) *British Broadcasting.* Newton Abbott. David & Charles.

Daly, .A. (1982) IBA/EBU Pan-European Experiment 24–30 May 1982 Interpretation Report. (Unpublished.)

de Bock, H. (1983) *Eurikon Considered: The Eurikonsumers' Perspective.* Mimeo.

Denys, M. (1991) 'News inflation – the EBU on a war footing'. In *Espace.* No. 2. June: 4–5. Geneva. EBU

Department of National Heritage (1992) *The Future of the BBC.* Cm 2098. London. HMSO.

Desgraupes, P. (1985) *Etude sur un projet de Chaine Culturelle Européenne pour le Canal 1 du Satellite TDF 1.* Mimeo. Paris.

Dibie, J.-N. (1993) *Aid for Cinematographic and Audio-visual Production in Europe.* London. John Libbey.

Dill, R. (1986) 'Europa TV – the real thing from Hilversum'. In *Forum* 2/86. Strasbourg. Council of Europe.

Docker, J. (1991) 'Popular culture versus the state'. In *Media Information Australia.* No. 59. February: 7–26.

Dondlinger, J. (1989) 'Europe's media future'. In *Media Bulletin.* Vol. 6, No. 2: 3. Manchester. European Institute for the Media.

EBU (1982) *Television Programme Committee Meeting on the Future of Eurovision.* 9.12.82. SPG 2130.

—— (1982a) *The EBU Statutes Revision. Presentation Report.* Geneva. EBU.

—— (1983) Unpublished letter dated 3.3.83 from de Kalbermatten to Directors General and TV Programme Executives of active members. Results of the special meeting of member organizations interested in the use of the L-Sat satellite of the European Space Agency. SG/1357.

—— (1984a) *Minutes of the EBU General Assembly 29.6.84–2.7.84.* AG 561 (pv) SPG 2652 June 84.

—— (1986) *Note for the 76th meeting of the Administrative Council. Direct Broadcast Satellites.* CA 1810 (dt) SPG 3312

—— (1987) *Report of the Working Party on Television News.* Com.TV/GT TV News (r) SPG 3543/March 87.

—— (1987a) *Television Programme Committee* Com. TV (dt) SPG 3577/April 87.

—— (1989) 'Declaration by public service broadcasters members of the EBU meeting at the 1989 Brussels Symposium'. In *EBU Review. Programmes, Administration, Law.* Vol. XL, No. 3. May: 15–16.

—— (1989a) *Brussels 21–23 March 1989. Public Service Broadcasting: An Appointment with Europe.* In *EBU Review. Programmes, Administration, Law.* Vol. XL, No. 3 May: 10–14.

—— (1990) *Statistics of Eurovision Programmes And News Exchanges, 1.1.89–31.12.89.* In *EBU Review. Programmes, Administration, Law.* Vol. XLI, No. 3. May: 23–4.

—— (1992) *Statutes of the European Broadcasting Union.* Geneva. EBU.

EBU/OTS Operations Group (1983) Eurikon DBS Pan-European Broadcasting. A Summarised Report on the EBU/OTS Experiment '82. Unpublished mimeo.

EBU (1984) L-Sat Finance Group Report. June. 13pp and 13pp attachments. (Unpublished.)

Elsaesser, T. (1989) *New German Cinema. A History.* Basingstoke. Macmillan.

Emanuel, S. (1991) *La Sept: Television and Culture in France: 1981–1991.* English language version of a dissertation submitted to the Université de Rennes II under the supervision of Professor A. Mattelart. December.

*Espace.* Ten times a year. Geneva. EBU.

Eugster, E. (1983) *Television Programming Across National Boundaries: The EBU and OIRT Experience.* Dedham. Artec House.

*European.* Weekly. London.

European Commission (1994) *Strategy Options to Strengthen the European Programme Industry in the Context of the Audiovisual Policy of the European Union.* [The Audiovisual Green Paper]. Brussels. Commission of the European Communities.

—— (1997) *European Community Competition Policy 1996.* Luxembourg. Office for Official Publications of the European Communities.

European Movement (n.d. [1950]) *The European Movement and the Council of Europe.* London. Hutchinson.

—— (1948) *Europe Unites.* London. Hollis & Carter.

European Parliament (1982) *Report on Radio and Television Broadcasting in the European Community on Behalf of the Committee on Youth, Culture, Education, Information and Sport.* [The Hahn Report]. Document 1–1013/81. 23.2.82. PE 73.271 final.

—— (1982a) *Resolution on Radio and Television Broadcasting in the European Community.* [The Hahn Resolution]. OJ C 87 5.4.82: 110–12.

—— (1984) *Report on a Policy Commensurate with New Trends in European Television on Behalf of the Committee on Youth, Culture, Education, Information and Sport.* [Arfé Report]. 16.3.84. PE 85.902 final.

—— (1984a) *Resolution on Broadcast Communication in the European Community (The Threat to Diversity of Opinion Posed by Commercialisation of the New Media).* [The Hutton Resolution]. OJ C 127 14.5.84: 147–50.

—— (1984b) *Hutton Report on Behalf of the Committee on Youth, Culture, Education, Information and Sport.* 15.3.84. PE 78.983 final.

—— (1985) *Resolution on a Framework for a European Media Policy Based on the Establishment of a Common Market for Broadcasting especially by Satellite and Cable.* OJ C 288 11.11.85: 113.

—— (1985a) *Proposal for a Council Regulation on a Community Aid Scheme for Non-documentary Cinema and Television Co-productions.* (COM(85) 174 final) OJ C. 288 8.10.85: 28–41.

—— (1985b) *Report on a Framework for European Media Policy especially on the Establishment of a Common Market for Broadcasting, Especially by Satellite and Cable on Behalf of the Committee on Youth, Culture, Education, Information and Sport.* [Second Hahn Report]. PE Document A2–75/85.

—— (1987) *Audio-Visual Policies of the Community. The Role of the European Parliament.* Research and Documentation Papers. Economic Series No. 10. 8–1987. European Parliament Secretariat. Directorate General for Research.

—— (1987a) *Resolution on the European Community's Information Policy.* [The Baget Bozzo Resolution]. OJ C 7 12.1.87: 111–14.

—— (1987b) *Audio-Visual Policies of the Community. The Role of the European Parliament.* Research and Documentation Papers. Economic Series No. 10. 8–1987. European Parliament Secretariat. Directorate General for Research.

—— (1989) *Report on the European Film and Television Industry.* [The de Vries Report]. 09.01.89. PE Document A2–0347/88.

—— (1990) *Report of the Committee on Youth, Culture, Education, the Media and Sport on the Proposal from the Commission to the Council Concerning the Implementation of an Action Programme to Promote the Development of the European Audiovisual Industry (1991–1995).* [The Barzanti Report]. 3.11.90. PE 144.275/fin. PE a 3–0293/90.

—— (1991) *Opinion for the Committee on Institutional Affairs of the Committee on Youth, Culture, Education, the Media and Sport on the Annual report by the Council of the European Communities on European Union. Part A: Activities in the Community framework.* PE Doc 153.030/def. 25.9.1991.

*Evening Standard.* Six days a week. London.

Falkenberg, H.-G. (1983) 'No future? a few thoughts on public broadcasting in the Federal Republic of Germany, Spring 1983'. In *Media Culture and Society.* Vol. 5, No. 3/4. July/October: 235–45.

Fichera, M. (1989) 'The new self-confidence in public service broadcasting in Italy'. In *EBU Review. Programmes, Administration, Law.* Vol. XL, No. 3. May: 21–4.

*Financial Times.* Six times a week. London.

Fiske, J. (1987) *Television Culture.* London. Methuen.

Fleming, R. (1982) Note for the attention of Madame van Hoof. Director-General Commission of the European Communities Joint Service Interpretation-Conferences. Subject EBU-OTS experiment in London. 8.6.1982. (Unpublished.)

Flournoy, D. (1992) *CNN World Report. Ted Turner's International News Coup.* London. John Libbey.

Fowler, R. (Chairman) (1965) *Report of the Committee on Broadcasting.* Ottawa. Queen's Printer.

Fraser, N. (1992) 'Rethinking the public sphere: a contribution to the critique of actually existing democracy'. In C. Calhoun (ed.) *Habermas and the Public Sphere.* Cambridge. MIT Press.

Freeman, C. (1994) 'The diffusion of information and communication technology and the world economy in the 1990s'. In R. Mansell (ed.) *The Management of Information and Communication Technologies. Emerging Patterns of Control.* London. ASLIB: 8–41.

Friedman, M. and R. Friedman (1981) *Free to Choose.* New York. Avon.

279

Frost, R. (1946 [1930]) *The Poems of Robert Frost*. New York. The Modern Library. Random House.

Garnham, N. (1983) 'Public service versus the market'. In *Screen*. Vol. 24, No. 1: 6–27.

—— (1983a) 'Editorial'. In *Media Culture and Society*. Vol. 5 No. 1: 1–5.

—— (1984) 'Introduction'. In A. Mattelart, X. Delcourt and M. Mattelart (eds) *International Image Markets*. London. Comedia.

—— (1986) 'The media and the public sphere'. In P. Golding *et al.* (eds) *Communicating Politics*. Leicester. Leicester University Press.

—— (1990) *Capitalism and Communications*. London. Sage.

—— (1992) 'The media and the public sphere'. In C. Calhoun (ed.) *Habermas and the Public Sphere*. Cambridge. MIT Press.

Gavin, B. (1991) *European Broadcasting Standards in the 1990s*. Oxford. NCC Blackwell.

Gellner, E. (1983) *Nations and Nationalism*. Oxford. Blackwell.

Gentikow, B. (1993) 'Oversettelse av film og fjernsyn. Dialog eller kulturell hegemoni?' In *Nordicom-Information*. No. 2: 1–14.

George, S. (1990) *An Awkward Partner. Britain in the European Community*. Oxford. Oxford University Press.

Golding, R. (1982) *A View of the EBU/OTS 'Eurikon' Project*. Central Television Typescript.

Great Britain. Parliament. House of Commons. Home Affairs Committee. (1988) *The Future of Broadcasting*. 262-I and II. London. HMSO.

Great Britain. Parliament. House of Commons. Select Committee on National Heritage. (1993) *The Future of the BBC*. 77-I and II and III. London. HMSO.

Great Britain. Parliament. House of Lords (1985) *Fourth report. Television Without Frontiers*. Select Committee on the European Communities. (HL 43) London. HMSO.

—— (1987) *4th Report*. Select Committee on the European Communities. European Broadcasting (HL 67) London. HMSO.

Guback, T. (1969) *The International Film Industry*. Bloomington. Indiana University Press.

GUMG (Glasgow University Media Group) (1976) *Bad News*. London. Routledge & Kegan Paul.

GUMG (Glasgow University Media Group) (1980) *More Bad News*. London. Routledge & Kegan Paul.

Gunter, B. (1982) *Audience Reactions to Eurikon. Evidence on UK Viewer Ratings of a New Pan-European TV Service*. London. IBA Audience Research Department.

—— (1982a) *Measurement of Audience Ratings of Eurikon Programming from the First Demonstration Week (24–30 May 1982): A Report on Three Pilot Experiments and Some Preliminary Research Findings*. July. IBA Typescript.

—— (1982b) *Audience Reactions to Eurikon. Impressions of Programmes from Week Two*. November. IBA Typescript.

—— (1983) *Audience Reactions to Eurikon. Further Evidence on UK Viewer Ratings of a New Pan-European TV Service*. London. IBA Audience Research Department.

—— (1991) *The Television Audience in Europe*. ITC Research Paper. London. Independent Television Commission.

Habermas, J. (1974) 'The public sphere'. In *New German Critique*. No. 3. Fall: 49–55.

—— (1989 [1962]) *The Structural Transformation of the Public Sphere*. Polity. No place of publication [Cambridge].

Haley, W. (1948) 'The Lewis Fry Memorial Lecture'. Extracts in A. Smith (ed.) (1974) *British Broadcasting*. Newton Abbott. David & Charles.

Hall, S. *et al.* (eds) (1980) *Culture, Media, Language*. London. Hutchinson.

Hartz, L. (1964) *The Founding of New Societies: Studies in the History of the United States, Latin America, South Africa, Canada and Australia*. New York. Harcourt Brace and World.

Hayek, F. (1972 [1944]) *The Road to Serfdom*. Chicago. University of Chicago Press.

Hearst, S. (1988) *Neighbourhood Watch*. In *Guardian*. 4.7.1988: 23.

Heller, C. (1978) *Broadcasting and Accountability*. London. British Film Institute.

Herbst, T. (1987) 'A pragmatic translation approach to dubbing'. In *EBU Review. Programmes, Administration, Law*. Vol. XXXVIII, No. 6. November: 21–3.

Hindriks, K-J (n.d. c.Jan 1985) *Olympus TV*. Mimeo EBU Pan-European Satellite Broadcast Project. Hilversum.

Hjarvard, S. (1991) *Pan European Television News. Towards a European Political Public Sphere?* Paper at the Fourth International Television Studies Conference London 1991. Revised version published in P. Drummond, R. Paterson and J. Willis (eds) (1993) *National Identity and Europe*. London. British Film Institute.

Hodgson, P. (1992) 'Foreword'. In T. Congdon *et al. Paying for Broadcasting. The Handbook*. London. Routledge.

Home Office (1981) *Direct Broadcasting by Satellite*. London. HMSO.

Hoskins, C. and S. McFadyen (1991) *International Joint Ventures in Television Program Production. National Centre for Management Research and Development*. Working Paper NC 91–21. University of Western Ontario.

Hoskins, C. and R. Mirus (1988) Reasons for the US domination of the international trade in television programmes. In *Media Culture and Society*. Vol. 10, No. 4: 499–515.

*Independent*. Daily. London.

Internationes (1989) *Broadcasting Laws. Documents on Politics and Society in the Federal Republic of Germany*. Bonn. Internationes.

Jarvie, I. (1965) 'Limits to functionalism and alternatives to it in anthropology'. In *Functionalism in the Social Sciences*. Monograph No. 5. Academy of Political and Social Science. Philadelphia. February: 18–34.

—— (1966) 'The social character of technological problems: comments on Skolimowski's paper'. In *Technology and Culture*. Vol. vii, No. 3. Summer: 384–90.

Jay, M. (1973) *The Dialectical Imagination*. London. Heinemann Educational Books.

Johnston, S. (1979) 'The author as public institution. In *Screen Education*. No. 32/33. Autumn/Winter: 67–78.

Jones, K. and R. Cere (1991) *A Comparative Study of British and Italian TV News*. Paper given at the Fourth International Television Studies Conference. London.

Kant, I. (1949 [1788]) *Critique of Practical Reason*. Trans. L.W. Beck. Chicago. University of Chicago Press.

—— (1959 [1784]) 'What is enlightenment?' In *Foundations of the Metaphysics of Morals*. Trans. and ed. L.W. Beck. Indianapolis. Bobbs-Merrill.

Katz, E. and T. Liebes (1985) 'Mutual aid in the decoding of "Dallas"'. In P. Drummond and R. Paterson (eds) *Television in Transition*. London. British Film Institute.

Keane, J. (1991) *The Media and Democracy*. Cambridge. Polity.

Kedourie, E. (1966) *Nationalism*. London. Hutchinson.

Kilborn, R. (1991) *'Speak my language'. Current Attitudes to Television Subtitling and Dubbing*. Paper presented to the Fourth International Television Studies Conference. London.

Kimmel, H. (1982) *What is Public Service Broadcasting (PSB) Now and Tomorrow?* Evidence to the Perez Group. ZDF mimeo 6.9.1982 Mainz.

Komiya, M. (1990) 'Intelsat and the debate about satellite competition'. In K. Dyson and P. Humphreys (eds) *The Political Economy of Communications*. London. Routledge.

Kumar, K. (1986) 'Public service broadcasting and the public interest'. In C. MacCabe and O. Stewart (eds) *The BBC and Public Service Broadcasting*. Manchester. University of Manchester Press.

Lang, J. (1988) 'The Future of European film and television'. In *European Affairs*. Vol. 2, No. 1: 12–20.

*Le Monde*. Daily. Paris.

Leapman, M. (1987) *The Last Days of the Beeb*. London. Coronet.

Luyken, G.-M. and T. Herbst, J. Langham-Brown, H. Reid and H. Spinhof (1991) *Overcoming Language Barriers in Television: Dubbing and Subtitling for the European Audience*. Manchester. European Institute for the Media.

MacCabe, C. and O. Stewart (eds) (1986) *The BBC and Public Service Broadcasting*. Manchester. Manchester University Press.

MacConghail, M. (1983) 'Pan-European TV'. In *Irish Broadcasting Review*. No. 16. Spring: 61–5.

Maggiore, M. (1990) *Audiovisual Production in the Single Market*. Luxembourg. Commission of the European Communities.

Maidment, K. (1985) Letter to Leon Brittain [*sic*]. In *Annual Report of the British Film and Television Producers' Association*. 1984/5. London.

Marcuse, H. (1972 [1964]) *One Dimensional Man*. London. Abacus.

McDonnell, J. (1991) *Public Service Broadcasting. A Reader*. London. Routledge.

McQuail, D. (1994) *Mass Communication Theory*. 3rd edn. Thousand Oaks. Sage.

*Media Policy Review*. Monthly. London.

Melich, A. (1990) *Identité Nationale et Media Contemporains*. Lausanne. Editions Loisirs et Pédagogie.

Melody, W. (1988) 'Pan-European television: commercial and cultural implications of European satellites'. In P. Drummond and R. Paterson (eds) *Television and its Audience*. London. British Film Institute: 267–82.

Mitrany, D. (1975) *The Functional Theory of Politics*. London. Martin Robertson.

Monnet, J. (1978) *Memoirs*. London. Collins.

Morley, D. (1980) *The Nationwide Audience. Structure and Decoding*. London. British Film Institute.

—— (1992) *Television Audiences and Cultural Studies*. London. Routledge.

Murdock, G (1990) 'Redrawing the map of the communications industries: concentration and ownership in the era of privatization'. In M. Ferguson (ed.) *Public Communiction. The New Imperatives*. London. Sage.

Negrine, R. (ed.) (1988) *Satellite Broadcasting. The Politics and Implications of the New Media*. London. Routledge.

Negrine, R. (1989) *Politics and the Mass Media in Britain*. London. Routledge.

Negrine, R. and S. Papathanassopoulos (1990) *The Internationalisation of Television*. London. Pinter.

*New Media Markets*. Fortnightly. London.

Noel, E. (1988) *Working Together. The Institutions of the European Community*. Luxembourg. Office for Official Publications of the European Communities.

NOS (1983) *Eurikon Considered, The Dutch Viewers' Perspective*. Hilversum. NOS.

—— (1984) *Europees Programma via Satelliet*. Mimeo dated 9.10.84. Hilversum.

—— (1986) Europa Television. Statement to President of the EBU dated 3.12.86. Hilversum. NOS.

—— (1990) 'Regulations covering "comprehensive programming"'. In *Hilversummary. Broadcasting News from the Netherlands*, 2: 4–5.

—— (1991) 'Dutch broadcasting and culture'. In *Hilversummary. Broadcasting News from the Netherlands*, 2: 4–5.

NTIA (1993) *Globalization of the Mass Media*. Washington DC. US Department of Commerce. National Telecommunications and Information Administration Special Publication 93–290. US Government Printing Office.

Papathanassopoulos, S. (1990) 'Towards European television: the case of Europa-TV'. In *Media Information Australia*. No. 56. May: 57–63.

Peacock, A. [Chairman] (1986) *Report of the Committee on Financing the BBC*. Cmnd 9824. London. HMSO.

Perez Group(1983) *Conclusions of the TV Programme Committee's Group of Experts on the Future of Public Service Broadcasting. (Chairman H. Perez)*. Submitted to the Television Programme Committee meeting April 1983. EBU Mimeo.

Perez Group(1983a) *Summary of the Discussions of the Last Meeting of the Perez Group (Chairman H. Perez) Geneva 9.12.83*. Presented to the 4th Meeting of the Study Group on Public Service Broadcasting, 25–26 January 1984.

Pilkington, H. [Chairman] (1962) *Report of the Committee on Broadcasting* (1960). Cmnd 1753. London. HMSO.

Porter, V. (1985) 'European co-productions: aesthetic and cultural implications'. In *Journal of Area Studies*. No. 12. Autumn: 6–10.

Porter, V. and S. Hasselbach (1991) *Pluralism, Public Service and the Marketplace. The Regulation of German Broadcasting*. Routledge. London.

*Producer News*. Monthly. London. The Producers Association.

Raboy, M. (ed.) (1996) *Public Broadcasting for the 21st Century*. London. John Libbey.

RAI (1983) *Research on Attitudes to Eurikon Television Programmes*. LCMIANUS Typescript. February.

—— (1983a) Experiment of the EURIKON Programs Transmitted via the OTS Satellite. LCMIANUS Typescript. April.

Rato, A. (1987) 'Europa TV. They shoot pioneers don't they?' In *Media Bulletin*. Vol. 4, No. 1: 2. Manchester. European Institute for the Media.

Reid, H. (1987) 'The semiotics of subtitling, or Why don't you translate what it says?' In *EBU Review. Programmes, Administration, Law*. Vol. XXXVIII, No. 6. November: 28–30.

Reiler, E. (1982) Report on the interpretation of multilingual programmes within the framework of a European satellite-television programme. Also version in German language. (Unpublished.)

—— (1983) Report on the problem of interpretation and translation of multilingual programmes during the ARD/SWF/OTS experimental week in Baden-Baden, W.-Germany. (Unpublished.)

Reith, J. (1949) *Into the Wind*. London: Hodder & Stoughton.

RTP (1983) Letter and 13 pp summary (translated into French from Portugese research report) attachment from M.M. Furtado RTP to N. Clarke 14.1.1983.

Schiller, H. (1969 and 1992) *Mass Communications and American Empire*. New York. A.M. Kelley. 2nd edn. Boulder. Westview.

Schlesinger, P. (1985) 'From public service to commodity: the political economy of tele-text in the UK'. In *Media Culture and Society*. Vol. 7, No. 4: 471–86.

—— (1991) *Media State and Nation*. Sage. London.

Schudson, M. (1992) 'Was there ever a public sphere? If so, when? Reflections on the American case'. In C. Calhoun (ed.) *Habermas and the Public Sphere*. Cambridge. MIT Press.

Schwarzkopf, D. (1986) 'Eins Plus und Europa Television'. In *Media Perspektiven*. 2/1986: 74–80.

Sepstrup, P. (1990) *Transnationalization of Television in Western Europe*. London. John Libbey.

Shaughnessy, H. and C. Fuente Cobo (1990) *The Cultural Obligations of Broadcasting*. Manchester. European Institute for the Media.

Silj, A. (ed.) (1992) *The New Television in Europe*. London. John Libbey.

Silj, A. and M. Alvarado (1988) *East of Dallas. The European Challenge to American Television*. London. British Film Institute.

Smith, A. (ed.) (1974) *British Broadcasting*. Newton Abbott. David & Charles.

Smith, A.D. (1991) *National Identity*. London. Penguin.

*Stage and Television Today*. Weekly. London.

Stephane, R. (1988) 'The cinema and television in Europe. Present situation and future prospects. In *EBU Review. Programmes, Administration, Law*. Vol. XXXIX, No. 2. March: 14–20.

Stoop, P. (1986) 'Arche Noah vor der Flut. Das Europa-TV in seiner präoperationalen Phase'. In *epd Kirche und Rundfunk*. No. 27: 3–6.

—— (1986a) 'Wenig Geld und grosse Pläne. Zum Programme von Europa-TV'. In *epd Kirche und Rundfunk*. No. 43: 4–6.

*Television Business International*. Monthly. London.

*Television Week*. Weekly. London.

*Television World*. Monthly. London.

Thompson, Lord G. (1985) 'A new role for regulation?' In *Airwaves*. Winter 84/5: 10–11. London. IBA.

Tongue, C. (n.d. [1997]) *The Future of Public Service Broadcasting Television in a Multi-channel Digital Age*. [The Tongue Report]. Ilford. The Office of Carole Tongue, MEP.

Tracey, M. (1992) 'Our better angels. The condition of public service broadcasting'. In *Media Information Australia*. No. 66. November: 16–27.

UNESCO (1982) *Three Weeks of Television. An International Comparative Study*. UNESCO. Paris.

UNESCO (1989) *World Communication Report*. Paris. UNESCO.

UNESCO, International Commission on Communication Problems (MacBride Commission) (1980) *Many Voices: One World*. London. Kogan Page.

Underhill, F. (1966) 'Foreword'. In P. Russell (ed.) *Nationalism in Canada*. Toronto. McGraw Hill.

Ungureit, H. (1988) 'The programmes of the European Co-production Association'. In *EBU Review. Programmes, Administration, Law*. Vol. XXXIX, No. 3. May: 17–20.

UPITN (1983) Eurikon News. The Proposal. Unpublished tender dated 8.9.1983 for the provision of news services to Europa [then named Eurikon].

*Variety*. Weekly. New York.

Vasconcelos, A.-P. [Chairman] (1994) *Report by the Think Tank*. Mimeo. No place of publication.

Veil, S. (1988) 'European cinema and television year'. In *EBU Review. Programmes, Administration, Law*. Vol. XXXIX, No. 2. March: 9–10.

Verveld, C. (1986) 'Television by satellite. A common desire to be European but different approaches to programming'. In *Media Bulletin*. Vol. 3, No. 1: 2. Manchester. European Institute for the Media.

Wankell, S. (1986) 'Kennen Sie Europa TV? Ein Programm mit hohem Anspruch und wenig Zuschauern'. In *Funk-Korrespondenz*. Vol. 34, No. 36: 1–4.

Waters, G. (1986) 'The spirit of public service broadcasting'. In *International Broadcasting*. September: 19–20.

Wendelbo, H. (1986) *What Audience for European Television?* Paper at the First International Television Studies Conference 1986. London.

White, J. (1980) 'At 30 the EBU needs creative fire'. In *Irish Broadcasting Review*. No. 7. Spring: 57–60.

Whyte, N. (1989) *Europe and Space*. European Dossier No. 13. Polytechnic of North London Press. London.

Williams, R. (1963) *Culture and Society*. Harmondsworth. Penguin.

Wilson, N. (1988) 'A sporting chance'. In *TV World*. February. London.

—— (1994) 'Eurovision. Forty years in the service of the public. 1954–1994'. In *Diffusion*. Spring: 4–38.

Wolton, D. (1992) 'Values and normative choices in French television'. In J. Blumler (ed.) *Television and the Public Interest*. London. Sage.

*World Broadcast News*. Monthly. London.

Wright, M. (1983) Eurikon Reviewed. In *EBU Review. Programmes, Administration, Law*. Vol. XXXIV, No. 4. July: 31–8.

Yvane, J. (1987) 'The treatment of language in the production of dubbed versions'. In *EBU Review. Programmes, Administration, Law*. Vol. XXXVIII, No. 6. November: 18–20.

# INDEX

ACT 47, 248n; ACT Charter 47, 63, 245n
active audience/weak effect thesis 17
Administrative Council, EBU 34, 42, 250n; beginning of Europa service 139–40; establishment of Euronews proposed by Fichera 169; for and against the Europa service 123–6; formal adoption of Wangermée report 46; membership 241n; received report from Euronews Study Group 167–8; recommendations of Wangermée Group 44–5; shocked by Europa's sudden closure 145–6; *see also* Enkelaar Group
advertising 130, 132, 133–4; failed to provide enough revenue for Europa 115, 149; and sport 157, 158; too few transnational products 140–1
American films/television programmes, increase in 2, 238n
American influence on Europa programming 143
anti-Americanism 259n
ARD 138, 143; commitment to vertical scheduling 110; Eurikon programming 92, *93*; Eurikon week 107, 109–12; fear of commercial TV 221–2, 259n; on pan-European services 178; re-languaging strategies in Eurikon week 182–4; symposium, 'Possibilities for a pan-European DBS Channel' 117–20; withdrew from Euronews 170
Arfé Resolution 26, 137
ARTE 116; re-languaging methods 266n
ASBU, visit to EBU 107
audience: hunger for more entertaining

and popular programmes 218–19; as market 210; potential for Europa, various claims 140; *see also* European television audiences; viewers
audience research, lacking for Europa 148
audio-visual policy, European 2, 24, 153, 238n
Autin, J.: possibly unwise statement on pan-European television 118–19; saw production as challenge not distribution 119; scepticism of 76, 113, 250n

BABEL re-languaging programme 16, 44
Bangemann Report 2
Barrand, C.: argued in favour of language channels 183–4; considered Eurikon too dependent on political institutions 88; description of Europa Television 141–2; on problems of constructing a European-wide news programme 89; saw improvements in Europa scheduling 142–3
Barzanti, R.: describing MEDIA programme 263n; made claim for European Parliament's importance 234; necessary to include culture within Maastricht Treaty 231
Barzanti Report 263n
BBC 50; and Channel 4, extensive commitment to cultural quality 59; declined invitation to participate in Eurikon 270n; given responsibility for UK's DBS service 224; the 'Himalayan option' 11; and the OTS initiative 82–3; participation in Eurosport 83; small exploratory group of experts 227;